AF803670

Palgrave Studies in the History of Social Movements

Series Editors
Stefan Berger, Institute for Social Movements, Ruhr University Bochum, Bochum, Germany
Holger Nehring, Contemporary European History, University of Stirling, Stirling, UK

Around the world, social movements have become legitimate, yet contested, actors in local, national and global politics and civil society, yet we still know relatively little about their longer histories and the trajectories of their development. This series seeks to promote innovative historical research on the history of social movements in the modern period since around 1750. We bring together conceptually-informed studies that analyse labour movements, new social movements and other forms of protest from early modernity to the present. We conceive of 'social movements' in the broadest possible sense, encompassing social formations that lie between formal organisations and mere protest events. We also offer a home for studies that systematically explore the political, social, economic and cultural conditions in which social movements can emerge. We are especially interested in transnational and global perspectives on the history of social movements, and in studies that engage critically and creatively with political, social and sociological theories in order to make historically grounded arguments about social movements. This new series seeks to offer innovative historical work on social movements, while also helping to historicise the concept of 'social movement'. It hopes to revitalise the conversation between historians and historical sociologists in analysing what Charles Tilly has called the 'dynamics of contention'.

Editorial Board
John Chalcraft (London School of Economics, UK)
Andreas Eckert (Humboldt-University, Germany)
Susan Eckstein (Boston University, USA)
Felicia Kornbluh (University of Vermont, USA)
Jie-Hyun Lim (Research Institute for Comparative History, Hanyang University Seoul, South Korea)
Marcel van der Linden (International Institute of Social History, The Netherlands)
Rochona Majumdar (University of Chicago, USA)
Sean Raymond Scalmer (University of Melbourne, Australia)
Alexander Sedlmaier (Bangor University, UK)

Jesper Jørgensen · Flemming Mikkelsen
Editors

Trade Union Activism in the Nordic Countries since 1900

palgrave
macmillan

Editors
Jesper Jørgensen
The Workers Museum
Copenhagen, Denmark

Flemming Mikkelsen
Copenhagen, Denmark

ISSN 2634-6559 ISSN 2634-6567 (electronic)
Palgrave Studies in the History of Social Movements
ISBN 978-3-031-08986-2 ISBN 978-3-031-08987-9 (eBook)
https://doi.org/10.1007/978-3-031-08987-9

© The Editor(s) (if applicable) and The Author(s), under exclusive license to Springer Nature Switzerland AG 2023, corrected publication 2023
This work is subject to copyright. All rights are solely and exclusively licensed by the Publisher, whether the whole or part of the material is concerned, specifically the rights of translation, reprinting, reuse of illustrations, recitation, broadcasting, reproduction on microfilms or in any other physical way, and transmission or information storage and retrieval, electronic adaptation, computer software, or by similar or dissimilar methodology now known or hereafter developed.
The use of general descriptive names, registered names, trademarks, service marks, etc. in this publication does not imply, even in the absence of a specific statement, that such names are exempt from the relevant protective laws and regulations and therefore free for general use.
The publisher, the authors, and the editors are safe to assume that the advice and information in this book are believed to be true and accurate at the date of publication. Neither the publisher nor the authors or the editors give a warranty, expressed or implied, with respect to the material contained herein or for any errors or omissions that may have been made. The publisher remains neutral with regard to jurisdictional claims in published maps and institutional affiliations.

Cover illustration: Danish National Archives

This Palgrave Macmillan imprint is published by the registered company Springer Nature Switzerland AG
The registered company address is: Gewerbestrasse 11, 6330 Cham, Switzerland

Preface

The anthology is a result of a growing interest in labor history and social movements. To paraphrase the credo of Palgrave Studies in the History of Social Movements, we are not only beginning to historicize labor market conflicts of the post-Cold War era and the post-Global Financial Crisis of 2008. We are also trying to relate recent contentious politics to a longer history of social movements, including traditional labor organizations, such as working-class parties and trade unions.

In a Nordic perspective, one of the first clear indications of this new research momentum was the XIV Nordic Labour History Conference (NLHC) in Reykjavik in 2016. The conference was bigger and wider in scope compared to the 1970s and 1980s and inspired the establishment of the Nordic Labour History Network in Stockholm in 2017 in line with the newly established European Labour History Network in 2013 and the Global Labour History Network in 2015. Indirectly, it was also a starting point for us as this publication is largely based on presentations planned for the conference track 'Political Activism and Labour Protest' at the XV NLHC in Copenhagen November 2020. Because of the COVID-19 epidemic, the conference was postponed to January 2022 and in the meantime, the idea of an anthology took form. In January 2021, we held an online workshop with most of the contributors, all leading historians and social scientist in the field of trade union activism in Denmark, Sweden, Norway, Finland, and Iceland. Later we found common ground with the series editors and Palgrave Macmillan. We hope the book can serve as inspiration for other regional studies and a steppingstone for further historical social movement research across the Nordic countries.

We thank The Workers Museum and the Danish Ministry of Culture's Research Committee for support.

Copenhagen, Denmark

Jesper Jørgensen
Flemming Mikkelsen

Contents

Notes on Contributors

Lars Berggren (born 1951), Ph.D., is professor emeritus in History at Lund University, Sweden. His research has mainly been focused on social and labor history, but also cultural history. Among other things, he has written about labor processes, trade union formation, work environment, labor migration, and management strategies. He wrote his thesis on Kockum's Shipyard in Malmö, Southern Sweden. Most recently, he has studied conditions among Levee camp workers in Mississippi during the 1920s and 1930s.

Tapio Bergholm (born 1958), Ph.D. in history and sociology, is docent at the University of Eastern Finland and at the University of Helsinki. His research interests are history of industrial relations, gender history, labor history, and transport history. He has published articles in Finnish, Nordic, and International journals and books. He is author of the four-volume History of the Central Organisation of Finnish Trade Unions (SAK) (2005, 2007, 2012, and 2018) and writing on a biography of the Finnish president Mauno Koivisto. First volume was published in 2020.

Peter Birke (born 1965), Ph.D., is senior researcher and coordinator of the research cluster "socio economy of work and labor" at the Sociological Research Institute, University of Göttingen, Germany. In his Ph.D. dissertation *Wilde Streiks im Wirtschaftswunder* (2007), he worked on comparison of strike movements and social movements in Denmark and Germany. He is co-editor of the journal *Social History Online*.

Martin Ericsson (born 1982), Ph.D., is associate professor of History at Lund University, Sweden. His research in contentious politics studies includes the co-authored article "Youth Riots" and the Concept of Contentious Politics in Historical Research: The Case of the 1948 Stockholm Easter Riots' in *Scandinavian Journal of History* (2019).

Mats Greiff (born 1955), Ph.D., is full professor in history at Malmö University, Sweden. His research has mainly been focused on modern social and cultural history. Gender and class are two main features in most of his research. Oral history is another speciality. Among other things, he has written about labor processes, trade union formation in both Sweden and Northern Ireland, sports history, and the relation between popular music and social change in different localities e.g., GDR, England, and the Appalachia. He wrote his thesis on changing work conditions for white-collar workers.

Jesper Hamark (born 1973), Ph.D., is researcher at the Unit for Economic History, Department of Economy and Society, University of Gothenburg, Sweden. Related work includes *Strejk: Från satans svarta kvarnar till gigekonomin* (2022), and 'Strikes and lockouts: The need to separate labor conflicts' in *Economic and Industrial Democracy* (online October 2021).

Idar Helle (born 1972) is research officer at De Facto Centre for trade unionists in Oslo, Norway. His field of research is Norwegian and international working life and labor movement history. He has been author and co-editor of, among others, *Kollektivkameratene. Oslo Sporveiers Arbeiderforening 1994–2019* (2019), *Labour and Transnational Action in Times of Crisis* (2015), *Historier om motstand. Kollektive bevegelser i de 20. århundret* (2010), and *Utfordrerne. Verkstedklubben og arbeiderne på Aker Verdal 1969–2009* (2009).

Laust Høgedahl (born 1983), Ph.D., is associate professor at the Centre for Labour Market Research (CARMA), Department for Politics and Society, Aalborg University, Denmark. He does research within the academic fields of industrial relations and labor market regulations including collective bargaining and unionization. He has published his work in *European Journal of Industrial Relations*, *British Journal of Industrial Relations*, *Journal of Industrial Relations*, *Industrial Relations Journal*, etc.

Jenny Jansson (born 1974), Ph.D., is associate professor and senior lecturer at the Department of Government, Uppsala University, Sweden. Her research interests include labor studies, digitalization, and e-archives. She has published in journals such as *International Labor and Working-Class History*, *Labor History* and *Economic and Industrial Democracy*. She is the author of *Crafting the Movement* published by Cornell University Press (2020).

Jesper Jørgensen (born 1975), historian, is archivist at The Workers Museum & The Labour Movement's Library and Archives in Copenhagen, Denmark. He has published in journals such as *Moving the Social*, *The International Journal of Intelligence, Security, and Public Affairs* and *Twentieth Century Communism*. He is co-author of *Den røde underverden. Hemmelig kommunistisk virksomhed i Skandinavien mellem to verdenskrige* (2019), and co-editor of the Danish labor history journal *Arbejderhistorie*.

Knut Kjeldstadli (born 1948), Dr.philos., is professor emeritus at University of Oslo, Norway. He has worked on general Norwegian history, and on labor history from his doctoral dissertation *Jerntid. Fabrikksystem og arbeidere ved Christiania Spigerverk og Kværner Brug fra om lag 1890 til 1940* (1989) to his latest book *Arbeid og klasse. Historiske perspektiver* (2018). Furthermore, on migration history where he has edited *Norsk innvandringshistorie, Vol. I-III* (2003).

Knud Knudsen (born 1951), Dr.phil., is former associate professor at Aalborg University, Denmark. He has been engaged in labor history since the 1970s and has published books and articles on local, national, and international labor history and historiography. His latest books are *Danish trade unionism 1870–1940. Work, workshop & society* (2021) and *Dansk fagbevægelses historie frem til 1950* (2011).

Ragnheiður Kristjánsdóttir (born 1968), Dr.phil., is professor of History at the University of Iceland. She has published works on nationalism, democracy, the politics of the left, and gender. She is country editor of the *Scandinavian Journal of History* and her most recent book is *Konur sem kjósa. Aldarsaga* [A Century of Women Voters] (2020), a co-authored work about the history of women voters in Iceland.

Flemming Mikkelsen (born 1946), Dr.scient.pol., is independent researcher. He is currently working in the fields of social movements, labor market relations, ethnic relations, and historical sociology. His latest publications include 'The Diffusion and Innovation of Muslim Organizations in Denmark,' *Journal of Muslim Minority Affairs* (2019), *Popular Struggle and Democracy in Scandinavia, 1700-Present* (2018), and 'Workers' Activism and Industrial Democracy in Denmark in the twentieth Century,' *Moving the Social* (2017).

Silke Neunsinger (born 1970), Ph.D., is director of research at the Swedish Labour Movement Archives and Library, Stockholm. Her current research is focused on the history of minimum wages in India. She has worked extensively on feminist labor history, global labor history, and methodology. She is the editor of the Swedish labor history journal *Arbetarhistoria.*

Stefan Nyzell (born 1975), Ph.D., is professor of History at Malmö University, Sweden. His research in contentious politics studies includes: Flemming Mikkelsen, Knut Kjeldstadli, and Stefan Nyzell (eds.) *Popular Struggle and Democracy in Scandinavia, 1700 to the Present* (2018); and Stefan Nyzell, 'A Fight for the Right to get Drunk: The Autumn Fair Riot in Eskilstuna, 1937' in Ilaria Fevretto and Xabier Itcania (eds.) *Protest, Popular Culture and Tradition in Modern and Contemporary Western Europe* (2017).

Finn Olstad (born 1950), Dr.philos., is former professor at The Norwegian School of Sport Sciences, Norway. He has written several books about Norwegian labor movement history, notably a political biography of late Prime Minister Einar Gerhardsen and the opening volume of the history of the Norwegian trade union movement (1891–1935). He has also written sports history, local history, and general history, including two volumes on Norwegian history in the twentieth and twenty-first centuries.

Katrin Uba (born 1978), Ph.D., is associate professor and senior lecturer at the Department of Government, Uppsala University, Sweden. Her research focuses on labor relations, social movements, political outcomes of environmental protests and climate strikes, and youth political activism. She has published in journals such as *Mobilization, Social Movement Studies, American Behavioral Scientist,* and *Politics*. Together with Jenny Jansson, she is author of *Trade unions on YouTube: online revitalization in Sweden* published by Palgrave Macmillan (2019).

List of Figures

List of Tables

CHAPTER 1

Trade Union Activism in the Nordic Countries: Introduction

Flemming Mikkelsen and Jesper Jørgensen

The formation of the Nordic labor movements and the Nordic welfare states has often been seen as a result of gradual forward-looking and rather peaceful processes without major obstacles and conflicts. No doubts, the Nordic trade union movements were successful, and the path toward democracy and prosperity was less conflictual and violent than in most other European countries. However, it does not mean that the development was without obstacles, regression, and marked by huge confrontations, on the contrary. That is why the purpose of this book is to take a closer look at the mobilization strategies of trade union activists and their organizations, formal or informal, and how they interacted with other major collective actors such as social movements, political

F. Mikkelsen
Copenhagen, Denmark
e-mail: fmmikk@gmail.com

J. Jørgensen (✉)
The Workers Museum, Copenhagen, Denmark
e-mail: jjo@arbejdermuseet.dk

© The Author(s), under exclusive license to Springer Nature Switzerland AG 2023

J. Jørgensen and F. Mikkelsen (eds.), *Trade Union Activism in the Nordic Countries since 1900*, Palgrave Studies in the History of Social Movements, https://doi.org/10.1007/978-3-031-08987-9_1

parties, pressure groups, and governments. A further step is to deconstruct the prevalent perception of the Nordic trade union movement as being a stable and homogeneous body. In a global perspective, the Nordic trade union movements have shown long-lasting unity and solidarity to a degree not found in most other countries. However, despite this mobilization capacity and consensus drive the Nordic trade union movements were marked by internal strifes that sometimes manifested themselves in the form of trade union opposition at the local, national, and international levels. In other words, what we are witnessing is alternative organization structures often, but not always, in opposition to mainstream mass organizations. In critical situations, such as the two World Wars and during major waves of internal disturbances, these alternative forms of organization significantly affected labor market relations and the political system. At other times and in other situations, they assumed a more marginal position, but constituted constantly a warning to the established centralized organizations not to distance themselves from their members.

This is the story we want to tell with this book; but it is also a history, which requires new perspectives and methods. The anthology builds on traditional and well-reputed methods but incorporates new approaches especially from the extensive literature on social movements. Therefore, this book can be seen as an extension of two other English-language publications—*Labour, Unions and Politics under the North Star* (2017) and *Popular Struggle and Democracy in Scandinavia* (2018)—that seek to provide an overview of the history of labor, unions, and social movements in the Nordic countries from the beginning of the eighteenth century to the present.[1]

Trade Union Activism in the Nordic Countries: Old and New Perspectives

The most thorough attempt to deliver a comparative historical analysis of 'radicalism' and the development of working-class movements in Scandinavia (Denmark, Sweden, and Norway) was done in 1922 by

[1] Hilson, M., Neunsinger, S. and Vyff, I. (eds.) (2017) *Labour, Unions and Politics under the North Star: The Nordic Countries, 1700–2000* (New York/Oxford: Berghahn); and Mikkelsen, F., Kjeldstadli, K. and Nyzell, S. (eds.) (2018) *Popular Struggle and Democracy in Scandinavia, 1700-Present* (London: Palgrave Macmillan).

the Norwegian historian Edvard Bull, Sr., since followed by the American labor economist Walter Galenson.[2] The so-called Bull-Galenson hypothesis emphasizes the connection between rapid industrialization and radicalism, "... explosive industrialization [...] recruitment of industrial workers from small farms without previous experience in steady employment, and the poor working and living conditions they found in the hastily constructed industrial towns, all contributed to the formation of an extreme radical ideology."[3]

Later, the American-Norwegian social scientist William Lafferty ignored the deprivation argument in favor of a Durkheim-inspired explanation that sees "labor response as being negative (radical) to the entire development process and [I] shall view this negative response as being primarily motivated by the anomic results of rapid and intense industrialization."[4] According to Bull, Galenson, and Lafferty, radicalism refers to the left-wing ideological turn of the Norwegian labor movement during the 1910s and 1920s caused by hasty industrialization, while the relatively moderate labor reaction in Denmark and Sweden stems from a more balanced and smooth economic modernization.

The Swedish political scientist Nils Elvander is more concerned with the Scandinavian labor movements since World War II, but explains likewise the deviant Norwegian path as a result of economic factors, but adds that political conditions must be included in the picture.[5] Based on a theory of power mobilization, the Danish sociologist Gøsta Esping-Andersen claims that it is not the pace of industrialization that matters, but instead the relative size of the working class, class coalitions and the role of the state, which determine the long-term success of the labor movement and ultimately the creation of a welfare state. And in the case

[2] Bull, E. (1922) 'Die Entwicklung der Arbeiterbewegung in den drei skandinavischen Ländern 1914–1920', *Archiv für die Geschichte des Sozialismus und der Arbeiterbewegung*, 10, pp. 329–61; and Galenson, W. (1952) 'Scandinavia' in Galenson, W. (ed.) *Comparative Labor Movements* (New York: Prentice Hall), pp. 104–72.

[3] Ibid., pp. 147–52.

[4] Lafferty, W. M. (1971) *Economic Development and the Response of Labor in Scandinavia* (Oslo: Universitetsforlaget), p. 19. Seymour Martin Lipset also highlights rapid industrialization as a radicalizing factor, see: Lipset, S. M. (1960) *Political Man* (London: Heinemann), pp. 68–72.

[5] Elvander, N. (1980) *Skandinavisk arbetarrörelse* (Stockholm: LiberFörlag).

of the post-World War II era, the new middle class "constitutes one of the most profound changes in the class structure."

The Danish social scientist, Flemming Mikkelsen, presents the latest large-scale comparative analysis of industrial conflict and power relations in Scandinavia since 1848.[6] The analytical framework is based on how class, industrialization, capital concentration, labor market organizations, political power structure, and world market prices affect the timing, magnitude, and shape of industrial conflict. One of the results is that the assumption of a particular Norwegian radicalism, measured as labor protest and other forms of contentious collective actions, is non-existing.[7] Danish, Swedish, and for that matter Finnish workers too would from time to time take action on a grand scale, which, even in a European context, testifies to the extraordinary capacity for social and political mobilization at the local and national levels. In short, it turns out that Bull, Galenson, and Lafferty saw the collective reaction of workers as a consequence of the dissolution of existing social bonds and norms, and unpleasant conditions by industrialization. In contrast to the 'breakdown' and 'deprivation' argument, we find Elvander, Esping-Andersen, and Mikkelsen who locate the sources of workers' collective action around an organized perception of their interests.

The distinction between breakdown, deprivation, and interest explanations has its origin in the international literature on workers' protest. With reference to the European working class, Clark Kerr et al. write that the "wrenching from the old and the groping for the new in the industrializing community create a variety of frustrations, fears, uncertainties, resentments [and] aggressions," which led to new problems, latent protest, and erupted in violence.[8] Val Lorwin elaborates on the argument claiming that it was the least stable and those most isolated

[6] Mikkelsen, F. (1992) *Arbejdskonflikter i Skandinavien 1848–1980* (Odense: Odense Universitetsforlag).

[7] According to Einar Terjesen "... the apparently exceptional strength of the radicalism in the 1920s was not an effect of exceptional radicalism in itself, but a result of the decentralized structure of the party and the lack of a strong social democratic leader." (Terjesen, E. (2017) 'Radicalism or Integration: Socialist and Liberal Parties in Norway, 1890–1914' in Hilson, Neunsinger and Vyff, *Labour, Unions and Politics*, pp. 218–36, p. 218.

[8] Kerr, C., Dunlop, J. T., Harbison, F. and Myers, C. A. (1960) *Industrialism and Industrial Man: The Problems of Labor and Management in Economic Growth* (Cambridge: Harvard University Press), p. 202.

from the general population who resorted to protest.[9] N.J. Smelser provides a more sociological interpretation, arguing that excessive differentiation in the form of rapid industrialization and urbanization and other societal changes challenges social cohesion and increases the risk of disturbances.[10]

This sort of reasoning has lost its appeal among historians and social scientists but has not completely disappeared. It was the English historian E. P. Thompson who formulated an alternative theoretical and historical narrative concerning working-class collective action. Thompson argues that during the early years of the industrial revolution in England, a variety of pre-industrial traditions coalesced into a unified working-class culture, and that the action of protestors is linked to their daily experiences, social networks, and interaction with other interest-oriented groups.[11]

Edward Shorter and Charles Tilly likewise combat "the idea of strikes as direct responses to dislocation and deprivation [...] Aggression may be channeled to collective ends only through the coordinating, directing functions of an organization, be it formal or informal."[12] It opens up further insights, which accentuate the power of social relations, the strategic character of collective action and the role of state institutions. "The frequency of industrial conflict fluctuates as power balances change – not only between workers and employers, but also with regard to officials, allies, and other parties to the conflict."[13]

A central focal point is about the accumulation and mobilization of resources, and it is assumed that formal mass organizations function as a vehicle of power and influence: First, they make possible the co-ordination of the economic and political resources of large numbers of people

[9] Lorwin, V. (1958) 'Working-Class Politics and Economic Development in Western Europe', *American Historical Review*, 63, pp. 338–51.

[10] Smelser, N. J. (1963) 'Mechanisms of Change and Adjustment to Change' in Hoselitz, B. and Moore, W. E. (eds.) *Industrialization and Society* (Paris: UNESCO-Mouton), pp. 32–54.

[11] Thompson, E. P. (1963) *The Making of the English Working Class* (New York: Vintage Books).

[12] Shorter, E. and Tilly, C. (1974) *Strikes in France 1830–1968* (Cambridge: Cambridge University Press), pp. 285, 338.

[13] Tilly, C. (1989) 'Theories and Realities' in Haimson, L. and Tilly, C. (eds.) *Strikes, Wars, and Revolutions in an International Perspective: Strike Waves in the Late Nineteenth and Early Twentieth Centuries* (Cambridge: Cambridge University Press), pp. 3–17, p. 11.

who, on their own, have few such resources. Second, formal organization permits the strategic use of these resources in labor market disputes and political actions. Third, formal organization ensures the continuity of mass mobilization over time;[14] and fourth, centralized bureaucratic organizations that escape factional splits are very likely to be successful.[15]

The importance of formal mass organizations is well documented. However, it is also a well-known fact that when trade unions grow, the leaders withdraw from the members and their immediate interests. Already Robert Michels presented the basic mechanisms in "das eiserne Gesetz der Oligarchie,"[16] and later, Frances Piven and Richard Cloward argued, "Organizers not only failed to seize the opportunity presented by the rise of unrest, they typically acted in ways that blunted or curbed the disruptive force which lower-class people were sometimes able to mobilize [...] for organization-building activities tended to draw people away from the streets and into the meeting rooms."[17] Piven and Cloward's main concern was about politics, power, and protest, not primarily about type of organization. They suggested a local, small, centralized, and less structured type, or what they called 'cadre organizations,' as the appropriate vehicle to disrupt the established political system, and to gain influence. Instead of cadre organization, we prefer the term 'action network'—that is, a rudimentary form of organization able to produce mobilization for collective action. The mobilization capacity of base organizations provides the cognitive base for collective action in accord with a 'frame alignment process' that makes people define situations in a new way, integrates their beliefs with those of a larger group, and develops a sense of shared injustice. Base organizations produce leaders and have access to

[14] Cronin, J. E. (1979) *Industrial Conflict in Modern Britain* (Croom Helm: London); Geary, D. (1981) *European Labour Protest 1848–1939* (Croom Helm: London); Katznelson, I. and Zolberg, A. R. (eds.) (1986) *Working-Class Formation: Nineteenth-Century Patterns in Western Europe and the United States* (Princeton: Princeton University Press); and Ahrne, G. (1994) *Social Organizations: Interaction Inside, Outside and Between Organizations* (London: Sage).

[15] Gamson, W. A. (1975) *The Strategy of Social Protest* (Homewood: The Dorsey Press), p. 108.

[16] Michels, R. (1970) *Zur Soziologie des Parteiwesens in der modernen Demokratie* (Stuttgart: Kröner Verlag).

[17] Piven, F. F. and Cloward, R. A. (1978) *Poor People's Movements: Why They Succeed, How They Fail* (New York: Vintage Books), p. xxii.

communication technologies, and they have the opportunity to generate innovative, tactical collective action.[18]

Workers in the periphery of mainstream labor movements must cultivate new means for claim-making, such as the sudden and illegal strike, public mass meetings, picketing, violent actions that expand the boundaries of industrial relations and politics beyond the formal arena.[19] If these activities and networks over a period manage to challenge the employers, the established unions, and the government, we may talk about 'social movement unionism.' It refers to union strategies that use social movement-type approaches, which typically operated outside established organizations.[20] However, these types of action are associated with high risks and may often result in backlash and eviction of social actors. Therefore, it is often seen that the challenge of the existing industrial order takes the form of a protest wave, which begins as a consequence of changes in opportunities and threats followed by a fast reshuffling of organizational resources among claim makers, their allies, their opponents, the government, and the mass public simultaneously with the expansion and innovation of the repertoire of contentious action.[21] From a methodological point of view, this means that theories of class formation, organization models, industrial relations schemes, and institutional histories of political parties and trade unions must be supplemented with ideas and concepts from social movement studies.[22]

We must acknowledge that, at the empirical level, classes do not exist as cohesive social collectivities, and they do not mobilize on shared common interests. Proletarians, workers, and employees have always been engaged

[18] McAdam, D., McCarty, J. and Zald, M. (1988) 'Social Movements' in Smelser, N. J. (ed.) *Handbook of Sociology* (Newbury Park: Sage), pp. 695–737.

[19] Chun, J. J. (2012) 'The Power of the Powerless: New Schemas and Resources for Organizing Workers in Neoliberal Times' in Suzuki, A. (ed.) *Cross-National Comparisons of Social Movement Unionism: Diversities of Labour Movement Revitalization in Japan, Korea and the United States* (Bern: Peter Lang), pp. 37–60.

[20] Waterman, P. (1993) 'Social-Movement Unionism: A New Union Model for a New World Order', *Review*, 16, 3, pp. 245–78.

[21] Tarrow, S. (1998) *Power in Movement: Social Movements and Contentious Politics* (Cambridge: Cambridge University Press), Ch. 9.

[22] Yon, K. (2016) 'A Long-Awaited Homecoming: The Labour Movement in Social Movement Studies' in Fillieule, O. and Accornero, G. (eds.) *Social Movement Studies in Europe: The State of the Art* (New York: Berghahn); and Berger, S. and Nehring, H. (eds.) (2017) *The History of Social Movements in Global Perspective* (London: Palgrave).

in extensive social and spatial networks with the purpose of utilizing economic opportunities in search of social and economic security. Over time, it has produced different labor processes, social hierarchies, employment statuses, labor markets, recruitment and supply networks, conditions of living, organizing capabilities, and political identities. In short, recent writing of working-class history has taken a step away from a narrow deterministic exploration of class structure to focusing on class action and the interaction of multiple actors at the micro, macro, and global levels.[23]

The Structure of the Book

The chapters in this book adhere closely to these methodological guidelines and present a picture of multiple actors, supporters as well as opponents. Thus, the deconstruction of the concept of class and a greater emphasis on interaction and transaction enables a greater insight into the constantly changing forces, attitudes, and strategies that workers, employees, and trade unions faced from around 1900 until today. The contributions cover studies of long historical trends including waves and fluctuations of strikes, lockouts, and other forms of collective actions, and in-depth case studies. Some have a quantitative approach, others a more qualitative. Most analyses are based on a local perspective or a single country either Denmark, Sweden, Norway, or Finland, whereas several studies also draw comparisons between Nordic countries including Iceland besides Germany and the USA. In other words, the methodological approach is wide-ranging and ensures a deeper understanding of labor market disputes and related conflicts.

After presenting old and new perspectives on trade union activism in this opening chapter, the editors in Chapter 2 give an overview of the conjunctures of labor market struggles across four Nordic countries: the three Scandinavian countries Denmark, Sweden and Norway, and Finland from the mid-nineteenth century until today. The aim is to give the

[23] Berger, S. and Broughton, D. (eds.) (1995) *The Force of Labour: The Western European Labour Movement and the Working Class in the Twentieth Century* (Oxford: Berg); Kalb, D. (1997) *Expanding Class: Power and Everyday Politics in Industrial Communities, The Netherlands, 1850–1950* (Durham: Duke University Press); van Voss, L. H. and van der Linden, M. (eds.) (2002) *Class and Other Identities: Gender, Religion and Ethnicity in the Writing of European Labour History* (New York: Berghahn); and Silver, B. J. (2003) *Forces of Labor: Workers' Movements and Globalization since 1870* (Cambridge: Cambridge University Press).

readers a diachronic and synchronic framework to evaluate and interpret phases and case studies covered by the authors. Part I deals with the early years of trade union activism when the labor movement fought for recognition on an equal footing with the employers and the state. Part II deals primarily with the time after World War II, when the labor movement became a leading co-player in the construction and administration of a welfare state. Part III expands the field of vision to other countries and consciously uses the comparative method to gain a better understanding of where the Nordic countries are similar but also differ from one another.

Even though Bull and Galenson have described Norway as a radical hotspot in the period around World War I, Norway has since then been considered a quiet and peaceful country, with relatively limited trade union activism. But as brought forward in Chapter 3, written by Finn Olstad, the interwar years in Norway experienced extensive strike activity and a trade union opposition that turned into a revolutionary alternative. The opposition united quite different groups with varying outlooks and strategic positions. The common issue was the opposition to union centralism and long-term collective agreements, accompanied by the support for political radicalism and membership of the Communist International during the 1920s. In Chapter 4, Knud Knudsen highlights the Syndicalist movement in Denmark, 1917–20, which contested both the employers, the Social Democratic trade union leadership, and the government. The career of the Syndicalists was short and intense, but with World War I and the European revolutions as a backdrop, they succeeded in forcing significant improvements in terms of wages and working hours before they were crushed by the Social Democratic leadership and swallowed by the upcoming Communist movement.

Mobilization from the bottom up is also the theme of Lars Berggren and Mats Greiff's Chapter 5 on labor market conflicts in Malmö, 1890–1910. In this early phase of the trade union movement, we see how workers gathered in streets and public places to put pressure on employers in the private and public sector, but also how youngsters and women, and even children were present at the site of demonstrations and clashes. The Swedish employers were keen to deploy strikebreakers, which set in motion a counter-offensive by workers and their families, a subject Martin Ericsson and Stefan Nyzell elaborate on in Chapter 6. Besides lockouts, the widespread use of strikebreakers was utilized by employers to limit the effect of strikes and to discipline the workforce. The workers, for their part, tried to prevent the "black souls" from entering the workplaces and to shame them in the public space, which frequently resulted in violent clashes between strikers, strikebreakers, and the police. Trade unions took precautions against strikebreakers, but it was often local working-class communities that directly confronted the strikebreakers; in other words, trade union culture and working-class culture were not always the same thing.

The outcome of World War II and the formation of a completely new international economic and political order changed the conditions for the trade union movements and the political parties. However, this does not mean that interwar political movements and political cleavages were put out of action. As Flemming Mikkelsen shows in Chapter 7, the Danish Communists played a decisive role in the mobilization of the resistance against the German occupation of Denmark and in the aftermath of the war. In Chapter 8, Jesper Jørgensen focuses his analysis on these critical, early post-war years in Copenhagen, when dissatisfaction with the deprivations of the war was widespread. He shows that when you get close to the course of events, it becomes clear that local union organizing and resource mobilization by both Communists and Social Democrats were decisive for generating large labor demonstrations and strikes. Later, the Soviet invasion of Hungary in 1956 seriously weakened the position of the Communists in the labor movement. And when a new third wave of labor protest unfolded in 1968–1985, as pointed out by Flemming Mikkelsen also in Chapter 7, a diversity of new action groups and organizations emerged with an alternative repertoire of contentious collective actions.

The abortive Civil War in Finland, 1917–1918, eroded the position and power of the labor movement for years and made Finland a special case among the Nordic countries. However, after World War II, the Finnish trade union movement gained renewed strength. In Chapters 9 and 10, Tapio Bergholm discusses how the leaders of two Communist dominated trade unions in Finland prepared, debated, and organized strikes in the 1950s–1960s, and why national and local collective bargaining was particular conflictual and fostered a true strike wave spearheaded by local wildcat strikes. State, employer organizations, and trade union confederations tried to enhance industrial peace but were only partially successful seen in the light of the events of 1970–1980, when strike level reached new heights. Greatest peculiarity of Finnish industrial conflict during these years, was the combination of unstable incomes policy and intense local strike activity resulting in a substantial number of working days lost. Finland was at that time the strike champion of the Nordic countries.

In Norway, the economic and political elites and the leaders within the labor movement supported capitalist restructuring and Norway's closer integration into the EU single market. However, as Idar Helle shows in Chapter 11, union militancy at the local and national levels managed to protect jobs, wages, and self-determination under shifting economic and political circumstances, and to set up an alternative agenda for labor issues and union politics. At the same time, trade unions wrestled hard to organize the increasing number of foreign workers who entered the Norwegian labor market. In Chapter 12, we get a detailed understanding of the many obstacles trade unions were facing reaching out to migrant workers, among whom Poles were the dominant nationality. Knut Kjeldstadli's case is Oslo constructions workers, but his explanatory model could be used in the study of other trades and other Nordic countries that have received increasing numbers of immigrant workers.

After World War II, the Swedish labor market was characterized by cooperation and few conflicts that was interrupted by a minor conflict recovery, 1980–1990. In Chapter 13, Jenny Jansson and Katrin Uba investigate the changing opportunities for striking and the possibility to replace strikes with other forms of protest from 1980 to 2020. And although a significant decline in strike activity in 1990 and beyond, the number of trade union demonstrations did not decrease accordingly.

The national and local approaches offer a detailed entrance to the study of country-specific labor market policies, whereas the comparative approach highlights similarities and differences between the Nordic countries and where the Nordic countries differ from other industrialized countries. Thus, in Chapter 14, Jesper Hamark shows that lockout activity was substantial in all three Scandinavian countries, and that lockouts had a profound influence on labor market structures. The lockout was a feared weapon in the hands of the employers and their central organizations, while conversely the workers' wildcat strike, i.e., the sudden, non-legal, decentralized, and network-based venture, put extra pressure on the employers. In the Nordic countries, wildcat strikes flourished during the 1970s, but in Peter Birke's Chapter 15, on wildcat strikes in Denmark and the Federal Republic of Germany, we learn that decentralized workplace disputes prospered in both countries already from the late 1950s. Many strikes were carried out by so-called guest workers and unskilled female workers who protested against increasing workloads and demanded equal wages for equal work. These strikes relayed on extensive networks outside the unions and around 1970, some of the wildcat strikes were supported by and in some cases even merged with left-wing social movements.

Since the mid-1970s, wildcat strikes and other forms of contentious actions also gained a foothold in the public sector. In Chapter 16, Laust Høgedahl looks at the emergence of trade unionism among public employees in Denmark, Sweden, and Norway, and how new groups of public personnel were employed on collective agreements and not as civil servants from the 1950s onwards. This reorientation gave public employees some degrees of freedom, which they used to launch nonofficial strikes and to build powerful trade unions with strike funds that were channeled into legal strikes and secured the public employees a more advantage position in the collective bargaining process since the 1970s.

In the final Chapter 17 of this book, Ragnheiður Kristjánsdóttir and Silke Neunsinger closely explain how women trade unionists in Sweden and Island struggled for equal remuneration during the twentieth century. Due to different national and international opportunity structures Islandic and Swedish women embarked on various paths to equal pay, and at the same time demonstrate the importance of situating women's economic, social, and political rights in the wider global context.

References

Ahrne, G. (1994) *Social Organizations: Interaction Inside, Outside and Between Organizations* (London: Sage).

Berger, S. and Broughton, D. (eds.) (1995) *The Force of Labour. The Western European Labour Movement and the Working Class in the Twentieth Century* (Oxford: Berg).

Berger, S. and Nehring, H. (eds.) (2017) *The History of Social Movements in Global Perspective: A Survey* (London: Palgrave Macmillan).

Bull, E. (1922) 'Die Entwicklung der Arbeiterbewegung in den drei skandinavischen Ländern 1914–1920', *Archiv für die Geschichte des Sozialismus und der Arbeiterbewegung*, 10, pp. 329–61.

Chun, J. J. (2012) 'The Power of the Powerless: New Schemas and Resources for Organizing Workers in Neoliberal Times' in Suzuki, A. (ed.) *Cross-National Comparisons of Social Movement Unionism: Diversities of Labour Movement Revitalization in Japan, Korea and the United States* (Bern: Peter Lang), pp. 37–60.

Cronin, J. E. (1979) *Industrial Conflict in Modern Britain* (London: Croom Helm).
Elvander, E. (1980) *Skandinavisk arbetarrörelse* (Vällingby: LiberFörlag).
Galenson, W. (1952) 'Scandinavia' in Galenson, W. (ed.) *Comparative Labor Movements* (New York: Prentice Hall), pp. 104–72.
Gamson, W. A. (1975) *The Strategy of Social Protest* (Homewood: The Dorsey Press).
Geary, D. (1981) *European Labour Protest 1848–1939* (London: Croom Helm).
Hilson, M., Neunsinger, S. and Vyff, I. (eds.) (2017) *Labour, Unions and Politics Under the North Star: The Nordic Countries, 1700–2000* (New York/Oxford: Berghahn).
Kalb, D. (1997) *Expanding Class: Power and Everyday Politics in Industrial Communities, The Netherlands, 1850–1950* (Durham: Duke University Press).
Katznelson, I. and Zolberg, A. R. (eds.) (1986) *Working-Class Formation. Nineteenth-Century Patterns in Western Europe and the United States* (Princeton: Princeton University Press).
Kerr, C., Dunlop, J. T., Harbison, F. and Myers, C. A. (1960) *Industrialism and Industrial Man: The Problems of Labor and Management in Economic Growth* (Cambridge: Harvard University Press).
Lafferty, W. M. (1971) *Economic Development and the Response of Labor in Scandinavia* (Oslo: Universitetsforlaget).
Lipset, S. M. (1960) *Political Man* (London: Heinemann).
Lorwin, V. (1958) 'Working-Class Politics and Economic Development in Western Europe', *American Historical Review*, 63, pp. 338–51.
McAdam, D., McCarty, J. and Zald, M. (1988) 'Social Movements' in Smelser, N. J. (ed.) *Handbook of Sociology* (Newbury Park: Sage), pp. 695–737.
Michels, R. (1970) *Zur Soziologie des Parteiwesens in der modernen Demokratie* (Stuttgart: Kröner Verlag).
Mikkelsen, F. (1992) *Arbejdskonflikter i Skandinavien 1848–1980* (Odense: Odense Universitetsforlag).
Mikkelsen, F., Kjeldstadli, K. and Nyzell, S. (eds.) (2018) *Popular Struggle and Democracy in Scandinavia, 1700–Present* (London: Palgrave Macmillan).
Piven, F. F. and Cloward, R. A. (1978) *Poor People's Movements: Why They Succeed, How They Fail* (New York: Vintage Books).
Shorter, E. and Tilly, C. (1974) *Strikes in France 1830–1968* (Cambridge: Cambridge University Press).
Silver, B. J. (2003) *Forces of Labor: Workers' Movements and Globalization Since 1870* (Cambridge: Cambridge University Press).
Smelser, N. J. (1963) 'Mechanisms of Change and Adjustment to Change" in Hoselitz, B. and Moore, W. E. (eds.) *Industrialization and Society* (Paris: UNESCO-Mouton), pp. 32–54.

Tarrow, S. (1998), *Power in Movement: Social Movements and Contentious Politics* (Cambridge: Cambridge University Press).

Terjesen, E. (2017) 'Radicalism or Integration: Socialist and Liberal Parties in Norway, 1890–1914' in Hilson, M., Neunsinger, S. and Vyff, I. (eds.) *Labour, Unions and Politics Under the North Star: The Nordic Countries, 1700–2000* (New York/Oxford: Berghahn), pp. 218–36.

Thompson, E. P. (1963) *The Making of the English Working Class* (New York: Vintage Books).

Tilly, C. (1989) 'Theories and Realities' in Haimson, L. and Tilly, C. (eds.) *Strikes, Wars, and Revolutions in an International Perspective: Strike Waves in the Late Nineteenth and Early Twentieth Centuries* (Cambridge: Cambridge University Press), pp. 3–17.

van Voss, L. H. and van der Linden, M. (eds.) (2002) *Class and Other Identities. Gender, Religion and Ethnicity in the Writing of European Labour History* (New York: Berghahn).

Waterman, P. (1993) 'Social-Movement Unionism: A New Union Model for a New World Order', *Review*, 16, 3, pp. 245–78.

Yon, K. (2016) 'A Long-Awaited Homecoming: The Labour Movement in Social Movement Studies' in Fillieule, O. and Accornero, G. (eds.) *Social Movement Studies in Europe: The State of the Art* (New York: Berghahn).

CHAPTER 2

Labor Market Struggles and Labor Market Relations in the Nordic Countries, 1848–2020: Trends and Fluctuations

Flemming Mikkelsen and Jesper Jørgensen

This chapter provides a broad overview of the development of major labor market struggles and labor market institutions in the Nordic countries; the three Scandinavian countries Denmark, Sweden and Norway, and Finland.[1] It begins with a short review of the early years of the Nordic labor movements and the introduction of a new repertoire of contentious action with the strike, the lockout, and the mass demonstration as the most popular and effective collective manifestations. Then follows a description of the formative years of the labor movements

[1] Iceland, the fifth Nordic country, is only included in Chapter 17.

F. Mikkelsen
Copenhagen, Denmark
e-mail: fmmikk@gmail.com

J. Jørgensen (✉)
The Workers Museum, Copenhagen, Denmark
e-mail: jjo@arbejdermuseet.dk

© The Author(s), under exclusive license to Springer Nature Switzerland AG 2023

J. Jørgensen and F. Mikkelsen (eds.), *Trade Union Activism in the Nordic Countries since 1900*, Palgrave Studies in the History of Social Movements, https://doi.org/10.1007/978-3-031-08987-9_2

and the consolidation of the nationwide trade union organizations from 1900 until the end of Second World War. The final historical sections look at labor market disputes during the creation of the Nordic welfare states since 1945, when the trade union movements and the labor parties reached their zenith but also came under greater pressure due to declining support in the time leading up to the millennium.

From Hunger Riots to Strikes and Lockouts

> The wage earning, the working, and the poor part of the common people is called on to gather at the end of Slottsbacken on the 20th of August at eleven o'clock at night to destroy the below-mentioned bloodsuckers, who with high rates cause general times of high prices. – Hang them and tear down the houses to the ground. [...] Bring with you iron bars and axes: The hungry soldier may also be present.[2]

This call for a riot to be staged in Stockholm on August 20, 1798, did not trigger any popular uprising but is an expression of a clear warning to the authorities that food prices were out of control. According to Rolf Karlbom, it is also the manifestation of the protest tradition of humble people. "In this respect the working-class movement already had found its melody one hundred years ago, composed in the midst of bitter distress and thirst for brandy, broken illusions, and a feeling of brotherhood."[3]

Since the late eighteenth and mid-nineteenth centuries, Europe and the Nordic countries were ravaged by years of famine, which sometimes resulted in social unrest. It was often a partially unorganized, mixed group of proletarians who protested against the authorities and the grain dealers. However, because of changes in production and social structure it became more common with organized, homogeneous occupational groups that demonstrated and stopped work in order to carry through demands for 'fair pay and a fair price,' for wages corresponding to their work effort. In other words, the strike as a collective contentious action was taken shape. The first modern strikes gradually began to manifest themselves after the turbulent year 1848, but it was the business cycle from 1870 to 1874,

[2] Quoted from Karlbom, R. (1967) *Hungerupplopp och strejker 1793–1869* (Lund: Gleerups), p. 42. Translated by the authors.

[3] Ibid., p. 264. Translated by the authors.

which gave the impetus to the formation of trade unions and sparked the first real strike wave in Denmark, Sweden, and Norway.[4] When the economic cycle reversed most unions crumpled and strike activity fell. From 1880, however, renewed economic activity and steady economic growth created the precondition for the development of a solid organizational infrastructure with the strike as the main weapon. Until the turn of the century, Danish workers, with Copenhagen as epicenter, took the lead followed by Swedish, Norwegian, and Finnish workers (Table 2.1).[5]

To strengthen their position against the employers, the trade union movements centralized professional and technical expertise in nationwide federations: Denmark and Sweden in 1898 followed by Norway in 1899 and Finland in 1907. Around 1900, total membership figures for the Danish federal organization was approximately 77,000, for Sweden 66,000 and for Norway 4800,[6] whereas the Finnish Federation of Trade Unions claimed to represent 40,000 members.[7] The growing organizational strength of workers was to be faced quickly with countermobilization of the employers who established their own nationwide associations: by 1896 in Denmark, by 1900 in Norway, by 1902 in Sweden, and by 1907 in Finland.[8] With growing tensions between workers and employers toward the end of the nineteenth century, workers made use of strikes and demonstrations while the employers used the lockout in an attempt to subdue the other party.

[4] Mikkelsen, F. (1986) 'Workers and Industrialization in Scandinavia, 1750–1940' in Hanagan, M. and Stephenson, C. (eds.) *Proletarians and Protest: The Roots of Class Formation in an Industrializing World* (New York: Greenwood Press); Cederqvist, J. (1980) *Arbetare i strejk: Studier rörende arbetarnas politiska mobilisering under industrialismens genombrott: Stockholm 1850–1909* (Stockholm: LiberFörlag); and Olstad, F. (1981) 'Fra matopprør til streik', *Tidsskrift for Arbeiderbevegelsens Historie*, 1, pp. 115–30.

[5] Mikkelsen, F. (1993) 'Industrial Conflict in Scandinavia 1848–1990' in Kettunen, P. (ed.) *Strike and Social Change* (Turku: Turku Provincial Museum), pp. 27–52, pp. 32–35; and Soikkanen, H. (1993) 'Historical Review of Strikes in Finland', in Kettunen, *Strike and Social Change*, pp. 17–26.

[6] Galenson, W. (1952) *The Danish System of Labour Relations: A Study of Industrial Peace* (Cambridge: Harvard University Press), p. 283.

[7] Bergholm, T. (2016) *A History of the SAK* (Helsinki: SAK), p. 11.

[8] Jensen, C. S. (ed.) (2000) *Arbejdsgivere i Norden: En sociologisk analyse af arbejdsgiverorganiseringen i Norge, Sverige, Finland og Danmark* (Copenhagen: Nordisk Ministerråd).

Table 2.1 Major upheavals, movements, and industrial disputes in the Nordic Countries, 1848–present

Year	*Denmark*	*Sweden*	*Norway*	*Finland*
1848	The fall of the absolute monarchy and a constitution	Major popular disturbances and several people killed in Stockholm	Demonstrations in favor of the February revolution in France	
1850–1851			The Thrane movement	
1855		Food riots and violent confrontations		
1871–1874	Strike wave and the emergence of an embryonic trade union movement	Disturbances and strike wave	Popular disturbances and strike wave	
1879		The Sundsvall strike		
1885–1887	Major wave of popular mobilization The blacksmith lockout			
1899	The big lockout	The voting right movement		
1902		The big political strike		
1905				General strike and riots
1909		The general strike		
1911	Major lockout		Major lockout	
1917–1920	Strikes and Syndicalism	Strikes, food riots, Syndicalism, and soldiers' demonstrations	Strikes, political strikes, food protests, and workers' councils	Strikes and civil war
1920	The Easter crisis			
1921–1922	Major lockouts		Major lockout	

(continued)

Table 2.1 (continued)

Year	*Denmark*	*Sweden*	*Norway*	*Finland*
1923–1924			Major strike and lockout	
1925	Major strike and lockout	Major lockout		
1927–1928				Industrial conflicts
1928–1932		Strike activity		
1929–1935	Crisis movements, anti-democratic movements Anti-Nazi/German mobilization	Rural protest movements Communist, Fascist, and anti-Fascist movements	Rural protest movements Communist, Fascist, and anti-Fascist movements	The Lapua movement 1929–1932, and the Mutiny of Mäntsälä in 1932
1931			Major lockout	
1936	Major lockout			
1936–1938			Strike activity	
1940–1945	Indirect and more direct forms of popular mobilization against German occupation	Neutral The metal worker strike 1945	No political and organizational room for active resistance against the Germans	Engaged in war with Soviet Union
1946	Strikes and major demonstrations			Increasing strike activity
1947–1950	Scattered protests			Political strike 1948
1956	Major strike and violent confrontations		Major strike	General strike
1961	Major strike			
1968–1970s	Youth rebellion and new social movements	Youth rebellion and new social movements	New social movements and youth protests	New social movements and youth protests

(continued)

Most of these confrontations were rather small, but in 1879, more than 5000 workers in the forestry and sawmill industry in the Swedish Sundsvall region went on strike. They demanded higher wages, but when the governor called upon military forces the workers were forced to give up. Though the strike “did not lead to any immediate improvements for

Table 2.1 (continued)

Year	*Denmark*	*Sweden*	*Norway*	*Finland*
1970s–1986	Major strike wave and political demonstration strikes Wildcat strikes	Strike wave Wildcat strikes		Major strike wave Wildcat strikes
1985	Major industrial conflict			
1998	Major industrial conflict			
2000s	Moderate strike activity	Moderate strike activity	Low strike activity	Moderate strike activity

Sources Mikkelsen, F. Kjeldstadli, K. and Nyzell, S. (2018) *Popular Struggle and Democracy in Scandinavia, 1700–Present* (London: Palgrave); and Mikkelsen, F. (2022) 'The Nordic 'Sonderweg': Popular Struggle, State Building and Democracy in the Nordic Countries in a European Perspective, 1400–2000' (Working Paper)

the workers in Sundsvall, it became the preclude to a more organized trade union mobilization all over the country."[9] In Denmark, the Blacksmith lockout in 1885, resulted in a major setback for the trade unions in the important iron industry while the big lockout in 1899, culminated in a compromise named the September Agreement. The Agreement centralized industrial negotiations, guaranteed workers' rights to organize, and recognized employers' managerial rights.[10]

The relatively strong position of the trade union movement in Denmark was also reflected in the political arena. Here, the labor movement managed to emancipate itself from the Liberals and the Conservatives, and to form autonomous unions and political parties earlier than their Nordic counterparts.[11] In Denmark, the Social Democratic Party

[9] Berglund, M. (2018) 'Sweden 1740–1889: From Peasant Rebellion to Urban Riots—The Long Process of Democratization' in Mikkelsen, Kjeldstadli and Nyzell, *Popular Struggle*, pp. 279–318, p. 313.

[10] Christensen, L. K., Kolstrup, S. and Hansen, A. E. (2007) *Arbejdernes historie i Danmark 1800–2000* (Copenhagen: SFAH), pp. 58–59, 78–81; and Knudsen, K. (2021) *Danish Trade Unionism 1870–1940* (Aalborg: Aalborg University Press).

[11] Mikkelsen, F. (1992) *Arbejdskonflikter i Skandinavien 1848–1980* (Odense: Odense Universitetsforlag), pp. 45–75.

was founded in 1878, and the first election of a Social Democratic candidate to Parliament occurred in 1884. In Sweden, it happened in 1889 and 1896, in Norway in 1887 and 1903, whereas the Finnish Labour Party (SDP) was established in 1899 and entered parliament in 1907.[12]

However, it should be noted that the trade union movement was far from the only popular movement in the Nordic countries.[13] The temperance movements, the Free Church movements, the peasant movements, the cooperative movement, and the educational movements were active before and at the same time as the labor movement. Some of these had far more members than the trade union movement but owing to the unions' organic relationship to the production they constituted some of the most powerful and lasting movements that became visible after the turn of the century (Fig. 2.1).

The Great Test of Strength, 1900–1920

In Sweden, voting rights were still based on income and wealth but during the 1890s, the demand for an election reform grew. Inspired by the Chartists in England, liberals and social democrats organized so-called People's Parliaments and in 1899, a national petition under the slogan 'one man—one vote—one rifle' gathered almost 364,000 signatures for universal suffrage. In early 1902, when the government introduced compulsory military service, the Social Democratic Party (SAP) decided on a general strike for democratic rights.[14] Demonstrations and riots sprang up in Stockholm and Malmö, and a three-day long strike mobilized c. 90,000 workers, but was also met with great resistance from the

[12] Elvander, E. (1980) *Skandinavisk arbetarrörelse* (Vällingby: LiberFörlag), pp. 23–49; Esping-Andersen, G. (1985) *Politics Against Markets: The Social Democratic Road to Power* (Princeton: Princeton University Press), pp. 57–70; and Kirby, D. (2006) *A Concise History of Finland* (Cambridge: Cambridge University Press), pp. 150–51.

[13] Nielsen. N. K. (2009) *Bonde, stat og hjem: Nordisk demokrati og nationalisme – fra pietisme til 2. verdenskrig* (Aarhus: Aarhus Universitetsforlag); Alapuro, R. and Stenius, H. (eds.) (2010) *Nordic Associations in a European Perspective* (Baden-Baden: Nomos); and Mikkelsen, Kjeldstadli and Nyzell, *Popular Struggle*.

[14] Simonson, B. (1985) *Socialdemokratin och maktövertagandet: SAP:s politiska strategi 1889–1911* (Göteborg: Historiska institutionen); and Greiff, M. and Lundin, J. (2018) 'Sweden 1880–1910: The Age of the Labour Movement' in Mikkelsen, Kjeldstadli and Nyzell, *Popular Struggle*, pp. 319–55, pp. 326–29.

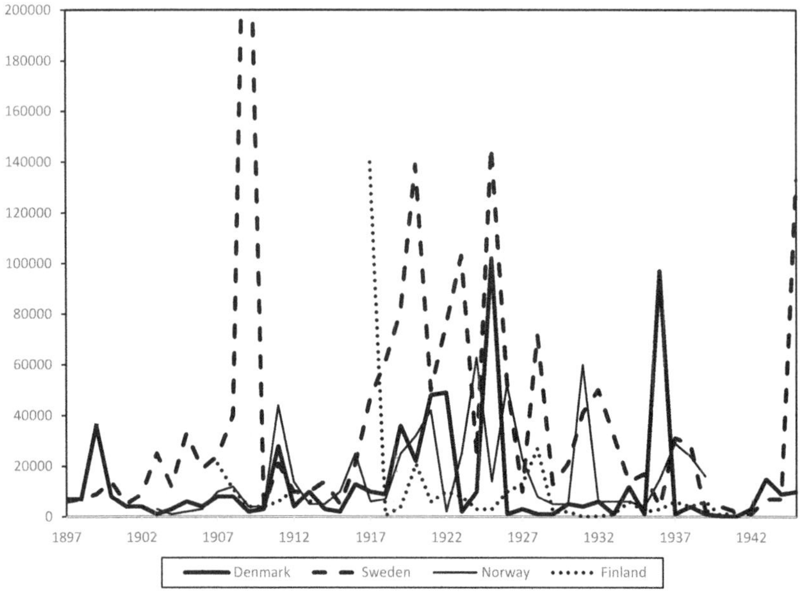

Fig. 2.1 Industrial conflicts in the Nordic Countries, 1897–1945 (number of participants) (*Sources* Statistics Denmark; Swedish National Mediation Office (*Medlingsinstitutet*); Statistics Norway; and Statistics Finland)

government and the employers.[15] Three years later, the first Russian revolution spread to Finland, where a general strike paved the way for a radical parliamentary reform based on a unicameral assembly and universal and equal suffrage for both men and women, although the Russian emperor still had the final legislative decision.[16]

After the political demonstration strike in 1902, Swedish workers struggled to obtain better wages and to regain control of the labor process with help from the advantageous economic conditions and a simultaneous

[15] Olofsson, M. (2016) 'Rösträttskravallerna i Stockholm 1902 och den återvunna demonstrationsrätten', in Ericsson, M. and Pinto, A. B. (eds.) *Politik underifrån: Kollektiva konfrontationer under Sveriges 1900-tal* (Lund: Arkiv förlag), pp. 31–54.

[16] Tikka, M. (2017) 'Strike in Finland, Revolution in Russia: The Role of Workers in the 1905 General Strike in the Grand Duchy of Finland' in Hilson, M., Neunsinger, S. and Vyff, I. (eds.) *Labour, Unions and Politics Under the North Star* (New York/Oxford: Berghahn Books), pp. 197–217.

increase in union membership. The employers reacted against this threat with several lockouts and transformed their associations into offensive conflict organizations, and in order to keep wages down they demanded uniform national collective agreements.[17] To put power behind their claims the employers lock-outed 70,000 workers what made the labor movement respond with a strike involving nearly 270,000 organized and non-organized workers. What should have been a short powerful strike lasted 2½ months and demobilized the labor movement for several years.

In Denmark and Norway, the employers also wanted to abolish local agreements. They pleaded for identical contracts with common expiration, long periods of agreements, a uniform wage structure, and a centralization of the negotiations in order to avoid wage drift. Therefore, when contracts were to be renegotiated in 1911, the employers launched a general lockout, which pointed to a common solution for the whole labor market. The lockout in Denmark lasted only two days, while the Norwegian workers could return to the workshops and factories after seven long weeks. The outcome of the conflict turned out quite well for the unions: higher wages and differentiated wage rates but acceptance of a five-year term of contract.[18]

Since the turn of the century, labor market relations in Denmark, Sweden, and Norway became increasingly centralized. However, the outbreak of World War I started a true protest cycle. The mobilization was bottom-up, decentral, and offensive. Most strikes were small and short, and based on wage demands though shorter working hours became an issue, too. Aside from strikes, different groups used political rallies, hunger marches, military demonstrations, and violence, and set up boards of workers, soldiers, and peasants. The strike movement was led by organized workers and was soon followed by the Syndicalists. They organized some of the larger strikes and profited by the widespread unrest. To control the strike movement and the left-wing mobilization, the established part of the labor movement tried to canalize the most

[17] Schiller, B. (1967) *Storstrejken 1909: Förhistoria och orsaker* (Göteborg: Elander); and Mikkelsen, *Arbejdskonflikter*, pp. 144–53.

[18] Knudsen, K. (1999) *Arbejdskonflikternes historie i Danmark: Arbejdskampe og arbejderbevægelse 1870–1940* (Copenhagen: SFAH), pp. 104–10; and Mikkelsen, *Arbejdskonflikter*, pp. 214–20.

radical demands through the existing central organizations from where they put pressure on the employers and the parliament.[19]

Even the peaceful Grand Duchy of Finland faced social and political disorder that turned into a bloody civil war in 1918. This was preceded by the economic transformation of Finland that mainly took place in rural areas dominated by forestry and sawmills. Along with changes in agricultural forms of production, it resulted in a fast-growing rural proletariat that became a political force. Within a few years, membership of the newly established Social Democratic Party rose from c. 16,000 in 1904 to almost 100,000 in 1906, and became the largest party with 80 of the 200 seats in parliament in 1907.[20] This enormous political mobilization of ordinary people took place in both urban and rural districts, but it was the fast increase of workers' associations, i.e., meeting halls in rural districts, that forged an alliance between industrial and agrarian workers and radicalized the working class.[21] This extraordinary expansion of political organization, and the "rapid and powerful penetration into the polity", argues Risto Alapuro, "made the Finnish working-class movement focus on the state rather than on direct confrontation with the capitalist class."[22]

So, in the early 1917, when the Social Democrats lost their absolute majority in parliament and were pushed aside, parliamentary procedures collapsed, and the bourgeois and the Socialist camps began to form civil guards and red guards and collect weapons. The reform demands of the Socialists and the general strike in November increased disorder. And when the disintegration of the Russian imperial regime made it impossible for the dominant elites in Finland to invoke armed forces from

[19] Ericsson, M. and Nyzell, S. (2018) 'Sweden 1910–1950: The Contentious Swedes—Popular Struggle and Democracy' in Mikkelsen, Kjeldstadli and Nyzell, *Popular Struggle*, pp. 337–46; Mikkelsen, F. (2018) 'Denmark 1914–1939: Popular Struggle in an Age of Mass Politics' in Mikkelsen, Kjeldstadli and Nyzell, *Popular Struggle*, pp. 73–102, pp. 81–85; Kjeldstadli, K. (2018) 'Norway 1850–1940: Six Types of Popular Resistance' in Mikkelsen, Kjeldstadli and Nyzell, *Popular Struggle*, pp. 201–44, pp. 227–31; and Mikkelsen, *Arbejdskonflikter*, pp. 153–57, 220–33, 294–306.

[20] Alapuro, R. (1988) *State and Revolution in Finland* (Berkeley: University of California Press), pp. 114–27.

[21] Alapuro, R. (1998) 'Artisans and Revolution in a Finnish Country Town' in Hanagan, M., Moch, L. P. and te Brake, W. (eds.) *Challenging Authority: The Historical Study of Contentious Politics* (Minneapolis: University of Minnesota Press), pp. 73–88.

[22] Alapuro, *State and Revolution*, p. 123.

Russia to defend the prevailing political system the scene was set to civil war, when the left launched its bid for power in Helsinki on January 27, 1918. The civil war lasted three months and ended with the total breakdown of the red forces due to the military capacity of the white armies under the command of General Carl Mannerheim.[23] The human costs were extensive. In a country of 3.1 million people, approximately 7000 died in battle, whereas 1500 Whites and 8000 Reds were executed in captivity; 2000 Reds were missing, and 12,500 Reds died in prison camps.

The abortive Finnish revolution in 1918 and the overwhelming White victory was followed by a drastic response: The Social Democratic Party was excluded from participating in the political process and the Communist Party was declared illegal. But, due to the German defeat, the victorious Entente alliance demanded democratic general elections in order to recognize Finnish independence.[24] The Social Democratic members stayed loyal to the party and a third of a million voted socialist in the 1919 elections. The party occupied 80 seats in parliament, and the same year a republican constitution was confirmed. The Social Democrats had decided on a policy of 'class peace,' and their role in labor struggles remained minor.

The employers accused the labor unions of carrying a heavy responsibility for the civil war and decided that they would not negotiate with trade unions and, furthermore, established some strong strikebreaking organizations. However, the employers could not prevent workers from organizing, and there were a few large industrial disputes in the late 1920s.[25] It looked different in the other Nordic countries, where the interwar years were marked by huge strikes and lockouts but also riots and demonstrations.

The Consolidation of the Trade Union Movement, 1920–1939

In Denmark, Sweden, and Norway, the employers watched with considerable anxiety the sprawling strike movement and the aggressive syndicalists. But they also knew that it could not continue like that. Therefore, the

[23] Ibid., pp. 167ff.

[24] Kirby, *A Concise History*, pp. 163–65.

[25] Soikkanen, 'Historical Review of Strikes', p. 19.

employers pursued a policy of procrastination: They reorganized their organization, accumulated conflict funds, and organized strikebreakers, on the assumption that the economic boom soon would be superseded by a recession. And when world market prices dropped and unemployment increased at the end of 1920, the employers demanded a reduction of wages backed up with lockouts in Denmark 1921 and 1922, and with partial lockouts in Sweden. In Norway, the unions attempted to stop employers' offensive with a general strike affecting 115,000 workers but failed. Two years later, the Norwegian employers' wage reduction generated a widespread lockout and strike activity centered round the metallic industry in Oslo, and only the intervention of the government was able to stop the conflict.

In 1924–1925, favorable market conditions put pressure on the cost-of-living, while the employers strived to forestall the widely dispersed strike activity and encountered the demands with a general lockout. In Denmark, the work stoppage lasted 2½ months and was brought to an end when the Social Democratic government threatened the unions with obligatory arbitration. In Sweden, the Social Democratic government accentuated the "interests of the society," which quickly brought the parties to the negotiating table and the conflict to an end.

Seven years after the last general lockout, the Norwegian employers' association mobilized its members for a huge lockout under impression of decreasing world market prices 1930–1931. The employers wanted to lower the cost of production by reducing wages. But what should have been an effect full and brief lockout lasted for nearly five months, where after the parties had to give up and enter a compromise. The last major labor conflict occurred in Denmark, when rising prices made the workers call for wage increase, and the employers answered with a general lockout in 1936. After 100,000 workers had been out of work for about two weeks the Social Democratic government passed a compulsory arbitration, which paid the workers higher wages much to the resentment of the employers.

In sum, it was the fluctuations of world market prices and their impact on the cost-of-living and cost of production, which triggered conflict activity, whereas the growth and centralization of labor market organizations made preparatory mobilization possible. The implementation of collective agreements restrained decentral strike and lockout activity and increased the size of the single work stoppage (Table 2.2). The situation in Finland was different. The Finnish labor market was characterized

Table 2.2 Number of workers covered by collective agreements

Year	*Denmark*	*Sweden*	*Norway*
1909	n.d	318,000	49,000
1914	108,000	233,000	89,000
1928	224,000	513,000	123,000
1938	n.d	1,016,000	361,000

Source Mikkelsen, 'Industrial Conflict in Scandinavia', p. 38

by low and temporary membership, and trade union activity was associated with the strong political labor movement. As consequent collective agreements were not very widespread until the 1940s.[26]

The labor market underwent an accumulation and centralization of resources, while the Social Democrats' success in elections and ultimate takeover of the state apparatus in Sweden, Denmark, and Norway from the 1920s restricted the power of the employers in favor of the trade unions.[27] The crisis agreements of the 1930s (the Kanslergade Agreement in Denmark 1933, The Cow Deal in Sweden 1933, the Crisis Agreement in Norway 1935, and the 'Red-Earth' coalition in Finland 1937), and separate labor market agreements such as the Saltsjöbad Agreement in Sweden 1933 and the main agreement in Norway 1935, strengthened the coalition between workers and farmers and loosened the tensions between employers and workers.[28] Overall, we can talk about class compromises

[26] Teräs, K. (1993) 'Industrial Actionism and Industrial Conflicts in Finland' in Kettunen, *Strike and Social Change*, pp. 71–76; and Bergholm, T. (2000) 'Historieforskning och fackföreningsrörelse i Finland', *Arbetarhistoria*, 26, 103–104, pp. 45–50, p. 47.

[27] Dahl, H. F. Dybdahl, V, Hentilä, S. and Torbacke, J. (1974) 'Krisen og det politiske liv' in *Kriser och krispolitik i Norden under mellankrigstiden* (Uppsala: Almqvist & Wiksell), pp. 71–104.

[28] Hilson, M. (2007) 'Scandinavia' in Gerwarth, R. (ed.) *Twisted Paths: Europe 1914–1945* (Oxford: Oxford University Press), pp. 8–32, pp. 20–22; Krake, K. (2016) *Skandinavien i ekstremernes tidsalder: Systemkritik og demokratiforsvar i mellemkrigstiden*, Ph.D. dissertation, University of Southern Denmark; and Österberg, M. (2017) 'Norden as a Transnational Space in the 1930s' in Hilson, Neunsinger and Vyff, *Labour, Unions and Politics*.

that stabilized the Nordic countries but also confirmed and laid the foundation for continuing strength of the labor movements, which surpassed the organizational strength of labor in all the other European countries.[29]

In spite of moderate strike peaks in Sweden in the late 1920s and early 1930s, and in Norway in the late 1930s, industrial conflicts were declining in Scandinavia. And in addition to a few violent strikes initiated or taken over by the Communists, like the seamen's strikes in Sweden 1933 and Denmark 1934,[30] the Nordic labor markets were purged of any major clashes.

Besides certain sectors, the Communists in Denmark, Norway, and Sweden lacked organizational support and fared poorly in the elections. Internal divisions and party splintering was widespread in the Scandinavian communist movements in the 1920s and 1930s, mostly because of their subordination to the international communist organization Comintern in Moscow.[31] Instead, they resorted to extra-parliamentary activities as demonstrations and riots that were mainly held in response to debates in parliament or took place in the context of labor disputes, whereas actual political uprisings were almost absent. One of the most violent clashes took place in the Swedish locality, Ådalen, in 1931, where one bystander and four demonstrating timber and pulp industry workers were killed by gunfire from deployed soldiers defending strikebreakers. The communists tried to capitalize on these conflicts but had neither the organizational strength nor the support of the workers to challenge the employers, the established political parties, or the governments. From the mid-1930s, the Comintern anti-fascist tactic boosted popular support for the communist parties, while attempts to achieve cooperation with the social democrats failed. Compared to the Scandinavian communist parties, the Finnish communists were in the most precarious situation. Because the authorities and "the whole bourgeoisie" were afraid of revolutionary uprisings as in 1917–1918, they only accepted indoor meetings, and throughout the 1930s, the Finnish historian, Tauno Saarela, writes,

[29] Mikkelsen, F. (2005) 'Working-Class Formation in Europe and Forms of Integration: History and Theory', *Labor History*, 46, 3, pp. 277–306.

[30] Weiss, H. (2021) *A Global Radical Waterfront: The International Propaganda Committee of Transport Workers and the International of Seamen and Harbour Workers, 1921–1937* (Leiden: Brill), pp. 344–48, 405–06.

[31] Elvander, *Skandinavisk arbetarrörelse*, pp. 50–56.

"demonstrations by Finnish communists were mainly limited to raising a Red flag somewhere or painting slogans on walls."[32]

When a fall in world market prices set in from 1930, we can observe a simultaneous escalation in the number of forced sales, contentious rallies, and agrarian crisis movements. The farmers organized demonstrations, public meetings, petition drives, dispatched threatening letters, and tried to hinder forced sales. Some of the crisis movements did voice proto-fascist ideas too. However, the Nordic states managed to contain the discontent and pressure from the right and the left, but with the outbreak of World War II, the way ordinary people mobilized changed fundamentally.

War, Occupation, and Opposition, 1940–1945

On April 9, 1940, German troops invaded the Norwegian territory, and in June, the country was entirely subjected to German rule. Norwegian military forces had fought bravely against a superior enemy but in vain. The King and the government fled to England and after some unsuccessful negotiations with the political parties, the German leadership appointed a puppet government led by Vidkun Quisling, head of the domestic national-socialist party *Nasjonal Samling* (NS).

With support from the German occupying forces, the Quisling government tried to Nazify local and national administration and civil society. NS used the censored press to promote its own mass meetings and street processions, whereas the harsh German occupation did not leave much room for organized resistance not even industrial conflicts.[33] Mostly passive resistance met the attempt to Nazify Norwegian society, while a few sabotage actions sought to derail German troops. The Norwegian exile authorities including the King, the business community, and

[32] Rønning, O. M. (2015) 'Communism in the Nordic Countries 1917–1990: Communist Parties—Organisational Development and Electoral Support' in Egge, Å. and Rybner, S. (eds.) *Red Star in the North: Communism in the Nordic Countries* (Stamsund: Orkana Akademisk), pp. 37–61, pp. 45–47; and Saarela, T. (2015) 'From Revolutions to Peaceful Roads—Communist Strategy in the Nordic Countries' in Egge and Rybner, *Red Star in the North*, pp. 120–57, pp. 135.

[33] Grimnes, O. K. (2010), 'Okkupation og politik', in Dahl, H. F., Kirchhoff, H., Lund, J. and Vaale, L.-E. (eds.) *Danske tilstande – Norske tilstande: Forskelle og ligheder under tysk besættelse 1940–45* (Copenhagen: Gyldendal), pp. 79–103.

most of the dominant Norwegian elite strongly dissuaded the population from sabotage, but concurrently with German defeats on the Eastern and Western fronts the Communists and some loosely organized groups stepped up their sabotage actions.[34]

Contrary to the fierce Norwegian military resistance, Danish military units provided minimal resistance, and the whole society adjusted quickly to cooperation with the Germans. The first years of the German occupation put a damper on open demonstrations and direct actions in favor of less provocative and stirring popular manifestation. However, from 1943, street fighting, riots, sabotage, barricades, political killings, and strikes characterized the Danish resistance.[35] The confrontations culminated during 9–29 August 1943, when a mixture of local strikes, demonstrations, meetings, and assaults on Nazi collaborators in several provincial cities caused a change in the relationship between ordinary Danes, the Danish authorities and the Germans.[36] Next year, a further step in that direction ensued, when another major outburst of protest and defiance toward the German occupation broke out, and this time with the epicenters in working-class neighborhoods and big industrial workplaces in Copenhagen. And when the dust had settled nearly 100 had been killed and more than 670 wounded.[37] Shortly after the Liberation on May 4, 1945, demonstrations and strikes broke out and continued into the next year; but as the established and centralized trade unions strengthened their grip on labor market negotiations, the number of strikes withered away.[38]

Soviet territorial claims on Finland and the prelude to World War II started a major crisis mobilization of the Swedish society. The state and the big organizations established close cooperation concerning economy

[34] Borgersrud, L. (2010) 'Modstandsbevægelsen i Norge' in Dahl, Kirchhoff, Lund and Vaale, *Danske tilstande*, pp. 177–99, pp. 193–95.

[35] Pedersen, B. S. and Holm, A. (1998) 'Restraining Excesses: Resistance and Counter-Resistance in Nazi-Occupied Denmark 1940–1945', *Terrorism and Political Violence*, 10, 1, pp. 60–89.

[36] Kirchhoff, H. (1979) *Augustoprøret 1943*, Vol. 1–3 (Copenhagen: Gyldendal); and Mikkelsen, F. (2018) 'Denmark 1940–1946: War, Occupation and Liberation' in Mikkelsen, Kjeldstadli and Nyzell, *Popular Struggle*, pp. 103–10.

[37] Kirchhoff, H. (2004) *Samarbejde og modstand under besættelsen* (Odense: University Press of Southern Denmark).

[38] Kjeldsen, M. (2010) 'Mellem oprør og demokrati: Om normaliseringen i Danmark maj-oktober 1945' in Dahl, Kirchhoff, Lund and Vaale, *Danske tilstande*, 282–308.

and industrial relations resulting in a sharp decline in strikes and lock-outs during 1939–1941.[39] However, cost of living continued to rise, and despite of a price freeze from 1942 the number of strikes increased and culminated in February–July 1945, when 123,000 metal workers went on strike for higher wages. Communist agitation and Communist union members played a major role and used the conflict to criticize the Social Democrats and the centralized union leadership.[40] But, it was the dissatisfaction of rank-and-files that kept the conflict going until union leadership used the veto to end the strike because the employers threatened to extend the conflict.

The Soviet invasion of Finland in 1939–1940 and the Finnish counter-attack from 1941–1944 put enormous pressure on Finnish economy and society and did not leave much space for open internal conflicts. The end of the war, however, led to a revival of left-wing parties and an increase in unionism, pay claims, and strikes.[41]

From Neo-Corporatism and Industrial Peace to Renewed Industrial Activity, 1946–1985

World War II had left Norway and Denmark with a worn but largely intact production apparatus and together with Sweden, which had successfully stayed out of the War, the Nordic countries soon fixed on an expansive economic growth model that transformed the industrial landscape, occupational structure, consumption patterns and, as a consequence, class organization.[42]

The number of trade union members increased steadily until the mid-1990s, followed by stagnation and incipient decline as shown in Table 2.3.

[39] Mikkelsen, *Arbejdskonflikter*, p. 160.

[40] Ericsson and Nyzell, 'Sweden 1910–1950', pp. 363–65.

[41] Bergholm, *A History of the SAK*, pp. 34–35, 41–42.

[42] Jörberg, L. and Krantz, O. (1976) 'Scandinavia 1914–1970' in Cipolla, C. M. (ed.) *The Fontana Economic History of Europe. Vol. 6, Part 2: Contemporary Economies* (Glasgow: Collins), pp. 377–459; Mjøset, L. (ed.) (1986) *Norden dagen derpå: De nordiske økonomisk-politiske modellene og deres problemer på 70- og 80-tallet* (Oslo: Universitetsforlaget); and Mjøset, L. (1987) 'Nordic Economic Policies in the 1970s and 1980s', *International Organization*, 41, 3, pp. 403–56.

Table 2.3 Trade union density rate in percent, 1980–2016

	1980	*1985*	*1995*	*1998*	*2016*
Denmark	75	77	76	76	67
Sweden	78	81	85	81	66
Norway	57	57	56	55	52
Finland	67	67	78	80	65

Sources For the years 1980–1998: Kjellberg, A. (2001) *Fackliga organisationer och medlemmar i dagens Sverige* (Lund: Arkiv), p. 27; and for the year 2016: Logue, J. (2019) 'Trade Unions in the Nordic Countries', *nordics.info* (https://nordics.info/show/artikel/trade-unions-in-the-nordic-region); the article has been updated by Einhorn. E. E., retrieved September 27, 2022

Until circa 1970, blue-collar workers were better organized compared to other occupational groups; but since then, white-collar and especially public sector employees have approached the union density of traditional industrial workers.[43]

The strength of the trade unions corresponded to Social Democratic success at the polls. Until the end of the 1970s, the Swedish and Norwegian parties managed to gain the support of about 45% of the electorate and the Danish party about 37%. This enabled the Scandinavian Social Democrats to assume office for longer periods. However, since the mid-1980s, the Social Democratic Parties in Sweden and Norway lost support among the electorate, including working-class voters, and have been out of office for several terms. This trend has been most pronounced in Denmark and started already in the early 1970s.[44] The Finnish left (including the Social Democrats) did not achieve the same powerful position as the Left in the other Nordic countries and was furthermore marked by a deep split between the Social Democrats and the Communist, which propagated to the labor market.

In contrast to most other European countries, high union density among almost all categories of workers, and a firm hand on government (at least until 1980), placed the labor movements in Sweden, Denmark,

[43] Mikkelsen, F. (2012) 'Class and Social Movements in Scandinavia Since 1945', *Moving the Social: Journal of Social History and the History of Social Movements*, 48, pp. 29–48.

[44] Cerny, K. H. (ed.) (1977) *Scandinavia at the Polls: Recent Political Trends in Denmark, Norway, and Sweden* (Washington: Amer Enterprise); and Knutsen, O. (2006) *Class Voting in Western Europe* (Oxford: Lexington Books).

and Norway in a unique and favorable position from where they formulated a policy which Walter Korpi has called "an economic growth strategy of class conflict" that also can be seen as a "welfare strategy."[45] According to this argument, the working-class movement aimed at applying its resources to gaining control of the state apparatus. State capabilities allowed it to limit the power of capital and to mitigate the social consequences of a partially free market for commodities and labor, regarded as a necessity for efficiency of production. The Social Democratic government guaranteed low levels of unemployment, social security, regulation of prices, and working conditions, while the central labor market organizations assured growth in production and real earnings, and low levels of strike and lockout activity. This social contract has also been referred to as neo-corporatism.[46]

These mutual obligations between Social Democratic governments, workers, and employers worked quite well until the end of the 1960s, to be interrupted only in 1956, when major strikes broke out in Denmark, Norway, and Finland.[47] Collective bargaining in Denmark was characterized by irreconcilable demands and on 17 March, 66,000 wage earners went on strike and blocked oil and gasoline supplies, which crippled much of public and private transport. To support their demands for higher wages and piece-rates 51,352 Norwegian workers in forestry, wood processing industry, and construction went on strike, while nearly 400,000 Finish workers started a three-week general strike when wartime price and wage control had been lifted. After this major outburst of union power class tensions diminished and both employers and employees "started to participate in the regulation of the national labor market and the economy on a more equal footing."[48]

It took about twelve years before the labor market bursted into a major protest cycle caused by international price inflation that put a strain on

45 Korpi, W. (1978) *The Working Class in Welfare Capitalism: Work, Unions and Politics in Sweden* (London: Routledge and Kegan Paul), Ch. 4; and Korpi, W. (1983) *The Democratic Class Struggle* (London: Routledge and Kegan Paul).

46 Crouch, C. (1982) *Trade Unions: The Logic of Collective Action* (Glasgow: Fontana), pp. 206–07.

47 Mikkelsen, *Arbejdskonflikter*; and Soikkanen, 'Historical Review of Strikes'.

48 Nieminen, A. (2000) 'Finnish Employer Confederations—Streamlining Inner Organization and Regulating National Capitalism' in Jensen, *Arbejdsgivere i Norden*, pp. 287–371, p. 305.

real wages at the same time as the employers intensified the modernization of the production plant. It resulted in a moderate increase in strike activity in Norway, while the number of strikes and strikers in Denmark and Sweden, and especially in Finland rocketed.[49] It was not an isolated Nordic phenomenon but an international trend induced by a price-wage-strike spiral that escalated tensions on the labor market and other parts of society referred to as 'The Resurgence of Class Conflict' by Colin Crouch and Alessandro Pizzorno.[50]

In Denmark and Sweden, the existing unions were tied to long-term wage contracts at the national level that strongly restricted their mobilization capacity. Therefore, the number of legal union-sponsored strikes remained low, whereas unofficial strikes grew during the protest wave. These strikes were not officially supported or otherwise subsidized by the trade unions, but relied on small, local and somewhat unstructured types of organizations also called 'action networks.' In Sweden, wildcat strikes broke out across the country and "the shop floor became more and more at odds with central union leadership."[51] Some of the protracted conflicts were supported by groups, which in Denmark constituted a real alternative to the established trade union movement. In Norway, wildcat strikes did not reach anywhere near the same extent as in the other Nordic countries. But in the peak year 1976, most of the company-based strikes were under influence by the Maoist party.[52]

Especially Finland and Denmark were exposed to politicization and polarization of labor market relations after 1968. In Denmark, the leading Social Democratic Party lost ground to left-wing parties just as the split

[49] Mikkelsen, *Arbejdskonflikter*, pp. 363–420; Mikkelsen, F. (1997) 'Cycles of Struggle and Innovations in Industrial Relations in Denmark After World War II, *Scandinavian Journal of History*, 22, pp. 31–51; Thörnqvist, C. (1994) *Arbetarna lämnar fabriken: Strejkrörelser i Sverige under efterkrigstiden, deres bakgrund, förlopp och føljder* (Göteborg: Historiska institutionen); and Stokke, T. Aa. and Thörnqvist, C. (2001) 'Strikes and Collective Bargaining in the Nordic Countries', *European Journal of Industrial Relations*, 7, 3, pp. 245–267.

[50] Crouch, C. and Pizzorno, A. (eds.) (1978) *The Resurgence of Class Conflict in Western Europe Since 1968*, Vol. 1–2 (New York: Holmes & Meier).

[51] Peterson, A., Thörn, H. and Wahlström, M. (2018) 'Sweden 1950–2015: Contentious Politics and Social Movements Between Confrontation and Conditioned Cooperation' in Mikkelsen, Kjeldstadli and Nyzell, *Popular Struggle*, pp. 377–432, p. 386.

[52] Helle, I. and Matos, T. (2018) 'Norway 1945–2015: Contention and Democracy' in Mikkelsen, Kjeldstadli and Nyzell, *Popular Struggle*, pp. 245–75, p. 248.

between the Social Democrats and the Communists in Finland weakened the institutional and organizational control mechanisms that had moderated industrial conflicts. Besides, in Denmark, many short strikes were legalized and, in practice, accepted in Sweden and Finland. In Norway, on the other hand, the tolerance level for unofficial strikes was low and sanctions against such strikes were very high.[53] Because most unofficial strikes were declared illegal by the authorities, unions were barred from providing support to the striking workers. However, it cleared the way for other actors especially left-wing unions and action networks. They stepped in with economic, moral, and intellectual resources, and, during the 1970s and 1980s, there was a close collaboration between conflict-ridden workplaces and branches, leftist shop stewards, academics, and the student movement.

Changing Classes and Labor Market Structures Since 1985

Although the volume of participants and lost working days declined after the mid-1980s (Fig. 2.2), strike activity did not return to the pre-1968 level but remained high, even in a European context.[54] When the length and seriousness of the economic recession of the 1980s became clear, industrial policy and managerial investment strategies became more important. Neoliberal thoughts and policies gained renewed attention among private and public employers, just as the established trade union organizations once again got the upper hand. The challenges but also the opportunities offered by the European Single Market and the expanding global economy became some of the major problems trade unions and their members had to take into account, and which left its mark on labor conflicts far into the twenty-first century. Another far-reaching change

[53] Stokke and Thörnqvist, 'Strikes and Collective Bargaining', p. 256; Mattila, Aa. (1993) 'Industrial Conflicts and Their Mediation in the Finnish Labour Market from the 1800's to the 1980's' in Kettunen, *Strike and Social Change*, pp. 53–70; Lilja, K. (1998) 'Finland: Continuity and Modest Moves Towards Company-Level Corporatism' in Ferner, A. and Hyman, R. (eds.) *Changing Industrial Relations in Europe* (Oxford: Blackwell), p. 177; and Bergholm, T. and Jonker-Hoffrén, P. (2012) 'Farewell to the Communist Strike Hypothesis?—The Diversity of Striking in Finland Between 1971–1990' in van der Velden, S., Varela, R. and Simões do Paço, A. (eds.) *Strikes and Social Conflict: Towards a Global History* (Lisbon: International Association Strikes and Social Conflict), pp. 401–13.

[54] Scheuer, S. (2004), *Strejker i Europa*, LO-Dokumentation 2 (Copenhagen: LO).

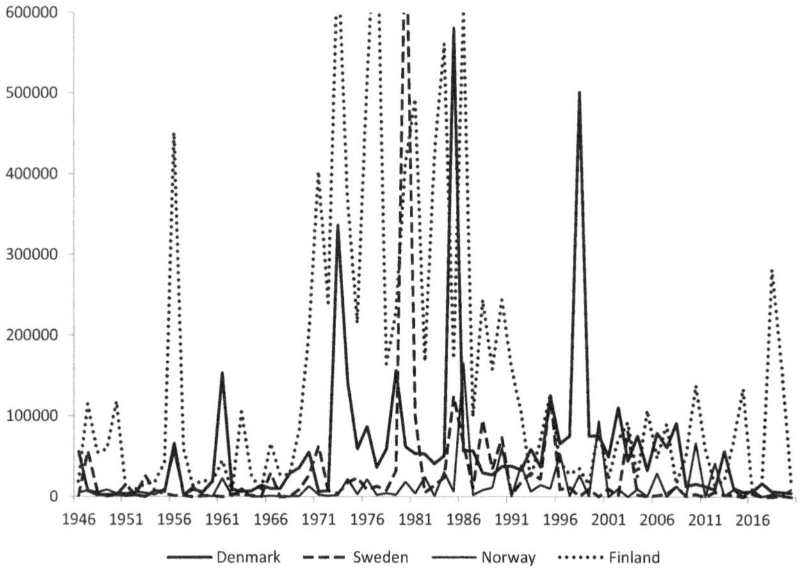

Fig. 2.2 Industrial conflicts in the Nordic Countries, 1946–2020 (number of participants) (*Sources* Statistics Denmark; *Medlingsinstitutet*; Statistics Norway; and Statistics Finland)

and innovation was the growing professional activity and in some cases militant behavior of public employees.

It already began in the mid-1960s, when public employees (and to a lesser extent other parts of the service sector) displayed a more independent bargaining position. They adopted the working class' preferred mode of organization, the trade union, and learned to use the strike-weapon.[55] Since then, teachers, social workers, bus drivers, nurses, junior doctors, and many other (semi) professional categories have acted as challengers, striving for a more advanced position on the labor market;[56] and in the first decades of the twenty-first century, it has been public employees who

[55] Ozaki, M. (1987) 'Labour Relations in Public Service', *International Labour Review*, 126, 3 and 4.

[56] Thörnqvist (1994) *Arbetarna*, pp. 128–30; and Mikkelsen, F. (1998) 'Unions and New Shopfloor Strike Strategies and Learning Processes among Public Employees', *Economic and Industrial Democracy: An International Journal*, 19, 3, pp. 505–38.

most often went on strike and protested in the streets. One explanation is that the number of public employees has increased quite considerably at the local and national levels. But even more important is that public employees have created large, centralized organizations, expanded the use of shop stewards, established strike funds, and managed to form radical action networks. Besides, many public employees have strong trade unions based on their education, such as teachers and nurses.

The growing public sector has also gone hand-in-hand with a feminization of public employment just as old idealistic association with an emphasis on ethical and professional questions turned into modern trade unions negotiating wages and other working conditions.[57] A driving force for many female employees has been the deep wage gap between male and female occupations and professions. The segregated labor market has created large pay differences, but just as decisive has been the state's determination of hierarchical wage categories to the great disadvantage of female employees. In Denmark, for instance, hospital nurses and their organization, *Dansk Sygeplejeråd* (DSR), had long been unhappy with their ranking on the wage scale and in 1973, 1000 nurses at the 'nerve centres' of the hospitals stopped working after unsuccessful negotiations with the state representatives. Since then, hospital nurses—sometimes in cooperation with other healthcare workers—have repeatedly left the workplace and demonstrated for better working conditions and against austerities within the public sector. A recent event occurred in 2008, when the nurses went on strike and demonstrated together with c. 75,000 public health care servants.[58] The result was meager and in 2021, the nurses attempted yet another strike, in spite of the fact that the other public sector organizations and the nurses own organization (DSR) had accepted the mediation proposal. The strike was followed by numerous demonstrations and public attention but after two months, the government passed a legislative intervention that ended the strike.

The above case reveals how difficult it is for public sector employees and organizations to achieve better working conditions. Labor market partners have agreed that public sector salaries were not allowed to exceed wage increases in the private sector. In addition, public employers were

[57] Julkunen, R. and Rantalaiho, L. (1993) 'Women on Strike—Nonexistent or Silenced?' in Kettunen, *Strike and Social Change*, pp. 97–114.

[58] Sørensen, A. E. (2014) 'Fra velfærdsbevægelse til ligelønsbevægelse', *Temp*, 9, pp. 142–69.

barred from favoring selected occupations, because wage increases in one area would quickly spread to other sections and thus burden the public finances. The problem has only grown with the extension of the welfare state.

The radicalization of public employees was an international trend, which was also the case with immigrant workers, who entered the Nordic labor force in greater numbers since the mid-1960s.[59] At the beginning they arrived from the European periphery and neighboring areas, but after some years immigrant workers and refugees came from countries outside of Europe, such as Turkey, Chile, Pakistan, Iran, Somalia, and Iraq. Labor market integration went well, but with the international economic crisis of the late 1970s and increasing unemployment, tensions rose and spread to the political sector. The trade union movements were caught in a quandary:[60] On the one hand, increasing immigration put pressure on real wages; on the other hand, immigrants contributed to the countries' overall economy and increased wage mobility for native workers. In general, the unions opted for a controlled immigration and that foreign workers should be subject to collective agreements in order to avoid social dumping. As an important part of this strategy, the unions sought to organize labor migrants, but with mixed results. It seems that labor markets with high union density and long-time stable relationship between trade unions and employers have done better compared to branches with unstable working conditions and low union density.

Since the late 1980s, major labor disputes have been rare but not impossible. It happened in 1998 in Denmark, when 450,000 private employees stopped work demanding a sixth holiday week. The conflict also affected the supply of groceries and public transport, and after an 11-day strike, the prime minister intervened and enforced the mediation proposal into law. In 2018, a growing number of Finnish unions engaged in industrial action against the government's reform proposal of dismissal protection, which they regarded as an unacceptable weakening of employment security. Next year, a conflict in the postal sector escalated into a strike wave, when several unions, particularly in the transport

[59] Hilson, M. (2008) *The Nordic Model: Scandinavia Since 1945* (London: Reaktion Books), pp. 157–74.

[60] Kjeldstadli, K. (2015) 'A Closed Nation or an Open Working Class? When Do Unions Opt for Including Labour Migrants?' in Bieler, A. et al. (eds.) *Labour and Transnational Action in Times of Crisis* (London: Rowman & Littlefield), pp. 83–98.

sector, joined the Finnish Post and Logistics Union in solidarity. At the core of the labor dispute was the announcement that the Finnish state-owned company, Posti, planned to transfer 700 employees working in mail sorting to a new collective agreement with lower labor costs. Eventually, a solution was found, and industrial action called off when both parties accepted the national conciliator's third mediation proposal.

So, in spite of declining strike activity private and public employees and their unions still had the capacity and the determination to launch major strikes, including solidarity strikes, both in defense of established rights but also in the attempt to improve their living conditions. In other words, one of our era's great achievement and innovation, the trade union, still has an important role to play.

References

Alapuro, R. (1988) *State and Revolution in Finland* (Berkeley: University of California Press).

Alapuro, R. (1998) 'Artisans and Revolution in a Finnish Country Town', in Hanagan, M., Moch, L. P. and te Brake, W. (eds.) *Challenging Authority: The Historical Study of Contentious Politics* (Minneapolis: University of Minnesota Press), pp. 73–88.

Alapuro, R. and Stenius, H. (eds.) (2010) *Nordic Associations in a European Perspective* (Baden-Baden: Nomos).

Bergholm, T. (2000) 'Historieforskning och fackföreningsrörelse i Finland', *Arbetarhistoria*, 26, 103–104, pp. 45–50.

Bergholm, T. (2016) *A History of the SAK* (Helsinki: SAK).

Bergholm, T. and Jonker-Hoffrén, P. (2012) 'Farewell to the Communist Strike Hypothesis?—The Diversity of Striking in Finland Between 1971–1990' in van der Velden, S., Varela, R. and Simões do Paço, A. (eds.) *Strikes and Social Conflict: Towards a Global History* (Lisbon: International Association Strikes and Social Conflict), pp. 401–13.

Berglund, M. (2018) 'Sweden 1740–1889: From Peasant Rebellion to Urban Riots—The Long Process of Democratization' in Mikkelsen, F., Kjeldstadli, K. and Nyzell, S. (eds.) *Popular Struggle and Democracy in Scandinavia, 1700–Present* (London: Palgrave Macmillan), pp. 279–318.

Borgersrud, L. (2010) 'Modstandsbevægelsen i Norge' in Dahl, H. F., Kirchhoff, H., Lund, J. and Vaale, L.-E. (eds.) *Danske tilstande – Norske tilstande. Forskelle og ligheder under tysk besættelse 1940–1945* (Copenhagen: Gyldendal), pp. 177–99.

Cederqvist, J. (1980) *Arbetare i strejk: Studier rörende arbetarnas politiska mobilisering under industrialismens genombrott: Stockholm 1850–1909* (Stockholm: LiberFörlag).
Cerny, K. H. (ed.) (1977) *Scandinavia at the Polls: Recent Political Trends in Denmark, Norway, and Sweden* (Washington: Amer Enterprise).
Christensen, L. K., Kolstrup, S. and Hansen, A. E. (2007) *Arbejdernes historie i Danmark 1800–2000* (Copenhagen: SFAH).
Crouch, C. (1982) *Trade Unions: The Logic of Collective Action* (Glasgow: Fontana).
Crouch, C. and Pizzorno, A. (eds.) (1978) *The Resurgence of Class Conflict in Western Europe Since 1968*, Vol. 1–2 (New York: Holmes & Meier).
Dahl, H. F., Dybdahl, V., Hentilä, S. and Torbacke, J. (1974) 'Krisen og det politiske liv' in *Kriser och krispolitik i Norden under mellankrigstiden* (Uppsala: Almqvist & Wiksell), pp. 71–104.
Elvander, E. (1980) *Skandinavisk arbetarrörelse* (Vällingby: LiberFörlag).
Ericsson, M. and Nyzell, S. (2018) 'Sweden 1910–1950: The Contentious Swedes—Popular Struggle and Democracy' in Mikkelsen, F., Kjeldstadli, K. and Nyzell, S. (eds.) *Popular Struggle and Democracy in Scandinavia, 1700–Present* (London: Palgrave Macmillan), pp. 337–75.
Esping-Andersen, G. (1985) *Politics Against Markets: The Social Democratic Road to Power* (Princeton: Princeton University Press).
Galenson, W. (1952) *The Danish System of Labor Relations: A Study in Industrial Peace* (Cambridge: Harvard University Press).
Greiff, M. and Lundin, J. (2018) 'Sweden 1880–1910: The Age of the Labour Movement' in Mikkelsen, F., Kjeldstadli, K. and Nyzell, S. (eds.) *Popular Struggle and Democracy in Scandinavia, 1700–Present* (London: Palgrave Macmillan), pp. 319–55.
Grimnes, O. K. (2010) 'Okkupation og politik' in Dahl, H. F., Kirchhoff, H., Lund, J. and Vaale, L.-E. (eds.) *Danske tilstande – Norske tilstande. Forskelle og ligheder under tysk besættelse 1940–45* (Copenhagen: Gyldendal), pp. 79–103.
Helle, I. and Matos, T. (2018) 'Norway 1945–2015: Contention and Democracy' in Mikkelsen, F., Kjeldstadli, K. and Nyzell, S. (eds.) *Popular Struggle and Democracy in Scandinavia, 1700–Present* (London: Palgrave), pp. 245–75.
Hilson, M. (2007) 'Scandinavia' in Gerwarth, R. (ed.) *Twisted Paths: Europe 1914–1945* (Oxford: Oxford University Press), pp. 8–32.
Hilson, M. (2008) *The Nordic Model: Scandinavia Since 1945* (London: Reaktion Books).
Jensen, C. S. (ed.) (2000) *Arbejdsgivere i Norden: En sociologisk analyse af arbejdsgiverorganiseringen i Norge, Sverige, Finland og Danmark* (Copenhagen: Nordisk Ministerråd).

Jörberg, L. and Krantz, O. (1976) 'Scandinavia 1914–1970' in Cipolla, C. M. (ed.) *The Fontana Economic History of Europe. Vol. 6, Part 2: Contemporary Economies* (Glasgow: Collins), pp. 377–459.

Julkunen, R. and Rantalaiho, L. (1993) 'Women on Strike—Nonexistent or Silenced?' in Kettunen, P. (ed.) *Strike and Social Change* (Turku: Turku Provincial Museum), pp. 97–114.

Karlbom, R. (1967) *Hungerupplopp och strejker 1793–1869* (Lund: Gleerups).

Kirby, D. (2006) *A Concise History of Finland* (Cambridge: Cambridge University Press).

Kirchhoff, H. (1979) *Augustoprøret 1943*, Vol. 1–3 (Copenhagen: Gyldendal).

Kirchhoff, H. (2004) *Samarbejde og modstand under besættelsen* (Odense: University Press of Southern Denmark).

Kjeldsen, M. (2010) 'Mellem oprør og demokrati: Om normaliseringen i Danmark maj-oktober 1945' in Dahl, H. F., Kirchhoff, H., Lund, J. and Vaale, L.-E. (eds.) *Danske tilstande – Norske tilstande: Forskelle og ligheder under tysk besættelse 1940–45* (Copenhagen: Gyldendal), pp. 282–308.

Kjeldstadli, K. (2015) 'A Closed Nation or an Open Working Class? When Do Unions Opt for Including Labour Migrants?' in Bieler, A. et al. (eds.) *Labour and Transnational Action in Times of Crisis* (London: Rowman & Littlefield), pp. 83–98.

Kjeldstadli, K. (2018) 'Norway 1850–1940: Six Types of Popular Resistance' in Mikkelsen, F., Kjeldstadli, K. and Nyzell, S. (eds.) *Popular Struggle and Democracy in Scandinavia, 1700–Present* (London: Palgrave Macmillan), pp. 201–44.

Kjellberg, A. (2001) *Fackliga organisationer och medlemmar i dagens Sverige* (Lund: Arkiv).

Knudsen, K. (1999) *Arbejdskonflikternes historie i Danmark: Arbejdskampe og arbejderbevægelse 1870–1940* (Copenhagen: SFAH).

Knudsen, K. (2021) *Danish trade unionism 1870–1940* (Aalborg: Aalborg University Press).

Knutsen, O. (2006) *Class Voting in Western Europe* (Oxford: Lexington Books).

Korpi, W. (1978) *The Working Class in Welfare Capitalism: Work, Unions and Politics in Sweden* (London: Routledge and Kegan Paul).

Korpi, W. (1983) *The Democratic Class Struggle* (London: Routledge and Kegan Paul).

Krake, K. (2016) *Skandinavien i ekstremernes tidsalder: Systemkritik og demokratiforsvar i mellemkrigstiden*, Ph.D. dissertation, University of Southern Denmark.

Lilja, K. (1998) 'Finland: Continuity and Modest Moves Towards Company-Level Corporatism' in Ferner, A. and Hyman, R. (eds.) *Changing Industrial Relations in Europe* (Oxford: Blackwell), pp. 171–89.

Logue, J. (2019) 'Trade Unions in the Nordic Countries', *nordics.info* (https://nordics.info/show/artikel/trade-unions-in-the-nordic-region); updated by Einhorn, E. E., retrieved September 27, 2022.

Mattila, Aa. (1993) 'Industrial Conflicts and Their Mediation in the Finnish Labour Market from the 1800's to the 1980's' in Kettunen, P. (ed.) *Strike and Social Change* (Turku: Turku Provincial Museum), pp. 53–70.

Mikkelsen, F. (1986) 'Workers and Industrialization in Scandinavia, 1750–1940', in Hanagan, M. and Stephenson, C. (eds.) *Proletarians and Protest: The Roots of Class Formation in an Industrializing World* (New York: Greenwood Press), pp. 21–54.

Mikkelsen, F. (1992) *Arbejdskonflikter i Skandinavien 1848–1980* (Odense: Odense Universitetsforlag).

Mikkelsen, F. (1993) 'Industrial Conflict in Scandinavia 1848–1990' in Kettunen, P. (ed.) *Strike and Social Change* (Turku: Turku Provincial Museum), pp. 27–52.

Mikkelsen, F. (1997) 'Cycles of Struggle and Innovations in Industrial Relations in Denmark After World War II', *Scandinavian Journal of History*, 22, pp. 31–51.

Mikkelsen, F. (1998) 'Unions and New Shopfloor Strike Strategies and Learning Processes Among Public Employees', *Economic and Industrial Democracy: An International Journal*, 19, 3, pp. 505–38.

Mikkelsen, F. (2005) 'Working-Class Formation in Europe and Forms of Integration: History and Theory', *Labor History*, 46, 3, pp. 277–306.

Mikkelsen, F. (2012) 'Class and Social Movements in Scandinavia Since 1945', *Moving the Social: Journal of Social History and the History of Social Movements*, 48, pp. 29–48.

Mikkelsen, F. (2018a) 'Denmark 1914–1939: Popular Struggle in an Age of Mass Politics' in Mikkelsen, F., Kjeldstadli, K. and Nyzell, S. (eds.) *Popular Struggle and Democracy in Scandinavia, 1700–Present* (London: Palgrave Macmillan), 73–102.

Mikkelsen, F. (2018b) 'Denmark 1940–1946: War, Occupation and Liberation' in Mikkelsen, F., Kjeldstadli, K. and Nyzell, S. (eds.) *Popular Struggle and Democracy in Scandinavia, 1700–Present* (London: Palgrave Macmillan), 103–10.

Mikkelsen, F. (2022) 'The Nordic 'Sonderweg': Popular Struggle, State Building and Democracy in the Nordic Countries in a European Perspective, 1400–2000' (Working Paper).

Mikkelsen, F., Kjeldstadli, K. and Nyzell, S. (eds.) (2018) *Popular Struggle and Democracy in Scandinavia, 1700–Present* (London: Palgrave Macmillan).

Mjøset, L. (ed.) (1986) *Norden dagen derpå. De nordiske økonomisk-politiske modellene og deres problemer på 70- og 80-tallet* (Oslo: Universitetsforlaget).

Mjøset, L. (1987) 'Nordic Economic Policies in the 1970s and 1980s', *International Organization*, 41, 3, pp. 403–56.

Nielsen. N. K. (2009) *Bonde, stat og hjem. Nordisk demokrati og nationalisme – fra pietisme til 2. verdenskrig* (Aarhus: Aarhus University Press).

Nieminen, A. (2000) 'Finnish Employer Confederations – Streamlining Inner Organization and Regulating National Capitalism' in Jensen, C. S. (ed.) *Arbejdsgivere i Norden. En sociologisk analyse af arbejdsgiverorganiseringen i Norge, Sverige, Finland og Danmark* (Copenhagen: Nordisk Ministerråd), pp. 287–371.

Olofsson, M. (2016) 'Rösträttskravallerna i Stockholm 1902 och den återvunna demonstrationsrätten' in Ericsson, M. and Pinto, A. B. (eds.) *Politik underifrån. Kollektiva konfrontationer under Sveriges 1900-tal* (Lund: Arkiv förlag), 31–54.

Olstad, F. (1981) 'Fra matopprør til streik', *Tidsskrift for Arbeiderbevegelsens Historie*, 1, pp. 115–30.

Österberg, M. (2017) 'Norden as a Transnational Space in the 1930s' in Hilson, M., Neunsinger, S. and Vyff, I. (eds.) *Labour, Unions and Politics Under the North Star: The Nordic Countries, 1700–2000* (New York/Oxford: Berghahn).

Ozaki, M. (1987) 'Labour Relations in Public Service', *International Labour Review*, 126, 3 and 4.

Pedersen, B. S. and Holm, A. (1998) 'Restraining Excesses: Resistance and Counter-Resistance in Nazi-Occupied Denmark 1940–1945', *Terrorism and Political Violence*, 10, 1, pp. 60–89.

Peterson, A., Thörn, H. and Wahlström, M. (2018) 'Sweden 1950–2015: Contentious Politics and Social Movements Between Confrontation and Conditioned Cooperation' in Mikkelsen, F., Kjeldstadli, K. and Nyzell, S. (eds.) *Popular Struggle and Democracy in Scandinavia, 1700–Present* (London: Palgrave), pp. 377–432.

Rønning, O. M. (2015) 'Communism in the Nordic Countries 1917–1990: Communist Parties—Organisational Development and Electoral Support' in Egge, Å. and Rybner, S. (eds.) *Red Star in the North: Communism in the Nordic Countries* (Stamsund: Orkana Akademisk), pp. 37–61.

Saarela, T. (2015) 'From Revolutions to Peaceful Roads—Communist Strategy in the Nordic Countries', in Egge, Å. and Rybner, S. (eds.) *Red Star in the North: Communism in the Nordic Countries* (Stamsund: Orkana Akademisk), 120–57.

Scheuer, S. (2004) *Strejker i Europa, LO-Dokumentation 2* (Copenhagen: LO).

Schiller, B. (1967) *Storstrejken 1909: Förhistoria och orsaker* (Göteborg: Elander).

Simonson, B. (1985) *Socialdemokratin och maktövertagandet: SAP:s politiska strategi 1889–1911* (Göteborg: Historiska institutionen).

Soikkanen, H. (1993) 'Historical Review of Strikes in Finland' in Kettunen, P. (ed.) *Strike and Social Change* (Turku: Turku Provincial Museum), pp. 17–26.

Stokke, T. Aa. and Thörnqvist, C. (2001) 'Strikes and Collective Bargaining in the Nordic Countries', *European Journal of Industrial Relations*, 7, 3, pp. 245–67.

Sørensen, A. E. (2014) 'Fra velfærdsbevægelse til ligelønsbevægelse', *Temp*, 9, pp. 142–69.

Teräs, K. (1993) 'Industrial Actionism and Industrial Conflicts in Finland' in Kettunen, P. (ed.) *Strike and Social Change* (Turku: Turku Provincial Museum), pp. 71–76.

Thörnqvist, C. (1994) *Arbetarna lämnar fabriken. Strejkrörelser i Sverige under efterkrigstiden, deres bakgrund, förlopp och følјder* (Göteborg: Historiska institutionen).

Tikka, M. (2017) 'Strike in Finland, Revolution in Russia: The Role of Workers in the 1905 General Strike in the Grand Duchy of Finland' in Hilson, M., Neunsinger, S. and Vyff, I. (eds.) *Labour, Unions and Politics Under the North Star* (New York/Oxford: Berghahn Books), pp. 197–217.

Weiss, H. (2021) *A Global Radical Waterfront: The International Propaganda Committee of Transport Workers and the International of Seamen and Harbour Workers, 1921–1937* (Leiden: Brill).

PART I

National and Local Trade Union Activism, 1900–1939

CHAPTER 3

The Norwegian Experience: Trade Union Opposition and Local Activism, 1900–1939

Finn Olstad

Norway is generally considered a quiet and peaceful country with relatively little trade union activism. This may be right for the period from the 1930s but is not wholly accurate for the preceding period. Norway was, in fact, in the early decades of the twentieth century a country with relatively widespread strike activity and even a revolutionary movement characterised by its link to trade union activism. Different social forces were eager to channel and control this activism: revolutionary socialists and later The Communist Party, trade union officials aiming at establishing and maintaining a collective bargaining system, and employers who were desperate to curb local activism to maintain stability and secure profit.

F. Olstad (✉)
Oslo, Norway
e-mail: fiolstad@online.no

© The Author(s), under exclusive license to Springer Nature Switzerland AG 2023

J. Jørgensen and F. Mikkelsen (eds.), *Trade Union Activism in the Nordic Countries since 1900*, Palgrave Studies in the History of Social Movements, https://doi.org/10.1007/978-3-031-08987-9_3

Trade Union Centralism

Norway in the first decades of the twentieth century was a small country in the periphery of Europe and in many ways the little brother of its Scandinavian neighbours. Up to 1814, Norway had been virtually a part of Denmark and subject to the Danish crown. Then it became junior partner in a union with Sweden. (The two countries had the same king and certain other institutions in common.) When the union was dissolved in 1905, Norway was for the first time since the Middle Ages on its own as a wholly independent country. At the same time, there was an unprecedented industrial development. Much more than before, Norway became an industrial and capitalist country, also marked by industrial conflicts of a new kind and magnitude.

The Norwegian labour movement was initially not very well prepared for this development. In comparison with its Scandinavian colleagues, it was a latecomer, small, weak and inclined to copying the role models of Germany, Denmark, and Sweden. Local trade unions and some national federations had emerged in the 1880s and 1890s. However, these unions represented primarily three groups of workers: artisans, iron- and metalworkers, and miners. The Confederation of Trade Unions (*Arbeidernes faglige Landsorganisasjon*), established in 1899 as a joint organisation for all the unions, numbered in 1905 no more than 16,000 members, compared to 76,000 registered factory workers at the same time.[1] The Confederation as well as the national federations were based in the capital Oslo (until 1925 Kristiania).

Overall, the trade unions could not match the employers, either on the local or national scale. The Norwegian Employers' Confederation (*Norsk Arbeidsgiverforening*) was established in 1900 to counter the demands of the trade unions. The Employers' Confederation pursued a policy of unbridled capitalism. In comparison with the trade unions, it had superior resources and a crucial means of power in the lockout. It is fair to say that the employers were dominant in the field of industrial struggle.

How to cope with this situation, seen from the perspective of trade union officials? How to come to terms with industrial capitalism? The answer was not to be found in increased strike activity and anti-capitalism,

[1] This chapter is based on Olstad, F. (2009) *LOs historie, Vol. 1: 1899–1935: Med knyttet neve* (Oslo: Pax), which deals with the history of the Norwegian trade union movement until 1935.

according to Marius Ormestad, the leader of The Iron- and Metalworkers' Union during the years 1898–1909. Capitalist development had to be accepted, but the workers were entitled to get a share of the profits, with higher wages, shorter working hours, and other improvements. In this perspective, the preferred means of struggle was not collective conflicts, but rather a regulated individual strategy, as the union members were supposed to move to companies with higher wages and better working conditions. Ideally, the union officials should be able to direct the workforce in a way that made them masters of the labour market in their field. This was, of course, a strategy made for skilled and well-qualified workers.

This strategy presupposed peaceful negotiations. Ormestad wanted diplomacy and peace, but to achieve this, the organisation had to prepare for war and to be strong enough to stand up to the employers. It is perhaps one of the paradoxes of trade unionism that The Iron and Metalworkers' Union in these years grew significantly in membership numbers and strength, not because of Ormestad's visions, but because of ordinary workers' need to come together and pool resources to counter the employers' attacks on traditional working conditions. In 1907, the employers were ready to strike a bargain with Ormestad and his union.

This year, The Employers' Confederation and the unions of the iron industry made the first collective agreement of a whole branch of industry in Norway. The agreement was instrumental in shaping the field of industrial struggle for years to come. The employers would have full opportunity to lead and distribute the work ("*lede og fordele arbeidet*"), as the phrase was. This meant that the workers would not resist new methods of work, including stricter work discipline and piecework. However, they would get their share of greater productivity with the prospect of steady wage increase. A minimum wage was introduced to protect lower-paid unskilled workers, but not so much that it really mattered for the companies. The agreement laid the basis for a compromise between capital and labour on the terms of capitalist expansion. In a way, this also meant a tacit understanding between skilled workers and large industrial companies at the expense of smaller companies and unskilled workers, striving to keep afloat in the development of modern industrial capitalism.

This was the starting point for a transformation and regulation of industrial relations in the years to come, as the employers were able to force similar conditions on the greater part of Norwegian trade unions. However, there were limits to the employer dominance, as workers in large numbers joined the unions and submitted to the necessary union discipline. The Confederation of Trade Unions grew to 60,000 members in 1912. This was in the wake of the lockout of 1911, which affected more than 32,000 workers and provoked stubborn resistance. The result was a draw, after pressure from public opinion and politicians, appalled by the sufferings of class war. Shortly after, The Labour Disputes Act (*Arbeidstvistloven*) of 1915 to some degree regulated the right to strike and introduced the institution of the State Conciliator of Norway, as keeper of the peace in the industrial field. Industrial relations had become a game with three main players.

The central union officials were determined to play by the rules. The central union strategy was, as was stated by the editor of the main Labour Party newspaper, to promote the interests of the workers by "wise diplomatic negotiation", preferably without strikes and lockouts.[2] This also meant that the workers had to trust their leaders, who was supposed to have the knowledge and insight in what was possible to achieve. Local activism and the fire of class hatred was to be sacrificed to the cool assessment of overall costs and benefits. It was a strategy of plan, order and reason.

This is not to say that the central strategy was not based on class consciousness and class interests, only that this might look different from different perspectives. The central strategy did certainly not rule out conflicts, as it might be necessary to put up strong and organised resistance, as shown by the lockout of 1911. However, the relevant class interests were chiefly modelled on well-paid, skilled factory workers. For some workers, this meant exclusion, opposition, and local activism in defiance of employers and central union officials.

The Trade Union Opposition

Union growth and centralisation, proliferation of collective agreements and involvement of politicians and government in labour disputes characterised the years 1905–1915. Still, there was widespread local activism, as in the small town of Odda in western Norway in 1913.

The smelter in Odda, with its carbide production, was part of the new modern hydroelectrical industry in Norway. Semi-skilled workers,

[2] Kringen, O. (1905) *Fagorganisationen: Dens teorier og principer* (Kristiania: Det norske Arbeiderparti), p. 64. Cf. Olstad, *LOs historie*, p. 87.

who had migrated from different parts of Norway, operated the furnaces. Knowledge and experience were required to keep up the quantity and quality of production, and a shutdown would cause major problems. This gave the workers a strong bargaining position, as the company was dependent on their cooperation.

The strike originated in the workers' demand for respect, as the foreman had told one of them to leave the work. The local union demanded an apology, or the workers would go on strike within four hours. This, of course, was a violation of the collective agreement, and the local union had to back down. A mass meeting of the workers repeated the demands, and soon all the 600 workers of the smelter were on strike. However, the company did not give in. Without any outside support, the workers had to go back to work.

The strikers in Odda and other workers who had similar experiences easily gravitated towards the so-called Trade Union Opposition of 1911 (*Fagopposisjonen av 1911*) and its rallying cry of handing power back to the members ("*makten tilbake til medlemmene*"). The Trade Union Opposition violently opposed the centralism of the national unions and their strategy of negotiations and binding collective agreements. In short, the opposition wanted to replace the national unions with local councils or confederations of different kinds of workers (*samorganisasjoner*). It also wanted to get rid of the unions' health insurance and similar arrangements, which supposedly distracted them from the present class struggle. The trade union movement was like a standing army, where the workers as ordinary soldiers had to submit to the central strategy of the union generals. The Trade Union Opposition wanted to be an instrument for more spontaneous rebellion from below, in which the attitude, will and power of the local workers would be the decisive factors.

The challenge of this locally based opposition was a peculiar feature of the Norwegian labour movement. This was also true for the leading personality, if not the formal head of the movement, Martin Tranmæl. As the son of a bankrupt farmer, he had to make his living as a carpenter and construction worker in Trondheim, the third largest city of Norway. Later, travelling in the United States and in Europe profoundly influenced his opinions on trade unionism and politics. As a working immigrant in the United States, he had first-hand experience of the harsh oppression and fierce class struggle of American capitalism, and he witnessed the foundation of the syndicalist International Workers of the World in 1905. Eventually, he settled as a journalist and from 1913 editor of a newspaper called New Times (*Ny Tid*) in Trondheim, where he made himself noticed as a fierce critic of union centralism and the lacking radicalism of the labour movement. As a public orator, Tranmæl was extremely charismatic, powerful and influential. At the same time, he was a shrewd network builder with a special gift to attract oppositional and radical youth.[3]

Tranmæl was indeed influenced by syndicalism, as was The Trade Union Opposition. It proclaimed direct action and new and more radical means of struggle like sabotage, boycott and obstruction. Above all, it wanted to get rid of the long-lasting collective agreements, which made the workers inactive and complacent. All agreements should be provisional and prone to renegotiation at any time. In other words, local workers should be able to strike whenever they had the opportunity and a good chance of success. The idea was that local activists would bring the mass of ordinary workers with them in the attack on capitalist exploitation and privileges.

It is obvious that the programme of The Trade Union Opposition would appeal to workers like the furnace operators in Odda, who wanted the freedom to strike at any time, without the rigorous procedures of collective agreements. Even miners and construction workers, especially those highly mobile workers who helped build the new large electrochemical and electrometallurgical industrial plants, easily gravitated towards The Trade Union Opposition. Mobility was a source of freedom and bargaining power if you were not constrained by union centralism and discipline.

The strength and radicalism of The Trade Union Opposition in Norway have attracted the interest of historians and social scientists, and interpretations have focused on both the deprivation and on the alleged rootlessness and anomie of their core members of highly mobile workers.[4]

[3] The career and political standpoints of Martin Tranmæl until 1918 are analysed by Bjørgum, J. (1998) *Martin Tranmæl og radikaliseringen av norsk arbeiderbevegelse 1906–1918* (Oslo: Scandinavian University Press). My interpretations in Olstad, *LOs historie* and here may differ somewhat from those of Bjørgum.

[4] Some relevant works are Bjørgum, J. (1977) 'Industrialisering og radikalisme: Replikk til William M. Lafferty', *Tidsskrift for arbeiderbevegelsens historie*, 2, pp. 131–42; Bull, E. (1976) 'Arbeiderbevegelsens stilling i de tre nordiske land 1914–1920', *Tidsskrift for arbeiderbevegelsens historie*, 1, pp. 3–28 (originally published 1922); Fure, O.-B. (1976) 'Synspunkter og historieteoretiske tendenser I forskningen om den norske arbeiderklasse og -bevegelse i den radikale fase 1918–1933', *Tidsskrift for arbeiderbevegelsens historie*, 1, pp. 29–62; Fure, O.-B. (1983) *Mellom reformisme og bolsjevisme: Norsk arbeiderbevegelse*

However, these groups also had a highly developed sense of identity and a rather rigorous set of norms attached to work and to the living in barracks. At the core, there was a youthful, aggressive masculinity. The programme of The Trade Union Opposition may have been well suited to this kind of masculinity with its emphasis on strength and roughness. The show of physical strength and verbal aggression of direct action may have been more satisfactory than the relative caution and courtesy of union negotiations and highly disciplined strikes. The demand for respect in the face of condescending employers and others may have contributed to the will of uncompromising struggle. Rather than settling for a compromise, the right thing to do was to deliver a fast blow and move on.[5]

However, The Trade Union Opposition attracted several different groups. Its core area was in the region around Trondheim, which was renowned as the stronghold of radicalism in Norway. Strong demands and loud shouts masked that this radicalism was associated with weakness, rather than strength. The workers here were to a lesser degree organised than, e.g. the workers of Oslo. They were also more exposed to strikebreaking, and they frequently experienced defeat. To be blunt, they wanted the freedom to local activism, but with the help and support of The Confederation of Trade Unions. Their organisational weakness may further contribute to explain a certain attraction to radical politics. In large, The Trade Union Opposition stood out from international syndicalism with its demands for a strong national confederation and its emphasis on political struggle.

In conclusion, The Trade Union Opposition united quite different groups with varying outlooks and strategical positions. The common factor was the opposition to union centralism and long-term collective agreements, accompanied by the support for political radicalism. This also meant a rejection of central features of society and placed The Trade Union Opposition in the larger context of social rebellion.

1918–1920. Teori. Praksis (doctoral dissertation, University of Bergen); Lafferty, W. M. (1971) *Economic Development and the Response of Labor in Scandinavia: A Multi-Level Analysis* (Oslo: Universitetsforlaget); Lafferty, W. M. (1974) *Industrialization, Community Structure and Socialism: An Ecological Analysis of Norway, 1875–1924* (Oslo: Universitetsforlaget); and Lafferty, W. M. (1977) 'Industrialisering og radikalisme: En kort kommentar', *Tidsskrift for arbeiderbevegelsens* historie, 1, pp. 199–208.

[5] Olstad, *LOs historie*, p. 187. Cf. Bjørnson, Ø. (1990) *Arbeiderbevegelsens historie i Norge, Vol. 2: På klassekampens grunn (1900–1920)* (Oslo: Tiden), p. 48ff.

The Trade Union Opposition from the start declared the need for more "revolutionary" means of struggle and placed itself in a revolutionary tradition. It was not at all clear what that really meant. For many workers the self-proclaimed revolutionary attitude may simply have meant more aggressive and efficient class struggle, and it is striking how many workers applauded the revolutionary message of Tranmæl and others while at the same time preparing negotiations and collective agreements with the employers.

Martin Tranmæl was indeed more of a politician than a trade unionist and became the central and unifying figure for The Labour Party members who worked for revolution. His strategy was to bind local trade union activism to revolutionary politics. This made the Norwegian labour movement somewhat different from the labour movements of other Western European countries in the crucial years during and shortly after the First World War.

Hard Times and Increased Activism

The horrors of the First World War changed the face of Europe, with material, economic and social devastation, the fall of great empires, the creation of new national states, the Russian Revolution and revolutionary movements elsewhere. As Norway was able to keep out of the war, it was less affected, but in some ways more so than its Scandinavian neighbours. Trade union activism and the split between the central union leadership and The Trade Union Opposition contributed to the somewhat special course of the Norwegian labour movement.

Dramatically rising prices undermined the long-lasting collective agreements and spurred local activism, especially in 1917 and 1918. At the same time, there was significant union membership growth, and the distinction between skilled and unskilled workers became less obvious. The employers complained about frequent local actions, which might proceed somewhat like this: a local union or workshop club presented its demands with an extremely short deadline. If the employers resisted, the workers left the workplace on short notice, either individually or collectively. Then there were conferences with the unions, which regularly ended with the workers returning and the employers raising the payment.

In this precarious situation, the national unions tacitly supported local actions. In fact, some unions even encouraged local activism. The central union strategy was flexible enough to allow for such changes if the union hierarchy remained unchallenged. This of course meant that groups with strong bargaining power would have the advantage. Some groups resorted to actions which long had been used by, e.g. skilled ironworkers and were part of a formally individual strategy. The workers simply left the job, one after another, and pressure was put on those who did not at first comply with the common cause. However, the workers did not define this as a strike, and the unions were not officially involved. Often, the company had no alternative but to negotiate with an ad hoc group of workers and raise the payment to get the workforce back to work.[6]

In this way, groups of workers managed to compensate for the rising costs of living. Real wages decreased significantly during the years 1914–1916. During the next two years, there was an increase in real wages, although not quite enough to bring them back to the level of 1914.[7] However, activism made for big differences between groups and branches. There were winners, like the typographers, and losers. In fact, groups that supported the national unions and adhered to the central union strategy seem overall to have been more able to take advantage of the situation than those gravitating towards The Trade Union Opposition.

The opposition grew in numerical strength and launched a campaign to take over the national unions and even The Confederation of Labour. To some degree, it succeeded. The national leaders had to make compromises, e.g. by giving local workers' confederations a certain role to play. In 1918, The Trade Union Opposition gained the majority at the national meetings of two of the main unions, The Norwegian Union of General Workers and The Iron- and Metalworkers' Union. Both unions voted in favour of abolishing binding collective agreements. However, the new principles were not put into practice, as the more radical leaders had no more power or resources to combat the employers than the previous leadership.

In the end, The Trade Union Opposition as such withered away, while many of the leaders won important positions in the trade union movement, as well as in The Labour Party. By this time, much of the energy of

[6] Cf. examples in Olstad, *LOs historie*, pp. 212–13.

[7] *Lønninger og levekår* (1918), published by *Statistisk sentralbyrå* (Statistics Norway) (Olstad, *LOs historie*, p. 214).

the opposition was diverted to politics with the aim of overthrowing capitalist society. The cause of revolution in Norway received strong support from trade union activists under the guidance of Martin Tranmæl.

A Revolutionary Alternative

For Martin Tranmæl and his companions in The Trade Union Opposition, trade union activism and revolution were two sides of the same coin. A revolution was, according to Tranmæl, both necessary and possible in the near future. Trade union activists would play a key role in this revolution. "Revolutionary mass action" ("*revolusjonær masseaksjon*") was the slogan. What this would mean in practice, was never clearly defined.

In 1917, there were reasons to believe in an imminent revolutionary development. In addition to rising prices, there were food shortages and rationing. On 6 June 1917 demonstrations all over the country gathered 300,000 people. In Oslo 40,000 took part in the largest demonstration in the city ever. Among the protesters were many housewives and other women. As we know from the history of the French and Russian revolutions, when women march in the streets the authorities have reason to fear.

Tranmæl and his revolutionary comrades were ready to take advantage of the situation. In a brochure written in March 1917, they called for action. The plan was to summon a general workers' congress, which was to make the necessary decisions and preparations. The outcome would be a general strike, which eventually would force the government to back down.

In this brochure, Tranmæl came closer than ever to develop a theory of revolutionary takeover. The general strike would be the starting point. It was to be accompanied by an "antimilitary action" as the government undoubtedly would try to use military forces to break the strike. Soldiers from the working class were expected to gather in soldiers' councils and to refuse mobilisation. Tranmæl thought that this would lead to major confrontations. In this situation, trade union activists would have a key role by causing local disturbances and rebellions, which would eventually turn the general strike into a full-scale revolution.[8]

[8] The brochure *Til handling!* (1917), published by Norges socialdemokratiske ungdomsforbund (Olstad, *LOs historie*, pp. 260–62).

The leaders of The Confederation of Trade Unions, however, did not favour such a development. In short, they countered the attempts to summon a general workers' congress. Instead, they made sure that the matter was handed over to an extraordinary congress of the Confederation. Here, of course, the Confederation leaders had the upper hand. This would not be the last time national union leaders intervened against revolutionary preparations. The Confederation of Trade Unions proved to be a solid support for the authorities against the threat of revolution.

The resentment and anger against capitalism and society had to be channelled elsewhere. Tranmæl's masterpiece was to unite the forces of local activists in The Trade Union Opposition with the revolutionary opposition of The Labour Party, chiefly to be found in its youth organisation (*Norges socialdemokratiske ungdomsforbund*). This resulted in a majority at the congress of The Labour Party in spring 1918. The party declared itself as revolutionary, with a proclamation that the party would "reserve the right to use revolutionary mass action in the struggle for the economic liberation of the working class".[9] The revolutionaries took over the party management. Tranmæl, as usual, did not want to be at the forefront. As a party secretary, he was still the actual leader and the main force of revolution.

Under the auspices of the new leaders, the programme and the rhetoric of the party became more and more revolutionary. Lesser known is that they on a couple of occasions even thought of the possibility of revolution and attempted some revolutionary planning. In November/December 1918, after what was thought to be the start of a socialist revolution in Germany, they predicted the advent of the world revolution and wanted to call for workers' and soldiers' councils to take the lead. Tranmæl said that "we are facing the final preparations" and had to be ready for "the march towards the new society".[10] However, Ole O. Lian, the formidable leader of The Confederation of Trade Unions, summoned the party leaders to his office and told them not to publish any appeals to form workers' councils. In the face of opposition from the trade unions, the party leaders had little choice but to cooperate, and, as we know, the world revolution did not materialise.

[9] According to the minutes of the congress. The whole text is reproduced in Lorenz, E. (ed.) (1970) *Norsk sosialisme En dokumentasjon* (Oslo: Pax).

[10] *Solidaritet* (radical newspaper), November 23, 1918 (Olstad, *LOs historie*, p. 263).

Later, during the period from autumn 1920 to spring 1921, there seem to have been serious preparations for a revolutionary attempt. By this time, The Labour Party was affiliated to The Communist International of Moscow. However, there was a gap between the localist, and union-based revolutionary approach of Tranmæl and his followers and the more elitist revolutionary demands of The Communist International. Still, preparations seem to have continued until the international revolutionary leadership (that is to say a revolutionary central in Berlin) put the brakes on, shortly after the disastrous "March Action" in Germany.[11] A proposed general strike in Norway in May/June 1921 came to no more than an ordinary and non-revolutionary strike.

At this point, Martin Tranmæl had taken over the post as editor of the chief Labour Party newspaper *Arbeiderbladet* (a post that he held until 1949). It seems that he wanted to take advantage of the situation to arouse a more long-term revolutionary spirit among the workers, and he especially argued for factory occupations (according to Italian model). In this way, he reverted to the strategy of local activism and revolution from below.

These attempts were in vain, as the ordinary trade unionists and party members did not follow. The strike of 1921 ended in defeat, resignation, and a significant loss of union membership. In short, local union activism was not easily translated into revolutionary rebellion. The more or less ideological positions at the top of the labour movement related to a limited extent to the experiences, interests and views at the local level. In the end, it turned out that the revolutionary practice had no real popular backing. More generally, when in position, The Trade Union Opposition failed to find a course of action that was compatible with the different local perspectives. It did not survive the acquisition of national positions and power.

In the end, The Labour Party could not reconcile the approach of Tranmæl with communist revolution as advocated by Moscow. The Party split on the issue in November 1923, with a small majority following

[11] This interesting development is outside the scope of this article. See Olstad, *LOs historie*, pp. 273–284; and Olstad, F. (2018) 'Spørsmålet om revolusjon i Norge og Skandinavia 1917–1921. En oppsummering og mulig ny begynnelse', *Arbeiderhistorie*, pp. 127–141. Cf. Kan, A. (2005) *Hemmabolsjevikarna: Den svenska socialdemokratin, ryska bolsjeviker och mensjeviker under världskriget och revolutionsåren 1914–1920* (Stockholm: Carlssons Bokförlag).

Tranmæl. The sympathisers of The Communist International formed The Norwegian Communist Party, trying hard to thrive on trade union activism. The ironworkers' strike in 1923/24 became the first major showdown.

Activism and Communism

The ironworkers' strike in Oslo 1923/24 was the most intense case of trade union activism in the interwar period. It had all the ingredients of the hard-fought class struggles of the time. First, there was the feeling of abuse and injustice. The strike started spontaneously as the employers in late October 1923 put up posters telling the workers that they had decided to turn down wages. This they had the right to do according to the collective agreement, as the cost-of-living index had fallen below a certain limit. However, the fall was largely due to certain formalities and did not correspond to the real cost of living. More importantly, for the workers, these posters meant a command from above, treating them not as equals, but as subordinates. They simply retaliated by leaving the work.[12]

The ironworkers' strike was more long lasting and exhausting than any other local conflict at the time. The workers were out of job for seven months. The later Labour Party secretary, Haakon Lie, recalls in his memoirs how they had to sell their furniture and pawn their watches. He saw single girls faint as they cued up for the meagre strike contribution. When they had paid the rent, there was not enough money left for food.[13]

The strike even meant confrontations with the police and the judiciary. According to the authorities, leading or joining the strike was a criminal offence, and 29 of the activists received fines or imprisonment. As

[12] Olstad, F. (1990) *Jern og Metall 100 år, Vol. 1: 1891–1940* (Oslo: Tiden), pp. 353–380; and Olstad, *LOs historie*, pp. 294–307. The ironworkers' strike is described in detail in Bjørnhaug, I. (1975) *Jernstreiken og arbeiderbevegelsen. En undersøkelse av jernstreiken 1923–24 og dens betydning for utviklinga av norsk arbeiderbevegelse* (master's thesis, University of Oslo). My interpretations are somewhat different from those of Bjørnhaug. On the history of The Norwegian Communist Party, see Lorenz, E. (1978) *Norwegische Arbeiterbewegung und Kommunistische Internationale 1919–1930. Untersuchung zur Politik der Kommunistischen Internationale* (Oslo: Pax); and Lorenz, E. (1983) *Det er ingen sak å få partiet lite. NKP 1923–1931* (Oslo: Pax).

[13] Lie, H (1980) *Loftsrydding* (Oslo: Tiden), p. 149.

the sentences were read out, there was some unrest and clashes with the police, in which the young Labour Party secretary and Tranmæl disciple, later Prime Minister Einar Gerhardsen, played a major part. As an editor, Tranmæl himself was fined for "glorification" of the strike.

In the mythology of the labour movement, the ironworkers' strike has signified sacrifice and heroism. However, at the time, it also meant internal strife. The strike activism challenged the system of collective agreements and the established hierarchy of the trade union movement. The leader of The Iron- and Metalworkers' Union Halvard Olsen, ironically an earlier chairman of The Trade Union Opposition, might sympathise with the strikers. Still, he had to condemn the strike as illegal and order the workers back to job. (Illegal in this context means contrary to the collective agreements.)

The ironworkers' strike entered a field of political tension, at a time when the so-called "tranmælites" and the Moscow-oriented communists of The Labour Party were about to split up. The strike was led by an action committee, in which communists had control. This did not mean that The Communist Party had the power to direct the action committee. Rather, it was the other way round. An alliance between the leaders of the strike and the left wing of The Communist Party took control over relevant party affairs. Halvard Olsen, who by the time was vice chairman of The Communist Party, was formally excluded.

At the same time, leading representatives of the iron industry wanted to teach radical workers a lesson. The workers should understand "that it is not quite harmless to make use of the revolutionary institutions of the Bolsheviks".[14] After New Year 1924, The Norwegian Employers' Confederation put in effect a major lockout, which in the end affected more than 50,000 workers. They even pushed for a law against strikes contrary to collective agreements. The Confederation of Trade Unions retaliated with a sympathy strike of 20,000 workers.

In the end, the government had to intervene. Despite the fact of being a right-wing government, it did not, or did not dare to follow the lead of The Employers' Confederation. It would seem unfair, as the ironworkers' grievances had proved to be correct. The prices had risen, and the initial wage cut appeared as unreasonable. Moreover, the ironworkers'

[14] Minutes of Mekaniske Verksteders Landsforening (*The Federation of Norwegian Manufacturing Industries*), December 17, 1923 (Olstad, *LOs historie*, p. 298).

strike was no longer to be classified as illegal, as the collective agreement had expired. In this situation, there was no moral justification to punish the workers. Instead, the government acted in consultation with The Confederation of Trade Unions and put pressure on the employers. This paved the way for a compromise, even if the ironworkers were against it. The action committee wanted to go on striking but was overruled by a small majority of the ironworkers of Oslo.

The ironworkers' strike proved to be a significant episode in trade union history in Norway, but not quite as the action committee and the politically motivated activists had intended. The overwhelming support for the action committee was more situational than principally justified. The radical course of the action committee may have suited the ironworkers in the present situation when their resentment and despair resulted in an illegal strike. Obviously, many workers at the time were looking for something new. However, the ironworkers' strike and the action committee brought no victory. For most of the workers, the radical and revolutionary alternative would seem like a blind alley. It promised and demanded too much, with intensified class struggle and prolonged strikes in a period of economic distress, perhaps resulting in a dramatic and possibly even violent confrontation with the authorities. The preferred alternative was the old, predictable and relatively safe course of the union leadership and The Confederation of Trade Unions.

Perhaps an action like the ironworkers' strike may be judged more as a sort of catharsis than as a support for a radically new course of trade unionism. The strike was an outlet for intense feelings of honour, masculinity, class hatred, solidarity and comradeship. This was not something that the workers would easily repeat on command. Instead, as the struggle was over, they could go on with their heads raised to the everyday world of traditional trade unionism.

From this time, The Labour Party was wedded to trade union centralism and left political support for irregular local actions to The Communist Party. The communists, in fact, tried to use local actions to recruit and mobilise workers for their own purposes. This was clearly visible during the third period of the Communist International 1928–33, with renewed militancy and revolutionary rhetoric.[15] By far and large, this strategy failed. As local activism became too much politicised, the bulk of

[15] McDermott, K. and Agnew, J. (1996) *The Comintern: A History of International Communism from Lenin to Stalin* (London: Macmillan), p. 81ff.

workers retreated. In most cases, the political struggle within the labour movement was an obstacle, rather than an asset for trade union activism.

The Final Showdown

Even more than the illegal iron strike, the so-called battle of Menstad (*Menstad-slaget*) looms large in Norwegian labour movement memory and mythology. That this minor skirmish has gone down in history as the "battle", testifies that labour relations of Norway have been mostly non-violent.

What happened, was that a group of 2000 demonstrators, with music, flags and a small uniformed force ("*arbeidervern*"), marched to confront some strike breakers at Menstad, a loading place between the towns of Skien and Porsgrunn. Halfway it met a local police force, and the fighting began. The police with their water hoses had no chance against rough workers armed with sticks and firewood. After some five minutes of fighting, the police retreated to Menstad, calling for reinforcements and revolvers. Luckily, the leaders of the demonstration managed to calm down some hot-headed workers who wanted to pursue the police force and continue fighting.[16] After the "battle", the government sent the hated state police and military troops to control the situation. This would add to the position of the battle of Menstad in labour movement mythology, especially as the minister of defence was major Vidkun Quisling, later infamous as the national traitor of the Second World War.

This episode of local activism took place during the lockout of 1931. This was in a Norwegian context a gigantic labour struggle, by far the largest in Norwegian history. It affected 60 000 workers for five months, which amounts to 7.5 million lost working days. Both parts had planned for the tariff settlement of 1931 in relatively bright economic times, which was a problem as the economic crisis struck. The major ambition of the employers was to reduce wages, which since the outbreak of the First World War had risen to a level considerably higher than in countries like Sweden, England, and Germany.[17] This meant trouble, as workers always had fiercely resisted demands to cut back on wages.

[16] For a detalied analysis, see Johansen, P. O. (1977) *Menstadkonflikten 1931* (Oslo: Tiden).

[17] According to the internal statistics of The Norwegian Employers' Confederation, the wages were 15–20% higher than in Sweden, 20–25% higher than in England and 40%

After four months, both The Employers' Confederation and The Confederation of Trade Unions, now headed by Halvard Olsen, were ready to make peace. This once again revealed the schism between the perspectives of nation union leaders and local workers, who were determined to fight for the upholding of their standard of living and for their honour as working men and women facing the brutality of capitalism. The stage was set for local resistance and activism.

This also meant political confrontations, as the communists regularly backed local actions, while The Labour Party sided with the union leadership. The Communist Party prior to the lockout had organised sympathetic workers in opposition groups and communist fractions, with a Revolutionary Trade Union Opposition (*Den revolusjonære fagopposisjon*) at the top. The communists had their strongholds in the chemical industry, construction and above all in shipping, with communist cells and from New Year 1931 communist clubs in several ports.

The communist strategy was to encourage and mobilise local resentment and activism, as can be shown in the case of shipping. The sailors themselves were to adopt and lead strikes and other forms of labour struggle, at least formally. The plan was to form local action committees, elected at mass meetings and not in the local unions. These committees were to visit ships, hold meetings and deal with claims and actions. At the end, they were to lead the actions, while a central committee was to lead nationwide struggles. These actions would continue regardless of unions support and regardless of union collective agreements. A main point was the collaboration of organised and non-organised workers in a so-called united front from below.

Again, it turned out that workers, who welcomed communist support and initiatives, backed down when actions became too demanding and when the political purpose became too obvious. Rather than principal socialism or communism, they were motivated by a fighting spirit that was grounded in local interests and traditions. The action committees did not become the expected force, even if there was some local activity. In Bergen, the main bastion of communism in Norway, the local branch of The Seamen's Union in May 1931 voted for strike in defiance of the

higher than in Germany, while Danish workers were on the same level as Norwegian (Olstad, *LOs historie*, p. 334).

national union leadership. The communist opposition urged the sailors: Every man ashore. Only a single ship followed the call.[18]

Communists also were active at the battle of Menstad. All the prominent union leaders who attended were in fact communists. The communist press considered the incident as the starting point of "independent, directly rebellious struggle in Norway".[19] However, there was no such breakthrough, and the communist connection was soon forgotten as the battle of Menstad was exalted into the memory of great moments in Norwegian labour history. The communists did never overcome the basic ambiguity of local class interest and rebellious politics. Even union communists deserted as the unions became the main target for criticism and they had to collaborate with the non-organised. They wanted no "wild west", as one of them said before leaving the party.[20]

The challenges from below made a compromise between the employers' and the workers' central organisations necessary. However, the workers would not easily give in. Twice they discarded an agreement proposal before finally consenting, as the unions threatened stop strike contributions. In the end, the lockout of 1931 highlighted the problems of large nationwide labour struggles and the need to control local activism. In this way, it was an important driving force behind the settlements of the 1930s, which laid the foundations of the present so-called Norwegian model of labour relations.

Postscript: The Norwegian Model

A kind of war fatigue characterised both camps after the lockout of 1931. As the later chairman of The Confederation of Trade Unions, then leader of the iron- and metalworkers Konrad Nordahl writes in his memoirs, there had been ten years of almost uninterrupted conflict. Even if the conflicts were well justified, they did not help to build the general prosperity. Therefore, there was an agreement to have a prolonged period of peace, of at least ten years.[21]

[18] Olstad, F. (2006) *Norsk Sjømannsforbunds historie, Vol. 1: Vår skjebne i vår hånd* (Oslo: Pax), p. 213ff.

[19] *Arbeideren* (communist newspaper) July 18, 1931 (Olstad, *LOs historie*, p. 339).

[20] Idar Hamsås quoted from *Den internasjonale transportarbeider* (communist periodical), 1, 1930 (Olstad, *Norsk Sjømannsforbunds historie*, p. 221).

[21] Nordahl, K. (1967) *Minner og meninger* (Oslo: Tiden), p. 177.

The leading employers had reached a similar conclusion, after years of trying to bring wages down. This formed the basis of an understanding that shaped the labour relations for years to come. There would be no more large-scale and devastating conflicts. (An exception did not happen until 1986.) There was a tacit understanding that employers and workers would cooperate in the modernisation of Norwegian industry, to make it efficient and competitive. In return for their cooperation, the workers would have their fair share of the gains.

This situation and the economic crisis of the 1930s made little room for trade union activism, although there were some irregular local conflicts. In fact, there was a marked tendency for local workers to agree to reduce their wages to preserve jobs. Even this might lead to conflicts with the national unions, as it was contrary to union politics and challenged the established order.

Trade union centralism prevailed, and trade union activism was reduced to a more marginal position than ever. Still, activism may have been a crucial factor in the establishment of the new industrial relations of the 1930s. In dealing with the unions and negotiating peace, the employers always had to consider the guerrilla of local activism.

To a certain degree, the employers and their organisations controlled the unions and their members through the introduction of large-scale collective agreements. The great danger was that uncontrolled trade union activism would undermine this solution. The fear of losing control was even greater when local activism linked up with political, even revolutionary ambitions. This prompted the employers to make concessions to support the central union strategy and preserve the dominance of the national leadership of the unions. In 1919, the employers agreed to considerably higher wages, the eight-hour day, paid vacation and other benefits, as a "a sort of insurance".[22]

In 1931, local unrest and communist activity was a major encouragement to employer cooperation with The Confederation of Trade Unions to put an end to the conflict. The chairman of The Employers' Confederation emphasised the need to "strengthen the present leadership" of the unions. "If this is to be destroyed or weakened, if the elements that at present ravage down there come to power, things will look very dark for us". ("*Skal den ødelegges eller svekkes, skal de elementer som nu raser*

[22] The chairman of The Employers' Confederation, Lars Rasmussen, quoted from the minutes of the commitee of representatives, May 22, 1919 (Olstad, *LOs historie*, p. 245).

dernede komme til makten, så vil det se meget mørkt ut for oss".)[23] There was always some sort of tacit understanding between the main leaders of both parts to uphold the rules of the game, and this was especially clear in times of crises.

In conclusion, The Norwegian Model of relative peace, modernisation of the industry and economic gains for the workers came to characterise labour relations, even if that did not mean the end to class politics or class consciousness. At the same time, the former revolutionary Labour Party completed its reversion to parliamentary politics by taking over government in 1935, despite not having a majority. Generally, labour movement politics at the time was an attempt to deal with the great challenges of the time, as the need to combat the economic crisis and the fear of fascism. However, even trade union activism played its part, in a perhaps paradoxical way. It strengthened the bargaining position of the unions and contributed to the willingness of the dominant employers to concessions and cooperation. The existence of both a central union strategy and local trade union activism proved to be an important asset for the labour movement.

References

Bjørgum, J. (1977) 'Industrialisering og radikalisme: Replikk til William M. Lafferty', *Tidsskrift for arbeiderbevegelsens historie,* 2, pp. 131–42.

Bjørgum, J. (1998) *Martin Tranmæl og radikaliseringen av norsk arbeiderbevegelse 1906–1918* (Oslo: Scandinavian University Press).

Bjørnhaug, I. (1975) *Jernstreiken og arbeiderbevegelsen: En undersøkelse av jernstreiken 1923–24 og dens betydning for utviklinga av norsk arbeiderbevegelse* (Master's Thesis, University of Oslo).

Bjørnson, Ø. (1990) *Arbeiderbevegelsens historie i Norge, Vol. 2: På klassekampens grunn (1900–1920)* (Oslo: Tiden).

Bull, E. (1976) 'Arbeiderbevegelsens stilling i de tre nordiske land 1914–1920', *Tidsskrift for arbeiderbevegelsens historie*, 1, pp. 3–28.

Fure, O.-B. (1976) 'Synspunkter og historieteoretiske tendenser i forskningen om den norske arbeiderklasse og -bevegelse i den radikale fase 1918–1933', *Tidsskrift for arbeiderbevegelsens historie*, 1, pp. 29–62.

Fure, O.-B. (1983) *Mellom reformisme og bolsjevisme: Norsk arbeiderbevegelse 1918–1920. Teori. Praksis* (Doctoral Dissertation, University of Bergen).

[23] Finn Dahl quoted from the minutes of the executive committee, August 14, 1931 (Olstad; *LOs historie*, p. 336).

Johansen, P. O. (1977) *Menstadkonflikten 1931* (Oslo: Tiden).

Kan, A. (2005) *Hemmabolsjevikarna: Den svenska socialdemokratin, ryska bolsjeviker og mensjeviker under världskriget och revolutionsåren 1914–1920* (Stockholm: Carlssons Bokförlag).

Kringen, O. (1905) *Fagorganisationen: Dens teorier og principer* (Kristiania: Det norske Arbeiderparti).

Lafferty, W. M. (1971) *Economic Development and the Response of Labor in Scandinavia: A Multi-Level Analysis* (Oslo: Universitetsforlaget).

Lafferty, W. M. (1974) *Industrialization, Community Structure and Socialism: An Ecological Analysis of Norway, 1875–1924* (Oslo: Universitetsforlaget).

Lafferty, W. M. (1977) 'Industrialisering og radikalisme: En kort kommentar', *Tidsskrift for arbeiderbevegelsens historie*, 1, pp. 199–208.

Lie, H. (1980) *Loftsrydding* (Oslo: Tiden).

Lorenz, E. (ed.) (1970) *Norsk sosialisme: En dokumentasjon* (Oslo: Pax).

Lorenz, E. (1978) *Norwegische Arbeiterbewegung und Kommunistische Internationale 1919–1930: Untersuchung zur Politik der Kommunistischen Internationale* (Oslo: Pax).

Lorenz, E. (1983) *Det er ingen sak å få partiet lite: NKP 1923–1931* (Oslo: Pax).

McDermott, K. and Agnew, J. (1996) *The Comintern: A History of International Communism from Lenin to Stalin* (London: Macmillan).

Nordahl, K. (1967) *Minner og meninger* (Oslo: Tiden).

Olstad, F. (1990) *Jern og Metall 100 år, Vol. 1: 1891–1940* (Oslo: Tiden).

Olstad, F. (2006) *Norsk Sjømannsforbunds historie, Vol. 1: Vår skjebne i vår hånd* (Oslo: Pax).

Olstad, F. (2009) *LOs historie, Vol. 1: 1899–1935. Med knyttet neve* (Oslo: Pax).

Olstad, F. (2018): 'Spørsmålet om revolusjon i Norge og Skandinavia 1917–21. En oppsummering og mulig ny begynnelse', *Arbeiderhistorie*, pp. 127–41.

CHAPTER 4

Syndicalism and Strikes in Denmark, 1917–1920: The Syndicalist Challenge to Social Democratic Trade Union Leadership

Knud Knudsen

By the end of the First World War, a wave of strikes, including wildcat strikes, swept across the Danish labor market. Some regarded the strikes—and the wildcat strikes in particular—as the result of syndicalist agitation and a threat to the existing system of labor relations based upon collective agreements between the associations of employers and the trade unions. The wildcat strikes culminated in 1919–1920, as did the confrontation between the syndicalist trade union opposition and the social democratic leadership of the unions. The aim of this chapter is to examine the strikes

The original version of this chapter was revised: Incorrect author name has been updated. The correction to this chapter is available at https://doi.org/10.1007/978-3-031-08987-9_18

K. Knudsen (✉)
Aalborg, Denmark
e-mail: kchrknudsen@gmail.com

© The Author(s), under exclusive license to Springer Nature Switzerland AG 2023, corrected publication 2023

J. Jørgensen and F. Mikkelsen (eds.), *Trade Union Activism in the Nordic Countries since 1900*, Palgrave Studies in the History of Social Movements, https://doi.org/10.1007/978-3-031-08987-9_4

1917–1920, in particular the role of the syndicalist opposition in the strikes and the confrontation between syndicalism and social democracy in the Danish labor movement. After a brief historiographical review and an introduction to the historical context, there will be, first, a general examination of the strikes in Denmark 1917–1920 and second, a closer look at four major "syndicalist strikes" 1919–1920.

Historiography

In Denmark, syndicalism was rediscovered by the new labor history in the 1970s. The historian per excellence of Danish syndicalism was Carl Heinrich Petersen (1915–1988), apprenticed cigarmaker and self-taught labor historian who had been a friend to leading Danish syndicalists. For half a century he lived as a journalist and a historian of the revolutionary tradition in the Danish labor movement.[1] He explained the growth of syndicalism during the war as the result of both "objective" and "subjective" factors, both the rising prices and declining real wages, and syndicalist agitation. According to him the defeat of the dockers and seamen's strike in 1920 contributed to the rapid decline of syndicalism. Further, he regarded the syndicalists' theoretical weakness and lack of historical knowledge as another cause of the demise of syndicalism in the early 1920s. Widely historians in the 1970s followed in the track of Carl Heinrich Petersen.[2] In labor history a new social historical literature on syndicalism emerged in the 1960s and 1970s, seeking to locate syndicalism in the social history of capitalism and the labor movement in late nineteenth and early twentieth century. Altogether, the 1970s witnessed an upsurge of interest in the history of European syndicalism. Several authoritative accounts of European and American syndicalism were published, and important debates took place. A new history of syndicalism emerged, breaking the traditional straitjacket of identifying syndicalism as a particular Romance phenomenon, influential

[1] Petersen, C. H. (1970) *Danske Revolutionære* (Copenhagen: Borgen); Petersen, C. H. (1973) *Fra klassekampens slagmark i Norden* (Aarhus: Modtryk); and Petersen, C. H. (ed.) (1979) *Christian Christensen og den danske* syndikalisme I–II (Aarhus: Modtryk). Cf. Engberg, J. (1985) 'Carl Heinrich – et flittigt liv som arbejdssky' in Pedersen, K. and Stræde, T. (eds.) *Anarki og arbejderhistorie. Festskrift for Carl Heinrich Petersen* (Copenhagen: Tiderne Skifter), pp. 9–17.

[2] Petersen, E. S. (1981) 'Historieskrivningen om den danske arbejderbevægelse i perioden 1871–1914/20' in Callesen, G., Caspersen, H. and Knudsen, K. (eds.) *Fremad og aldrig glemme* (Copenhagen: SFAH), pp. 74–76.

in France, Italy, and Spain, and elsewhere only as minority groups on the fringes of the labor movement.

In a historiographical review of the studies of syndicalism in the European labor movement, Peter Schöttler (1986) summarized the contributions of social history to the historiography of syndicalism, in particular regarding France, England, and Germany.[3] In France, the only country where syndicalism became a dominant current in the labor movement before the First World War, syndicalism was seen as part of a radical tradition in French society. In the English-speaking world, Peter N. Stearns' *Revolutionary Syndicalism and French Labor* (1971) presenting syndicalism as "a cause without rebels" was a much-disputed contribution. Stearns dismissed the idea of French radicalism and opposed the revolutionary syndicalist leadership to the moderation of French workers.[4] In England Bob Holton sought to portray British syndicalism as a movement in its own right, not only as a precursor of the shop steward movement or English communism. In Germany, the pioneering work of Hans Manfred Bock rescued German syndicalism from oblivion. In the social historical studies focus shifted from ideology and philosophy to syndicalism as part of the social history of society—toward the "Realgeschichte" of syndicalism. In his review, Schöttler also discussed the various attempts to suggest structural explanations of syndicalism as an international phenomenon. In 1977, Georges Haupt called for an international perspective and suggested a social historical explanation, which located revolutionary syndicalism in the complex transition from liberal to organized capitalism, appealing in particular to craftsmen who had experienced the degradation of work and to new groups of unskilled workers. Historians such as Wayne Westergaard-Thorpe, Larry Peterson, and Peter Lösche pursued such ideas further.[5]

In the 1990s and the early twenty-first century, labor history turned in new transnational directions. Marcel van der Linden and Wayne Thorpe's *Revolutionary Syndicalism: An international Perspective* (1990) heralded

[3] Schöttler, P. (1986) 'Syndikalismus in der Europäischen Arbeiterbewegung: Neue Forschung in Frankreich, England und Deutschland' in Tenfelde, K. (ed.) *Arbeiter und Arbeiterbewegung im Vergleich. Historische Zeitschrift. Sonderheft 15* (München: Oldenburg), pp. 419–75.

[4] Stearns. P. N. (1971) *Revolutionary Syndicalism and French Labor: A Cause without Rebels* (New Brunswick: Rutgers University Press).

[5] Schöttler, *Syndikalismus*, pp. 469–75.

the global and transnational turn in the 1990s. In the book, they also made an attempt to provide a cross-national set of explanations for the international syndicalist movement as a whole. They suggested a number of long-term developments that encouraged the spread of syndicalism across the world: the growth of a radical mood among workers as expressed in the rising level of strikes; the changes of labor processes and labor relations, intensifying the pressure of work and enhancing managerial control; the critique and rejection of the dominant strategy of existing trade unions and labor parties; the feasibility of general strikes as an alternative strategy; and spatial and geographical influences. The ideas were elaborated by Marcel van der Linden in his "Second Thoughts" (1998), where he discussed issues such as definitions of revolutionary syndicalism, the shopfloor perspective, organization and ideology, culture, international diffusion, and variations.[6] Discussing definitions of syndicalism, van der Linden suggested a shift of focus from the ideology of syndicalism to practice. "My personal inclination is to regard the ideological criterion as the least important; what counts is what the movement does in practice and not how it justifies what it does."[7]

The transnational turn had various faces: One has been a return to biography and ideology, a second a shift of focus from the European and Western world toward non-Western societies, and a third the emphasis on international comparison.[8] A similar global trend has taken place in the study of strikes and social conflicts, switching focus from the Global North to the Global South. In 2013, a special issue of *International Labor and Working-Class History* published contributions on strikes and social conflicts, among these Ralph Darlington's "Syndicalism and Strikes" in which he presented the main findings of his book *Radical Unionism:*

[6] van der Linden, M. and Thorpe, W. (1990) 'The Rise and Fall of Revolutionary Syndicalism' in Linden, M. van der and Thorpe, W. (eds.) *Revolutionary Syndicalism: An International Perspective* (Aldershot: Scolar Press), pp. 4–17; and van der Linden, M. (1998) 'Second Thoughts on Revolutionary Syndicalism', *Labor History Review*, 63, 2, pp. 182–96.

[7] https://libcom.org/library/second-thoughts-revolutionary-syndicalism-marcel-van-der-linden.

[8] Berry, D. and Bantman, C. (eds.) (2010) *New Perspectives on Anarchism, Labor and Syndicalism: The Individual, the National and the Transnational* (Newcastle on Tyne: Cambridge Scholars Publishing); and Ness, I. (ed.) (2014) *New Forms of Worker Organization: The Syndicalist and Autonomist Restoration of Class-Struggle Unionism* (Oakland: PM Press).

The Rise and Fall of Revolutionary Syndicalism (2008) which is of special interest in a study of syndicalism and strikes.[9]

The book is a comparative study of syndicalism in France, Italy, America, England, and Ireland. Darlington sees the growth of syndicalism, which he defines as "radical unionism," as a reflection of workers' growing discontent with the social democratic parties and the failure of mainstream trade unions to deliver real improvements. Though syndicalism was not a doctrine, rather "a practice in search of a theory," Darlington insists that syndicalism was not atheoretical. He regards the emergence of revolutionary syndicalism as part of a wider upsurge in workers' militancy across the world in the years preceding the First World War. "In fact, as we have seen, the emergence and subsequent growth of syndicalist organization was itself a response to the growing labor unrest and political radicalization that occurred, rather than being its cause." To wholly attribute the industrial and political militancy of the period to syndicalist agitators, would be to exaggerate their influence.[10] In his analysis of syndicalism and strikes Darlington seeks to balance two basic ideas, on the one hand, that syndicalists were not the instigators of strikes, and on the other, that syndicalists exerted a radicalizing influence upon the strikes. Though syndicalism benefitted from the upsurge of strikes and syndicalists played an important role in strikes, both as leaders and organizers, they were not the instigators of strikes. In order to rescue the revolutionary element of syndicalism, Darlington refuses to dismiss ideology and theories, while at the same time seeing syndicalism as a movement of class-practice.

Examining strikes in Denmark during the First World War we might draw attention to the comparative project organized by Haimson and Tilly (1989) on strikes, wars, and revolutions in late nineteenth and early twentieth centuries, including Russia and various industrialized countries in Western Europe. One general conclusions on strikes in the belligerent Western countries was that in the context of the war economy, "all strikes automatically assumed political, if not a potentially revolutionary

[9] Velden, S. van der and Varela, R. (2013) 'Introduction: Strikes and Social Conflicts', *International Labor and Working-Class History*, 83, pp. 31–36.

[10] Darlington, R. (2013) *Radical Unionism: The Rise and Fall of Revolutionary Syndicalism* (Chicago: Haymarket Books), pp. 8, 83.

character."[11] The question might be asked whether the strikes and the radicalization of trade union struggle in Denmark 1917–1920, a non-belligerent country, in the context of war, did assume a similar political character, or whether the influence of syndicalism should be regarded as an indication of the non-political nature of labor unrest in Denmark? Before examining the strikes 1917–1920, a brief introduction to the Danish context might be useful.

Syndicalism, Social Democracy, Trade Unions, and Strikes in Denmark

In contrast to Norway and Sweden the influence of syndicalism was weak in Danish trade unions before 1914. In the 1950s, the American sociologist Walter Galenson argued that Danish economic development was "much less favorable to the spread of syndicalist influence than that of either Norway or Sweden." Furthermore, he referred to the slow growth of the Danish working class and better labor conditions. Altogether, Danish trade unionism was much the strongest when syndicalism made its bid for power in Scandinavia; Danish trade unions had achieved a stability of collective bargaining relationships which the trade unions in Norway and Sweden required several more decades to obtain. According to Galenson, "Danish labor did not provide fertile ground for the growth of syndicalism."[12]

Danish syndicalism had its roots in the socialist youth organizations in the early twentieth century. The first explicitly syndicalist association in Denmark was formed in December 1908, the Federation of Syndicalism (*Syndikalistisk Forbund*). Leading figures were tobacco-worker Sophie Falck and joiner H. P. Willumsen. The editor of the magazine published by the syndicalist federation was Christian Christensen (1882–1960) who later became the undisputed leader of the syndicalist movement in

[11] Haimson, L. H. and Tilly, C. (eds.) (1989) *Strikes, Wars, and Revolutions in an International Perspective: Strike Waves in the Late Nineteenth and Early Twentieth Centuries* (Cambridge: Cambridge University Press), p. 532.

[12] Galenson, W. (1969) *The Danish System of Labor Relations: A Study of Industrial Peace* (New York: Russell & Russell), p. 46.

Denmark.[13] In 1910, he took the initiative to establish the Federation of Trade Union Opposition (*Fagoppositionens Sammenslutning*) which became the syndicalist association in Denmark for the next decade. From December 1911 the federation published the weekly journal *Solidarity* (*Solidaritet*). Ideological influences were American and British syndicalism rather than French ideas. In particular Tom Mann, who was invited to speak in Denmark in 1912, was an important source of inspiration.[14] Chr. Christensen had strong Norwegian connections too.

At the beginning the Federation of Trade Union Opposition counted only few members, approximately 30–40, most of them soil and concrete workers in Copenhagen. Progress was slow. At the outbreak of war in August 1914, the federation counted approximately 300–400 members. In the provinces, very few had ever heard of syndicalism. The early phase of Danish syndicalism was devoted to agitation which, however, did not prevent the syndicalist opposition from intervening in the general lock-outs in the spring 1911. To support the conflicting unions the syndicalists advocated sympathy strikes by other trades: "Stop the Machines! Turn out the Light in Copenhagen!"[15] In 1912 an attempt was made to gain a foothold in the major provincial towns, another tour was arranged in November 1914.[16] At such meetings the ideas of syndicalism were presented, sometimes rather complicated issues.

The syndicalist opposition was not restricted to only propaganda. As early as 1911 the newly established syndicalist federation became involved in a conflict among the soil and concrete workers in Copenhagen. During the conflict the social democratic leaders of the union resigned in protest and left a new untrained syndicalist leadership with the ungrateful task of conducting a strike in the middle of the winter. During the strike Christian Christensen spoke at meetings in the union. He refused the allegations of the social democrats that the soil and concrete workers were ruled by syndicalists, that was not true. "Even though the syndicalist might be splendid agitators, no one would believe that a new idea could convince 1200 comrades who do not even have the time to seek

[13] Arbejdermuseet & Arbejderbevægelsens Bibliotek og Arkiv (ABA), Landsorganisationen i Danmark, Archive no. 1500, Box 1252: *The Syndicalist*, No. 9, 1909, and Box 1253: Newspaper clippings on anarchists and syndicalists.

[14] ABA, 1500, Box 1253: The syndicalist meetings 1911/12.

[15] ABA, 1500, Box 1253: Newspaper clippings on the syndicalists 1910/11.

[16] ABA, 1500, Box 1254: A syndicalist agitation tour (November 1918).

information." The specter of syndicalism was intended to separate the soil and concrete workers from the rest of the working class and to enforce them to give in. He, Chr. Christensen, was a syndicalist, the striking soil and concrete workers were not.[17] By stamping the strike as "syndicalist" opponents sought to delegitimize the strike, insinuating that the striking workers were manipulated by a syndicalist minority.

Though syndicalism was weak before 1914, some progress was made in a number of trade unions—the soil and concrete workers in Copenhagen, the blacksmiths and mechanics in Copenhagen, the dockworkers and longshoremen, the bricklayers and other building trades, most of these in Copenhagen but in some provincial towns too. However, difficulties were obvious, as mentioned by Walter Galenson: "The skilled crafts were devoted to collective bargaining and impervious to the alleged advantages of more militant procedures. The unskilled workers had also benefited from collective bargaining and were, moreover, staunch opponents of the industrial unionism advocated by the syndicalists."[18] The drive for industrial unionism was weak in Denmark.

Despite the insignificant membership of the opposition before 1914, syndicalism was perceived as a threat by the social democrats and syndicalist activities were followed closely by both the party and the leadership of the unions. Social democratic observers were present at syndicalist meetings; they were instructed to oppose the syndicalist agitators and to report back to the party or the trade union leadership. At a meeting where Christian Christensen spoke about the strength of syndicalism in France, the social democratic opponent stood up and asserted that the German and the Danish trade unions had achieved much better results than the syndicalist CGT in France.[19]

In 1912, Carl Gran, secretary of the Danish Federation of Trade Unions (*De samvirkende Fagforbund*), examined the syndicalist program and writings and set up a document summarizing the social democratic critique of syndicalism: In a society with less developed industry as in Denmark, it did not make sense to go for "industrial unionism"; the syndicalist ideas of "autonomous organizations" would result in dissolution and more unions in the same trades; the syndicalist opposition to

[17] ABA, 1500, Box 1253: The syndicalist meetings 1911/12.

[18] Galenson, *The Danish System*, p. 46.

[19] ABA, 1500, Box 1254: A syndicalist agitation tour (November 1914).

centralization and centralized strike funds would have a similar effect, dissolution instead of unity. "By breaking up the economic community between the organizations we would undermine the moral community too. The empty propaganda in which the syndicalists build their public agency will never pervade the working class, in contrast the mandatory and mutual strike support is true solidarity." He did not believe in the sudden strike; it was a remnant of the past. Altogether, the social democrats found nothing new in syndicalism, not a single new idea, just old deposited and rejected methods, "cheap phrases" and "empty propaganda."[20] At the core of the social democratic critique was the syndicalist opposition to the centralized strike funds. Syndicalist methods challenged the core of social democratic tactics. Direct actions were irreconcilable with the system of collective agreements which the social democratic trade unions had struggled to achieve.

During the war syndicalism became stronger. Membership of the Federation of Trade Union Opposition rose to 3000 in 1918. In 1914, the weekly paper sold 1500 copies, in 1915 it rose to 3000 copies, in 1916 to 9000 copies and in 1918 to approximately 18,000.[21] Unquestionably, the rise of syndicalism in Denmark resulted from the extraordinary circumstances of the war. In the Danish case, it makes sense to regard the growth of syndicalism as a reflection of the radicalization of the working class during the war and as a response to the failure of social democratic tactics.

By the outbreak of war in August 1914 the Social Democratic Party engaged in a parliamentarian truce to bring Danish society safely through the war. The so-called Extraordinary Commission was set up in August 1914 to regulate prices and supplies, and to some extent the efforts of public regulations were successful, but only to some extent. As the war progressed, the discrepancy between declining wages and rising prices accelerated and dissatisfaction increased. The trade unions became involved in unending negotiations on cost-of-living allowances, which, however, could not keep pace with the rising prices. The contrast between the grievances of working people and the fortunes of "the new rich,"

[20] ABA, 1500, Box 1523: Secretary Gran's comments to the syndicalist program (1912).

[21] Petersen, *Christian Christensen*, Vol. I, p. 44.

farmers and speculators, enhanced the radicalization of the working classes thereby providing the preconditions of the growth of syndicalism.

The syndicalist opposition arranged meetings protesting the humbug and bogus of cost-of-living allowances and organized the rising numbers of unemployed after 1917. Syndicalists also campaigned against militarism. 1918 became a year with numerous public meetings and demonstrations in Copenhagen and other provincial towns, against militarism, unemployment, and rising prices, demonstrations which often ended up in violent clashes with the police. Carl Heinrich Petersen depicted 1918 as "the revolutionary year 1918."[22] Mass-meetings and demonstrations in January and February culminated when a group of leading syndicalists succeeded in entering the Stock Exchange and attempted to throw the stockbrokers out of the hall. The police arrived before the door was shut by a board with the inscription: "the gambling den is closed." In the summer new mass-meetings and demonstrations were organized in the center of Copenhagen, which ended in violent clashes with police, and four syndicalists were arrested and imprisoned, among them the leader Christian Christensen. New mass-meetings for the release of the four syndicalists culminated in violent tumults in November 1918. A photo in the national papers of the syndicalist John Sperling standing on top of a tram and waving the red flag symbolized the revolutionary mood and has become iconic. A general strike was called a few days later to claim the release of the four syndicalists.

As the disturbances in November became increasingly violent—it should be remembered that the "battles at the vegetable market" in Copenhagen were concurrent with the outbreak of revolution in Germany—both bourgeois politicians and social democrats feared that events might slip out of control. A social democratic gathering on November 14, 1918, exposed the anxiety of the social democratic leadership. The question was whether the social democrats should ignore the syndicalists or stand up publicly against them. Some spoke in favor of ignoring them; the syndicalists might be able to mobilize a majority in 20 unions, but social democrats could muster 2000. Thorvald Stauning, the general secretary of the party, was not convinced. He feared that violence would spread and spoke in favor of more radical measures. In the end a resolution was passed warning in strong words against participating in

[22] Petersen, *Fra klassekampens slagmark*, pp. 60–74.

the syndicalist protest-strike.[23] The question of fighting syndicalism was also discussed in a publication of the socialist youth organization in 1918: Should the social democrats fight syndicalism? The answers were all affirmative, but most advocated information and debate as the best means to fight syndicalism.[24] The protest-strike ended in failure, but from 1919 the social democratic counter-offensive assumed an increasingly uncompromising character. The syndicalists were denounced as a splinter group, their methods as disruptive and fractional—similar terms as used later about communism.

The mass-demonstrations in the streets of Copenhagen, from time-to-time violent clashes with the police, provided the backcloth to the industrial unrest culminating in 1919. The failure of the general strike in November 1918 did not put a stop to the wildcat strikes. Increasingly syndicalist methods were used at the shop floor—and with success. In the summer of 1918, the bricklayers in Copenhagen initiated their campaign for an eight-hour working day—the so-called weekend movement: They simply stopped working at noon on Saturdays. The action was suspended in November 1918 but resumed in February 1919, the employers' response was a lockout in the building trades. Concurrently, syndicalist strikes put a stop to work in the docks and at major shipyard in Copenhagen, in both the outcome was the dissolution of the existing unions and formation of new ones. In September 1919, the Federalist Association in Denmark (*Føderalistisk Sammenslutning*) was established, a syndicalist central organization in embryo.

Syndicalist progress came to a halt in 1920. The Easter Crisis in late March turned out to be a serious challenge to the syndicalist opposition. The king Christian X. dismissed the radical-liberal government including Thorvald Stauning. The issue at stake was the redrawing of the national borderline between Germany and Denmark in accordance with the Treaty of Versailles. The response of the social democratic labor movement was radical and dramatic: If not the king accepted the claims of the labor movement, a general strike would be launched. The syndicalist response was groping, first rejecting altogether to participate in a general strike for

[23] ABA, 1500, Box 1256: Board Meeting, November 1918.

[24] ABA, 1500, Box 1256: 'Should we fight the syndicalist movement? The Socialist Youth Organization (1918)'.

the reinstalment of a bourgeois government, however, soon the syndicalist position changed, and it was decided to participate in the general strike on certain conditions, one of these was the release of all political prisoners. The syndicalist paper declared that the red flag of revolution was raised: Bourgeois and capitalist society should be removed by means of the general strike. It did not happen. The general strike was canceled as compromises were negotiated during the Easter days. However, syndicalist groups of workers had been among the first to lay down work, and several of these strikes continued after the cancelation of the general strike. The seamen and the dockers' strike ended after three months in defeat. Carl Heinrich Petersen regarded the defeat of the seamen's strike in 1920 as a contributing factor to the decline of syndicalism in Denmark.[25]

Internal divisions played a role too. Half a year later Christian Christensen published a series of articles in *Solidarity* in which he argued for seeking cooperation with the communist party and explained the reasons why.[26] According to Christensen anarchists had taken over the syndicalist federation, while he and others had been imprisoned. The anarchists sought to turn the syndicalist trade union opposition into a movement outside the existing trade unions. The Federalist Association was an invention of the anarchists. Their aim was to substitute the old syndicalist federation of 1910 by the new Federalist Association of 1919. By merging with the communists, he sought to rescue syndicalism from being taken over by anarchism, it was, in fact, a rescue operation. He argued that Danish syndicalism had never been anti-political, and he referred to the program of 1910, written by himself, anti-parliamentarianism was not mentioned at all. He also called attention to the Bolshevik revolution in 1917. True revolutionaries were enthusiastic and remained so, in contrast to the anarchists who soon lost faith and became pessimists. To rescue true syndicalism from anarchism Christian Christensen turned to communism. In 1921, the syndicalist federation merged with the newly established communist party into the so-called Communist Federation in Denmark (*Danmarks kommunistiske Føderation*). In the moment of defeat, Danish syndicalists turned toward communism and syndicalism vanished as an independent current in the labor movement. Later he

[25] Petersen, *Christian Christensen*, Vol. 1, p. 56.

[26] Published in Petersen, *Christian Christensen*, Vol. 2, pp. 520–550.

offered a more pragmatic explanation for his decision to join communism: He went for a share of the gold from Moscow to rescue the syndicalist paper in Denmark.

The sudden demise of syndicalism in 1921 might disclose the fact that syndicalism, when it was at its height in 1919–1920, was taken serious as a threat to society, not only because of the demonstrations and disturbances in the streets but also, maybe not least, due to the increasing influence of syndicalism in the trade unions and the wildcat strikes at the workshops.

Strikes in Denmark 1917–1920

After three peaceful years 1914–1916, the number of strikes exploded 1917–1920. At the culmination in 1919, 472 work stoppages were registered, approximately the double of the total number of strikes in the preceding five-year period 1911–1915. According to the statisticians at the Danish Statistical Office, the rapidly increasing number of strikes was caused, firstly, by the rising prices and declining real wages, and secondly, by the impact of syndicalist propaganda; the syndicalist influence might explain the numerous "illegal strikes." Furthermore, the statisticians added the influx of large numbers of new members to the trade unions at the end of the war; new, "unschooled" members who did not have the usual discipline of ordinary trade union members. The pattern of strikes 1917–1920 broke with the prevailing trends of labor conflicts. Most of the stoppages were strikes involving only a single employer, most were of a relatively short duration, and in contrast to the usual pattern, the strikes 1917–1920 were spread across the year and not concentrated in the spring and early summer.[27] According to official statistics more than 35,000 workers were affected by strikes in 1919.

According to the employers' reports, the number of strikes was much higher. In the annual report of the Danish Association of Employers (*Dansk Arbejdsgiverforening*) 1917–1918, the picture was alarming:

> Without exaggerating it can be asserted that working conditions have never been as unruly as in the preceding year. The Association of Employers has received approximately 150 reports on illegal strikes, and the number of

[27] 'Strejker og Lockouter i Danmark 1916–1920' (1922), *Statistiske Meddelelser*, 4, 66, 2, p. 9.

illegal strikes which have occurred without reaching the central organizations is of course much higher. A very substantial part of the illegal strikes has been purely syndicalist, that is sudden stoppages of work to obtain higher wages or other concessions. Apparently, the syndicalist movement has gained a not insignificant upsurge and it is directed in particular against the leadership of the labor movement.

The employers acknowledged that times were difficult for the leadership of the trade unions. In numerous unions, they experienced the syndicalist influence, in particular the construction trades, bricklayers, carpenters, and bricklayers' workmen had moved into anarchy; in several other trades there seemed to be a fertile breeding-ground for syndicalism too. The employers also pointed to the problem of the new members who had become unionized to obtain unemployment benefits. In the report examples of the syndicalist practice of "direct actions" were presented. Working conditions were characterized as "an eternal boiling unrest of sudden illegal work stoppages to enforce a higher wage than in the collective agreement."[28] Trade union discipline was breaking down.

The annual report of the industrial employers the following year confirms this picture. According to statistics collected by the industrial employers, approximately 67,000 workers were involved in 1100 illegal strikes between June 1919 and June 1920, most of these of short duration, on average lasting 4 days, affecting 28 workers per strike. In Denmark such numbers were extraordinary. Most of these illegal strikes took place in the iron- and metal industries.[29] Industry complained about the numerous strikes, in particular the wildcat strikes: "In 1919 the labor market was characterized by a boiling unrest. Legal and illegal strikes were the order of the day, and if, finally, there was a break without a major industrial conflict, you could be certain that it was only a breathing space, preparing for the next stoppage. It might even be said that the big official strikes were not the worst, it was the intolerable tone which dominated at the workshops, where workers conscious of their position of power in every way sought to compel their dominance." The report continued: "It would be a mistake to claim that public opinion in 1919 was characterized by sympathy for the workers' claims as they were put forward. It

[28] *Beretning om Dansk Arbejdsgiver- og Mesterforenings Virksomhed 1917–18* (1918) (Copenhagen: Dansk Arbejdsgiver- og Mesterforening), pp. 22–23.

[29] *Industrifagenes Beretning for 1919–20* (1921) (Copenhagen: Industrifagene).

was not the case that people sympathized with the workers but that they were frightened. Revolutions and risings around Europe were perceived as a "memento" of what might be expected, and major parts of society were imbued with a nervous anxiety for what the "unknown" working class might come up with. In consequence, all infringements on the side of the workers were tolerated, everyone longed for only one thing, peace, no matter what."[30] As the war progressed, the political dimension of the strikes became increasingly manifest. Strikes were seen in the context of revolution abroad as more than just industrial conflicts.

The problem was also addressed in a speech by the chairman of the Labor Court (*Den faste Voldgiftsret*), C. Th. Ussing, at a meeting in the Association of Social Politics in November 1919: Trade union discipline was breaking down and the system of collective agreements was threatened by dissolution. The decisions of the Labor Court were not respected, fines were not paid because unions went bankrupt which only made things even worse. Ussing, too, blamed syndicalist agitation.[31] From the perspective of the Labor Court the years after 1916 were "difficult times" due to "the syndicalist movements among the workers"—and "exceptional"; it was not the rule that the decisions of the Court were not obeyed by the workers.[32]

The Eight-Hour Campaign and "Syndicalist Strikes" 1919–1920

It was the general perception among employers and authorities that the influence of syndicalism was a major cause of the numerous strikes 1917–1920. A closer examination of the most conspicuous "syndicalist strikes" 1919–1920 supports the view that syndicalists played an active role. The first of these was the building and construction workers' "week-end-movement" in the autumn of 1918 and early 1919—mentioned above. At the general assembly of the bricklayers in Copenhagen in late May 1918, the well-known syndicalist Chr. Rassow advanced the proposal

[30] *Dansk Industriberetning for Årene 1919 og 1920* (1923) (Copenhagen: Industriforeningen i Danmark), pp. 74–76.

[31] Ussing, C. Th. (1919) *De kollektive Arbejdsaftalers Fremtid* (Copenhagen: Gads Forlag).

[32] Topsøe-Jensen, V. (1935) *Den faste Voldgiftsret gennem 25 Aar* (Copenhagen: Gads Forlag), pp. 26–27.

to introduce an "English week." Support was unanimous, and as the employers rejected the proposal, direct action was initiated.[33] The bricklayers resolved to stop work at noon on Saturdays. After the bricklayers had taken the initiative, other trades followed. The unions were taken to the Labor Court and heavily fined. In late 1918, the bricklayers' union went bankrupt and was dissolved. A new union, the Bricklayers' Union of 1919 (*Murersvendenes Fagforening af 1919*), was formed and Rassow elected secretary. In February 1919, the action was resumed; the employers' response was a lockout of the building and construction workers all over Copenhagen.

The direct action of the building and construction workers was regarded as a rejection of the collective agreement on the gradual reduction of working hours which the Danish Association of Employers and the Danish Federation of Trade Unions had agreed upon in January 1919. The building and construction workers were not satisfied with a gradual reduction of working hours, they claimed the 8-h working day. In April the leadership of the Danish Federation of Trade Unions had to acknowledge that dissatisfaction with the January agreement was widespread among Danish workers, and negotiations with the employers were resumed. In May, a general agreement on the 8-h working was carried through. Afterward the syndicalists claimed that the building workers in Copenhagen deserved the honor of having carried the unrestricted 8-h day to victory, the social democrats that it was the concerted action of party and trade unions. No doubt, it was the pressure from below—some of which was organized by the syndicalists—which compelled the social democratic leadership to take action.

The second "syndicalist strike" was the dockworkers' strike in Copenhagen. In May 1919, the dockworkers rejected a proposal for a new general agreement and laid down work immediately after. A second proposal was accepted, the strike was called off, however, soon new stoppages occurred, and "illegal strikes" became the order of the day. The Federation of General Workers (*Dansk Arbejdsmandsforbund*) initiated a campaign to make the dockers expel the syndicalist troublemakers from the port and resume work, but all in vain. Apparently, no one was really in control of events in the port, except perhaps a group of "syndicalist

[33] Grelle, H. (2019) *Murersvende – Forrest i kampen, stolte i faget: Københavnske murersvendes historie* (Copenhagen: Murersvendenes Brancheklub København), pp. 24–27.

elements" with a strong fighting spirit who seemed to control the meetings in the union.[34] In the end the dockworkers union went bankrupt, due to heavy fines in the Labor Court, and afterward a new Federation of Transport Workers (*Dansk Transportarbejderforbund*) was formed.

The third "syndicalist strike" started a week later at a shipyard in Copenhagen. A group of mechanics claimed an increase of wages, the employers refused, and the mechanics laid down work. Several attempts were made by the Federation of Blacksmiths and Mechanics (*Dansk Smede- og Maskinarbejderforbund*) to induce the striking mechanics to resume work, however, without success. During the strike, the "syndicalist elements" rejected all initiatives on the side of the national federation. Here too, as in the port, no one seemed to be in control, meetings at the shipyard were controlled by the syndicalists, and here too the outcome was the dissolution of the union—the large union of blacksmiths and mechanics in Copenhagen. A new union was established, the Metalworkers Union in Copenhagen (*Københavns Metalarbejder Forbund*), 1300 of the approximately 7000 members of the old union joined the new union of 1919.

The inevitable result of these major "syndicalist strikes" was the dissolution of the unions and formation of new ones without influence upon conditions of work and pay, as collective agreements remained with the existing organizations. In 1919, the tone of the confrontations between syndicalism and social democracy became increasingly crude and malignant. As the social democrats recognized that the improvements which the trade unions had obtained in the collective agreements in the spring of 1919 had not diminished the followings of syndicalism, a pamphlet was distributed to warn trade union members against the syndicalist troublemakers and to explain social democratic tactics as the lesson of the past: The "sudden strike" advocated by syndicalism was not a new weapon in the struggle against capital; it was an obsolete and outworn method, a remnant of the past which was of no use in the modern age of organized capitalism.[35] In the preceding two years, however, direct action had proved effective.

[34] ABA, Dansk Metalarbejderforbund, Archive no. 855, Box 28: The conflict at the Shipyard.

[35] *Hvilken vej skal fagforeningerne?* (1919) (Copenhagen: De samvirkende Fagforbund).

A fourth "syndicalist strike" occurred in the spring and summer of 1920, the seamen and transport-workers' strike—in connection to the Easter Crisis. The strike began in late March, when it was resolved to launch a general strike if not the king accepted the claims of the labor movement before the end of the Easter days. Following the resolution of the general assembly several workers and trades stopped work, among these were the transport workers and the seamen. Although the general strike canceled, large groups of workers were already on strike and several others followed Easter days—loudly complained by the employers. After a few weeks, most workers were back but not the transport workers and the seamen; they remained on strike for months.

It was a bitter fight, the striking workers felt betrayed by the social democratic politicians and trade union leaders. The strike turned into a confrontation between the syndicalist opposition and the social democratic trade union leadership which refused to have offered special promises to the seamen and the transport workers. The social democrats rejected all accusations, however, they recognized that the claims of the striking workers were justified and encouraged the strikers to return to work and enter negotiations with the employers. The striking workers decided to put extra pressure upon the social democrats by extending the strike to include deliveries of coal to the capital. Now the strikers, identified as syndicalists, were accused of having allied with capital in an assault upon the workers of Copenhagen. The social democratic press wrote about the syndicalists' "mean conspiracy against the workers in Copenhagen" and "The capitalist-syndicalist plot against the city of Copenhagen."[36] In the most embittered phase of the conflict, the striking unions published a handbill posing the question: "Are the seamen and transport workers syndicalists? – No!" It was not a "syndicalist strike." "We strike for strictly trade union and economic goals." They were not, as claimed by the social democratic press, a bunch of ruthless revolutionaries paid by the opponents of the social democratic labor movement. "Our organizations are neither socialist nor syndicalist; the political convictions of our members are a private matter."[37] The strike ended in defeat, and the seamen lost the 8-h day which they had just obtained the year before.

[36] ABA, 1500, Box 747: The transport workers' strike.

[37] ABA, 1500, Box 747: The transport workers' strike.

In the summer of 1920 syndicalism emerged from the confrontation with the social democratic labor movement as the weaker part. The trade unions turned toward their "natural" enemy, the employers who no longer feared revolution and were determined to put a stop to wage increases. By August 1920 the "illegal strikes" came to an end. Hereafter, it was the Associations of the Employers who orchestrated the centralized confrontations between workers and capital in the massive lockouts in 1921 and 1922, and here there was no room left for the syndicalist opposition and wildcat strikes. Altogether, the Easter Crisis in 1920 was a turning point in a more general sense between the offensive of the working class and the capitalist counter-offensive.

The four examples examined above leave no doubt that syndicalists played a significant role in the strikes, but in different ways. The campaign of the building and construction workers for the 8-h day was resolved at a general assembly of the unions; the strikes of the transport workers and the seamen in 1920 were also conducted with the leadership of the unions in command. In contrast, the strikes in the docks and at the shipyard in Copenhagen were both beyond union control. The activities and the meetings during the strikes seemed to be controlled by a group of syndicalists eager to fight to the bitter end, inevitably causing the dissolution of the existing unions and leaving the new organizations isolated at the periphery of the trade union movement—and causing divisions within the syndicalist movement, however, not between anarchists and syndicalists as claimed by Christian Christensen in 1921. The embittered confrontation between syndicalism and social democracy at the culmination of the strikes 1919–1920 proved that syndicalism had become a movement of influence in Denmark, but also that the social democratic response to the syndicalist challenge cannot be ignored in explanations of the fall of syndicalism.

Conclusion

The strikes 1917–1920 were exceptional in the history of Danish trade unionism. The well-organized and disciplined normality of Danish trade unions was substituted by a wave of sudden work stoppages at the workshops, a mixture of legal and illegal strikes. The examination of the strikes leaves no doubt that syndicalists were active in the strike movement, both as instigators of strikes and as examples inspiring others, not necessarily syndicalist workers. Apparently, syndicalism offered answers to the grievances of working people, which the social democrats were unable to deliver. Direct action and illegal strikes were effective, employers gave in to striking workers' claims, while the endless negotiations between trade unions and the employers always lagged behind. Evidently syndicalists played an important role in some of the major "syndicalist strikes" 1918–1919, exerting a radicalizing influence. It has been argued too that the involvement in the strike movement also caused divisions within the syndicalist movement.

Considering that the growth of syndicalism in Denmark reflected the extraordinary circumstances of the war, the general theories of international syndicalism referred to in the historiographical section may seem irrelevant. Nonetheless, some of the factors suggested by van der Linden and Thorpe (1990) were at play in the Danish case: the growth of a radical mood, the rejection of the strategy of existing trade unions, and the feasibility of an alternative strategy. Van der Linden's "second thoughts" on shop floor policies and on praxis instead of ideology are important too. As in several other countries the strongholds of syndicalism in Denmark were the building and construction workers, dockers, and seamen, and the iron and metal industries, to some extent crafts and trades with a considerable degree of workshop autonomy which favored local and illegal actions. However, there is little evidence to support the idea of syndicalism as a response to structural changes of industry or management. Nothing indicates that the strikes in Denmark assumed a political character as in the belligerent countries—as claimed by the employers. Rather, the strikes should be seen as a revolt against the reluctance of the social democratic leadership to assert the interests of working people during the war.

In the Danish case, the rise and fall of syndicalism cannot be explained without considering the role of the social democratic labor movement. During the war the syndicalist opposition benefitted from the restraints of the Social Democratic Party due to the parliamentarian truce and the policy of regulations. It made sense that workers turned to the trade unions and to the syndicalist opposition under the circumstances of the war when the contrasts and disparities of society increased. From 1919 to 1920 the social democratic counter-offensive contributed to the decline of syndicalism. Furthermore, the syndicalist opposition was tormented by internal divisions between those who regarded syndicalism as an association of propaganda and the trade union activists. Basically, however, it was crucial that in 1920–1921 the working-class offensive had come to an end and was substituted by a bourgeois counter-offensive. In the defensive struggles of labor, revolutionary syndicalism offered no convincing answers. Syndicalism in Denmark disappeared almost overnight. Within a year after the dramatic Easter Crisis in April 1920—when the syndicalist newspaper *Solidarity* claimed that the general strike would overthrow capitalism in Denmark—the syndicalist opposition approached communism was embraced by Moscow, and then disappeared. On the face of it, the differences between communism and syndicalism were considerable, in practice, however, differences might be insignificant. Former syndicalists could continue as before, practicing radical unionism. Communism had no problem in establishing a synthesis of both industrial militancy and revolutionary politics.

References

Archives

The Workers Museum & The Labour Movement's Library and Archive (*Arbejdermuseet & Arbejderbevægelsens Bibliotek og Arkiv, ABA*):
Landsorganisationen i Danmark, Archive no. 1500.
Metal København, Archive no. 855.

Serials

Arbejderen
Arbejdsgiveren
Solidaritet

Literature

Bang et al. (1975) *Fagoppositionens Sammenslutning 1910.1921 – de danske syndikalister* (Aarhus: Modtryk).

Beretning om Dansk Arbejdsgiver- og Mesterforenings Virksomhed 1917–18 (1918) (Copenhagen: Dansk Arbejdsgiver- og Mesterforening).

Berry, D. and Bantman, C. (eds.) (2010) *New Perspectives on Anarchism, Labor and Syndicalism: The Individual, the National and the Transnational* (Newcastle on Tyne: Cambridge Scholars).

Dansk Industriberetning for Aarene 1919 og 1920 (1923) (Copenhagen: Industriforeningen i Danmark).

Darlington, R. (2013a) *Radical Unionism: The Rise and Fall of Revolutionary Syndicalism* (Chicago: Haymarket Books).

Darlington, R. (2013b) 'Syndicalism and Strikes, Leadership and Influence: Britain, Ireland, France, Italy, Spain and the United States', *International Labor and Working-Class History*, 83, pp. 37–53.

Engberg, J. (1985) 'Carl Heinrich – et flittigt liv som arbejdssky' in Pedersen, K. and Stræde, T. (eds.) *Anarki og arbejderhistorie: Festskrift for Carl Heinrich Petersen* (Copenhagen: Tiderne Skifter), pp. 9–17.

Galenson, W. (1969) *The Danish System of Labor Relations: A Study in Industrial Peace* (New York: Russel & Russel).

Grelle, H. (2019) *Murersvende – forrest i kampen, stolte i faget. Københavnske murersvendes historie* (Copenhagen: Murersvendenes Brancheklub København).

Hvilken vej skal fagforeningerne? (1919) (Copenhagen: De samvirkende Fagforbund).

Industrifagenes Beretning for 1919–20 (1921) (Copenhagen: Industrifagene).

Kuhn, G. (2014) 'Syndicalism in Sweden: A Hundred Years of the SAC' in Ness, I (ed.), pp. 168–83.

van der Linden, M. (1998) 'Second Thoughts on Revolutionary Syndicalism', *Labor History Review*, 63, 2, pp. 182–96.

van der Linden, M. and Thorpe, W. (1990) *Revolutionary Syndicalism: An International Perspective* (Aldershot: Scolar Press).

Ness, I. (ed.) (2014) *New Forms of Worker Organization: The Syndicalist and Autonomist Restoration of Class-Struggle Unionism* (Oakland: PM Press).

Petersen, C. H. (1970) *Danske revolutionære: Ideer, bevægelser og personligheder* (Copenhagen: Borgen).

Petersen, C. H. (1973) *Fra klassekampens slagmark i Norden* (Aarhus: Modtryk).

Petersen, C. H. (ed.) (1979) *Christian Christensen og den danske syndikalisme*, Vol. I–II (Aarhus: Modtryk).

Petersen, E. S. (1981) 'Historieskrivningen om den danske arbejderbevægelse i perioden 1871–1914/20" in Callesen, G., Caspersen, H. and Knudsen, K. (eds.) *Fremad og aldrig glemme* (Copenhagen: SFAH).

Schöttler, P. (1986) 'Syndikalismus in der Euroäischen Arbeiterbewegung: Neue Forschung in Frankreich, England und Deutschland', in Tenfelde, K. (ed.) *Arbeiter und Arbeiterbewegung im Vergleich: Historische Zeitschrift. Sonderheft 15.* (München: Oldenburg), pp. 419–75.

Stearns, P. N. (1971) *Revolutionary Syndicalism and French Labor: A Cause without Rebels* (New Brunswick: Rutgers University Press).

'Strejker og Lockouter i Danmark 1916–20' (1922) *Statistiske Meddelelser*, 4, 66, 2.

Stræde, T. (1978) 'Syndikalismen blandt lager- og pakhusarbejderne i København', *Årbog for arbejderbevægelsens historie*, 8, pp. 55–96.

Thorpe, W. (2010) 'Uneasy Family: Revolutionary Syndicalism in Europe from the *Charter of Amiens* to World War I' in Berry, D. and Bantman, C. (eds.)

(2010) *New Perspectives on Anarchism, Labor and Syndicalism: The Individual, the National and the Transnational* (Newcastle on Tyne: Cambridge Scholars), pp. 16–42.

Topsøe-Jensen, V. (1935) *Den faste Voldgiftsret gennem 25 Aar* (Copenhagen, Gads Forlag).

van der Velden, S. and Varela, R. (2013) 'Introduction: Strikes and Social Conflicts', *International Labor and Working-Class History*, 83, pp. 31–36.

CHAPTER 5

Trade Unions, the Social Democratic Party and Labor Market Conflicts in Malmö, 1890–1910

Lars Berggren and Mats Greiff

According to labor movement historian Axel Uhlén, two local conflicts in Malmö have created a huge interest all around Sweden.[1] The first labor dispute is the woodworker's strike in 1890, called the Malmö revolt when thousands of people demonstrated in the streets and squares in the city center. Both local police and military forces met the demonstrators. The other one is a strike among municipal workers in 1908. It has sometimes been characterized as a wildcat strike. It was contested within the labor

[1] Uhlén, A. (1949) *Facklig kamp i Malmö under sju decennier* (Malmö: Framtiden), p. 259.

L. Berggren
Lund University, Lund, Sweden
e-mail: lars.berggren@hist.lu.se

M. Greiff (✉)
Malmö University, Malmö, Sweden
e-mail: mats.greiff@mau.se

© The Author(s), under exclusive license to Springer Nature Switzerland AG 2023

J. Jørgensen and F. Mikkelsen (eds.), *Trade Union Activism in the Nordic Countries since 1900*, Palgrave Studies in the History of Social Movements, https://doi.org/10.1007/978-3-031-08987-9_5

movement but was also encountered with hard reactions from the local authorities.

The aim of this chapter is to highlight trade union activism and its relation to social movement activities, namely how a social political struggle is connected to conflicts in the labor market. We carry out the analysis by looking at the mobilization of organizational resources, and how strikes interacted with other forms of social and political protest.

The State of the Labor Movement in Malmö Around 1890

At the end of the 1880s, the labor movement in Malmö, as well as nationally, was on the rise. In April 1889, the Social Democratic Workers' Party of Sweden (*Sveriges socialdemokratiska arbetareparti*, SAP) was established at the national level. Smaller regional or local social democratic associations joined the national party, and so did the Malmö Social Democratic Association.[2] At the same time, there were strong contradictions within the local community between employers and workers who set up mass organizations to strengthen their position. Between 1882 and 1889, about thirty unions were founded in Malmö. In the year 1889, two national unions were established, including the woodworkers', which increased the total number of national unions to seven. Part of the strategy to strengthen the class-consciousness of workers was the establishment of the local daily paper The Labour (*Arbetet*) in 1887.[3]

Class struggle became very intense with an increasing number of conflicts. Contradictions between labor and capital often resulted in strikes and lockouts when employers refused to negotiate with trade unions and tried to prevent workers from organizing. One notable conflict was the so-called Lomma lockout in 1889, which is sometimes referred to as Sweden's first real lockout. The conflict started with masons demanding higher wages at a factory construction site. The harsh response from the employer was to lockout 500 workers. However, the

[2] Billing, P. (1989) *Hundra år med SAP i Skåne. En årskrönika över Skånes socialdemokratiska partidistriktsverksamhet 1889–1988* (Malmö: Partidistriktet), p. 5.

[3] Ibid.

real background to the conflict was that a workers' union had been formed, which the leading capitalist Rudolf F. Berg wanted to curb.[4]

In 1889, the Southern District of SAP held its first annual congress. In the newly formed party, important strategical issues were highlighted on this occasion. Among other things, two resolutions on the significance of the strike as a tool for the transformation of society in a socialistic direction were passed. Here, the influence from *Arbetet's* editor-in-chief Axel Danielsson was sharp:

> Since the socialist workers' movement, which is essentially a social and not a political popular movement, ultimately aims at not a political reformation, but a social transformation, this agitation, maintained by the laborer's Party, should as far as possible avoid inciting the working masses to fish for so-called political reforms through participation in a political comedy, but instead directly teach scientific socialism and familiarize the masses with the plan for the coming society, while at the same time not neglecting to point out the possibilities that exist for the working class by strikes and demonstrative behavior to make conquests from the ruling classes and strengthen the working class' power.[5]

The resolution points out both strikes and demonstrations as strategically important tools in the effort to transform society. Additionally, a special resolution was formulated on the strike issue:

> The congress regards the strike as the working class' natural means of struggle and its development into ever larger dimensions as the most powerful lever for the socialist transformation of society. The training of the working class in the tactics of stopping work is so much more necessary since all indications are that the ruling system is facing its rapid downfall precisely through the stubborn strike war of the organized working class.[6]

Obviously, there is a syndicalist ambience in these resolutions, which became visible in the contradictions that arose when the issue of participation in the forthcoming parliamentary elections was discussed. Nevertheless, there was a great deal of agreement on the significance of strikes

[4] Uhlén, *Facklig kamp i Malmö*, p. 75.

[5] Cf. Ibid., pp. 81–82.

[6] Ibid., p. 82.

as a strategy to transform society. This does not appear to be particularly controversial as the local social democracy had its origin in the trade unions that created the political party. In this light, it will also be easier to understand the strong anti-union stance of capital interests and attempts to stifle the formation of unions.

The Woodworker's Strike in 1890

When the woodworkers' decided to commence the strike that broke out in Malmö at the end of April 1890, it could be interpreted as a reflection of the resolution on the strike as an essential weapon in the struggle for a socialistic society. At that time, about 140 workers went on strike to reduce working hours, to increase wages and overtime pay. To these requirements was added one that was more related to the labor-process, namely the addition of a 25% wage supplement when they worked with the assembly of machine-made carpentry instead of carrying out this work by themselves.[7] In that way, the strike was not just about wage increases and shorter working hours, but also an attempt to gain influence over the work process so that rationalizing measures would benefit the workers and not only the capitalists. If the building contractors wanted the work to be done with prefabricated material, workers who were deprived of these tasks would be compensated financially. In doing so, the strike was also an attack on one of the core principles of industrial capitalism, the prerogatives of management to lead and organize the labor-process.[8]

In addition, it must be pointed out that alongside the strike other strategies were in play. For example, on April 10, 1890, the Wood Workers' Union (*Träarbetarefackföreningen*) in Malmö discussed the question of starting a cooperative construction company.[9] Similar considerations took place within the Masonry Workers' Union (*Murarefackföreningen*) in Malmö.[10] These discussions might be interpreted as another strategy

[7] Tidman, Y. (1982) *Byggnads avd 2 100 år. Minnesskrift* (Malmö: Avd.), p. 37.

[8] Ekdahl, L. (1983) *Arbete mot kapital. Typografer och ny teknik. Studier av Stockholms tryckeriindustri under det industriella genombrottet* (Lund: Arkiv), p. 86.

[9] The Labour Movement's Archive in Scania, Malmö (*Arbetarrörelsens arkiv i Skåne, Malmö*, AAS), Träarbetarefackforeningen, avdeling 13's arkiv, Minutes 1890–1893.

[10] Ekström, G. (2016) *En förändrad scen? Strejk och upplopp i Malmö 1890*, unpublished master's thesis, Lund University, p. 20.

to break the power of capital and eventually transform society in a socialist-cooperative direction.

After a cautious start in 1882, the masonry trade union had increasingly assumed a very clear socialistic character. The union supported the establishment of the newspaper *Arbetet*, and it became a member of the Social Democratic Workers' Party when it was formed in 1889. In other words, class struggle was a clearly visible phenomenon in Malmö in 1890, and the power of capital was limited in several ways by the growing labor movement that applied different kinds of strategies in its attempts to transform society. Strikes and demonstrations were just some of several other strategies. It is in the light of this societal context we must consider the dramatic events that unfolded in the streets and squares of Malmö.

The woodworkers' strike began on April 30, when workers shut down the work and presented their demands. The strike issue was intensely discussed also within the masonry union. One proposal that was put forward was whether the masons also should go on strike at the same time as the woodworkers. After intense discussions in the mason union, members decided not to go on strike but to continue negotiating a wage increase and shorter working hours. The argument for this solution was that the building constructors were weakened by the action of the woodworkers. This meant that the bargaining position of the masons was strengthened. However, they decided to launch a very limited sympathy action at a single workplace.[11]

The woodworkers' strike was launched on the Walpurgis Night, and the next day the labor movement in Malmö would, for the first-time, participate in an extensive May 1 demonstration demanding shorter working hours. The inspiration came from the Second International's decision in Paris, the year before, to make the first of May into an international workers' day. Here, union formation and political struggle were united through different kinds of activities and narratives. The party district's resolution on the significance of the strike and demonstration in the transformation of society came to concrete expression in the city during the spring of 1890.

[11] AAS, Murarbetarefackföreningen i Malmös arkiv, Minutes May 8 and 11, 1890.

The Battle

In mid-May, the construction companies' association responded to the union's demand, partly by a letter to the woodworkers' union, partly by a message in the press threatening the striking workers with dismissal. If the work was not to resume the following Monday, the constructors intended to recruit labor from outside. The woodworkers refused to resume work, whereupon the building company employed six strikebreakers who would work at constructor Skytte's building site under police protection. About the same time, constructor J. Andersson terminated his previous agreement with the woodworkers' association.[12]

The conflict became even more intense when constructor Nils Stenmarck employed additional strikebreakers, recruited from Småland and Blekinge, at a workplace in the city center. These strikebreakers were escorted to the workplace under police protection. A crowd of three to four hundred protesting participants followed the strikebreakers on the road between the workplace and their accommodation.[13] Gradually, protests against the employers' strategy to hire strikebreakers grew and the demonstrations escalated rapidly. On June 2, the number of protesters in the central part of the city amounted to several thousands. The city authorities then called out all available police personnel who were reinforced with a significant military force, something that was allowed if the situation required it. However, the escalation led to even more people taking to the streets.[14]

The next day, June 3, more people joined. On this day, it is estimated that between 7,000 and 8,000 people had been on the streets in the central parts of the city. The clashes between protesters, on the one hand, and police and military units on the other became violent. The bourgeoisie paper The South Swedish Daily News (*Sydsvenska Dagladet*) reported about the clashes where the demonstrators used strategies like singing and shouting, while mounted police officers attempted to disperse the crowd.[15]

Sydsvenska Dagbladet was particularly displeased by the fact that women and children had been visible at the site of demonstrations and

[12] Uhlén, *Facklig kamp i Malmö*, p. 84.

[13] Ibid., pp. 84–85.

[14] Ibid., p. 85.

[15] *Sydsvenska Dagbladet*, June 4, 1890.

clashes. The paper pointed out the danger to women and children and that they stirred up anger among other people. Particularly, upset was the paper over youngsters' participation in the events. Boys from different social classes between the age of ten and sixteen were pointed out as not only spectators but also as active participants in the clashes between protesters and the police. Some of them were said to only tease the police officers as in a hide-and-seek game, but others were alleged to throw stones and gravel against the police.[16]

The police authority used mounted police, a strategy that they considered useful to disperse crowds. Together with hussars stationed in the city, they tried to disperse the masses with the help of their sabers. Protesters responded by making clatter, loud noise and throwing stones. They tore out paving stones from the streets and used it as weapons. The demonstrators not only attacked police officers but also the police station, which became a target for stone-throwing workers. In *Arbetet*, as well as in *Sydsvenska Dagbladet* the situation was compared to the street fights of Paris during the Commune in 1871.[17]

The following day, June 4, additional military forces had been requisitioned to the city in the form of 200 artillerymen from nearby Landskrona. They were equipped with carbines, bayonets and ten sharp shots each. The authorities mobilized for new clashes and strengthened their combat capacity. The same afternoon, an extra sheet published by *Arbetet* was printed and distributed, in which the editor-in-chief Axel Danielsson, after explaining the situation, urged all workers to stay at home:

> During today's negotiation between employers and the union, the workers of Malmö should not demonstrate at Gustaf Adolfs Torg [the main square]. The best way to demonstrate today is that the square and adjoining streets will be as empty as possible. Therefore, the workers are advised to remain at home. But, if the negotiation will not lead to any result, then the workers of Malmö should know how to express their opinion. May the workers realize the situation in a correct way and let the police and the hussars be left alone in tonight's demonstration.[18]

[16] Ibid.

[17] Uhlén, *Facklig kamp i Malmö*, p. 8; and *Arbetet*, June 5, 1890.

[18] *Arbetet*, extra sheet, June 4, 1890.

The workers followed Danielsson's message. No significant demonstrations took place, and it was quiet in the streets. The cavalrymen from Landskrona never had to use their carbines or ammunition. Danielsson's motive might have been to avoid bloodshed. However, the event also attracted strong symbolic meaning. The labor movement could discipline itself and maintain societal order without threats from the police or the military. *Sydsvenska Dagbladet* expresses concerns that new disturbances would take place, while *Arbetet* responded with the argument that new demonstrations were not a problem if the labor movement was in charge and not the police or military forces. "When it was so calm and quiet in Malmö last night, the credit goes to the admirable, instinctively or considerable, visible or invisible *organization*".[19] In this way, the labor movement showed a high degree of organizational skill and discipline, when employers and authorities instead regarded the movement as a mob. Thereby, the actions may had become even more frightening for the establishment when they became aware that the actions of the labor movement were not spontaneous mob riots but instead part of a well-organized strategy including men, women and youngsters.

The Result of the Strike

The unrest led the governor to intervene in the strike to mediate. However, this did not lead to an immediate solution to the conflict. However, after a few more weeks, the entrepreneurs announced that they would agree to the demands for a wage increase, overtime supplement and reduced working hours. The union refused the offer and after a few more weeks, an agreement guaranteed the workers a 10% surcharge when working with machine-prepared material.[20] However, the political issue regarding demonstration as a strategy to transform the society was not solved. Instead, several workers were sentenced to prison. Seven, who were picked out as leaders, allegedly on a random basis, were convicted for altogether fourteen and a half years in prison. In addition, about ten of the workers were fined.[21]

[19] *Arbetet*, June 5, 1890: "För dagen".

[20] Uhlén, *Facklig kamp i Malmö*, p. 87.

[21] Ibid., p. 87.

Development After 1890

As the trade union movement in Malmö grew, it became increasingly important to create a stronger organization to coordinate activities. At the beginning of 1893, an umbrella organization, the Malmö Cooperating Unions (*Malmö samarbetande fackföreningar*), was formed by representatives of 16 trade unions. It was stated that, "the cooperating unions are obliged to support each other in the worker's common struggle against capital such as during strikes, lockouts etc."[22] In 1901, the political and trade union branches of the labor movement were further synchronized by the formation of the Malmö Commune of Workers (*Malmö arbetarekommun*). The decision to reorganize was taken at the national level and consisted of a board of 13 people: six belonged to a union committee and six to a political committee. Three of the board members were women.[23]

In the 1890s, the labor movement also created its own meeting places where it could hold mass meetings without interference from the police. As in other cities around the country these People's Houses (*Folkets Hus*) and People's Parks (*Folkets Parker*) became of great importance to the movement.

Several battles were fought during the first decade of the twentieth century. Some of these were about the right of workers—male and female—to belong to a trade union. Employers often hired strikebreakers to weaken workers' solidarity. The reactions from the workers against strikebreakers were often fierce and sometimes violent. An example from the Malmö area was the long-running conflict at the Ludvig Rössel's wagon factory in Arlöv 1900–1902, probably the first-time in Sweden strike breakers were recruited from other countries.[24] Another example was a dynamite attack on a strike-breaking accomodation-ship named Amalthea in the port of Malmö during the dock workers conflict in 1908.

For three days in May 1902, the national labor movement staged a nationwide political strike for universal suffrage. Demonstrations became an important way of raising public awareness of the demands of the labor movement, and in some places, such as Stockholm, violence took place

22 Ibid., p. 121.

23 *Minnesskrift 1901–1926. Malmö arbetarkommun* (1926) (Malmö: Framtiden), p. 2.

24 Uhlén, *Facklig kamp i Malmö*, pp. 202–05.

when the police attacked the demonstrators. In Malmö, several demonstrations were carried out during the general strike and the largest had a turnout of 21,000 participants, 94 flags and 4 orchestras. During the last day of the political strike, 800 female textile workers, who previously had been denied leaving the factory, walked in front of the demonstration. Now, they became the heroines of the great manifestation.

Although the general strike was political, it also had significance for the trade unions. Firstly, the labor movement showed its strength. Some historians have argued that it was the reason employers set up a nationwide organization, the Swedish Employers' Confederation (*Svenska Arbetsgivareföreningen*), the same year. Secondly, there were repercussions in some places including Malmö Wool Factory (*Malmö Yllefabrik*), where workers went on strike in protest against a couple of workers being fired as a reprimand for participating in the general strike.[25]

At the beginning of the twentieth century, a political battle was waged within the Swedish labor movement. The so-called Young Socialists (*Ungsocialisterna*) advocated an extra-parliamentary path to socialism, mainly through a general strike, and a pronounced anti-militarism. They were also influenced by anarchist and syndicalist currents. In 1903, the Swedish Socialist Youth Union (*Svenska socialistiska ungdomsförbundet*) did split into two parts. Three years later, some of the leading Young Socialists were suspended and later expelled from the party, just as the Malmö Commune of Workers distanced itself from the Young Socialists. After that, the Young Socialist movement developed in a syndicalist direction, and members performed a drastic action by the planting and detonation of a bomb on the ship Amalthea, that was used as accommodation for English strikebreakers in the harbor of Malmö.[26] Three Young Socialists with anarchistic sympathies were arrested.[27]

[25] Ibid., pp. 208–224; and Greiff, M. and Lundin, J. A. (2018) 'Sweden 1880–1910: The Age of the Labour Movement' in Mikkelsen, F., Kjeldstadli, K. and Nyzell, S. (eds.) *Popular Struggle and Democracy in Scandinavia, 1700–Present* (London: Palgrave Macmillan), pp. 319–35, pp. 326–29.

[26] Berggren, L. and Johansson, R. (2008) 'Bomben som skakade Sverige' in Larsson, P. (ed.) *Ekot från Amalthea. En bok om gränslös konkurrens, våld och 2000-talets nya strider* (Malmö: ABF Malmö), pp. 19–64, pp. 28–31.

[27] Ibid., pp. 21–25.

Municipal Workers on Strike, 1908

A couple of days before the Amalthea bomb attack, twenty municipal workers were dismissed as they refused to work alongside strikebreakers in the harbor.[28] A municipal Remunication Board claimed that the workers acted against an agreement, which had been signed a few months before, when workers at the Malmö Gas Works had launched a one-day-strike. The agreement regulated wages and working hours,[29] and, according to a paragraph, strikes and lockouts were not allowed.[30]

The strike that followed was launched in July 1908, and it lasted almost two months. It was proclaimed when the Remunication Board refused to negotiate with the local branch of the Manual and Factory Workers' Union (*Grov- och fabriksarbetareförbundet*) in Malmö concerning the dismissed workers as mentioned above. However, neither the national union leadership nor the Trade Union Confederation did sanction the strike.[31] The decision to strike was taken by the municipal workers themselves at a meeting in the People´s House, August 7. In a secret ballot, 603 workers voted for a strike and 143 against.[32] Some hundred workers went on strike; not only workers in the harbor but also workers from other areas of the Municipality: the Power Plant, Sanitation Works, Gas Works and the Slaughterhouse. Nearly 1,000 workers were on strike.[33] The historian Bernt Schiller characterizes the strike as a wildcat strike, as it took place in violation of a collective agreement and because it was not sanctioned by the unions at the national level.[34]

[28] Uhlén, *Facklig kamp i Malmö*, p. 258.

[29] Fogelberg, T. (1989) 'Den proletära rösten. Kommunalarbetarstrejken i Malmö 1908' in Berggren, B. and Modéer, K. Å. (eds.) *Motsättning och samverkan. Nya bidrag till Malmö historia. Festskrift till Einar Bager på 100-årsdagen 19 april 1987* (Malmö: Malmö Fornminnesförening and Malmö Förskönings- och Planteringsförening), pp. 229–42, p. 231.

[30] Gyllin, Y. (1950) *I stadens tjänst 1910–1950. Sv. kommunalarbetareförbundets avd. 13* (Malmö: Framtiden), p. 45.

[31] Uhlén, *Facklig kamp i Malmö*, p. 258; and Casparsson, R. (1947) *LO under fem årtionden 1898–1923*, Vol. 1 (Stockholm: LO), pp. 301–02.

[32] *Arbetet*, August 8, 1908.

[33] Fogelberg, 'Den proletära rösten', p. 234; and Uhlén, *Facklig kamp i Malmö*, p. 259.

[34] Schiller, B. (1967) *Storstrejken 1909. Förhistoria och orsaker* (Göteborg: Erlander), pp. 103, 106.

To combat the strike, the authorities in Malmö formed a Committee of Public Safety under the leadership of Edvard Lindahl, who was the city mayor but also a teacher of history. He was outspoken when he proclaimed that the strike was a matter of power: "Should we or the men in the People's House lead the city?"[35] Thereby, the conflict got a political dimension, just as in 1890. The Committee of Public Safety recruited strike breakers en masse. However, a vast majority was not experienced workers but students, officers and men from the bourgeoisie. Some of them came from the regiment in Malmö, the hussars. There are many stories about the variety of strike breakers, and the workers on strike often made fun of them.[36]

However, in the long run, the Committee on Public Safety seems to have succeeded in weakening the strength of the strikers. Though the workers did get some funding from local unions and other workers, they never gained considerable support from the national unions. Some of the leading Social Democrats were reluctant to support the strikers. The chief editor of *Arbetet* presumably resigned because he was against the strike, although he said his resignation has to do with parliamentary work. The paper was also heavily criticized, though a warning text was included, for publishing advertisements by the Committee of Public Safety trying to recruit new workers. The Workers' Municipality criticized this, and the Young Socialist newspaper New Popular Will (*Nya Folkviljan*) often mentioned it.[37] Thus, the contradictions within the labor movement were further exposed.

However, the strikers gained somewhat unexpected support from two lawyers. One of them, Henning Elmquist, had acted as an arbitrator in another conflict. According to him, the Remunication Board had violated the agreement when it refused to negotiate. At the same time, Elmquist was critical against the strikers because the strike was not sanctioned by the central trade unions. Another lawyer, Karl Schlyter, also criticized the Remunication Board for not wanting to negotiate, which it was obliged to do according to the agreement.[38]

[35] *Arbetet*, August 7, 1908.

[36] Schiller, *Storstrejken 1909*, pp. 235–36.

[37] AAS, Malmö arbetarekommuns arkiv, Minutes August 20, 1908; *Nya Folkviljan*, August 22 and 29, September 5, 1908; and cf. Fogelberg, 'Den proletära rösten', pp. 236–38.

[38] Ibid., pp. 234, 239.

The board of the national union did not support the strike, but was under pressure from its members, so it actually granted the strikers a loan.[39] The leadership of the Trade Union Confederation had a meeting with the local unionists in mid-September, and they criticized the Municipality in Malmö, and especially the Committee on Public Safety and the Renumeration Board for not respecting collective agreements and instead advocating individual contracts.[40] The strike ended on October 1 and out of a thousand striking workers about 200 or 300 could not get their jobs back as they had been replaced by other workers.[41]

Meetings and Activities Among the Strikers in 1908

On August 30, the Malmö Commune of Workers held a meeting in the People's Park. More than a thousand persons attended, and the meeting declared its support for the municipal workers.[42] This is just one example of a meeting organized by the workers during the strike. The importance of meeting places such as the Peoples' House and People's Park cannot be overrated. The strikers met nearly every day during the strike.[43]

Though the striking workers were male, women were mobilized in several ways. On September 2, a special festivity for the workers' wives were arranged at the Peoples Park and it was announced that a humorist should entertain the women.[44] Women were also present in street activities against strikebreakers. Students and other men without any experiences of manual labor replaced the striking sanitation workers. And when they collected barrels of latrine from working class residential areas, people reacted in many ways. One newspaper reported that "Workers' wives pushed against them with clasped hands, and a crowd of a thousand people gathered. This, however, was soon dispersed by a numerous police force and armed cavalry".[45]

[39] Gyllin, *I stadens tjänst*, p. 53.

[40] Fogelberg, 'Den proletära rösten', p. 239.

[41] *Skånska Dagbladet*, October 1, 1908.

[42] Ibid., August 31, 1908.

[43] Gyllin, *I stadens tjänst*, p. 50.

[44] *Arbetet*, September 1, 1908.

[45] *Skånska Dagbladet*, August 10, 1908.

Sometimes, the reactions could be violent, when strikebreakers carried out cleaning work in a street, and one of them was hit by an iron screw thrown on him from a carpenter's shop.[46] On September 10, the bourgeois paper Scanian Daily News (*Skånska Dagbladet*) reported on incidents of violence against strikebreakers working at the Sanitation Works.[47] A few days later, six workers were arrested for beating and kicking four "newly employed workers" at the Sanitation Works,[48] and some days later, a demonstration was organized against newly recruited workers, acting as strikebreakers. The police disbanded the demonstration.[49]

Humor was also applied as a weapon against strike breakers. On one occasion, a barrel full of latrine was put out in the street with a poem "the latrine student". However, the strike breakers refused to bring the barrel to the Sanitation Works.[50] That humor was used as a weapon is also illustrated in the magazine The Welfare Trap (*Välfärdsfällan*) published by the strikers. The publisher was called "Knight of the Broom" and the purpose of the magazine was formulated in the following words: "The Welfare Trap wants to express itself as a voice for the upside-down welfare. We promise that it will be scary and unreliable, and that it will shed light on today's burning issues as clear as the street lighting in the city and its outskirts".[51]

Eviction of Workers and Their Families

About 160 sanitation workers were on strike. Some of them rented apartments in houses belonging to the Sanitation Works in Malmö. In mid-August the city evicted workers' families from their apartments. However, when the workers refused to move, they were forced to leave their homes by police officers on September 19. A total of thirteen families, consisting of more than a hundred people, were thus evicted with the help of the police.[52] A journalist from *Arbetet* described what happened:

[46] Ibid., August 20, 1908.

[47] Ibid., September 10, 1908.

[48] Ibid., September 13, 1908.

[49] Ibid., September 19, 1908.

[50] Ibid., September 15, 1908.

[51] Gyllin, *I stadens tjänst*, pp. 50–51.

[52] *Arbetet*, September 19, 1908; and Fogelberg, 'Den proletära rösten', p. 240.

> On the roads leading to the sewage treatment plant, many policemen were seen, riding or walking, as well as hussars, anxiously riding from side to side. It almost looked like the authorities had a guilty conscience. No doubt, they expected a great battle, but nothing came of it. Self-control is the greatest strength; the workers know that.

Just as in 1890, *Arbetet* emphasized the ability of the labor movement to maintain self-control. Later in the article, the reporter wrote that an owner of a mansion nearby came to the place:

> With ill-concealed pleasure, she made her way forward, and from time to time cast a contented glance at the thrown-out furniture and the children crawling in the dirt, the children who will one day evict down the privileges which, contrary to the will of the majority, now rule society. And to this struggle they shall be spurred on by the strong outcry 'long live solidarity!' which their evicted mothers raised when the evictions were carried out.[53]

Conclusion

In this chapter, we have written about two different strike actions in Malmö. The first occurred in 1890 and the second 18 years later. Between them, much happened in the labor movement and in the labor market, both at the local and national level. The workers created congregation places such as *Folkets Hus* and *Folkets Park* and thereby got arenas where they could gather and manifest their solidarity and concrete demands. During the strike of 1890, the activities mainly took place in the city's central squares and streets. The unions founded a National Organization in 1898, and a few years later the employers organized themselves. Thus began a new, more institutionalized phase of class struggle. The unions' struggle for recognition was intense but was also opposed. However, in some locations, they succeeded in concluding agreements. By a compromise in December 1906, the right of association was recognized by the employers' organization and the employers' right to lead and distribute work was recognized by the unions. This did not prevent many individual employers from trying to break the trade union movement with lockouts and recruitment of strikebreakers. The battles were extremely fierce in some places.

[53] *Arbetet*, September 19, 1908.

The events we have written about differs partly from each other. In the first case, it is a battle against private capitalists, while the second is against a public employer. Through the resolutions adopted within SAP 1889, the first strike with its demonstrations in the central parts of the city can also be regarded as a political action with the aim of changing society in a socialist direction. The other battle could be described as a wildcat strike (although the term was not used at the time), that is, a strike that was in breach of an agreement. Although the strike did not lead to victory, the boundaries of trade unionism were tested through the strike, and it provided important lessons to the future. It also showed that there were contradictions and tensions within the labor movement.

In the first strike action, the united masses of workers in Malmö went out in large demonstrations in streets and on squares. In the second, numerous meetings were held in the Peoples' Park, an arena that was not available in 1890. However, there are also similarities. The mobilization from below is obvious in both cases. In 1908, the members decided on their own to strike, and to some extent they succeeded in getting the national union to make certain concessions. In both cases, strikebreakers were recruited, and the city authorities deployed police and military. While Axel Danielsson's intervention emptied the streets in 1890, the families of the sanitary workers showed a disciplined calm in connection with the evictions in 1908.

Women certainly took to the streets in 1890. They did so even though at the time there was an ideal of family support, and the unions had a strong male dominance. Women were not always welcome on the same terms as men in trade unions, but they were considered part of the working class. In 1908, women became an important factor in the creation of solidarity and mobilization.

References

Archives

The Labour Movement's Archive in Scania, Malmö (*Arbetarrörelsens arkiv i Skåne, Malmö*, AAS):

Malmö arbetarekommuns arkiv.

Murarbetarefackföreningen i Malmös arkiv.

Träarbetarefackforeningen, avdeling 13's arkiv.

Serials

Arbetet
Nya Folkviljan
Skånska Dagbladet
Sydsvenska Dagbladet

Literature

Berggren, L. and Johansson, R. (2008) 'Bomben som skakade Sverige' in Larsson, P. (ed.) *Ekot från Amalthea. En bok om gränslös konkurrens, våld och 2000-talets nya strider* (Malmö: ABF Malmö), pp. 19–64.

Billing, P. (1989) *Hundra år med SAP i Skåne. En årskrönika över Skånes socialdemokratiska partidistriktsverksamhet 1889–1988* (Malmö: Partidistriktet).

Bjurling, O. (1985) 'Stad i utveckling' in Bjurling, O. (ed.) *Malmö stads historia, Vol. 4: 1870–1914* (Malmö: Malmö stad).

Casparsson, R. (1947) *LO under fem årtionden 1898–1923*, Vol. 1 (Stockholm: LO).

Ekdahl, L. (1983) *Arbete mot kapital. Typografer och ny teknik. Studier av Stockholms tryckeriindustri under det industriella genombrottet* (Lund: Arkiv).

Ekström, G. (2016) *En förändrad scen? Strejk och upplopp i Malmö 1890*, unpublished master's thesis, Lund University.

Fogelberg, T. (1989) 'Den proletära rösten. Kommunalarbetarstrejken i Malmö 1908' in Berggren, B. and Modéer, K. Å. (eds.) *Motsättning och samverkan. Nya bidrag till Malmö historia. Festskrift till Einar Bager på 100-årsdagen 19 april 1987* (Malmö: Malmö Fornminnesförening and Malmö Förskönings- och Planteringsförening), pp. 229–42.

Greiff, M. and Lundin, J. A. (2018) 'Sweden 1880–1910: The Age of the Labour Movement' in Mikkelsen, F., Kjeldstadli, K. and Nyzell, S. (eds.) *Popular Struggle and Democracy in Scandinavia, 1700–Present* (London: Palgrave Macmillan), pp. 319–35.

Gyllin, Y. (1950) *I stadens tjänst 1910–1950. Sv. kommunalarbetareförbundets avd. 13* (Malmö: Framtiden).

Minnesskrift 1901–1926. Malmö arbetarkommun (1926) (Malmö: Framtiden).

Schiller, B. (1967) *Storstrejken 1909. Förhistoria och orsaker* (Göteborg: Erlander).

Tidman, Y. (1982) *Byggnads avd 2 100 år. Minnesskrift* (Malmö: Avd.).

Uhlén, A. (1949) *Facklig kamp i Malmö under sju decennier* (Malmö: Framtiden).

CHAPTER 6

Anti-Strikebreaker Protests and Collective Violence in Sweden, 1918–1939

Martin Ericsson and Stefan Nyzell

On May 14, 1931, Swedish military forces opened fire and killed four striking pulp factory workers and one bystander during a demonstration in the municipality of Lunde, in the Ådalen district outside of Kramfors in northern Sweden. The killings sent shock waves through the Swedish labor movement and significantly contributed to the Social democratic win in the general elections the next year. The event has become an iconic moment in modern Swedish historical culture, and the aftermath is often described as a turning point where Sweden left the social conflicts of the

M. Ericsson (✉)
Lund University, Lund, Sweden
e-mail: martin.ericsson@hist.lu.se

S. Nyzell
Malmö University, Malmö, Sweden
e-mail: stefan.nyzell@mau.se

© The Author(s), under exclusive license to Springer Nature Switzerland AG 2023

J. Jørgensen and F. Mikkelsen (eds.), *Trade Union Activism in the Nordic Countries since 1900*, Palgrave Studies in the History of Social Movements, https://doi.org/10.1007/978-3-031-08987-9_6

1920s and instead choose cooperation and peaceful solutions on the labor market, the so-called Swedish model.[1]

What happened in Ådalen was, of course, a clash between striking workers and the Swedish military—which was never again used during industrial conflicts.[2] But there was also a third party involved in the incident, which sometimes is almost forgotten: the c. 60 strikebreakers, recruited by the employers. The protesters in Lunde intended to pass by or possibly march up to the strikebreaker's lodgings, the military were there to protect the strikebreakers, and the killings on May 14 were actually preceded by a series of violent confrontations between strikers and strikebreakers.

The day before May 14, 400–500 people gathered in Kramfors and listened to a speech by the local communist leader Axel Nordström. They then marched to the nearby Sandviken harbor, where strikebreakers were loading pulp at the steamship *Milos*. The protesters decided to violently board the steamship. Many strikebreakers managed to escape, but some hid at the cargo deck. When they were discovered, the protesters first gave them a beating and then lifted them up in the air with the crane of the *Milos* in a public display. Four strikebreakers were then forced to march with the protesters back to Kramfors, where they were forcibly made to stand at a macadam heap while Nordström questioned them about their identities and the reasons why they had become strikebreakers—a kind of mock trial in front of a large crowd.[3]

These events illustrate, we would argue, two important elements in strikes that turned violent in Sweden between the first and second world wars. Violent strikes, while often portrayed by the labor movement as strikebreakers attacking workers, were, in effect, often workers attacking strikebreakers, or police and military forces using violence when protecting strikebreakers. Moreover, anti-strikebreaker violence was a

[1] Johansson, R. (2001) *Kampen om historien: Ådalen 1931 – Sociala konflikter, historiemedvetande och historiebruk 1931–2000* (Stockholm: Hjalmarson & Högberg), pp. 447, 451.

[2] Guillemot, A. (1997) 'Från Sundsvall 1879 till Ådalen 1931: Om militära kommenderingar vid strejker och sociala konflikter' in Ericsson, T. and Guillemot A. (eds.) *Individ och struktur i historisk belysning* (Umeå: Umeå universitet), pp. 67, 79.

[3] *Berättelse avgiven av den av Kungl. Maj:t tillsatta kommissionen för undersökning rörande oroligheterna i Gudmunrå m.fl. kommuner av Västernorrlands län i maj 1931* (1931) (Stockholm: Norstedt), pp. 22–30.

form of collective violence with its own repertoires and performances. It was, as we will argue later in this chapter, rooted not so much in Swedish trade union culture as in Swedish working-class culture. Thus, anti-strikebreaker violence was part of a working-class repertoire of contention, with several types of violent actions available for protesters to act upon.

However, although a few violent events have been analyzed before, there is a lack of systematical studies of this contentious repertoire.[4] This chapter is a first step in such a study. Here, we present a typology of the forms of collective violence used against strikebreakers in Sweden in the mid-war years, which we hope will inspire future investigations.

Aims and Methods

Our aim in this chapter is not to draw advanced conclusions about which types of collective violence were the most common, or how their prevalence differed over time. These kinds of quantitative analysis will have to wait until more events have been studied. Instead, our aim is to discuss which *types* of collective violence that were available for workers when they protested against strikebreakers.

Our typology is based on a sample of events which took place during 26 strikes in Sweden between the world wars. We have identified these strikes with the help of three kinds of sources. First, the historiographical literature on Swedish labor history. Second, the magazine *The Trade Union Movement* (*Fackföreningsrörelsen*), issued by the major Swedish trade union organization, The Swedish Confederation of Trade Unions (*Landsorganisationen i Sverige*, LO). Several violent events are mentioned in the publication. Third, we have read a large selection of trade union chronicles issued by national trade unions, often publicized at 25-, 50- or 100-year jubilees. These chronicles are very useful, mentioning events of violent confrontation while discussing inter-war industrial conflicts.

Hence, our study does not claim to draw quantitative conclusions but to present a rough working typology over the forms of collective violence used against strikebreakers. We discuss these forms below, analyzing them

[4] See for example: Andersson, K. (2002) 'Brädgårdskonflikten i Halmstad 1931', *Ale: Historisk tidskrift för Skåne, Halland och Blekinge*, 2, pp. 9–20; and Nyzell, S. (2009) *'Striden ägde rum i Malmö': Möllevångskravallerna 1926 – En studie av politiskt våld i mellankrigstidens Sverige* (Malmö: Malmö University Press).

by using two parameters suggested by Charles Tilly. He proposes that collective violence differ in the amount of physical and personal damage caused, and in the amount of coordination and planning among the participators required to carry it out.[5] As we will show in this article, Swedish protesters engaged in collective violence, with different levels of coordination and with low as well as high level of damage, during inter-war industrial conflicts.

Anti-Strikebreaker Violence in Context

Before we present the typology, we have to say something about the general prevalence of strikes in Sweden, the use of strikebreakers and the division of the Swedish labor movement in reformist, communist and syndicalist branches.

In the 1920s and 1930s, the Swedish labor market was one of the most confrontational in the world, and a very large number of strikes as well as lockouts occurred. Strike frequency was especially high in the politically unstable 1920s and early 1930s, a period marked by recessions as well as economic booms. From the first half of the 1930s, the number of labor market confrontations slowly began to drop. This has been explained by several factors, such as the Social Democratic Workers Party of Sweden's (*Sveriges socialdemokratiska arbetareparti*, SAP) rise to power and negotiations between LO and the most important organization of employers, The Swedish Employers' Confederation (*Svenska Arbetsgivareföreningen*, SAF), resulting in the so-called Saltsjöbaden agreement in 1938.[6]

Most strikes were not violent. Therefore, strike frequency does not necessarily correlate with the frequency of collective violence. Collective violence did not occur during strikes per se but could occur during strikes in which the employers hired strikebreakers. This was something that some, but certainly not all, Swedish employers did in the 1920s and 1930s, just as in the other Nordic countries.[7]

[5] Tilly, C. (2003) *The Politics of Collective Violence* (Cambridge: Cambridge University Press), pp. 13–15.

[6] Hamark, J. (2014) *Ports, Dock Workers and Labour Market Conflicts* (Gothenburg: University of Gothenburg), pp. 141–51; and Mikkelsen, F. (1992) *Arbejdskonflikter i Skandinavien 1848–1980* (Odense: Odense Universitetsforlag), pp. 93, 111, 370.

[7] See for example: Bergholm, T. (1996) 'Masculinity, Violence and Disunity: Waterfront Strikers and Strikebreakers in Finnish Ports in the 1920s and 1930s', *International*

Another thing that must be emphasized is that trade union tactics against strikebreakers most often was non-violent. Since its formation in the 1880s, the Swedish trade union movement had developed a repertoire of anti-strikebreaker actions, aiming at social exclusion more than physical damage. For example, strikebreakers could have their portraits published, so that other workers would recognize them. During a railway strike in 1922, a booklet labeled *Svarta själar* (Black Souls) was published, with several portraits of railway workers who had done 'Judas work' during the strike.[8] Perhaps the most important strategy was to publish names and addresses of strikebreakers in labor movement newspapers, urging the readers to treat strikebreakers as traitors. This was a severe threat of social exclusion in working-class milieus, although there was a way out. Strikebreakers could 'confess' and 'apologize' (*göra avbön*) by publicizing statements in the press in which they condemned their previous actions. As an example of such a 'confession', we can pick one of many statements reproduced in a government report from 1927:

> We undersigned, who acted as strikebreakers at Holmsjön during the log-driving strike in the summer of 1921, have come to realize that our actions were an un-solidary way of attacking our fighting comrades in the back. We ask for forgiveness and promise that we will (if allowed) enter chapter 454 [of the forest worker's union] and always obey the union's decisions. Österström, Holm, March 21, 1925.[9]

Somewhat paradoxically, it seems as if strikebreaking as such was a more common practice before the first world war, but that anti-strikebreaker collective violence became more common in the 1920s and 1930s.[10]

Journal of Maritime History, 8, 1, pp. 23–42; Mikkelsen, *Arbejdskonflikter i Skandinavien*, pp. 212, 227, 232; and Silvennoinen, O. (2018) 'Demokratins framgångshistoria? Skogsindustrin, arbetsmarknaden och en fascistisk samhällssyn 1918–1940' in Meinander, H., Karonen, P. and Östberg, K. (eds.) *Demokratins drivkrafter: Kontext och särdrag i Finlands och Sveriges demokratier 1890–2020* (Stockholm: Appell), pp. 189–224, pp. 192, 215.

[8] *Svarta själar: Fotografiskt album med register över personer som arbetade 'på sitt sätt' under järnvägsstrejken 1922* (1922) (Stockholm: Politikens tryckeri).

[9] *Utredningar till belysande av arbetsfredsfrågan* (1927) (Stockholm: Socialdepartementet), p. 160.

[10] See for example: Cederqvist, J. (1980) *Arbetare i strejk: Studier rörande arbetarnas politiska mobilisering under industrialismens genombrott, Stockholm 1850–1909* (Stockholm: Liber), pp. 55, 79, 87, 92.

This is probably because of the more organized form of strikebreaking that occurred after the first world war, with the founding of large strikebreaker-recruiting organizations. This created a situation in which strikebreakers no longer were members of the local community where strikes were carried out but recruited from far-away places and thus viewed as outsiders even more than before.[11]

Finally, in the mid-war years, the Swedish labor movement consisted of three groups. The first and largest was the reformists, who dominated LO and had firm links to SAP. The second and smaller was the communists, who opposed the Social Democrats but fought with them within the formal boundaries of LO. The third and smallest was the syndicalists, a trade union and a revolutionary, political movement at the same time. The syndicalists were organized in The Central Federation of Swedish Workers (*Sveriges Arbetares Centralfederation*, SAC) and had a relatively strong position among some occupational categories, for example, forest workers.[12]

In historical chronicles written by Social Democrats, a recurring theme is to blame strike violence on communist activity.[13] Communists were, without a doubt, sometimes very confrontational during strikes in this period. But at the same time, as historian Tom Olsson points out, confrontational tactics could be advocated by reformists as well, at least on a local level.[14] In Sweden as well as in other Western countries, reformists, politicians and police also had a tendency to 'see' communist activity almost everywhere, sometimes regardless of the real amount of communist involvement.[15] Of course, we cannot solve the question

[11] Flink, I. (1978) *Strejkbryteriet och arbetets frihet: En studie av svensk arbetsmarknad fram till 1938* (Uppsala: Almqvist & Wiksell International), p. 143; and Nyzell, *'Striden ägde rum'*, pp. 128–67.

[12] Ericsson, M. and Nyzell, S. (2018) 'Sweden 1910–1950: The Contentious Swedes—Popular Struggle and Democracy' in Mikkelsen, F., Kjeldstadli, K. and Nyzell, S. (eds.) *Popular Struggle and Democracy in Scandinavia: 1700–Present* (London: Palgrave Macmillan), pp. 346–357.

[13] See among many examples: Casparsson, R. (1951) *LO under fem årtionden: 1924–1948* (Stockholm: Tiden), pp. 251–53.

[14] Olsson, T. (1980) *Pappersmassestrejken 1932: En studie av facklig ledning och opposition* (Lund: Arkiv), pp. 299–303.

[15] For one example, see: Laybourn, K. and Taylor, D. (2011) *Policing in England and Wales, 1918–39: The Fed, Flying Squads and Forensics* (Basingstoke: Palgrave Macmillan), pp. 72, 79.

in this chapter, but we think that some of our examples shows that the connections between communist activity and strike violence is much more complex than sometimes supposed, at least in the Social Democrats own historiographical tradition.

26 Strikes

Our sample consists of 26 strikes in which events of collective anti-strikebreaker violence occurred. As mentioned above, our aim is not to use this sample to draw quantitative conclusions. Nonetheless, we must mention something of the strikes, put them in context and discuss some major patterns.

Six strikes were organized by SAC or by syndicalists acting together with a reformist trade union. This is not very surprising, as syndicalists tended to strike often and in confrontational ways, especially in the early 1920s.[16] The rest of the strikes were organized by LO unions.

But interestingly, the largest LO-union—The Metal Workers Union—is absent in the sample. Instead, many strikes were launched by relatively small unions, organizing workers in small workplaces such as forest work, agriculture, stores and small industries. This hints at something important. The strong Metal Workers Union gained the right to organize already in 1905, through a central agreement with industrial employers. But in the 1920s and 1930s, there were still sectors on the Swedish labor market, such as in agriculture and retail business, where workers right to organize was not recognized.[17] In fact, half of the 26 strikes in our sample were fights over the right to organize unions and gain the right to collective bargaining. As noted by historian Klas Åmark, such strikes tended to become extra bitter.[18] Several international studies show the same.[19]

[16] Hamark, J. (2018) 'From Peak to Trough: Swedish Strikes and Lockouts in the First Half of the Twentieth Century', *Workers of the World*, 1, 9, pp. 145–47.

[17] Mikkelsen, *Arbejdskonflikter i Skandinavien*, pp. 387–88.

[18] Åmark, K. (1992) 'Social Democracy and the Trade Union Movement: Solidarity and the Politics of Self-Interest' in Misgeld, K., Molin, K. and Åmark, K. (eds.) *Creating Social Democracy: A Century of the Social Democratic Labor Party in Sweden* (University Park: Pennsylvania State University Press), p. 70.

[19] Lipold, P. (2014) '"Striking Deaths" at Their Roots: Assaying the Social Determinants of Extreme Labor-Management Violence in US Labor History 1877–1947', *Social Science History*, 38, 3–4, pp. 566–68; and Sherman Grant II, D. and Wallace, M. (1991)

Hence, a hypothesis that should be tested in forthcoming research is that collective anti-strikebreaker violence was especially prevalent in smaller workplaces and during strikes for the right to organize—a struggle that was by no means over in Sweden in the 1920s and 1930s, at least not for all workers.

Threats and Physical Intimidations

In January 1923, the Swedish Forest Workers Union, in cooperation with SAC, fought a strike for the right to collective bargaining in the province of Hälsingland in northern Sweden.[20] Strikebreakers were lodged in barracks at Selmbärget outside the village of Voxna. For many days, there were tensions between strikers and strikebreakers. On Saturday, January 27, things started to escalate.

That morning, c. 250 striking workers gathered outside the barracks, forming lines. When the strikebreakers opened the doors and started walking toward the stables to get to their workhorses, they had to walk between these lines. At the same time, the strikers, standing very close to the strikebreakers, started to sing "Arbetets söner" (Sons of labor), one of the social democratic labor movements most important songs.[21]

This is one of many examples of a form of collective violence which we call threats and physical intimidations. It had a low level of physical damage, since the purpose was not to inflict such damage but to intimidate, threat and frighten. The level of coordination could be very low and spontaneous, but also higher depending on situation—the forest workers at Voxna coordinated their actions well and even sang in unison.

In our sample, we have identified 20 events of threats and physical intimidations, making it the most common among the strikes that we have studied. Exactly, what workers did when they participated in this form of collective action varied, but all events share a common feature: striking workers or their sympathizers came physically very close to strikebreakers, trying to make them feel scared and humiliated. This was most

'Why Do Strikes Turn Violent?', *American Journal of Sociology*, 96, 5, pp. 1117–50, p. 1147.

[20] Karlbom, T. (1968) *Skogens arbetare: Till minnet av Svenska skogsarbetareförbundets 50-åriga verksamhet 1918–1968* (Stockholm: Svenska skogsarbetareförbundet), pp. 167–79.

[21] *Hälsinglands Folkblad*, January 30, 1923: "Skogskonflikten i Voxna",

often done simply by the display of overwhelming numbers and verbal insults. But there could also be small-scale physical violence. For example, during a municipal workers strike in Sundsvall in 1924, protesters threw snowballs at strikebreakers who were cleaning a street and at the police protecting them, until the police dispersed the crowd with sabers.[22] And at the farm Hamra in the region of Uppland, during a farm worker's strike in the summer of 1925, c. 30 striking farmhands gathered around a group of strikebreakers in a field, shouting at them and bombarding them with dirt and pebbles. In Malmö in 1926, several months of threats and intimidations against strikebreakers by striking workers were frequently interrupted by episodes of small-scale physical violence until it finally evolved into large scale confrontations after an especially violent episode.[23] This form of violence was, in most cases, not dangerous in a life-threatening way but must have created a toxic working milieu for the strikebreakers.[24]

'Following the Strikebreakers Home'

The next form of collective violence, making up 14 events in our sample, had a higher level of coordination, although not necessarily a much higher level of physical damage. It was practiced in a more uniform way than the intimidations mentioned above—indeed, in such a uniform way that we would argue that this was an important and well-known part of the Swedish working-class repertoire of contention between the first and second world wars.

An excellent and brief account of this form of collective violence is given in a report written by the police department in the city of Borås. In the winter of 1931, the city's textile workers went on strike, but the white-collar employees at the textile factories continued working and were seen as strikebreakers by many strikers. A police detective described what happened next:

22 *Sundsvalls-Posten*, January 18, 1924: "Polisrapport om uppträdet igår"; and Lindbom, T. (1935) *Svenska Kommunalarbetareförbundet 1910–1935: Historik* (Stockholm: Tiden), pp. 176–85.

23 Nyzell, *'Striden ägde rum'*, pp. 148–67.

24 *Upsala Nya Tidning*, August 4, 1925: "Överfallen på de arbetsvilliga jordbruksarbetarna"; and Johanson, C. (1970) *Lantarbetarna i Uppland 1918–1930: En studie i facklig taktik och organisation* (Stockholm: Svenska bokförlaget), pp. 255–56.

> The striking workers started to 'follow them home'. Crowds of striking men and women gathered outside the workplaces and followed their antagonists on the way to their homes. During the walk, they insulted and assaulted them by jostling and pushing them around, stamping at their feet, and spitting at them. In some cases, snowballs as well as pieces of ice and coal were thrown at them.[25]

'Following the strikebreakers home' was a form of collective violence occurring time after time, almost always combined with the same small-scale physical assaults as in Borås. Protesters shouted insults, spat at strikebreakers and stamped at their feet. In one case in 1926, female retail strikebreakers in Malmö were even photographed at close range and responded by showing their tongues at the photographer.[26]

The violence was seldom more severe than that, but sometimes 'home-followings' escalated, as small-scale violence evolved into fistfights or worse. During a factory-workers strike in Falkenberg in 1922, protesters followed strikebreakers from a lunch restaurant to the factory. Close to the gates, some protesters started kicking and headbutting the strikebreakers, and the city police commissioner himself had to save one of them.[27] Similar things happened in Malmö in both 1926 and 1935.[28] The latter episode occured during a market-garden workers' strike. 15 strikebreakers were 'followed' by c. 200 protesting workers on the way from a dinner restaurant to their employer's private villa, where they were lodged. Outside the entrance, a brawl started. One of the strikebreakers drew a knife but dropped it as he was punched in the face by a police officer. Workers started throwing rocks at the strikebreakers and one was hit, falling unconscious to the ground. At the same time, the sound of

[25] Swedish National Archives (*Riksarkivet*, RA), Kommittén angående statsfientlig verksamhet, YK 676, Box 6: Letter from Borås Detective Police, July 19, 1933. See also: *Betänkande med förslag angående åtgärder mot statsfientlig verksamhet* (1935) (Stockholm: Justitiedepartementet), p. 391.

[26] Malmö City Archives (*Malmö Stadsarkiv*, MS), Kriminalpolisen i Malmö, Box A2a, 42: Police report, October 28, 1926. See also Uhlén, A. (1949) *Facklig kamp i Malmö under sju decennier* (Malmö: Framtiden), p. 360.

[27] Lund Regional Archives (*Landsarkivet i Lund*), Stadsfiskalen i Falkenberg, Box E3a, 14: Police report, May 10, 1922; *Falkenbergs Tidning*, April 29, 1922: "Svårartade strejkuppträden i Falkenberg"; and Lantz, S. W. (1947) *De Förenade Förbundens organisationshistoria 1875–1945* (Stockholm: Tiden), pp. 333–35.

[28] Nyzell, *'Striden ägde rum'*, pp. 160–64.

gun shots was heard, and the crowd dispersed. It is unclear whether real shots were fired, but the police later found a revolver at the strikebreakers' lodgings.[29]

Of all the events in our sample, 'homefollowings' involved the highest number of participants, and the display of numbers was a major factor making this form of collective violence effective. Perhaps the most extreme event, in this respect, occurred during the retail strike in Malmö mentioned above. One night in October 1926, four female strikebreakers were followed on their way from a tram stop to their apartments by a crowd of at least 3,000 persons.[30]

Several large crowds in our sample consisted of women as well as men, which is interesting considering that almost all the strikes occurred at workplaces with a male workforce. As historian Tapio Bergholm notes, strikebreaking as well as anti-strikebreaker violence could function as a way of displaying a rough, working-class masculinity in the first half of the twentieth century.[31] However, not only men but also women 'followed strikebreakers home'. For example, newspapers noted the presence of 'many women' in Falkenberg in 1922, and the same observation was made during another retail workers strike in Malmö in 1928.[32]

Expulsions

Sometimes, protesters used violence to stop strikebreakers from working, physically expulsing them from the workplace. This, of course, meant a higher level of physical damage but not necessarily a higher level of coordination. Expulsions, as we call these events, could be more or less planned. We have found ten such events in our sample.

[29] MS, Kriminalpolisen i Malmö, Box A2a, 72: Police report, March 11, 1935; MS, Statspolisen i Malmö (kriminalavdelningen), Box A1, 5: Memorandum, March 8, 1935; and Sundell, Å. (1997) *Patriarkalism och föreningsrätt: Om production och facklig kamp inom handelsträdgårdsnäringen i Malmö med omnejd fram till 1936* (Lund: Lund University), pp. 114–21.

[30] *Sydsvenska Dagbladet*, October 9, 1926: "Kritiska ögonblick i går afton i Limhamn"; and *Arbetet*, October 9, 1926: "Sk. Aftonbladet har serverat lögnhistorier".

[31] Bergholm, 'Masculinity, Violence and Disunity', pp. 23, 34–35, 41.

[32] *Falkenbergs Tidning*, April 29, 1922: "Svårartade strejkuppträden i Falkenberg"; and *Skånska Aftonbladet*, October 24, 1928: "Nytt gatuspektakel i går afton på Östra förstadsgatan".

In Gothenburg, a big exposition of trade and culture was to be opened in May 1923. At the same time, there was a waterfront strike going on and many strikebreakers were present in the docks. The day before the opening of the exposition, strikebreakers were transported from the docks to the exposition hall to hurry up the final works. When the strikebreakers arrived, all workers in the hall (including the female cleaners) stopped working as a protest. They then approached the strikebreakers, and one of the strikebreakers fired a revolver as a warning. A fistfight broke out between the two groups, ending in a victory for the workers. All strikebreakers were withdrawn, never to return.[33]

This expulsion was rather violent but not very coordinated. Other expulsions had a significantly higher level of planning. One such event occurred during the 1923 forest workers strike mentioned earlier in this chapter. In late January that year, 16 strikebreakers were traveling in the woods with horses and equipment from Järvsö to the village of Hamra. They were ambushed by 300–400 striking workers, who forced them to return. The strikers then took all the forage that the strikebreakers had brought for their horses and soaked it in kerosene, making it unusable.[34]

Not surprisingly, when striking workers tried to expulse strikebreakers, the chance of success depended on the nature of the workplace. Strikebreakers working inside a building were hard to expulse. During a municipal workers strike in Kalmar in 1925, large crowds tried to stop strikebreakers from working at the local gas company and bombarded the building with rocks for several nights. However, the police could easily protect the premises.[35] It was far easier to disperse strikebreakers working outside, as in the agricultural strike in Uppland in the same year. For example, when six strikebreakers from Stockholm walked on the road to the mansion of Säbyholm, they were beaten up so hard by a crowd of c. 50 striking farmhands and sympathizers that they immediately returned to the capitol.[36]

[33] *Stockholms Dagblad*, May 8, 1923: "Vernissagen blev stormig"; and *Väst-Svenska Kuriren*, May 12, 1923: "En kort strejkbrytarvisit på utställningen".

[34] *Söderhamns Tidning*, February 1, 1923: "Upprörande övergrepp i Loos-skogarna".

[35] *Barometern*, July 27, 1925: "Blodiga kravaller utanför gasverket på lördagskvällen"; and *Fackföreningsrörelsen*, August 6, 1925: "Strejkuppträden i Kalmar".

[36] *Upsala Nya Tidning*, July 20, 1925: "Strejkuppträde vid Säbyholm".

Abductions and Forced Marches

Expulsions were a very instrumental form of collective violence. The aim was to stop strikebreakers from working and nothing else. In a few cases (five events in our sample), strikers used a more elaborate method, not only stopping strikebreakers from working but also humiliating them in a rather ritualized way, by forcing them to take part in anti-strikebreaker demonstrations and marches. We saw one such example in the beginning of this chapter, when we discussed what happened before the Ådalen killings in 1931. But that is not the only case.

For example, when the singing forest workers outside Voxna were unsuccessful in their efforts to stop strikebreakers in January 1923, they shifted tactics, escalating the level of physical damage. In the afternoon of January 31, a crowd of 300–500 protesters approached the strikebreakers' barracks. The strikebreakers were given two hours to leave the place, and when they finally refused, protesters entered the barracks. Four police officers present did not (or dared not) stop what happened next. All strikebreakers were abducted and forced to march with the strikers in an anti-strikebreaker protest march around the municipality of Voxna.[37]

These violent actions were quite ritualized, tended to look very similar, had a high level of coordination and at least a potentially high level of physical damage. A demonstration in itself is a ritualized form of collective action, with protesters marching in an orderly way, carrying banners and sometimes singing or performing music. All these elements were present in an abduction that took place during a strike outside Brännhult in the County of Kronoberg in southern Sweden in 1925. The Swedish Union of road- and waterworks construction workers fought a strike over the right to organize, and a local employer hired a few strikebreakers from outside the county. Saturday, September 5, c. 200 sympathizing workers marched with red banners and a brass band to the house in Brännhult where the strikebreakers were lodged. According to an eyewitness account, one of the banners had the text "Down with the strikebreakers, long live solidarity".[38] The protesters threatened the overseer, who eventually unlocked the doors of the building, and the

[37] *Hälsinglands Folkblad*, February 3, 1923: "En stor demonstration i Voxna"; and *Söderhamns Tidning*, February 2, 1923: "Våldsamma strejkuppträden I Voxna".

[38] Palm, G. (1982) *Det röda Kronoberg: Om arbetarrörelsen i Kronobergs län* (Växjö: Kronobergs socialdemokratiska partidistrikt), p. 60. See also: Nilsson, N. (1941) *Svenska*

strikebreakers were forced to join the demonstration and march all the way to the nearest railway station in Älmhult. There, the protesters scrambled money to buy tickets and put the strikebreakers on a train.[39]

Interestingly, forcing persons to join marches was not a unique form of collective action for anti-strikebreaker violence in the 1920s and 1930s. There are some events hinting that the method was part of a broader, and perhaps older, working-class repertoire of contention. At least in 1917, during the food-shortage at the end of the first world war, farmers in northern Sweden were forced to join rural marches and even to carry flags and banners. During these marches, hungry workers 'investigated' farms to see if the farmers had hidden any food.[40] However, the exact nature of the connections between the pre-1918 repertoire and the anti-strikebreaker protests after 1918 is not yet studied.

Mock Trials

Two forms of collective violence—mock trials and bombings—are rare in our sample, consisting of only two events each. They are interesting nonetheless, for different reasons. The staging of mock trials, with a high level of coordination but not necessarily a high level of physical damage, is the only form of collective violence in our sample correlating with communist-dominated strikes.

One of the mock trials has already been mentioned. It was the event at Kramfors in Ådalen, where communist strike-leader Axel Nordström 'questioned' strikebreakers. The other mock trial that we have found occurred two years later, during the seamen's strike of 1933.

The strike was launched by the Swedish Union of Seamen, one of the unions in LO. Hence, it was not a communist strike per se, as reformists as well as communists were active in the union. But from the beginning, the strike turned into a fight not only between strikers and employers but between reformists and communists inside the union as well. During the strike, the communists organized separately under the name of Red Trade Union Opposition (*Röd Facklig Opposition*, RFO), advocating

väg- och vattenbyggnadsarbetareförbundets historia 1914–1939 (Gävle: Arbetarbladet), pp. 453–54.

[39] *Arbetet*, September 9, 1925: "En lyckad demonstration i Brännhult".

[40] Andrae, C. (1998) *Revolt eller reform: Sverige inför revolutionerna i Europa 1917–1918* (Stockholm: Carlsson), pp. 48–54.

more far-reaching demands than the reformist union leaders, and certainly adopting more militant tactics against the strikebreakers, which were lodged onboard ships anchoring in the harbor of Gothenburg.[41]

During a subsequent razzia, the police discovered a leaflet issued by 'The national leadership of RFO' and dated in Gothenburg, March 20, 1933. In the leaflet, local RFO strike committees were called on to "organize one or more chock-brigades in every harbor" and "seize the strikebreakers from the ships and take them ashore".[42] Two days later, this is exactly what happened. On March 22, striking seamen used motorboats to reach and then enter the steamship *Kjell* in the harbor of Gothenburg. Five strikebreakers were abducted and brought ashore. At the docks, strikers arranged a mock trial, questioning the strikebreakers about their identities and whether they had participated in strikebreaking before. After the trial, the strikebreakers were transported by car to a nearby forest. There, they were given a beating and then permitted to leave.[43]

This event, as well as the one in Ådalen, seems to correlate well with communist activity. But at the same time, there are indications hinting that the situation might have been more complex. Six members of the Seamen's union were later sentenced in court for participating in anti-strikebreaker violence during the strike, but none of them were organized communists.[44] But exactly what crimes they were sentenced for is not known, and the Seaman's strike of 1933 is not yet thoroughly studied.

Bombings

The last form of collective violence had a high level of coordination and a potentially extremely high level of physical damage but did not necessarily take many persons to carry out. It was the use of bombs and explosives.

[41] Weiss, H. (2019) *För kampen internationellt! Transportarbetarnas globala kampinternational och dess verksamhet i Nordeuropa under 1930-talet* (Turenki: Työväen historian ja perinteen tutkimusen seura), pp. 325–27, 343.

[42] RA, YK 676, Box 1: "Den röda fackliga oppositionens (RFO) organisation och verksamhet i Sverige", p. 31.

[43] *Betänkande med förslag angående åtgärder mot statsfientlig verksamhet* (1935) (Stockholm: Justitiedepartementet), pp. 398–99.

[44] Svensson, B. and Svensson, E. (1972) 'Sjömansstrejken 1933', *Arkiv för studier i arbetarrörelsens historia*, 2, p. 14.

Even if we have found only two such events in our sample, the occurrence of bombings in the 1920s and 1930s is an interesting result of our ongoing study. This form of collective violence is otherwise associated mainly with the period before the first world war. The probably most well-known attack on strikebreakers in Sweden is the bombing of the strikebreaker-ship *Amalthea* in Malmö harbor in 1908, resulting in the death of an English strikebreaker.[45] The bombings of the 1920s and 1930s are less well-known, perhaps because no one was killed.

In one case, the lack of fatal victims probably depended on sheer luck. In the spring of 1929, agricultural workers employed by Degerfors Ironworks in the region of Värmland fought a strike for the right to form a union. On April 13, the strike had lasted almost 8 months and production had been carried on with the use of strikebreakers. That night, the ultra-conservative National Youth Movement (*Nationella ungdomsförbundet*) arranged a dance for the strikebreakers and the white-collar personnel at the Ironworks' canteen. When night fell, c. 200 protesters gathered outside the canteen, throwing rocks and smashing windows. Suddenly, someone (the police never found out who) throw a pipe bomb, made of an iron rod filled with dynamite. The bomb landed inside the canteen and an explosion was heard. However, the dynamite charge had failed to ignite, and the only thing that really exploded was the percussion cap. Therefore, the only victim was a dancing woman who injured her arm. Had the dynamite charge exploded, people might very well have died.[46]

The risk of fatal injuries is harder to assess in the second event, which took place during a syndicalist forest worker strike in Lillånäs in the region of Västerbotten. In early June 1923, three strikebreakers were working with log-driving, when a small group of masked protesters attacked them. One of the strikebreakers fired a warning shot with his rifle, but immediately after that, one of the attackers lighted a fuse and throw a bottle filled with explosives (probably dynamite) in the direction of the strikebreakers. However, the bottle missed them and exploded at the ground

[45] Tidman, Y. (1998) *Spräng Amalthea! Arbete, facklig kamp och strejkbryteri i nordvästeuropeiska hamnar 1870–1914* (Lund: Lund University), pp. 11–13. Indeed, anti-strikebreaker actions in the harbors often proved violent in the early decades of the twentieth century. See for example: Mikkelsen, *Arbejdskonflikter i Skandinavien*, pp. 138–39.

[46] *Örebro-Kuriren*, April 15, 1929: "Elakartat uppträde i Degerfors"; and Back, P. (1961) *En klass i uppbrott: Den fackliga lantarbetarrörelsens uppkomst och utveckling* (Malmö: Framtiden), p. 265.

several meters away. The explosion blew a hole in the ground, but no one was injured.[47]

A Repertoire of Anti-Strikebreaker Collective Violence

Our research is not yet finished. Therefore, we cannot say anything certain about the exact number of violent labor market confrontations in Sweden, nor about their geographical and temporal variations. However, the many examples given in this chapter show that the violent events preceding the killings in Ådalen in 1931 was only the top of an iceberg. Collective anti-strikebreaker violence might not by any means have occurred in most of the many Swedish strikes between the world wars, but it was not a rare phenomenon either.

In this chapter, we have created a typology, analyzing different forms of anti-strikebreaker violence varying in level of physical damage as well as in level of coordination: Threats and physical intimidations, 'following the strikebreakers home', expulsions, abductions and forced marches, mock trials, and bombings. In our forthcoming research, we will elaborate on this typology and hopefully be able to draw quantitative conclusions as well.

Although we abstain from drawing quantitative conclusions, a few qualitative observations should be highlighted before we end this chapter. First, we would stress that collective violence against strikebreakers formed a Swedish *working-class* repertoire of contention rather than a trade union repertoire. Trade unions publicized the names of strike-breakers in newspapers, as mentioned earlier. But trade union chapters did not in general vote and decide on the arrangement of anti-strikebreaker violence. This was something that workers did, and workers did not always act inside trade unions. Hence, although we of course must acknowledge that formal trade unions were strong and important in the Swedish 1920s and 1930s, trade union culture and working-class culture was not always the same thing, and both affected what happened during strikes.

[47] *Jämtlands-Posten*, June 6, 1923: "Häktade för mordförsök och brott mot Åkarpslagen"; and Bergkvist, K. (1935) *Sverges Arbetares Centralorganisation: Minnesskrift med anledning av tjugofemårsjubileet 1910–1935* (Stockholm: Federativs), pp. 311–12.

Second, the correlation between communist-dominated strikes and anti-strikebreaker violence seems to have been rather complicated, and more complex than Social Democratic historiography claims. True, the two mock trials in our sample occurred during strikes in which communists played important roles. But many violent strikes were not at all dominated by communists. For example, the many cases of 'following the strikebreakers home' in Malmö occurred during strikes dominated by reformists. Malmö, an industrial center where several of our examples took place, had almost no communists at all at the time.

Third, an important question to answer in future studies is the connections between the repertoire of contention in the 1920s and 1930s and older repertoires. Although we know a lot of how trade unions acted in strikes before the first world war, we know far less about how *workers* acted when confronting strikebreakers. Already in Malmö in 1890, striking workers is known to have 'followed the strikebreakers home'.[48] But was that a common or a rare form of collective violence? Was it a national or a local repertoire of contention? We do not know that yet.

Fourth, the events in our sample (maybe with mock trials as an exception) generally lack the more expressively ritualistic and sometimes even carnivalesque features present in, for example, the older repertoire that English workers used when they attacked strikebreakers in the nineteenth century, such as 'rough music' and 'donkey riding'.[49] They also lack some of the symbolic elements of the early twentieth century anti-strikebreaker repertoire in parts of the United States, such as the creation and destruction of strikebreaker effigies.[50] Hence, future studies should compare the Swedish repertoire of contention used against strikebreakers with the repertoires used by workers in other countries, in order to elucidate differences as well as similarities.

[48] Greiff, M. and Lundin, J. (2018) 'Sweden 1880–1910: The Age of the Labour Movement' in Mikkelsen, Kjeldstadli and Nyzell, *Popular Struggle*, p. 323.

[49] Linehan, T. (2018) *Scabs and Traitors: Taboo, Violence and Punishment in Labour Disputes in Britain, 1760–1871* (London: Routledge), pp. 116–70.

[50] Norwood, S. (2002) *Strikebreaking and Intimidation: Mercenaries and Masculinity in Twentieth Century America* (Chapel Hill: University of North Carolina Press), pp. 41, 55, 214.

References

Archives

The Swedish National Archives (*Riksarkivet*, RA)
Kommittén angående statsfientlig verksamhet, YK 676.
Lund Regional Archives (*Landsarkivet i Lund*)
Stadsfiskalen i Falkenberg.
Malmö City Archives (*Malmö Stadsarkiv*, MS)
Kriminalpolisen i Malmö.
Statspolisen i Malmö (Kriminalavdelningen).

Serials

Arbetet
Barometern
Fackföreningsrörelsen
Falkenbergs Tidning
Hälsinglands Folkblad
Jämtlands-Posten
Skånska Aftonbladet
Stockholms Dagblad
Sundsvalls-Posten
Sydsvenska Dagbladet
Söderhamns Tidning
Upsala Nya Tidning
Väst-Svenska Kuriren
Örebro-Kuriren

Literature

Åmark, K. (1992) 'Social Democracy and the Trade Union Movement: Solidarity and the Politics of Self-Interest' in Misgeld, K., Molin, K. and Åmark, K. (eds.) *Creating Social Democracy: A Century of the Social Democratic Labor Party in Sweden* (University Park: Pennsylvania State University Press), pp. 67–96.

Andersson, K. (2002) 'Brädgårdskonflikten i Halmstad 1931', *Ale: Historisk tidskrift för Skåne, Halland och Blekinge*, 2, pp. 9–20.

Andrae, C. (1998) *Revolt eller reform: Sverige inför revolutionerna i Europa 1917–1918* (Stockholm: Carlsson).

Back, P. (1961) *En klass i uppbrott: Den fackliga lantarbetarrörelsens uppkomst och utveckling* (Malmö: Framtiden).

Berättelse avgiven av den av Kungl. Maj:t tillsatta kommissionen för undersökning rörande oroligheterna i Gudmunrå m.fl. kommuner av Västernorrlands län maj 1931 (1931) (Stockholm: Norstedt).

Bergholm, T. (1996) 'Masculinity, Violence and Disunity: Waterfront Strikers and Strikebreakers in Finnish Ports in the 1920s and 1930s', *International Journal of Maritime History*, 8, 1, pp. 23–42.

Bergkvist, K. (1935) *Sveriges Arbetares Centralorganisation: Minnesskrift med anledning av tjugofemårsjubileet 1910–1935* (Stockholm: Federativs).

Betänkande med förslag angående åtgärder mot statsfientlig verksamhet (1935) (Stockholm: Justitiedepartementet).

Casparsson, R. (1951) *LO under fem årtionden: 1924–1948* (Stockholm: Tiden).

Cederqvist, J. (1980) *Arbetare i strejk: Studier rörande arbetarnas politiska mobilisering under industrialismens genombrott, Stockholm 1850–1909* (Stockholm: Liber).

Ericsson, M. and Nyzell, S. (2018) 'Sweden 1910–1950: The Contentious Swedes—Popular Struggle and Democracy' in Mikkelsen F., Kjeldstadli, K. and Nyzell, S. (eds.) *Popular Struggle and Democracy in Scandinavia: 1700–Present* (London: Palgrave Macmillan), pp. 337–75.

Flink, I. (1978) *Strejkbryteriet och arbetets frihet: En studie av svensk arbetsmarknad fram till 1938* (Uppsala: Almqvist & Wiksell International).

Greiff, M. and Lundin, J. (2018) 'Sweden 1880–1910: The Age of the Labour Movement' in Mikkelsen, F., Kjeldstadli, K. and Nyzell, S. (eds.) *Popular Struggle and Democracy in Scandinavia: 1700-Present* (London: Palgrave Macmillan), pp. 319–35.

Guillemot, A. (1997) 'Från Sundsvall 1879 till Ådalen 1931: Om militära kommenderingar vid strejker och sociala konflikter' in Ericsson, T. and Guillemot, A. (eds.) *Individ och struktur i historisk belysning* (Umeå: Umeå universitet), pp. 53–90.

Hamark, J. (2014) *Ports, Dock Workers and Labour Market Conflicts* (Gothenburg: University of Gothenburg).

Hamark, J. (2018) 'From Peak to Trough: Swedish Strikes and Lockouts in the First Half of the Twentieth Century', *Workers of the World*, 1, 9, pp. 137–66.

Johanson, C. (1970) *Lantarbetarna i Uppland 1918–1930: En studie i facklig taktik och opposition* (Stockholm: Svenska bokförlaget).

Johansson, R. (2001) *Kampen om historien: Ådalen 1931 – Sociala konflikter, historiemedvetande och historiebruk 1931–2000* (Stockholm: Hjalmarson & Högberg).

Karlbom, T. (1968) *Skogens arbetare: Till minnet av Svenska skogsarbetarförbundets 50-åriga verksamhet 1918–1968* (Stockholm: Svenska skogsarbetarförbundet).

Lantz, S. W. (1947) *De Förenade Förbundens organisationshistoria 1875–1945* (Stockholm: Tiden).

Laybourn, K. and Taylor, D. (2011) *Policing in England and Wales, 1918–39: The Fed, Flying Squads and Forensics* (Basingstoke: Palgrave Macmillan).

Lindbom, T. (1935) *Svenska Kommunalarbetareförbundet 1910–1935: Historik* (Stockholm: Tiden).

Linehan, T. (2018) *Scabs and Traitors: Taboo, Violence and Punishment in Labour Disputes in Britain, 1760–1871* (London: Routledge).

Lipold, P. (2014) '"Striking Deaths" at Their Roots: Assaying the Social Determinants of Extreme Labor-Management Violence in US Labor History 1877–1947', *Social Science History*, 38, 3–4, pp. 541–75.

Mikkelsen, F. (1992) *Arbejdskonflikter i Skandinavien 1848–1980* (Odense: Odense Universitetsforlag).

Nilsson, N. (1941) *Svenska väg- och vattenbyggnadsarbetareförbundets historia 1914–1939* (Gävle: Arbetarbladet).

Norwood, S. (2002) *Strikebreaking and Intimidation: Mercenaries and Masculinity in Twentieth Century America* (Chapel Hill: University of North Carolina Press).

Nyzell, S. (2009) *'Striden ägde rum i Malmö': Möllevångskravallerna 1926 – En studie av politiskt våld i mellankrigstidens Sverige* (Malmö: Malmö University Press).

Olsson, T. (1980) *Pappersmassestrejken 1932: En studie av facklig ledning och opposition* (Lund: Arkiv).

Palm, G. (1982) *Det röda Kronoberg: Om arbetarrörelsen i Kronobergs län* (Växjö: Kronobergs socialdemokratiska partidistrikt).

Sherman Grant II, D. and Wallace, M. (1991) 'Why Do Strikes Turn Violent?', *American Journal of Sociology*, 96, 5, pp. 1117–50.

Silvennoinen, O. (2018) 'Demokratins framgångshistoria? Skogsindustrin, arbetsmarknaden och en fascistisk samhällssyn 1918–1940' in Meinander, H., Karonen, P. and Östberg, K. (eds.) *Demokratins drivkrafter: Kontext och särdrag i Finlands och Sveriges demokratier 1890–2020* (Stockholm: Appell), pp. 189–224.

Sundell, Å. (1997) *Patriarkalism och föreningsrätt: Om produktion och facklig kamp inom handelsträdgårdsnäringen i Malmö med omnejd fram till 1936* (Lund: Lund University).

Svarta själar: Fotografiskt album med register över personer som arbetade 'på sitt sätt' under järnvägsstrejken 1922 (Stockholm: Politikens tryckeri, 1922).

Svensson, B. and Svensson, E. (1972) 'Sjömansstrejken 1933', *Arkiv för studier i arbetarrörelsens historia*, 2, pp. 99–110.

Tidman, Y. (1998) *Spräng Amalthea! Arbete, facklig kamp och strejkbryteri i nordvästeuropeiska hamnar 1870–1914* (Lund: Lund University).

Tilly, C. (2003) *The Politics of Collective Violence* (Cambridge: Cambridge University Press).

Uhlén, A. (1949) *Facklig kamp i Malmö under sju decennier* (Malmö: Framtiden).
Utredningar till belysande av arbetsfredsfrågan (1927) (Stockholm: Socialdepartementet).
Weiss, H. (2019) *För kampen internationellt! Transportarbetarnas globala kampinternational och dess verksamhet i Nordeuropa under 1930-talet* (Turenki: Työäven historian ja perinteen tutkimuksen seura).

PART II

National and Local Trade Union Activism, 1940–2020

CHAPTER 7

Social Movement Unionism in Denmark, 1940–1985

Flemming Mikkelsen

Around the turn of the century, local trade unions joined forces in nationwide central organizations. The employers formed large-centralized organizations, too, and both parties grew in membership. The centralized labor market organizations were tied into long-term wage contracts at the national level that guaranteed moderate wage increases and tolerable working conditions but restricted the use of strikes and lockouts. From time to time, however, the labor market erupted into outburst of protest, and to capture this development I introduce the notion of 'social movement unionism', tantamount to a bottom-up approach. The concept of 'social movement unionism' (SMU) was introduced by the American labor scholar, Lowell Turner, who defines SMU as "an activist mobilization-based unionism that, in contrast to established

F. Mikkelsen (✉)
Copenhagen, Denmark
e-mail: fmmikk@gmail.com

© The Author(s), under exclusive license to Springer Nature Switzerland AG 2023

J. Jørgensen and F. Mikkelsen (eds.), *Trade Union Activism in the Nordic Countries since 1900*, Palgrave Studies in the History of Social Movements, https://doi.org/10.1007/978-3-031-08987-9_7

insider unionism, pushes for substantial social change".[1] This definition can be applied to historical cases and transformations where the repertoire of collective action and forms of organization occupy a central position. Regarding Denmark, social movement unionism followed the international trend and manifested itself strongly in 1917–1920, in 1943–1946 and again in 1968–1985. During these strike waves the decision to go on strike moves down the hierarchy: from centralized unions, tied into long-term wage contrasts at the national level, to the shop-floor with radicalized workers and shop stewards in a central position.[2]

In Chapter 4 of this book, the Danish historian Knud Knudsen has shown how the Syndicalists managed to force through higher wages and an 8-hour working day. They also succeeded in putting anti-militarism, poverty and housing problems on the national agenda. The Syndicalists' determined behavior challenged the workers' central organizations, i.e., the DsF, and the Social Democratic Party, that were pressured to raise questions about wages, work councils and control of corporate finance. The Syndicalists also played an important role in the reaction against the king's dismissal of the government in 1920 and functioned as early risers to the Communists movement.

However, after some very turbulent years, the established part of the labor movement including the Social Democratic Party and the employers' central organization, DA, had restored power in the labor market. The lockouts in 1921 and 1922, the big strike and lockout in 1925 and the lockout in 1936 were fought between the central organizations on behalf of their members. The Arbitration Act of 1934, which adopted the concatenation of labor market agreements, set off a development that gradually and systematically reduced direct member influence, widened the gap between top and bottom of the trade union movement, and finally weakened the interest of the members to participate in union

[1] Lowell Turner, L. (2007) 'An Urban Resurgence of Social Unionism' in Turner, L. and D.B. Cornfield, D.B. (eds.) *Labor in the New Urban Battle Grounds. Local Solidarity in a Global Economy* (London: ILR Press), p. 15.

[2] Soskice, D. (1978) 'Strike Waves and Wage Explosions, 1968–1970: An Economic Interpretation' in Crouch, C. and Pizzorno, A. (eds.) *The Resurgence of Class Conflict in Western Europe Since 1968*, Vol. 1–2 (New York: Holmes & Meier).

Table 7.1 Strikes, protest events, sabotage and real wages, 1939–1946

Year	*Strikes*[a]	*Participants in strikes*[a]	*Protest events*[b]	*Participants in protest events*[b]	*Sabotage*[d]	*Real wages*[e]
1939	19	523	26	254.530	–	157
1940	9	257	37	960.700	10	138
1941	2	65	25	351.600	19	130
1942	7	3.155	21	111.400	122	131
1943	91	14.795	19	163.000[c]	969	138
1944	62	8.885	37	300.800[c]	867	146
1945	85	9.656	48	941.825	687	160
1946	108	56.304	36	957.370	–	171

Sources and *Note* [a]Statistics Denmark; [b]The Protest-Database-DK, see Mikkelsen (1999) 'Contention and Social Movements'; [c]These figures include both number of strikers and number of demonstrators; [d]Alkil, N. (1945–1946) *Besættelsestidens fakta*, Vol. 2 (Copenhagen: Schultz Forlag), p. 1206; and [e]Olsen, E. (1967) *Danmarks økonomiske historie siden 1750* (Copenhagen: Gads Forlag), p. 212. The two general political strikes in 1943 and 1944 are not included in the official strike statistics but listed under 'Participants in protest events'

activities.[3] To limit possible damages associated with prolonged strikes and lockouts the Social Democratic government regularly intervened in ongoing conflicts, during the 1930s. However, the tendency for further centralization was upset by the German occupation of Denmark. Trade union leaders were forced on the defensive and decisions concerning labor market regulations moved once again to the workplaces and to the labor union opposition this time with the Communists in a leading role.

Occupation, Collaboration and General Strikes, 1943–1946

During the first years of the occupation, the number of strikes declined as it appears from Table 7.1. But after some quiet years the labor market burst into flames with extensive strike activity, street riots, barricades and sabotage. It was the transition from passive to active resistance and from collaboration with the Germans to direct hostility.

[3] Mikkelsen, F. (1992) *Arbejdskonflikter I Skandinavien 1848–1980* (Odense: Odense Universitetsforlag), Ch. 8; Knudsen, K. (1999) *Arbejdskonflikternes historie i Danmark* (Copenhagen: SFAH), pp. 308–09.

Of great importance to preserve peace in the labor market was the Working Conditions Act of September 14, 1940.[4] The law stated that a Labor and Conciliation Board should be set up with the authority to make a final decision in disputes regarding pay and working conditions. It became illegal to launch work stoppages within the law. The relatively unanimous adoption of the law and the joint enactment of the main central organizations have probably put a damper on the unions' and workplaces' strike zeal. Uncertainty about how the Germans would react to lengthier strikes in armistice industries also lowered strike activity. Add to this the tighter regulation of labor market conditions, especially the so-called 'work card' or 'dog tag', which every wage earner over 18 years should have to receive unemployment benefit. The cards were kept by the employer, who controlled workplace shift and in reality, the political activities of the workers, too. Finally, the imprisonment of the leading Communists on August 20, 1941, and the cooperation with the German authorities during the early years of the occupation deprived many of the desire to challenge the Germans.[5]

In such a situation, a majority of the Danish population refrained from overt direct action and instead used more passive forms of resistance. Thus, hundred thousand of people participated in community singing and community walks. They attended the burial of the Prime Minister Th. Stauning; celebrated the king's birthday and sang the Norwegian national anthem during large sporting events and other rallies. Actual demonstrations occurred, but they were few, small and without political sting. The Communists on their side were clipped but not defenseless. In contrast to the adaptation strategy of DsF and the Social Democratic Party, the Communists arranged alternative trade union conferences and sought to influence public opinion in connection with local elections in March 1943 despite the party's illegal status. The Communist party initiated a reorganization plan through a construction of cells at workplaces and local neighborhoods. Illegal couriers with cover names and the Communist newspaper *Land og Folk* tied them together.[6]

[4] *Beretning* (1940) (Copenhagen: Dansk Arbejdsgiverforening), pp. 31–38.

[5] Nielsen, H. J. (1977) *Besættelse og befrielse. Den danske arbejderklasses historie 1940–1946* (Aarhus: Modtryk).

[6] Nielsen, *Besættelse*, pp. 58–70; and Christensen, L. K., Kolstrup, S. and Hansen, A. E. (2007)*Arbejdernes historie i Danmark 1800-2000*. (Copenhagen: SFAH), pp. 188–90.

In March 1943, the national election gave an overwhelming victory to the established political parties and the policy of collaboration. The Social Democratic and trade union leaders preached patience, moderation and discipline and condemned striking workers and sabotage but their credibility was declining. Falling or stagnant real wages, poor working conditions but also fewer unemployed made the workers more daring. After some strikes December 1942 a real strike wave spread across the country in the early 1943, fronted by the machine workers and in opposition to traditional collective agreements.[7] After reaching its nadir in June 1943 due to summer vacation strikes again flourished, and especially work stoppages at the shipyard in Odense and two factories in Aalborg on July 30 and August 9 ended with a "convincing victory". These collective manifestations meant a dramatic escalation of the strike as a political weapon and stand, as formulated by the historian Hans Kirchhoff, as "a transition from the single industrial strike to the city or general strike during the August-insurrection".[8] From August 9 to 29 strikes, closing of shops and offices, and mass demonstrations spread to major provincial towns but never reached Copenhagen. Kirchhoff estimates that about 390,000 people took part in the rebellion.

Workers occupied in the metal industries and the big fortifications took the lead and led the fight into the streets. They demanded danger money, more and cheaper homes, shelters, and improvements of living conditions; others required Germans and their sympathizers removed from the workplaces and the streets. Employers, white-collar workers and tradesmen followed the workers, stopped the production and closed the stores. Pro-German Danes were persecuted, and a few German soldiers assaulted. Political proclamations occurred but few dreamed of an open confrontation with the occupying forces.

Everywhere we see the Communists in the front line. The Communist Party "became the shock troops and true cadre organization of the general strike". The Communists bolstered the illegal newspapers, flyers and the formulation of strike plans.[9] Besides, during these intense days, the Social Democratic leadership, and the trade union central organization, DsF, lost control of essential resources such as buildings, member

[7] Kirchhoff, *Augustoprøret 1943*, Vol. 1 (Copenhagen: Gyldendal), pp. 247–50.

[8] Kirchhoff, *Augustoprøret*, Vol. 1, p. 294.

[9] Kirchhoff, *Augustoprøret*, Vol. 2, pp. 243–52.

lists, telephone and cash registers. They were bureaucratic and reformist institutions with great social and economic responsibility and commitment. They were neither tuned nor mentally equipped to fight against police and soldiers or were in no way prepared for any kind of illegality. This locked position caused a split in the labor movement, and we see that several local trade union federations, and many Social Democratic shop stewards joined the strike movement and instructed workers to rebel in the streets.

The whole protest movement was an attack on the politics of collaboration and had to be controlled and ultimately stopped. The leaders of the labor organizations tried to clip the fighting spirit and to stop the conflict as fast as possible. Anxiety for German military intervention and possible takeover of state power played a major role, but equally important was the fear of the Communists' growing importance. They grew in strength as the insurrection evolved from day to day. The strikes were declared illegal, and the Danish state deployed police forces to quell the uprising in the streets. However, when the state and the establishment did not manage to stop the August-rebellion, the Germans declared martial law after which the strikes and disturbances ended. The Germans also announced that sabotage, attacks on the Wehrmacht and other illegal actions were a capital crime. The Danish government rejected the German claims and consequently resigned.[10] From then on, Denmark was administered through the heads of departments with the Germans as the real rulers.

The August-insurrection led to an organizational and political breakthrough for the Communist movement. In the capital, its membership increased from 2,600 in 1943 to 25,000 in 1945, and the party moved from scattered groups to becoming a political factor challenging the position of the Social Democratic Party.[11] The Communists were seated in the Freedom Counsel (*Frihedsrådet*, founded in September 1943) and after the German defeat at Stalingrad February 1943, the party embarked on a more aggressive course with sabotage and urged workers to join the struggle for freedom. The Communists' strategy was to isolate the Social Democratic Party leadership and create a united front from below

[10] Christensen, C. B., Lund, J., Olesen, N. W. and Sørensen, J. (2009) *Danmark besat. Krig og hverdag 1940–45*, 3rd ed. (Copenhagen: Informations Forlag), pp. 467–72.

[11] Christensen, Kolstrup and Hansen, *Arbejdernes historie*, pp. 192–94.

under the leadership of the Communists. An important step in that direction came in the summer of 1944, when communist workers were at the forefront of the so-called part time strikes.

Prior to the incident the Germans had launched a crackdown on sabotage and executed eight freedom fighters, decreed a prohibition of public meetings, and imposed a curfew between 8 p.m. and 5 a.m. Four days later June 26, 1944, workers at B&W (a big shipyard in Copenhagen) went home at 2 p.m., and in the following days the strikes spread to other workplaces. From being a local phenomenon in "the troubled corner of Copenhagen", the strike soon included 80,000 workers. It had its center of gravity in the iron industry but quickly spread to other branches such as dock laborers and post workers. Shops were closed and public transport was stopped. People began to make bonfires in the streets, to build barricades and use firearms against German patrols and Nazi collaborators who shot back, and when the dust had settled about 90 civilians had been killed and 670 wounded.[12] On June 30, the Germans had laid an iron ring around the city, and blocked the supply of gas, water and electricity; they also threatened with direct military intervention. However, at the request of Danish politicians (who entered the political arena for the first time since the August-rebellion) and trade union leaders the Germans decided to raise the blockade, and when they also lifted the state of emergency people resumed work.

What happened in the summer of 1944 was a wake-up call for especially the Social Democratic leadership. There was only one thing to do, namely, to identify with the resistance movement. They contacted the Freedom Council and supplied the resistance movement with extra weapons, but to reach ordinary people and especially the workers the Social Democratic Party, in close collaboration with the DsF, pleaded for higher wages and better living, and they appointed a committee with the object of formulating a reform program more inclined to full employment, social security, shop committees, work councils and in general a more socialist policy.[13]

[12] Thing, M. (1987) *En analyse af Folkestrejken juni-juli 1944 med henblik på gadedemonstrationernes rolle og funktion* (unpublished master thesis, Københavns Universitet); and Kirchhoff, H. (1996) 'Folkestrejken 1944' in Karl-Erik Frandsen, K.-E. (ed.) *Kongens og folkets København – gennem 800 år* (Copenhagen: Forlaget Skippershoved).

[13] Christensen, Kolstrup and Hansen, *Arbejdernes historie*, pp. 195–98; and Dalgaard, N. (1995) *Ved demokratiets grænser. Demokratisering af arbejdslivet i Danmark 1919–1994* (Copenhagen: SFAH), pp. 104–14.

Next year, strikes and demonstrations for higher wages continued. The labor market was still characterized by decentralized negotiations where decisions about wages, working conditions and strikes were taken at the plant level, whereas the unions and their competent bodies were pushed into the background. After the end of the War, it was normal to continue with protest strikes, demonstrations in front of the parliament, deputations and mass fabrication of resolutions in all kinds of occasions.[14] After 1947, however, collective bargaining was more centralized, and in 1950, nearly all questions were settled with the help of the central labor market organizations and the conciliation board.

Industrial Conflict and Industrial Relations, 1947–1967

The Second World War had left Denmark with a worn but largely intact production apparatus, and the lack of foreign currency especially dollars meant that the reconstruction of the economy especially the industrial sector was very slow. From the late 1940s, the Marshall Plan sparked an industrial development, which slowly raised real wages and limited unemployment.[15] The War had weakened the trade unions, but soon after the peace trade union membership increased steadily, whereas the number of work stoppages, after the hectic strike days in 1946, reached a very low level until 1956, when 66,000 workers went on strike.[16]

It was disagreements between workers' and employers' central organizations about pay and working hours that triggered the conflict; but it was the shortage of oil and gasoline that caused the Social Democratic government to stop the oil blockade, which caused demonstrations and illegal strikes all over the country. It was Communist and Social Democratic shop stewards who agreed on short protest strikes, but there was no basis for a broader political mobilization against the Social Democratic government. Indeed, the Communists increased their share of union trust posts in 1956, but already the following year they lost terrain due to their

[14] *Under Samvirkets Flag* (1948) (Copenhagen: De samvirkende Fagforbund), p. 219.

[15] During the 1940s and 1950s the average rate of unemployment was about 10%.

[16] Mikkelsen, *Arbejdskonflikter*, pp. 324–26; and Christensen, Kolstrup and Hansen, *Arbejdernes historie*, pp. 224–26.

unconditional support for the Soviet invasion of Hungary. Since then, the Communists have played their part in the Danish labor movement.

Since 1956, economic output accelerated and unemployment fell. In 1960, a lesser strike wave spread across the country, and next year's collective bargaining quickly ran into problems.[17] A proposal for a settlement was rejected by the workers and soon close to 140,000 went on strike. To further press the employers striking seamen and dockworkers prevented unloading and loading ships in several ports while transport workers were blocking access to the gasoline harbor. At the request of the prime minister, the central labor market organizations agreed on an amended proposal that was accepted by a new ballot, which granted workers large wage increases both in the private and public sector.

The years between the early 1950s and early 1970s were the golden age of the labor movement. It established a close collaboration with the Social Democratic government and laid the foundation for a welfare state guaranteeing social security, regulating of prices and working conditions and low levels of strike and lockout activity.[18] These obligations, which relied on the ability of labor market organizations to control the actions of their members, worked quite well until the end of the 1960s, when international price inflation put a strain on real wages, and the employers intensified the modernization and reorganization of the production apparatus. Strike activity began to climb concomitant with other forms of collective contentious actions. It was not only a Danish phenomenon, but also spread to most of the Western industrialized world and made some social scientists to write about "the resurgence of class conflict".[19]

Industrial and Social Upheaval 1968–1985

The overall structural explanation of the industrial upheaval in Denmark was the expansive economic growth after 1965 that caused prices, wages and strikes to go up, starting an ongoing strike-wage spiral also named

[17] Mikkelsen, *Arbejdskonflikter*, pp. 327–28; and Christensen, Kolstrup and Hansen, *Arbejdernes historie*, p. 258.

[18] Mikkelsen, F. (2012) 'Class and Social Movements in Scandinavia Since 1945', *Moving the Social. Journal of Social History and the History of Social Movements*, 48, pp. 29–48.

[19] Crouch, C. and Pizzorno, A. (eds.) (1978) *The Resurgence of Class Conflict in Western Europe Since 1968*, Vol. 1–2 (New York: Holmes & Meier).

an industrial 'protest cycle'. The overheating of the economy and the resulting worsening of the balance of payments made the government to intervene in labor market negotiations. And together with other strong measures against an inflationary economy, it gave rise to a serious politicization of industrial relations and the upcoming of an alternative labor movement.

During the years of the protest cycle, old types of industrial conflict were activated, and new forms of labor actions entered the arena. The main categories can be described in this way: Strikes against contract renewal (few; very large; long). Lockouts against contract renewal (very few; very large; long). Political demonstration strikes (few; large; very short). Informal plant level strikes (many; small; short). To these well-known forms of dispute, we can add meetings during working hours, collective absenteeism, boycotts, work-to-rule, pickets, blockades and occupation of factories. Therefore, what happened during the 1970s was not only a major increase in strike activity but also a change in the repertoire of collective action including new forms of organization.[20]

In chronological order, we can see that from 1968 until 1979 thousands of workers strove for wage increases and protested contract renewal, political-economic decisions and the government in office. Left-wing trade unions and militant political groups in the private and public sector played an important part in organizing these strikes that often were followed by demonstrations in the center of the larger cities. Another important innovation imported from abroad was the physical blockade and factory occupation that time and again resulted in violent confrontations with the police.[21]

In the early 1980s, the violence came to a standstill and the last serious confrontation broke out on March 28, 1985, when more than 600,000 employees went on strike and the inner Copenhagen and above all the House of Parliament was blocked by thousands of demonstrators for several days in discontent with the labor market policy of the liberal government. Hence, strike activity declined, the left-wing action groups

[20] For an overview see: Mikkelsen, F. (2018) 'Denmark 1946–2015: Popular Struggle in an Era of Democracy' in Mikkelsen, F., Kjeldstadli, K. and Nyzell, S. (eds.), *Popular Struggle and Democracy in Scandinavia, 1700-Present* (London: Palgrave Macmillan).

[21] Jepsen, J. (1980) 'Policing Labour Conflicts', *Scandinavian Studies in Criminology*, 7, pp. 177–206.

demobilized and the centralized labor market organizations once again took control.

Industrial Conflict and Forms of Organization

The above description of strike patterns during the 1970s reveals not only an expansion and differentiation of the action repertoire but uncovers new actors and organizations as well. Initially, I distinguish between internal organizing and external organizing, which can be seen as a heuristic device going from less to more structural and bureaucratic actors. Below I have inserted the most important agents of mobilization between the two poles:

Internal organizing
- Informal groups
- Contacts between informal groups
- External support groups
- Trade unions
- Political organizations

External organizing

Trade unions and oppositional factions in the labor movement organized strikes against contract renewal and political demonstration strikes. And if we turn to informal plant level strikes, 1976–1979, the spectrum of organizational activity becomes more visible. Out of 1,970 cases, it appears that workers on their own initiative decided to go on strike on 1,406 (71%) occasions, whereas shop stewards and trade unions took the initiative in 293 and 259 events, respectively.[22] But this only tells us that external organizations played a minor role, and that ordinary workers were heavily involved in the decision to strike. However, with some manipulation, the data permit us to go a little beyond the wisdom on wildcat strikes as being unplanned, spontaneous and sudden eruptions of angry resentment on the part of workers without influence.

[22] Information on strikes and lockouts from Statistics Denmark is rather inadequate. Therefore, I have used other sources and databases. Consulting a wide range of newspapers, a group of students and researchers at the Department of Political Science, Aarhus University, compiled information on 2,986 plant level strikes 1976–1979. Of these industrial actions 1,490 involved between 1 and 20 plants and have been selected for detailed coding. This database was placed at my disposal and will be referred to as the *ST-database*. For an evaluation and recoding of the dataset see: Mikkelsen, *Arbejdskonflikter*, p. 432.

Table 7.2
Coordination of strike activity, 1976–1979

Number of plants	*Strikes*	*%*
1	728	24
2–4	317	11
5–7	78	3
8–10	83	3
11–20	284	10
21–50	452	15
51–100	302	10
101–200	160	5
201–350	582	20
Total	*2,986*	*101*

Source ST-database (see: note 22); and Mikkelsen (1992) *Arbejdskonflikter*, pp. 166–67

If action groups at different workplaces went on strike at the same time, and on the same issue, and if we can track down the presence of external supporting parties, it may be rather safely assumed that strikes were coordinated and planned. And that such a collaboration did take place is confirmed in Table 7.2.

In 728 events, or one-quarter, we cannot observe a connection with other conflicts; 317 strikes or 11% involved 2–4 plants; 78 strikes or 2.6% involved 5–7 plants, etc. In total, three-quarters of all strikes had an overlap in time and issue with other stoppages: It was the local rank and file shop committees and joint shop-steward committees within the same line of business that provided for regular contacts, security, condition of work and they also prepared the claims and the timing of strikes. If all the units of production in the same firm or company were closed simultaneously, the employers were prevented from transferring part of the manufacturing to other plants and were put under severe economic pressure. Therefore, many of these strikes tended to be very short.[23]

This pattern is found where strikes were launched in small groups, whereas multiple conflicts with more than twenty establishments clearly indicate the active presence of unions. Thus, we find several examples of union-sponsored strike activity within the metal industry, catering, service and security guards. In the public sector IT-personnel initiated several strikes against the state and the municipalities as did nurses, educators

[23] Mikkelsen, *Arbejdskonflikter*, p. 353.

and social workers. Workers' mutual solidarity is evident from Table 7.3, too.

Besides internal support activities, which amounted to 14%, and the strikers' own organization with 23%, workers in other plants (43%) backed up the strikers by stopping work or supplying them with men during flying pickets. Organizational support came mainly from the strikers' own trade union, which lent a hand or sometimes even took charge of the negotiations during and after a dispute. It might also, under cover, help with financial support.

Most short-lived stoppages did not need any organizational or financial support, for which reason it was around the long and heavy conflicts that external support networks tended to develop. Often these networks were of a mere ad hoc character, but if one of these struggles was superseded by another the support network would take on a more permanent form

Table 7.3 Support organizations and forms of support, 1976–1979

Support organizations	*Number of support activities*	*%*
Own workplace	91	9
Shop stewards	56	5
Workers in other plants	464	43
Own trade union	241	23
Other trade unions	74	7
Permanent support organization	29	3
Ad hoc support organization	108	10
Political organization	10	1
Forms of support		
Resolutions	92	9
Partial stoppage	32	3
Stoppage of work	428	42
Militant actions	49	5
Economic	130	13
Organizing	276	27
Others	17	2

Source and *Note* ST-database (see note 22). It was possible to record a maximum of four support activities for each single strike. The number of unsolved cases/strikes was high, so the number of support activities may be underestimated

Table 7.4 External support networks, 1979

Area	*Plant level*	*Support committees outside plants*
Copenhagen	357	261
Zealand	24	56
Funen	39	17
Jutland	193	78

Sources and *Note* Nielsen, H. H. and Rolighed, A. J. (1986) 'Strejker og fagopposition i 1970'erne' in Mikkelsen (ed.), *Protest og oprør* (Aarhus: Modtryk), p. 224; and Mikkelsen (1992) *Arbejdskonflikter*, p. 355. These figures refer to the number of support groups listed in selected newspapers in 1979

and become institutionalized. A survey of the support-structure, in 1979, can be found in Table 7.4.

As expected from Table 7.3, it was workers at other plants who constituted the backbone of the support network and, along with many of the support-committees, we can see the framework of a more permanent institutionalized structure of solidarity that developed in a communist, a federal and a left-wing movement.[24] Worker-Solidarity (*Arbejdersolidaritet, AS*) was the first alternative to arise from a strike in November 1970. AS prospered in the following months with strikes against the eroding of purchasing power but vanished as the first strike wave ended. By then the Foreman-Initiative (*Formandsinitiativet*, FI) had made itself conspicuous and achieved its largest extension with the strike at the Royal Porcelain Factory, the political strike against the Liberal government's tax measures in May 1974, and the unpopular 'August agreement' in 1976.[25]

FI coordinated the activities of the shop stewards but did not intervene directly in ongoing struggles. Instead, it became the object of the Socialist Workers' Club (*Socialistisk Arbejder Klub*, SAK), established after the strike at Sabro-ØB by the dismissed smiths in 1975. SAK interfered actively in many labor disputes but lost influence and backing because of internal faction and split. The same happened to FI, which nevertheless succeeded in preparing the way for the later shop-steward movement (*Tillidsmandsringen*). Shop stewards were not tied to the legal system

[24] Nielsen and Rolighed, 'Strejker og fagopposition', pp. 218–25.

[25] Logue, J. (1982) *Socialism and Abundance. Radical Socialism in the Welfare State* (Copenhagen: Akademisk Forlag), p. 147.

of industrial relations, and by forming movements in close contact with formal trade unions they were in an advantageous position when striking workers needed support from other colleagues and the public. The shop-steward movement was operative in many industries and had its heyday toward the end of the 1970s.

Public Employees Between Mass Organizations and Action Networks

Fully to understand the causes and intensity of the protest cycle 1968–1985 it is necessary to take a closer look at the public sector. In 1960 nearly 10% and in 1980 close to 30% of the workforce was employed in the public sector, while the number of organized employees in the public sector (transport and communication excluded) increased from 127,300 in 1960 to 612,600 in 1985, when union density reached 89%.[26] In general, a restructuring of public servants' trade unions followed this expansion: the semi-professional profile was strengthened, the administrative bureaucracy was modernized, the number of shop stewards increased and most unions built up strike funds. To strengthen their bargaining position, they also formed coalitions and cartels with other trade unions and sometimes resorted to strike action. Strikes and strike patterns can be seen as a result of these changes but, at the same time they also contributed to the transition.[27]

Strike action in the private sector paved the way for work stoppages among public employees in several ways: first, through intersector imitation; second, offering the possibility to join other large trade unions; and third, making it possible for the action networks to rely on support from left-wing trade unions and political parties, shop-steward movements, shop committees and the underlying growth of militant political groups. Public servants entered the arena of industrial action by making

[26] Bentzon, K.-H. (1984) 'Offentligt ansatte i Danmark i et internationalt perspektiv', *Økonomi og Politik*, 58, 3, p. 287; Visser, J. (1989) *European Trade Unions in Figures* (Deventer: Kluwer); and Scheuer, S. (1984) *Hvorfor stiger den faglige organisering? Om udviklingen i den faglige organisering i arbejdsløshedsperioden 1976–1982* (Copenhagen: Nyt fra Samfundsvidenskaberne), p. 50.

[27] Mikkelsen, F. (1994) *Radikaliseringen af de offentligt ansatte i Danmark* (Copenhagen: SFAH); and Mikkelsen, F. (1998) 'Unions and New Shopfloor Strike Strategies and Learning Processes Among Public Employees', *Economic and Industrial Democracy*, 19, pp. 505–38.

use of indirect, 'soft' forms of collective action such as moral boycotts, work-to rule and resignations. The strike became the most common form of collective action following one of the largest work stoppages ever in the private sector, in 1973. Most strikes in the public sector broke out over work conditions and not wage issues (as was the norm in the private sector); they were unofficial, and therefore not supported or subsidized by the official labor market organizations.[28]

Leaders of public sector unions were often reluctant to launch strikes. One thing is that the unions were tied to the system of negotiations; another is that public sector union leaders were unfamiliar with strike mobilization and feared the reaction of the state. Therefore, union members in many situations built up networks of (left-wing) activists who challenged the established union leaders and union bureaucracy to take a more active stance against the state and the municipality.

Alternative and often oppositional forms of organizations in the private and public sector peaked in the late 1970s and early 1980s. But after major strikes and demonstrations against collective bargaining and subsequent government intervention, in 1985, the alternative and often left-wing action networks faded away and surrendered the space to the established organizations. However, the protest cycle had not been in vain.

The largest strike upheaval since World War, II had warned trade union leaders and the government that workers on their own initiative still had the power to fight for higher wages, better working conditions and self-determination just as the strike wave had created a more advantageous opportunity structure for public employees. Through an ongoing process of imitation, network formation, alliances, and strikes, public sector organizations developed from small and weak associations placed in an inferior position facing the powerful state apparatus, to fully-fledged trade unions willing and able to back the interests of their members with strikes and militant actions.

[28] Nielsen and Rolighed, 'Strejker og fagopposition'.

Three Waves of Social Movement Unionism in Denmark

It was changes in the international economic and political system that fostered new forms of collective claim-making and new forms of organization referred to as social movement unionism. Shortly after the turn of the century, new socialist actors emerged on the national and international arena but it was the outbreak of World War I, which created the preconditions for a mobilization from below, new forms of organization and a new repertoire of contentious action. Next time the labor market burst into flames was during the Second World War, when the national political and economic elite was forced to retreat. The protests and the violent acts were directed against the German occupying forces but also against the established political parties and labor market institutions. Resistance in the form of sabotage, strikes and demonstrations but not least the general strikes and rebellions in 1943 and 1944 were strongly instrumental in acknowledging Denmark as a full member of the Western powers just as the resistance movement with support from the workplaces demanded civil, social and political reforms after the end of the War. In general, we may conclude that the leading role of the working class during the occupation secured workers and their organizations a central position in the regulation and management of the Danish society in the post-war years. These years brought welfare and affluence to many Danes but also prompted a true protest cycle, 1968–1985, that included the labor market and the social movement sector. It lasted for nearly 15 years with varying intensity, and besides increasing real wages and especially a lasting improvement in the bargaining position of public employees a substantial part of the working-class population moved into the middle class.

The apparent but time-limited success of SMU may not lead to the conclusion that social movement unionism represents an alternative to mass organizations. Social movement organizations relied heavily on the resources that trade unions, directly or indirectly, made available in the form of money, communication technologies, knowledge, political connections, strategies and staff, who often linked the different professions and workplaces to each other. In other words, the alternative forms of mobilization and organization acquired their main resources from, and partly owed their existence to the established mass organizations.

References

Literature

Alkil, N. (1945–1946) *Besættelsestidens fakta*, Vol. 2 (Copenhagen: Schultz Forlag).
Bentzon, K.-H. (1984) 'Offentligt ansatte i Danmark i et internationalt perspektiv', *Økonomi og Politik*, 58, 3.
Beretning (1940) (Copenhagen: Dansk Arbejdsgiverforening).
Christensen, C. B., Lund, J., Olesen, N. W. and Sørensen, J. (2009) *Danmark besat. Krig og hverdag 1940–45*, 3. ed. (Copenhagen: Informations Forlag).
Christensen, L. K., Kolstrup, S. and Hansen, A. E. (2007) *Arbejdernes historie i Danmark 1800–2000* (Copenhagen: SFAH).
Crouch, C. and Pizzorno, A. (eds.) (1978) *The Resurgence of Class Conflict in Western Europe since 1968*, Vol. 1–2 (New York: Holmes & Meier).
Dalgaard, N. (1995) *Ved demokratiets grænser. Demokratisering af arbejdslivet i Danmark 1919–1994* (Copenhagen: SFAH).
Jepsen, J. (1980) 'Policing Labour Conflicts', *Scandinavian Studies in Criminology*, 7, pp. 177–206.
Kirchhoff, H. (1979) *Augustoprøret 1943*, Vol. 1–2 (Copenhagen: Gyldendal).
Kirchhoff, H. (1996) 'Folkestrejken 1944' in Frandsen, K.-E. (ed.) *Kongens og folkets København – gennem 800 år* (Copenhagen: Forlaget Skippershoved).
Knudsen, K. (1999) *Arbejdskonflikternes historie i Danmark. Arbejdskampe og arbejderbevægelse 1870–1940* (Copenhagen: SFAH).
Logue, J. (1982) *Socialism and Abundance. Radical Socialism in the Welfare State* (Copenhagen: Akademisk Forlag)
Mikkelsen, F. (1992) *Arbejdskonflikter i Skandinavien 1848–1980* (Odense: Odense Universitetsforlag).
Mikkelsen, F. (1994) *Radikaliseringen af de offentligt ansatte i Danmark* (Copenhagen: SFAH).
Mikkelsen, F. (1998) 'Unions and New Shopfloor Strike Strategies and Learning Processes among Public Employees', *Economic and Industrial Democracy*, 19, pp. 505–38.
Mikkelsen, F. (1999) 'Contention and Social Movements in an International and Transnational Perspective: Denmark 1914–1995', *Journal of Historical Sociology*, 12, 2, pp. 128–57.
Mikkelsen, F. (2012) 'Class and Social Movements in Scandinavia Since 1945', *Moving the Social. Journal of Social History and the History of Social Movements*, 48, pp. 29–48.
Mikkelsen, F. (2018) 'Denmark 1946–2015: Popular Struggle in an Era of Democracy' in Mikkelsen, F., Kjeldstadli, K. and Nyzell, S. (eds.) *Popular*

Struggle and Democracy in Scandinavia, 1700–Present (London: Palgrave Macmillan).

Nielsen, H. J. (1977) *Besættelse og befrielse. Den danske arbejderklasses historie 1940–1946* (Aarhus: Modtryk).

Nielsen, H. H. and Rolighed, A. J. (1986) 'Strejker og fagopposition i 1970' erne' in Mikkelsen, F. (ed.) *Protest og oprør* (Aarhus: Modtryk), pp. 218–25.

Olsen, E. (1967) *Danmarks økonomiske historie siden 1750* (Copenhagen: Gads Forlag).

Scheuer, S. (1984) *Hvorfor stiger den faglige organisering? Om udviklingen i den faglige organisering i arbejdsløshedsperioden 1976–1982* (Copenhagen: Nyt fra Samfundsvidenskaberne).

Soskice, D. (1978) 'Strike Waves and Wage Explosions, 1968–1970: An Economic Interpretation' in Crouch, C. and Pizzorno, A. (eds.) *The Resurgence of Class Conflict in Western Europe Since 1968*, Vol. 2 (New York: Holmes & Meier), pp. 221–46.

Thing, M. (1987) *En analyse af Folkestrejken juni-juli 1944 med henblik på gadedemonstrationernes rolle og funktion* (unpublished master's thesis, Københavns Universitet).

Turner, L. (2007) 'An Urban Resurgence of Social Unionism' in Turner, L. and Cornfield, D. B. (eds.) *Labor in the New Urban Battle Grounds* (London: ILR Press).

Under Samvirkets Flag (1948) (Copenhagen: De samvirkende Fagforbund).

Visser, J. (1989) *European Trade Unions in Figures* (Deventer: Kluwer).

CHAPTER 8

Mass Labor Protest and Trade Union Activism in Early Post-War Copenhagen

Jesper Jørgensen

In the closing stages of the Second World War, a wave of labor unrest broke out all over the world, but most clearly in Europe, North America, and Australia/New Zealand.[1] The big industrial workplaces were often the centers of the revolts. In Denmark, the two general strikes, the August Uprising (*Augustoprøret*) of 1943 and the People's Strike (*Folkestrejken*) of 1944, were key flashpoints in this phenomenon, but the wave of labor protest did not end with the war. It continued until a political and

[1] An aggregate of labor unrest shows that the highest peaks in overall world labor unrest was in the ends and in the aftermaths of the two world wars (Silver, B. J. [2003] *Forces of Labor. Workers' Movements and Globalization Since 1870* [Cambridge: Cambridge University Press], pp. 125–27).

J. Jørgensen (✉)
The Workers Museum, Copenhagen, Denmark
e-mail: jjo@arbejdermuseet.dk

© The Author(s), under exclusive license to Springer Nature Switzerland AG 2023

J. Jørgensen and F. Mikkelsen (eds.), *Trade Union Activism in the Nordic Countries since 1900*, Palgrave Studies in the History of Social Movements, https://doi.org/10.1007/978-3-031-08987-9_8

economic power balance was firmly established with the beginning of the Cold War.[2]

The development was not unlike the one faced at the end of the First World War when across Europe there was a dramatic rise in the numbers of strikes and those taking part in them. Earlier it has led the American sociologist and historian, Charles Tilly, to theorize about a general societal tendency in the inter-relationship between industrial and political conflicts and between war and strikes:

> As a war draws to its close, both capitalist and organized workers often begin to press their suspended or repressed claims on the state. If the state has lost power – especially by starting to lose the war – its ability to meet those claims has declined just as it has become more vulnerable to claims; a war-shaken state often faces massive, politicized industrial conflict.[3]

Regarding Denmark, the last part of the war was in the same way marked initially by the declining military fortunes of the occupying power and an end to the Danish government's collaboration in August 1943, followed, after the liberation, by the formation of a war-shaken coalition government.

Concentrating on these developments, the analytical part of this chapter takes its inspiration from the theoretical approach of traditional sociology of social movements. In addition to Tilly's work are the path-breaking complimentary studies by American sociologists John D. McCarthy, Mayer N. Zald, and Doug McAdam where prominence is given to the forms of the protest actions taken (the repertoire of contention), organization and resource mobilization.[4] This paradigm saw

[2] Mikkelsen, F. (1992) *Arbejdskonflikter i Skandinavien 1848–1980* (Odense: Odense Universitetsforlag), p. 320. See also: Mikkelsen, F. (1997): 'Cycles of Struggle and Innovation in Industrial Relations in Denmark After World War II', *Scandinavian Journal of History*, 22, 1, pp. 31–51.

[3] Tilly, C. (1989) 'Introduction: The Effects of Short-Term Variation' in Haimson, L. H. and Tilly, C. *Strikes, Wars, and Revolutions in an International Perspective. Strike Waves in the Late Nineteenth and Early Twentieth Centuries* (Cambridge: Cambridge University Press), pp. 433–48, p. 444.

[4] McCarthy, J. D. and Zald, M. N. (1977) 'Resource Mobilization and Social Movements: A Partial Theory', *American Journal of Sociology*, 82, pp. 1212–41; McAdam, D. (1982) *Political Process and the Development of Black Insurgency, 1930–1970* (Chicago: University of Chicago Press); and Tilly, C. (1978) *From Mobilization to Revolution* (Reading: Addison-Wesly Publishing Company).

the aggregation of resources and the building of efficient organizations as key to the growth, success, and survival of political activism. Activism and protest do not simply occur where grievances are strongest, but where resources and organizational capacity can be mobilized to give voice to grievances. In other words, trade union activism grows when the right political opportunities emerge.[5]

The approach will be structured around an in-depth historical analysis of trade union activism in two of the most contentious and significant labor events in the period from the liberation in May 1945 to the consolidation of a political settlement in Denmark as part of the Western World with its accession to the European Recovery Program (the Marshall Plan) in 1948 and NATO membership in April 1949. Namely, the July 4 Demonstration of 1945 and the Typographical Conflict of 1947. Limiting the study to the immediate post-war years is in part inspired by the above-mentioned studies but is also influenced by the identification of this period as representing the second of three waves of social movement unionism in Denmark in the twentieth century (cf. Chapter 7).

The key actors of the two events were: (1) the joint union representatives (*fællestillidsmænd*) as heads of the combined union organizations (*fællesklubber*) at the biggest industrial and critical infrastructure workplace in Copenhagen, the shipyard and diesel engine manufacturer Burmeister & Wain (B&W), and (2) the trade unionists in the Communist-led Copenhagen branch of the Danish Typographical Union. The Communist trade union activists had key roles, but the picture was not a clear-cut. Social Democrats were involved as protesters and strikers too. A common cause was to regain benefits lost during the war.

The main primary source material used in this study has consequently been taken from an organizational middle level: B&W's combined union organizations and the Danish typographical union, Copenhagen branch. That is what McAdam, McCarthym and Zald have described as: "... the

[5] McAdam, D. (1996) 'Conceptual origins, current problems, future directions' in McAdam, D., McCarthy, J. D. and Zald, M. N. (eds.) *Comparative perspectives on social movements. Political opportunities, mobilizing structures, and cultural framings* (Cambridge: Cambridge University Press), pp. 23–40.

meso-level groups, organizations, and informal networks that comprise the collective building blocks of social movements and revolutions…”.[6]

The chapter will finally be rounded off with a critical discussion of the existing, mostly national grounded research on these events. This will be done partly by questioning the old but still prevailing assumption that sees popular grievances as decisive for the success of political protest as problematized by social movement theorists—partly by including recent transnational research in the discussion.[7]

The July 4 Demonstration

At noon on July 4, 1945, all work stopped at most of the large workplaces in Copenhagen. The workers assembled at a few central meeting points and marched in procession toward the parliament building in Copenhagen, Christiansborg. Included among the marchers were musical bands, choral groups, and the red banners of trade unions. An hour later, the first demonstrators arrived. There was no agreement on precisely how many were gathered. The Communist newspaper Land and People (*Land og Folk*) estimated the number as in the range of 100,000–125,000 while the paper of the Social Democratic Party *Social-Demokraten* was of the opinion there were only 20,000–30,000 contestants. From the government's side, the Social Democrat Hans Hedtoft-Hansen, Minister of Labor and Social Affairs, was designated to receive representatives from the demonstration. These were composed of a 10-member committee consisting of joint union representatives from the city's biggest workplaces with the Social Democrat Axel Jensen from B&W's iron foundry (*B&W Teglholmen*) in front. The delegation had with them a long list of demands for the improvement of wages and working conditions, including the implementation of a 40-hour working week with no reduction in wages, the repeal of the law against strikes from the time of the Occupation, the establishment of works committees, the abolition of the upper house

[6] McAdam, D., McCarthy, J. D. & Zald, M. N. (1996) 'Introduction: Opportunities, Mobilizing Structures, and Framing Processes—Toward a Synthetic, Comparative Perspective on Social Movements' in McAdam, McCarthy, and Zald, *Comparative perspectives*, pp. 1–20, p. 3.

[7] De Graaf, J. (2019) 'Strikes as Revolutionary History? Probing the Potential for a Revolution in Post-1945 Europe through Wildcat Strikes', *Archiv für Sozialgeschichte*, 59, pp. 229–51, pp. 229-31.

of the parliament (*Landstinget*), priority to be given to the provision of selected consumer goods, and the judicial action against collaborators, war profiters, and traitors. In response, the minister could not promise anything by, and pointed out that several of the demands raised fell under the aegis of the collective bargaining system of the labor market.

The almost non-existent results achieved gave rise to dissatisfaction among the crowd, spontaneous speeches were held, and the call for a general strike came from various sides. Individuals tried to break into the parliament. Axel Jensen and the Minister of Transport, the Communist Alfred Jensen, with limited effect called upon the discontented protestors to end the demonstration in peace and quiet, but this only eventually happened at about 5 p.m. A meeting of shop stewards was convened the same evening, where a resolution was adopted urging everyone to put their trust in the government and to resume work the next day. Finally, regret was expressed for "individual episodes" that took place at the end of the demonstration.[8]

The historical context of the protests was that of the war and German Occupation which had meant many deprivations for the working population. The summer of liberation was generally marked by unrest in the workplaces, and in the larger Copenhagen enterprises, there were many illegal stoppages. Discontent varied greatly but wages were in focus. During the war, working hours had been reduced through division of labor and Saturday closure without wage compensation at several of the capital's large industrial metal works. This led to a considerable fall in wages. In the months after the liberation, both sailors and brewery workers had achieved success with the same forms of protest, but the July 4 Demonstration failed in its formulated objectives. However, in his report, a half year after the events, Axel Jensen concluded that the demonstration had contributed to the decision to raise the cost-of-living supplement to wages in August.[9]

The mobilization of resources was mainly based on the organization of joint union representatives in the form of the network called the Association of Combined Union Organizations (*Fællesklubbernes Sammenslutning*). Here, Axel Jensen was the leading force as chief steward at one

[8] *Land of Folk* and *Social-Demokraten*, July 5, 1945.

[9] Arbejdermuseet & Arbejderbevægelsens Bibliotek og Arkiv (ABA), Fællesklubben, B&W Teglholmen, Archive no. 1347, Box 1: Minutes to "Ordinært Repræsentantskabsmøde", November 11, 1945.

of B&W's four workplaces in Copenhagen. The run-up to the organizing of the Copenhagen joint union representatives started from the beginning of the first half of 1943, when the war increasingly impinged on the workplaces. In January, the B&W machine factory in Christianshavn was bombed during a British air raid after which siren alarms and later also numerous telephoned bomb warnings began to pervade daily life, and conflicts arose as to who should pay for the numerous work stoppages and general decline in production. A wish therefore arose to be better informed about the situation in other workplaces and to coordinate common responses outside of the trade unions and the Danish Federation of Trade Unions (*De samvirkende Fagforbund*) which was felt not to be representing their interests under the Occupation. As representatives of the largest workplace in the country with around 4,000 workers, the joint union representatives of B&W felt they had a responsibility to take the lead.[10]

However, an inaugural meeting was canceled because of the general strikes and confrontations with Occupation forces in several urban centers throughout the country during the *Augustoprøret* which led to the resignation of the coalition government on August 29, 1943.

The first meeting of the joint union representatives in the iron industry was not held until March 3, 1944, when it was decided to establish a 5-man committee and a secretariat at B&W Teglholmen.[11] At the following meeting, a point was made of the fact that the network did not constitute a formal organization to placate fears that it could be seen as a challenge to the formal structure of the trade union movement. Therefore, no membership fee should be charged. Expenses arising from renting rooms, post, telephone, etc., should be shared among the combined union organizations as needs arose. There was, though, a procedure agreed upon that set down some rules for collaboration together with a resolution in

[10] ABA, 1347, Box 1: Minutes to "Udvidet Møde for samtlige Fællesklubber på Christianshavn", July 28, 1943. At the meeting, reference was made to a resolution they had previously adopted at a meeting in Tivoli. See also: Thomsen, P. (1973) *Øens folk. En beretning om Arbejdernes Fællesklub på Burmeister & Wains Skibsværft på Refshaleøen gennem 50 år* (Skærbæk: Forlaget Melbyhus), p. 46.

[11] ABA, 1347, Box 1: Minutes to "Møde for Fællestillidsmænd og Repræsentanter for de store Virksomheder indenfor Jernindustrien i København", March 3, 1944.

support of the demand of the national federation for an improvement of workers' pay and working conditions.[12]

It does not seem that the network played any significant role in the People's Strike that occurred at the end of June and at the beginning of July 1944. In due course, the exchange of information and co-ordination, or lack of, between the workplaces was criticized.[13] Only after the liberation on May 5 did the network launch joint, industrial protest activities that culminated in the July 4 Demonstration.

The first step was taken on May 17 when the combined union organization at Teglholmen held a meeting with the other B&W combined union organizations with the aim of passing a resolution demanding the enactment of a 40-hour week with no loss of pay. According to the resolution, it had the support from joint union representatives and shop stewards representing 25,000 workers in 32 enterprises in the iron industry primarily in the Copenhagen region but also in the shipyard town of Helsingør north of Copenhagen.[14]

The role of the Communists in the wider run-up to the demonstration on July 4 is worth looking at more closely, because they both played a key role in the August Revolt in 1943 and the People's Strike in 1944,[15] but also because in the literature on the industrial unrest in the months after liberation it is assumed that the Communists had "the

[12] ABA, 1347, Box 1: Minutes to "Møde for Fællestillidsmænd og Repræsentanter for de store Virksomheder i København", May 22, 1944.

[13] ABA, 1347, Box 1: Minutes to "Møde med Repræsentanter for Københavnske Virksomheder", August 24, 1944. The network did not have a formally adopted name. In August 1944 it was known as "The Ring". In 1945 it was called both "Fællesklubbernes Samvirke" and "Fællesklubbernes Sammenslutning". Sometimes with the addition of "in the iron industry".

[14] ABA, Arbejdernes Fællesklub, B&W Refshaleøen, Archive no. 1594, Box 1: Minutes to "Fællesudvalgsmøde for B&W", May 17, 1945; and ABA, 1347, Box 5: "Skrivelser til Fællesklubben Teglholmen fra fællestillidsmænd i jernindustrien", 1945. The number of workers represented was later raised to 32,000.

[15] Kirchhoff, H. (1979) *Augustoprøret 1943. Samarbejdspolitikkens fald. Forudsætninger og forløb. En studie i kollaboration og modstand*, Vol. 2 (Copenhagen: Gyldendal), p. 244; and Kjeldsen, M. (1993) *"Gå-tidlig-hjem"-strejkerne juni 1944. Om optakten til den københavnske folkestrejke. En studie i strejkebevægelsens struktur og organisering*, unpublished master's thesis, University of Copenhagen, p. 102.

greatest importance in the organization of shop stewards" in the summer of 1945.[16]

In January 1945, the Danish Communist Party's (*Danmarks Kommunistiske Parti*, DKP) clandestine trade union secretariat demanded full wage compensation for the reduced working hours in the coming negotiations in the state-run Work and Conciliation Council which with the Law on Working Conditions from 1940 had replaced the collective bargaining institution from before the war.[17] In their newspaper *Land og Folk,* the Communists threatened that the many illegal strikes of the summer of 1944 would quickly flare up again if major concessions were not forthcoming.[18] There was a direct call to the workplaces to take matters into their own hands if necessary:

> To this actual case it can also be added that the workplaces and trade unions will not this time be fobbed off with a pittance. It is most important that deputations and overtures from the workplaces to the employers and the conciliation board give renewed expression to this view.[19]

The newspaper highlighted that the demand was in alignment to the demands of B&W workers.

At the DKP's first public party meeting on June 19 after the liberation, the full focus was on the role of the Communist Party and the B&W workers under the Occupation:

> It was the workplaces that have saved the honor of Denmark. It was the People's Strike that crowned the work of the resistance and that was started at B&W with the "Go-home-early"-movement which culminated in the general strike. The Party was supportive from the very start.[20]

[16] Nielsen, H. J. (1977) *Besættelse og befrielse. Knudepunkter i den danske arbejderklasses historie* (Aarhus: Modtryk), p. 120; and Rostgård, M. (1980) 'Efterkrigsopgøret indenfor fagbevægelsen og socialdemokratiets økonomiske politik 1945–1950', *Historievidenskab*, 18–19, pp. 105–55, p. 110.

[17] ABA, Danmarks Kommunistiske Parti, Archive no. 921, Box 140: "Cirkulærer og løbesedler", 1941–1945.

[18] *Land og Folk*, February 1, 1945.

[19] *Land og Folk*, February 15, 1945.

[20] *Land og Folk*, June 20, 1945.

Undoubtedly, there was a great resonance between the politics of the Communists and the events in June and July 1945, but who exactly set off the spark that ignited the conflagration is more difficult to establish.

According to available primary sources, a central spark in action can be traced back to a poster put up June 25 on the wooden fencing surrounding the B&W's shipyard at the island Refshaleøen. The poster called on workers to go into action in protest that nothing had been done to dismiss collaborators, and the Law on Working Condition, etc., had still not been repealed. It seems obvious that things started at the shipyard. The shipyard was the largest of the four B&W workplaces, and its combined union organization was Communist-led, while the others were dominated by Social Democrats. On the face of it, the indications are that the first work stoppage at the shipyard on June 25 was spontaneous, but that the Communists was quick to follow up and support the action. The combined union organization at the shipyard was beforehand dissatisfied that the Association of Combined Union Organizations had not convened more meetings even though they had been strongly urged to do so. Now, there was the possibility of doing something. A strike of painters was already underway at the shipyard and there was a great deal of disgruntlement with a wage tariff among the shipyard workers. The organization therefore took the decision to initiate a demonstration to Christiansborg with the call on the government to place a "moral pressure" on the employers to meet the workers' demands.[21]

It cannot be unequivocally documented that the Communist Party stood behind the protest action on June 25, as it remains uncertain what role the DKP's industrial secretariat was. In this context, it is worth noting that the same is the case with the People's Strike in 1944, but here the historian Michael Kjeldsen assumes that the Communist faction at B&W met the DKP industrial secretary Svend Nielsen later the same day the first spontaneous work stoppages began at Refshaleøen. According to the recollections of one of the central participants, the industrial secretary chaired such meetings in a cafe in Amager under the Occupation, also during the People's Strike, and issued instructions to the Communists at B&W.[22] The same might be true a year later.

[21] ABA, 1594, Box 1: Minutes to "Udvalgsmøde", June 25, 1945, 10 a.m., and "Ekstra-ordinær Repræsentantskabsmøde", June 25, 1945, 11 a.m.

[22] Kjeldsen, *"Gå-tidligt-hjem"-strejkerne*, p. 27.

A short time after the demonstration commenced at Refshaleøen the combined union organization at Teglholmen joined in, even though Axel Jensen was not completely pleased with the uncontrolled course of events:

> There is, Ax. Jensen declared, something meaningless in the fact that a random man can put up a poster and thereby rile up a large workplace into taking this sort of action, but now it has happened. There is no time left for us to have a long discussion. We have to call the members to the canteen and hear their opinion.

The last B&W workplaces joined as well. At Christiansborg, they were received by the Prime Minister, Social Democrat Wilhelm Buhl, and several other members of the government, who promised to look into the problems, but for various reasons this could not come with any guarantees. In response, the representatives of the combined union organizations vowed that they would return if the demands of the workers were not met in the near future—and they would take all the Copenhagen workplaces with them.[23]

After this, the Association of Combined Union Organizations took over, and just three days later, Axel Jensen could inform his colleagues at Teglholmen that the secretariat of the association had resolved to call all the big workplaces to join a demonstration on July 4.[24] The Communist-led organization at the shipyard apparently did not play a leading role in the organization of the July 4 Demonstration.[25]

The Typographical Conflict of 1947

On May 14, 1947, a large protest meeting was convened for 6–7 p.m. by the Copenhagen branch of the Danish Typographical Union. The procession started off from the historic protest place the square *Grønttorvet* in the inner-city in the vicinity of the park *Fælledparken*, which since the 1880s has been another central meeting place for the labor movement. It was led by the Tramway Workers' Orchestra, with marchers carrying trade

[23] ABA, 1347, Box 1: Minutes to "Tillidsmandsmøde", June 25, 1945.

[24] ABA, 1347, Box 1: Minutes to "Forretningsudvalgsmøde", June 28, 1945.

[25] ABA, 1594, Box 1: Minutes to "Ekstra-ordinær Repræsentantskabsmøde", July 5, 1945.

union banners, and there was an open deck lorry where individuals were dressed to represent the enemies, the bourgeois newspapers with placards declaring "Break the No Policy". The meeting was opened with a musical prelude after which the branch treasurer welcomed those present and explained that the demonstration had been called to give an account of the typographers' hitherto ten week-long strike and to clear up any misunderstandings that had arisen. He then gave floor to the Norwegian Vålerengen Men's Chorus, who were on tour in Denmark and gave a rendition of the popular national song "There is a lovely country" ("*Der er et yndigt land*"). The audience answered by singing the Norwegian national anthem "Yes, we love this country ("*Ja, vi elsker dette landet*"). Each song had gained extra authority as important national symbols in their countries during their respective periods of occupation.

After yet another couple of songs from the Norwegian choir came the only speech of the day by the central figure and the public face of the strike, the chairman of Copenhagen typographers, the Communist Willy Bauer. In his speech, he made a great deal out of lamenting the campaign that had been waged against them from all sides, and he categorically denied that there was talk of a Communist-led strike and that the strike was a denial of the freedom of expression, because the bourgeois newspapers had been hit by stoppages. On the contrary, the strike was an expression of a legitimate fight for higher wages and better working conditions, not just for typographers, but in the long run for all Danish workers. Bauer, and as expressed by the resolution that was adopted by the assembly, found the backing given by the Copenhagen workers as an expression of solidarity and support for the continuation of the strike. The number of those taking part was hotly debated, but it was probably the largest trade union protest since the July 4 Demonstration of 1945. According to *Land og Folk*, the park keepers estimated that 100–150,000 participated, while the chairman of the event believed about 80–100,000 were gathered. *Social-Demokraten* referred to the resolution passed at the meeting which gave the number of participants as 80,000.[26]

The background to the great demonstration of solidarity was that the demands from the Occupation and the summer of 1945 on marked improvements in wages and working conditions had still not materialized.

[26] ABA, Dansk Typograf-Forbund, Archive no. 806, Box 348: "Scrapbog Typografkonflikten 1947 III" (*Land og Folk*, May 14 and 15, 1947, and *Social-Demokraten*, May 15, 1947).

Also, the unity discussions between the Social Democrats and DKP in late summer 1945 quickly stalled. The general election in October 1945 saw the coming to power of center-right government without the participation of workers' parties. The collective bargaining in 1946 despite both lawful and unlawful strikes only gave very modest rise in wages. Working hours remained virtually unchanged. The bad results further widened the split between Social Democrats and Communists, and it became more than ever obvious that they stood for two different strategies. In the leadership of the federation, the Social Democrats stood for a line that claimed that only if the unions, the local union branches, and the workshops stood together and in league with the Social Democrats, who were expected to enter government at some stage soon again, could any lasting results be achieved. Conversely, the Communists relied more upon their own power bastions concentrated in the metropolitan region, the large workplaces, and in particular unions. The thought behind this was that these forces should immediately take the lead and act as a lever and not wait for a coming Social Democratic government and the recovery of the national economy.[27]

Hardly surprisingly, both had in common that they were to be the leading force in collective bargaining but also in the labor movement and working class in general.

As well as in B&W, the Communists were also strong in the Copenhagen branch of the Danish Typographers' Union, which had seen a switch in power during the Occupation. From 1942, the Communist opposition had an increasing number of their members elected to leading positions culminating in the election of Willy Bauer as branch chairman at the end of 1944. At this point in time, he, together with many other typographers, was involved in the resistance movement's illegal printing works.[28] In the following years, the typographers in Copenhagen took to "the barricades" on several occasions. This included several days of illegal solidarity strikes in 1946 in support of slaughterhouse workers who got a rejected settlement proposal passed into law.[29]

[27] Rostgård, 'Efterkrigsopgøret', p. 124.

[28] Thomsen, P. (1991) *Typografen Willy Brauer: Det er resultaterne der tæller* (Copenhagen: Dansk Typograf-Forbund), pp. 17–19.

[29] Andersen, L. et al. (1969) *Danske typografers organisations historie*, Vol. 4 (Copenhagen: Dansk Typograf-Forbund), p. 18.

The conflict and the formal negotiations had their early origins in November 1946 when the Copenhagen Typographers' Wage Tariff Commission met. It was agreed that the situation was favorable in terms of getting results at the forthcoming collective bargaining negotiations, the first such free bargaining since the end of the war. The autumn's negotiations also included just 35,000 workers in the clothing industry and the Copenhagen typographic trade, so with any possible conflict there was no risk that the official conciliator would send a linked settlement proposal for ballot to several branches at one time. The chief claim was a general demand for a reduction of the daily work hours from 8 to 7 hours, i.e., from a 48-hour week to a 42-hour week. Individual members of the Commission, including the Social Democratic Union Chairman, K. A. Jørgensen, advised against making such a big demand, estimating it to be unrealistic.[30] After a lot of talks and 18 weeks strike the typographers returned to work again in July 1947 based on an expensively bought compromise. Working hours were reduced to 7 hours, but only when work started after 7 p.m. (i.e., it applied to those working on second and third shifts).[31]

Of interest here is the activities surrounding the formal negotiations. Therefore, it is noteworthy that the main player himself, Willy Brauer, many years later recalled that union activism had had a great significance for the way things unfolded:

> The conflict in 1947 became a new way of waging industrial disputes, building on getting the greatest possible number of members active through an on-going contact with them and their relatives personally and with gatherings of a social and informative nature.[32]

Already a few days into the dispute, the strikers and their families were invited to a film and entertainment event at the Saga Theatre. A new similar event was agreed with the theater for April starting with a report of the strike to date. The union branch also arranged for a choir concert, as well as the screening in May of an American sound film in the Workers'

[30] ABA, Dansk Typograf-Forbund, Københavns Afdeling, Archive no. 564, Box 27: Minutes to "Kommissionens 1. Møde", November 27, 1946.

[31] Thomsen, P. (1994) *Typografer i bevægelse. Fra Gutenberg til computeren* (Copenhagen: Den typografiske faggruppe i Grafisk Forbunds Kreds 1), p. 43.

[32] Thomsen, *Typografer i bevægelse*, p. 49.

Assembly Hall. In June, there was an invitation to several performances, among others a revue at Nørrebro Theatre, where Willy Brauer gave a welcome speech. The social initiatives were also apparently aimed at maintaining support from the typographers' married partners (wives), for as it was summed up: "The Entertainment Arrangements that had been held tied the Housewives to our Fight for just Wages and Working conditions in our Trade". Finally, typographers in the province were urged to take on a holiday child from the strike-affected families of the typographers in the capital city because the children needed sunshine and summer in the countryside and should not suffer unnecessarily during the strike.[33]

There was also an evident struggle over access to frame the conflict. This became apparent after the collective bargaining negotiations broke down and the strike was triggered on March 1 for approximately 4,000 members in 249 firms.[34] In the wake of this, a News Service under the leadership of the Union's Secretary had just been established with the task of regularly keeping the public informed of the course of the strike through the two workers' newspapers, *Land og Folk* and *Social-Demokraten*, which were not part of the Danish Employers' Association and were therefore excluded from the conflict, as was also the case with news agency *Ritzaus Bureau*. In addition, the Service was also tasked with counteracting incorrect information from the opposing parties in the conflict.[35]

However, this initiative did not go as everyone had expected. The opposition from the bourgeois press was especially fierce, even though they could not be published in their standard printed newspaper format. Those newspapers hit by the strike circulated leaflets, established news services via telephone, and newspapers like *Information* (independent) and *København* (affiliated to the liberal party *Venstre* in government) appeared in typewriter printed emergency format on a few pages, while the provincial newspapers, which were not encompassed by the strike, were undoubtedly read more than normal in the capital. Together they managed to create a massive campaign with the message that the "Communist strike" was an attack on the freedom of expression and that the

[33] ABA, 564, Box 11: Minutes to "Styrelsesmøde", March 6 and 26, and April 22, 1947; and *Typograf-Tidende* June 6 and 27, and July 18, 1947.

[34] ABA, Personal file of Willy Brauer (*personlæg*), notes on the 1947 Conflict, undated.

[35] ABA, 806, Box 346: "Scrapbog Typograf-konflikten 1947 I" (*Land og Folk*, March 3, 1947).

conflict was much too costly for both those directly involved but also for society as a whole. From early on, the typographers' News Service was constantly criticized by Brauer and his allies for being too passive. At the end of the conflict, they concluded that the Service had failed and that: "the conscious sabotage of the News Service by the *Social-Democrat* had been a contributory factor to the impending defeat".[36] What that sabotage amounted to was not further specified.

More clandestine methods were in fact used in the conflict, but it is unlikely that the leaders of Copenhagen typographers' branch, who formed the so-called Strike Committee, had anything to do with it. It is more likely that the perpetrators came from more radicalized elements of the conflict. It did not amount to much, but it surely aggravated the feelings of opponents of typographers. According to the emergency edition of *København* and a provincial newspaper, on March 11 one of *Information's* vehicles had had its tires punctured in four places with horse spikes preventing the distribution of its special strike newspaper. At the same time, accusations were made of a smear campaign by the workers' newspapers against those firms that produced the emergency newspapers as well as rumors that chemigraphers who had been responsible for printing them had been promised compensation if they refused the work. Later in the same month it was reported that the vehicles used to distribute *København* had also been sabotaged, that threatening letters had been sent to "the office ladies" who typed up the journalists' articles, and that there had been a break-in where the emergency newspapers were printed with the aim of sabotaging its rotary press.[37]

In response to the accusations, Willy Brauer denied that the threats and sabotage had come from "the responsible side", i.e., from the typographers' trade union representatives.[38] Those, on the other hand, who openly argued for such actions, were a tiny group, the Revolutionary

[36] ABA, 564, Box 11: Minutes to "Fællesmøde mellem Forretningsudvalg og Styrelse", June 9, 1947; and ABA, 806, Box 7: Minutes to "Forbundsstyrelsesmøde", June 28, 1947.

[37] ABA, 806, Box 346: "Scrapbog Typograf-konflikten 1947 I" (*København* og *Roskilde Dagblad*, March 11, 1947); and ABA, 806, Box 347: "Scrapbog Typograf-konflikten 1947 II" (*Thisted Amtstidende* og *Roskilde Dagblad*, March 14, 1947, and *Social-Demokraten*, March 17, 1947 (*Dansk Typograf-Forbunds Pressetjeneste*)).

[38] ABA, 806, Box 347: "Scrapbog Typograf-konflikten 1947 II" (*Information*, March 15, 1947).

Communists. In their own paper, the New Workers' Paper (*Det nye Arbejderblad*), they called for the halt of paper deliveries to the emergency papers and to their distribution. Possibly, there was a greater responsiveness to such radical proposed actions than normal. Many years later, one of the Trotskyist activists recalled that he sold 400 copies of their paper at one of the big venues of the typographers.[39]

To be able to carry out the strike, the Danish Typographers' Union was dependent on funding, especially when it came to providing economic support for those on strike. In his notes on the conflict, Willy Brauer jotted down a balance sheet for the 18 weeks which revealed that the result was a deficit of 1.5 million Danish crowns.[40] In other words, they ran out of money.

The decision to start the collection of voluntary contributions was taken at the second extraordinary general meeting held during the conflict on April 13 and received the backing of the annual meeting of the Workers' Joint Organization in Copenhagen on April 14. Collection lists were then printed with the heading "To all Copenhagen Workers!" and sent out to the Copenhagen workplaces. The approach taken was to mobilize broadly in the same way as in the summer of 1945. Thus, Willy Brauer visited B&W Refshaleøen where he received both moral support and economic support, and there was a proposal to convene a joint shop stewards meeting, but the old network of combined union organizations was not reactivated for the Typographical Strike.[41] In the last part of the conflict, an application was made for a loan of a million kroner from the Workers' National Bank (*Arbejdernes Landsbank*). However, it was turned down because the federation either could not or would not co-sign for the loan.[42]

[39] ABA, 806, Box 347: "Scrapbog Typograf-konflikten 1947 II" (*Information*, April 29, 1947); and *Klassekampen*, 126, 1979.

[40] ABA, Personal file of Willy Brauer (*personlæg*), notes on the 1947 Conflict, undated.

[41] However, the combined union organizations of B&W were still very active. On May 22, 1947, they took the lead of a government petition for basic supply, the so-called Potato Demonstration with participation of somewhere between "many thousands" (*Social-Demokraten*, May 23, 1947) and "almost 100.000" workers (*Land og Folk*, May 23, 1947).

[42] ABA, 564, Box 27: Minutes to "Kommissionens 10. Møde", June 24, 1947; ABA, Landsorganisationen i Danmark, Archive no. 1500, Box 1200: "Udtalelse fra Fællesklubben paa B&W Refshaleøen", June 6, 1947; and ABA, 564, Box 11: Minutes to

The role of the Communist Party in the conflict is difficult to document, but it is known that the Party's industrial secretariat had close contact with Communist union representatives in the various workplaces,[43] and moreover that Copenhagen members were directed to participate in the demonstration and mass meeting on May 14. In an internal communication, the Industrial Secretary, Hartvig Sørensen, also called for: "The deployment of the entire force of the Party to ensure the typographers‘ strike is won".[44] Of great importance was most likely also the secretary's relationship with the industrial editor of *Land og Folk*, David Hejgaard. In Hejgaard's memoirs, he emphasizes his dependence, as an inexperienced journalist, on the collaboration with Hartvig Sørensen as well as the fact that he was a member of the Party's Industrial Committee which was composed of leading trade unionists and shop stewards. Hejgaard also recounts that during the Typographers' Conflict he was given great help by Hartvig Sørensen and Willy Brauer. As regards the latter, Hejgaard had an agreement: "... that I should ring him every day at the typographers‘ office when I arrived at the newspaper to agree with him what I should write". Should an interview be required then they met at Brauer's office where he "... precisely and briefly dictated to me what I should write".[45]

Concluding Discussion

Until now the historical treatment by academics of the post-war labor protest has had the grievances of the working class as a causal explanation. According to the historian Hans Jørn Nielsen, who republished his book *Besættelse og befrielse* (Occupation and Liberation) from 1977 in 2020, the "summer of 1945" was a situation characterized by "the demands of the masses" and "a movement of progress in the workplaces", but that is was smothered by the DKP. The Party was committed to gaining political

"Fællesmøde mellem Forretningsudvalg og Styrelse", June 9, 1947. See also: ABA, 1500, Box 811: "Forretningsudvalgets stilling til Typografkonflikten", 1947.

[43] Schmidt, R. (2009) *PET's overvågning af arbejdsmarkedet 1945–1989. PET-kommissionens beretning, Vol. 8* (Copenhagen: PET-kommissionen), pp. 24–25.

[44] ABA, 921, Box 73: "Centralkomitemøde, May 17, 1947"; and Box 215: "Fagligt sekretariat".

[45] Hejgaard, D. (1981) *I det lange løb, Vol. 3: En kommunists erindringer fra maj 1945 til 1959* (Copenhagen: Forlaget Tiden), pp. 58–59, 68, 72.

influence through the National Unity Government and a United Front with the Social Democrats.[46]

This interpretation has been summed up by the historian Marianne Rostgård as an extreme position where it presupposes that there was a revolutionary situation. Conversely, the opposite view was one that saw the post-war unrest as a parenthesis, the repercussions of the abnormal wartime circumstances, and ripples on the surface caused by the intoxication of the liberation. She places herself in an intermediate position, one that sees the diffuse wants of the working class fusing into a number of demands for radical reform, but that this radicalization was not utilized through an "active working class policy of collaboration", because the Social Democrats and the Communist Party each pursued different strategies and worked against one another. She sees the defeat of the DKP in the Typographers' Conflict as crucial for the Social Democrats emerging best out of the post-war unrest and getting popular backing for a Left-Keynesian policy of reconstruction. However, if an "active working class policy of collaboration" had been pursued, the post-war period would have looked different and, it is implied, had been better.[47] In other words, the dissatisfaction of the working people constituted a potential for social change—an opportunity that was messed up and averted by the Communists and Social Democrats, respectively.

As a kind of "correction" to these Marxist-inspired class analyzes, Niels Jul Nielsen has found it more helpful to utilize an ethnological life-mode analysis, which points to how a specific life-mode can maintain its own continued existence. According to Nielsen, this implies the following: "If wage workers have the necessary requirements for their own reproduction (and continued existence) met – i.e. to have influence over the conditions in which they sell their time – then they will not put an end to the capitalist system (either through revolution or reform)". This perspective thus suggests another dynamic and explanation for why the Communists

[46] Nielsen, *Besættelse og befrielse, p.* 123. A similar conclusion can be found in Larsen, S. B. (1977) *Kommunisterne og arbejderklassen. En politisk biografi* (Copenhagen: Tiderne skifter), pp. 36–37; and Ege, L. and Hansen, N. H. (1978) *DKP 1945–46. For grundlov – og arbejdsro* (Copenhagen: Forlaget Oktober), pp. 35–48.

[47] Rostgård, 'Efterkrigsopgøret', pp. 105–06, 151–52. See also: Larsen, *Kommunisterne*, pp. 57–58.

in the end lost support. Wage workers were fundamentally interested in preserving the capitalist system.[48]

Again, however, it is the satisfaction or dissatisfaction of the masses that determinates the course of events and implicitly the preconditions for collective bargaining and trade union activism. It is not the intention here to reject these approaches or suggest that they do not contribute to an understanding of the protest processes, but rather to draw attention to supplementary perspectives that help us better understand the trade union activism of our time.

This chapter has picked up the thread from the work of Flemming Mikkelsen who—on the assumption that there will always be a varying degree of discontent or dissatisfaction in a population—is of the opinion that greater explanatory insight will come from looking at trade union organizing and the structural changes of the time. He refers to the tendency during the time of the Occupation and the first post-war years to transfer the settlement of industrial disputes to the workplaces and push the trade unions and their competent bodies into the background. For the trade union movement, this was advantageous during the Occupation, when with respect to the occupying power and the consequences of any confrontation, it was best not to take open responsibility for any industrial actions or protests. This meant that there was a rise in industrial conflicts once the power began to wane of first the Occupation administration and then the Unity Government due to the vicissitudes of war. However, the situation changed again with the reestablishment in 1947 of the collective bargaining system from the pre-war years.[49]

The two big manifestations of labor unrest in the early post-war time in Copenhagen were thus clearly two very different kinds of conflict that reflected the development in the structures of opportunity as outlined above. The first was an illegal strike directed at the government, while the second was a legal strike against the employers within the framework of the reconstituted collective bargaining system.

Whereas Flemming Mikkelsen has concerned himself with long waves of history, so the aim here has been to zoom in and give a richer description of a particular run of events. The focus has been on what forms of

[48] Nielsen, N. J. (2004) *Mellem storpolitik og værkstedsgulv. Den danske arbejder – før, under og efter Den kolde krig* (Copenhagen: Museum Tusculannums Forlag), pp. 24, 362–63.

[49] Mikkelsen, *Arbejdskonflikter*, p. 320.

action were in play and how they were organized, including the ability of the acting parties to mobilize resources. Here, it was not a case of the workers' parties contra the masses dominating proceedings but rather the contesting collective actors (the social movement organizations) without, however, arguing that the frame of mind in the broader population had no significance for the union activism. On the contrary, this perspective is linked to the question of framing—a process where the various actors consciously try to mediate common understandings of the world and themselves to legitimate and motivate collective actions.[50]

In this chapter, there has been a focus on the questions of organization and resources. In relation to the July 4 Demonstration, it is evident when looking deeper into the events that the Association of Combined Union Organizations played a very central role. Union representatives at the big Copenhagen ironworks, especially B&W, drew on their experiences from the war and other trades' recently petitions that had been successful in pushing through and achieving improvements. Not least they were able to mobilize quickly by virtue of their formalized network, even if the actions undertaken were not necessarily carefully planned beforehand. Even though the July 4 Demonstration did not achieve any concrete results, it undoubtedly helped to set a political agenda arguably contributing to long-term improvements. In 1947, the Typographical Conflict was a picture of the aforementioned "normalization" of the labor market with the built-in advantages and disadvantages it had. Among other things, it gave the possibility of drawing on considerable resources, both directly from members paying their union dues and from the federation, even if granted with certain reluctance. Additionally, the typographers union in Copenhagen was successful in initiating a series of social and political activities that doubtlessly helped maintain momentum in the protests. The fight for access to frame the conflict was clearly also crucial for those involved.

As previously mentioned, the role of the Communist Party is difficult to document. This is an obstacle for coming even closer to the heart of the matter. Even though the Party did not perform a completely dominant leading role in either the July 4 Demonstration in 1945 or the Typographers' Conflict in 1947, it was nevertheless a central actor in the trade union activism of the period. The industrial conflicts were covered

[50] McAdam, McCarthy and Zald, 'Introduction', pp. 5–6.

closely by the Party newspaper. They were framed in a Communist optic, with continuous encouragement of further struggles aimed against the Social Democratic trade union leadership and the employers. The Party's industrial secretariat had close contact with the Communist shop stewards in the workplaces, not least with those at B&W Refshaleøen, the country's largest workplace, where they had played a leading part in industrial unrest during the Occupation. It must also be assumed that Willy Brauer coordinated his efforts with the party in accordance with the Communist organizational principle of democratic centralism. Based on currently available sources, it is impossible to fully determine the significance of the work of the industrial secretariat, so it is best not exaggerate its role. The study also indicates that the period with a war-shaken or weakened state opened the possibility for a degree of practical co-operation between Social Democrat and Communist shop stewards in the trade unions and workplaces, despite having different ideological intentions with their trade union activism.

Despite the Communists' dominant role in the labor protests, the alleged revolutionary situation in the post-war years is difficult to detect. As Jan De Graff has shown on a European level, there were no clear calls for revolution from the shop floor workers. Even though the shop stewards were quite successful in organizing and mobilizing and in some cases indeed had revolutionary aspirations, the protests were less a show of strength than a gesture of suffering. According to De Graff, a pan-European characteristic was that there were profound divisions along lines of gender, generation, background, and skills within the post-war working class. Something the wildcat strikes only deepened and therefore in the eyes of the labor leaders had to be stopped as quickly as possible.[51]

As shown in this chapter, surely elements of desperation for getting better working and living condition, and internal labor movement divides were important to understand these labor market conflicts but with the amendment that without organization and mobilization at the meso-level there would not have been mass labor strikes in post-war Copenhagen. Neither "demands of the masses" nor pure desperation makes a significant strike.

Translated by Stephen R. Parsons

[51] For a historiographical account on European early post-war strike history, see: De Graaf, 'Strikes as Revolutionary History?', pp. 233, 250–51.

References

Archives

The Workers Museum & The Labour Movement's Library and Archive (*Arbejdermuseet & Arbejderbevægelsens Bibliotek og Arkiv, ABA*):
Arbejdernes Fællesklub, B&W Refshaleøen, Archive no. 1594.
Danmarks Kommunistiske Parti, Archive no. 921.
Dansk Typograf-Forbund, Archive no. 806.
Dansk Typograf-Forbund, Københavns Afdeling, Archive no. 564.
Fællesklubben, B&W Teglholmen, Archive no. 1347.
Landsorganisationen i Danmark, Archive no. 1500.
Personal file of Willy Brauer (*personlæg*).

Serials

Land og Folk
Social-Demokraten
Typograf-Tidende

Literature

Andersen, L. et al. (1969) *Danske typografers organisations historie*, Vol. 4 (Copenhagen: Dansk Typograf-Forbund).

De Graaf, J. (2019) 'Strikes as Revolutionary History? Probing the Potential for a Revolution in Post-1945 Europe through Wildcat Strikes', *Archiv für Sozialgeschichte*, 59, pp. 229–51.

Ege, L. and Hansen, N. H. (1978) *DKP 1945–46. For grundlov – og arbejdsro* (Copenhagen: Forlaget Oktober).

Hejgaard, D. (1981) *I det lange løb, Vol. 3: En kommunists erindringer fra maj 1945 til 1959* (Copenhagen: Forlaget Tiden).

Kirchhoff, H. (1979) *Augustoprøret 1943. Samarbejdspolitikkens fald. Forudsætninger og forløb. En studie i kollaboration og modstand*, Vol. 2 (Copenhagen: Gyldendal).

Kjeldsen, M. (1993) *"Gå-tidlig-hjem"-strejkerne juni 1944. Om optakten til den københavnske folkestrejke. En studie i strejkebevægelsens struktur og organisering*, unpublished master's thesis, University of Copenhagen.

Larsen, S. B. (1977) *Kommunisterne og arbejderklassen. En politisk biografi* (Copenhagen: Tiderne skifter).

McAdam, D. (1982) *Political Process and the Development of Black Insurgency, 1930–1970* (Chicago: University of Chicago Press).

McAdam, D. (1996) 'Conceptual Origins, Current Problems, Future Directions' in McAdam, D., McCarthy, J. D. and Zald, M. N. (eds.) *Comparative Perspectives on Social Movements. Political Opportunities, Mobilizing Structures, and Cultural Framings* (Cambridge: Cambridge University Press), pp. 23–40.

McAdam, D., McCarthy, J. D. & Zald, M. N. (1996) 'Introduction: Opportunities, Mobilizing Structures, and Framing Processes—Toward a Synthetic, Comparative Perspective on Social Movements' in McAdam, D., McCarthy, J. D. and Zald, M. N. (eds.) *Comparative Perspectives on Social Movements. Political Opportunities, Mobilizing Structures, and Cultural Framings* (Cambridge: Cambridge University Press), pp. 1–20.

McCarthy, J. D. and Zald, M. N. (1977) 'Resource Mobilization and Social Movements: A Partial Theory', *American Journal of Sociology*, 82, pp. 1212–41.

Mikkelsen, F. (1992) *Arbejdskonflikter i Skandinavien 1848–1980* (Odense: Odense Universitetsforlag).

Mikkelsen, F. (1997): 'Cycles of Struggle and Innovation in Industrial Relations in Denmark After World War II', *Scandinavian Journal of History*, 22, 1, pp. 31–51.

Nielsen, H. J. (1977) *Besættelse og befrielse. Knudepunkter i den danske arbejderklasses historie* (Aarhus: Modtryk).

Nielsen, N. J. (2004) *Mellem storpolitik og værkstedsgulv. Den danske arbejder – før, under og efter Den kolde krig* (Copenhagen: Museum Tusculannums Forlag).

Rostgård, M. (1980) 'Efterkrigsopgøret indenfor fagbevægelsen og socialdemokratiets økonomiske politik 1945–1950', *Historievidenskab*, 18–19, pp. 105–55.

Schmidt, R. (2009) *PET's overvågning af arbejdsmarkedet 1945–1989. PET-kommissionens beretning, Vol. 8* (Copenhagen: PET-kommissionen).

Silver, B. J. (2003) *Forces of Labor. Workers' Movements and Globalization Since 1870* (Cambridge: Cambridge University Press).

Tilly, C. (1978) *From Mobilization to Revolution* (Reading: Addison-Wesly Publishing Company).

Tilly, C. (1989) 'Introduction: The Effects of Short-Term Variation' in Haimson, L. H. and Tilly, C. *Strikes, Wars, and Revolutions in an International Perspective. Strikes Waves in the Late Nineteenth and Early Twentieth Centuries* (Cambridge: Cambridge University Press), pp. 433–48.

Thomsen, P. (1973) *Øens folk. En beretning om Arbejdernes Fælleskiub på Burmeister & Wains Skibsværft på Refshaleøen gennem 50 år* (Skærbæk: Forlaget Melbyhus).

Thomsen, P. (1991) *Typografen Willy Brauer: Det er resultaterne der tæller* (Copenhagen: Dansk Typograf-Forbund).

Thomsen, P. (1994) *Typografer i bevægelse. Fra Gutenberg til computeren* (Copenhagen: Den typografiske faggruppe i Grafisk Forbunds Kreds 1).

CHAPTER 9

Reluctant Vanguard? Finnish Building Workers' Unions and Strikes, 1949–1973

Tapio Bergholm

The discussion about outsider, especially Communist, involvement in strike movements is an old and ongoing debate. Researchers have looked at correlation between the strength of communism and how strike-prone trade unions are. Richard Hyman opposes ideas of outside influence on the making of strikes, and Paul Edwards has argued that industrial conflict is not party politically motivated but connected to structural features of production relations in different industries and sectors.[1]

In Finland, there was a tradition among the Finnish Security Intelligence Service and its predecessors to believe that Communists were always planning strikes. From the 1920s, the Security Police reported quite often that Communists had plans to organize gradually growing

[1] Hyman, R. (1977) *Strikes* (London: Fontana/Collins); and Hamark, J. (2014) *Ports, Dock Workers and Labour Market Conflicts* (Gothenburg: University of Gothenburg), pp. 143–52, 155–57.

T. Bergholm (✉)
University of Eastern Finland, Joensuu, Finland
e-mail: tapio.bergholm@uef.fi

© The Author(s), under exclusive license to Springer Nature Switzerland AG 2023

J. Jørgensen and F. Mikkelsen (eds.), *Trade Union Activism in the Nordic Countries since 1900*, Palgrave Studies in the History of Social Movements, https://doi.org/10.1007/978-3-031-08987-9_9

strike movements, which, according to somereports, should grow to revolutionary general strike or to general strike to enhance Communist political ambitions.[2]

It is easy to find open criticism of Communist trade union activists and trade union leaders when it comes to collective agreements or incomes policy arrangements. In these public statements, Communists argue that Social Democratic leaders are afraid to take advantage of the strength of the unions, and they often accused the Social Democratic leadership of restraining the activities of rank and file. This persistent and tough charges rise the question: Were Communist trade union leaders prone to resort to industrial action when they had the power.[3]

Klaus Schönhoven and Pauli Kettunen argue that there are inherent mechanisms in the trade unions to safeguard the future of the organization apparatus. Therefore, trade unions avoid revolutionary action or other excessive risks. Compromises and collective agreements were meant to ensure stability for organizations and members. Strikes and other forms of industrial conflict were used very economically and as a last resort. According to Kettunen, this applied to Finnish unions led by left-wing socialists and Communists between the World Wars.[4]

Compared to other Nordic Countries, the Finnish Communist movement was strong. After the Civil War in 1918, the Finnish labor movement gradually split into a reformist wing (the Social Democrats) and revolutionary wing (Communists and left-wing socialists). During the period from the 1950s to 1970s, the Social Democrats gained about 22–24% support in general elections and Communist around 20%. Until the

[2] The National Archives of Finland (*Kansallisarkisto*), Finnish Security Intelligence Service's archive (*Suojelupoliisin arkisto*), Report "Lakkoliikkeiden painopiste valtiojohtoisissa laitoksissa", March 19, 1973; Hakalehto, I. (1966) *Suomen kommunistinen puolue ja sen vaikutus poliittiseen ja ammatilliseen työväenliikkeeseen 1918–1928* (Helsinki: WSOY); and Kettunen, P. (1986) *Poliittinen liike ja sosiaalinen kollektiivisuus. Tutkimus sosialidemokratiasta ja ammattiyhdistysliikkeestä Suomessa 1918–1930* (Jyväskylä: SHS).

[3] Bergholm, T. (2005) *Sopimusyhteiskunnan synty I. Työehtosopimusten läpimurrosta yleislakkoon. Suomen Ammattiyhdistysten Keskusliitto 1944–1956* (Keuruu: Otava); Bergholm, T. (2007) *Sopimusyhteiskunnan synty II. Hajaannuksesta tulopolitiikkaan. Suomen Ammattiyhdistysten Keskusliitto 1956–1969* (Keuruu: Otava); and Bergholm, T. (2012) *Kohti tasa-arvoa. Tulopolitiikan aika I, Suomen Ammattiliittojen Keskusjärjestö 1969–1977* (Keuruu: Otava).

[4] Kettunen, *Poliittinen liike*; and Schönhoven, K. (1980) *Expansion und Konzentration. Studien zur Entwicklung der Freien Gewerkschaften im Wilhelminischen Deutschland 1890–1914* (Stuttgart: Verlag Klett-Cotta).

1980s, Communists had also a strong position in the Finnish trade union movement, even though the Social Democrats had the upper hand.[5]

Although there has been a comparatively high propensity of industrial conflict in Finland, I challenge the straightforward link between Communism and strike activity. In Finland, many groups and occupations with very low support or no support at all for Communism organized strikes.[6]

The Finnish Communist Party (*Suomen Kommunistinen Puolue*, SKP) was a founding member of the Finnish People's Democratic League in October 1944. The League was the official political front of Finnish Communism. It complicated negotiations when decisions were made in the League as well in the SKP. This was not the case in the trade union movement where SKP took care of unions. Therefore, I have excellent sources that inform about the connections between unions and SKP. The description and analysis in this chapter are based on sources from the political committee and trade union section of the SKP, and my earlier research.

I look at strikes not from a statistical or societal angle but from the perspective of the Communists within the strike-prone Finnish building sector. How the leaders of the Finnish Construction Workers' Union (*Rakennustyöläisten Liitto*)—the strongest Communist-led trade union in Finland—and the Finnish Bricklayers' Union (*Suomen Muurarien Liitto*), also led by Communists, did prepare, analyze, and organize strikes in the 1950s, 1960s, and 1970s. Could SKP influence the decisions of these unions? Were the Communist leaders of building workers' unions eager, cautious, or even reluctant to muster their organizations as vanguard

[5] Bergholm, T. (2016) *A History of the SAK* (Helsinki: SAK).

[6] Bergholm, T. (1988) *Kovaa peliä kuljetusalalla I. Kuljetusalan ammattiyhdistystoiminta vuoteen 1924* (Helsinki: Auto- ja kuljetusalan Työntekijäliitto); Bergholm T. (1997) *Ammattiliiton nousu ja tuho. Kuljetusalan ammattiyhdistystoiminta ja työmarkkinasuhteiden murros 1944–1949* (Helsinki: Suomen Historiallinen Seura and Työministeriö); Bergholm, T. (1998). 'Uho, vastuuntunto ja hapuilu—SKP, palkkaliikkeet ja lakot 1944–1947' in Saarela, T., Krekola, J., Parikka, R. and Suoranta, A. (eds.) *Aave vai haave* (Saarijärvi: Työväen historian ja perinteen tutkimuksen seura), pp. 203–36; Bergholm. T. (1997) *Kovaa peliä kuljetusalalla II. Kuljetusalan ammattiyhdistystoiminta vuosina 1925–1960* (Turenki: Auto- ja kuljetusalan Työntekijäliitto); Bergholm, *Sopimusyhteiskunnan synty I*; Bergholm T. and Jonker-Hoffrén P. (2012)'Farewell to the communist strike hypothesis?—The diversity of striking in Finland between 1971–1990' in Simões do Paço, A., Varela, R. and van der Velden, S. (eds.) *Strikes and Social Conflicts. Towards a global history* (Lisbon: International Association Strikes and Social Conflict); and Bergholm, T. (2020) *Kiihkeä Koivisto. Nuoruus, sota, onni 1923–1959* (Keuruu: Otava).

of strike mobilization to achieve wage demands made by the Finnish Communist Party?

Bitter Experience

After World War II, Communists gained legal rights to operate. Communists, left-wing socialists, and some Social Democratic dissidents founded the Finnish People's Democratic League (*Suomen Kansan Demokraattinen Liitto*) in 1944. Social Democrats had been part of government since 1937. They have supported war efforts against the Soviet Union during the Winter War 1939–1940 and the Continuation War 1941–1944.[7] After armistice in 1944, the Social Democratic Party was in a difficult and defensive position, and the Finnish People's Democratic League in the offensive.[8]

As the Cold War gradually heated in 1947–1949, Finnish Communists became marginalized in parliamentary politics after the general election in 1948, and in the Confederation of Finnish Trade Unions (*Suomen Ammattiyhdistysten Keskusliitto*, SAK) . From 1969 this organisation got new name The Central Organisation of Finnish Trade Unions (*Suomen Ammattiliittojen Keskusjärjestö*, SAK). The Communists decided to challenge the Social Democratic minority government and the Social Democratic leadership of SAK.

SKP started to plan strike action in the spring of 1949. Reluctance of unions and their members was obvious, when economic conditions were deteriorating, and unemployment was rising. Seven unions led by Communists withstood the persistent pressure from the party leadership and organized strikes in August and September 1949. Some avoided getting involved by organizing membership vote that turned out to be against strike mobilization. However, the Construction Workers' Union and the Bricklayers' Union took part in strike action which ended in defeat. Participation led to expulsion from SAK and then re-entry into SAK with humiliating terms. This was a bitter experience for Communist union leaders.[9]

[7] Soviet and Russian historiography has different names for these wars.

[8] Rentola, K. (1994) *Kenen joukoissa seisot? Suomalainen kommunismi ja sota 1937–1945* (Juva: WSOY), pp. 473–538.

[9] Bergholm, *Ammattiliiton nousu ja tuho*, pp. 236–40, 313–75; and Bergholm, *Sopimusyhteiskunnan synty I*, pp. 186–255.

Most plumbers who belonged to the Metal Workers' Union (*Metallityöväen Liitto*), joined the building site strikes in 1949. The Metal Workers' Union expelled local trade unions, which supported strike actions. The leadership of SKP advised plumbers to return to the Metal Workers' Union and was against the constitution of an alternative trade union. However, the Communist plumbers did not care much about democratic centralism and created a new independent union in 1950,[10] which tried to get collective agreement from Metal Workers' Union into their own hands. The plumbers' union pursued this aim with a long, bitter, and unsuccessful strike in February-October 1951. Solidarity from the Construction Workers' Union and the Bricklayers' Union did not prevent the ultimate defeat of the plumbers, when SAK, the Metal Workers' Union, and the employers were against their demands. This was a bitter lesson to SKP and other building workers unions.[11]

The tension inside the Communist movement between the high hopes of eruptions of discontent among workers and the worker's voluntary strike actions, and, on the other hand, the gray passivity of rank and file, and the fear of defeat of Communist trade union leaders was omnipresent also in the Finnish trade union movement. The Construction Workers' Union was on guard after this defeat. It feared disintegration organized by breakaway unions with Social Democratic leadership in the early 1950s.[12] Despite growing unemployment and poor economic conditions, the SKP tried to persuade local trade unions to demand higher wages in 1952. The campaign failed, and the trade union secretary of SKP, Paavo Koskinen, was extremely disappointed with the meager collective agreements,

[10] People's Archives (*Kansan Arkisto*, KA), Minutes to "Suomen Kommunistisen Puolueen sihteeristö", September 10, 1949; KA, SKP järjestöjaosto C11, Minutes to "Piirisihteerien neuvottelukokous", March 13, 1950; KA, SKP ay-jaosto Cb5, Minutes to "Putkimiesten ja työvaliokunnan jäsenten yhteisestä kokouksesta", May 27, 1950, and Minutes to "SKP ammatillisen jaoston työvaliokunta (tvk)" June 12 and 15, 1950; KA, Minutes to"SKP poliittinen jaosto", May 31, 1950; and Minutes to "SKP puoluetoimikunta", June 7, 1950; and Bergholm, *Ammattiliiton nousu ja tuho*, pp. 307–08.

[11] Bergholm, *Ammattiliiton nousu ja tuho*, pp. 308–309.

[12] KA, SKP ay-jaosto Ca2, Minutes to "KK:n [Central Committee of SKP] ammatillinen osasto", February 4, 1952.

because he claimed that there was growing wage discontent among most workers.[13]

In the autumn of 1952 and the winter of 1952–1953, the executive of the SKP trade union section discussed and planned wage actions, although members of the executive were aware that fighting spirit was missing at workplaces and building sites. During the discussions, Paavo Koskinen reminded that strikes do not start by command, and that the Construction Workers' Unions were cautious and unwilling to strike. Besides, negotiations dragged on because the employers did not offer any improvements. And due to pressure from SKP the building workers' unions postponed the signing of agreements until the autumn 1953. In the end the employers got what they wanted.[14]

In January 1954, the trade union section of SKP came to the conclusion that the building workers should not fight alone for the party's very inflated wage demands.[15] The building workers' approach was first of all pragmatic not combative as they postponed the closing of collective agreements, because employers preferred to negotiate new collective agreements without termination.[16] Negotiations were long and difficult, because unions pushed for a shorter working day. However, after some local strikes and a one-day national strike both parties accepted an agreement, which meant a 45-h week for 1 ½ months longer period each year. The Social Democratic leaders of SAK set strict limits to wage demands made by the affiliated unions. Therefore, results of collective bargaining in the building industry were far from satisfactory from the perspective of SKP.[17]

In April 1955, the political committee of SKP discussed targets of the next collective agreements for the Construction Workers' Union, which

[13] KA, SKP ay-jaosto Cb6, Minutes to "KK:n ammatillinen osasto tvk", February 14, 15, 20 and March 8, 1952".

[14] Ibid., September 22, October 31 and December 10, 1952, and January 8 and 16, February 17, April 25 and July 8, 1953; and Helin, J. (1998) *Rakentajien liitto. Rakennusalan työläisten järjestötoiminta Suomessa 1880-luvulta vuoteen 1995* (Jyväskylä: Rakennusliitto ry), pp. 193–194.

[15] KA, SKP ay-jaosto Cb6, Minutes to "KK:n ammatillinen osasto tvk", January 15, 1954.

[16] Ibid., February 25, 1954.

[17] Ibid., June 3, 12, 29, 30 and July 6 and 10, 1954; and Helin, *Rakentajien liitto*, p. 194.

issued a strike warning together with the Bricklayers' Union. Strike preparations and involvement of SAK led to limited success. However, the Communist were not willing to risk expulsion from SAK again and made collective agreement without industrial action.[18]

In summary, after 1949, the two Communist-controlled building workers' unions were very reluctant to spearhead wage and other demands made by SKP due to previous strike defeats and humiliation. These unions behaved cautiously. The Communist leaders of these unions were unwilling to risk union recourses in brave defeats. High wage demands on behalf of SKP, and modest achievements of the Communist-led building workers unions created tensions. The rank-and-file members received support from the Communist Party to their criticism of the meager achievements they obtained in connection with the negotiations.

Reluctant Vanguard of the Working Class

After the Second World War, there was a long period with a wage control system. The legal base for this arrangement was renewed annually but in 1955, there was no longer a majority in the Finnish parliament to prolong the regulations. Prices rose and SAK demanded wage compensation. The employers refused because a hard winter was closing harbors and restricted trade, which caused a general strike that started on March 1, 1956. A general strike was the Communists' fulfillment of the dreams of class unity, even though the Social Democrats of SAK kept national leadership of strike action in their firm grip.[19]

After a successful strike, price inflation increased, and wage gains were lost in a few months. The Communist demanded determined action from SAK to obtain full wage compensation. Still, the Communist trade union leaders saw no possibilities of successful industrial action before next year. The political committee of SKP was cautious and decided that if a common front could not be established consisting of the Construction Workers' Union, the Bricklayers' Union, the Food Workers' Union, and some other unions, there were no possibilities for isolated industrial

[18] KA, Minutes to "SKP poliittinen toimikunta", April 6, 1955, Appendix (*Liite*) 20/LJ/EA-AM/4.4.1955 P.M.: "Rakennusalan työehtosopimuskamppailu"; and Helin, *Rakentajien liitto*, p. 194.

[19] Bergholm, *Sopimusyhteiskunnan synty I*, pp. 473–91.

actions without support from SAK and its unions with Social Democratic leadership.[20]

Some Communist trade union leaders argued in favor of a new general strike, but the majority thought that it was an unrealistic way to solve wage negotiations. During a meeting with the SKP trade union section in March 1957, chairperson Aarne Saarinen made it crystal clear that the Communist building workers should not be thrown into a labor struggle as the first. Chairperson of the Bricklayers' Union, Urho Kilpinen, made the same point. He said that they (i.e., Communists) should not throw the building unions into battle as the first because the construction sector was economically weakened. In time of high unemployment, the Communist leaders of the Construction Workers' Union and the Bricklayers Union tried to avoid open conflict. However, to please the Communist party and some dissatisfied members, the unions organized a one-day demonstration strike on Saturday May 11, 1957, to put pressure on the employers who answered with a two-day lockout. After the strike and lockout, the trade union section of SKP decided that unions no longer should organize strikes alone and that the Communist should speak out against compromises in the forthcoming rounds of negotiation. The tactic did not work very well. Collective agreements in building trades followed the line agreed with the metal industry.[21]

This decision was criticized and met with opposition. Due to a new wage fixing system, earnings of concrete reinforcement workers fell by 20%, which led to a sharp critique of the union leaders. Thus, in November 1957, the executive committee of the trade union section of SKP evaluated that the authority of the trade union movement among workers had declined. This was also the case in the Construction Workers' Union.[22]

[20] KA, SKP ay-jaosto Ca2, Minutes to "KK:n ammatillinen jaosto", November 24 and 29, 1956; KA, SKP ay-jaosto Cb6, Minutes to "SKP KK:n ammatillinen osasto tvk", November 27 and 28, 1956; and KA, Minutes to "SKP poliittinen toimikunta", November 29, 1956".

[21] KA, SKP ay-jaosto Cb6, Minutes to "KK:n ammatillinen osasto tvk", March 2, May 2 and July 24, 1957; KA, SKP ay-jaosto Ca2, Minutes to "KK:n ammatillinen jaosto", May 14, 1957"; KA, Minutes to "SKP poliittinen toimikunta", August 2, 1957; and Helin, *Rakentajien liitto*, pp. 241–42.

[22] KA, SKP ay-jaosto Cb6, Minutes to "KK:n ammatillinen osasto tvk", November 13, 1957; KA, Minutes to "SKP poliittinen toimikunta", August 2, 1957 and April 12, 1958; and Helin, *Rakentajien liitto*, p. 242.

In March 1958, the executive of the trade union section of SKP accepted ambitious negotiation demands on employers in the building industry. The agency also accepted the bricklayers' and construction workers' action plan in May 1958, and the building workers voted twice with substantial majority in favor of industrial action. The first ballot was open for workers outside unions and the second was members only.

A strong mandate from the workers to strike did not end industrial peace in the building trades. However, the situation was not straightforward. Chairperson of the Construction Workers Union, Aarne Saarinen, told the political committee of SKP that there was no great enthusiasm among workers to go on strike. He also made it clear that with meager strike funds major struggles were impossible. New collective agreement was achieved in the beginning of August after long drawn negotiations. Results were far from the determined demands put forward in the first place.[23]

Strategically Targeted Strikes Instead of Political Education of Workers by Mass Strike Experience

In November 1958, the executive trade union section of SKP agreed that unions dominated by Communist should not rush negotiations with the employers' organizations. The delay should guarantee that the unions did not solve difficult situation with collective mobilization alone. Half a year later, Aarne Saarinen reported to the political committee of SKP that negotiations were difficult in the building industry. The Construction Workers' Union and the Bricklayers' Union planned united, limited, and targeted strike actions. The caution of Communist leaders was obvious. The chairperson of the Bricklayers' Union, Urho Kilpeläinen, commented, at a later executive meeting of SKP's trade union section, that employers could enlarge planned industrial conflict by declaring lockout. This time pressure for action came from the rank and file. Therefore, the aim of the unions was to restore traditional wage gap compared to the wages in the metal industry.[24]

[23] KA, SKP ay-jaosto Cb6, Minutes to "KK:n ammatillinen osasto tvk", March 8, May 5 and June 9, 1958; KA, Minutes to "SKP poliittinen toimikunta" July 6, 1958; and Helin, *Rakentajien liitto*, p. 242.

[24] KA, SKP ay-jaosto Cb6, Minutes to "KK:n ammatillinen osasto tvk", November 5, 1958, and April 4 and June 23, 1959; and KA, Minutes to "SKP poliittinen toimikunta",

After a general ballot of organized and unorganized construction workers strikes started in three big cities and in the surrounding areas. The employers had political considerations and industrial relation motivations not to budge to trade union demands and to avoid strikes. They could not give Communists more than other workers. The strike plan was good and economically not too heavy for the unions, because most of their members could work and pay extra strike fees to unions involved in strike action.

One quarter of the strike costs of the Construction Workers' Union came from the Communist-dominated organization, i.e., the international World Federation of Trade Unions. Employers' organizations and unions settled collective agreements after little over a month of conflict. Employers were unable to use the lockout weapon due to lack of solidarity and discipline among their ranks. Another reason was the absence of proper conflict funds to compensate losses for companies involved in lockouts. Workers achieved substantial gains, and the chairperson, Aarne Saarinen, praised limited and targeted strike action as an effective weapon to achieve goals without too heavy costs for unions and burdens for workers.[25]

In 1963, the partial strike strategy was again successfully employed in the metropolitan area of Helsinki and remote building sites in Seitakorva (Lapland). This time the strike was during winter, and it lasted longer. On the other hand, benefits obtained were better, even though the gap to the metal workers' wage level did not diminish.[26]

From a political perspective, it is interesting, how little the Finnish Communist Party (SKP) and the strongest trade unions with Communist leadership matched with stereotype ideas and general perceptions about Communists and strikes. The Construction Workers' Union and the Bricklayers' Union were very pragmatic in their industrial action. Both in 1959 and 1963, strikes were limited, targeted, effective, and

April 10, 1959, Appendix (*Liite*): "Rakennustyöläisten työehtosopimuskysymys", April 7, 1959.

[25] KA, SKP ay-jaosto Cb6, Minutes to "KK:n ammatillinen osasto tvk", June 23 and 30, 1959; KA, Minutes to "SKP poliittinen toimikunta", May 21 and 27, June 2, 11 and 22, and July 9, 1959; Helin, *Rakentajien liitto*, pp. 242–46; and Mattila, M. (1992) *Työriitojen sovittelun historia* (Helsinki: Työministeriö), p. 317.

[26] Mattila, *Työriitojen sovittelun historia*, pp. 317–18; and Helin, *Rakentajien liitto*, pp. 267–70.

cheap. Their aim was to limit not to enlarge these strikes. Strike results were more important than educational strike experiences. It is, therefore, obvious that raising class consciousness with as many participants as possible was not the aim of the unions or the SKP.

Incomes Policy, the Construction Workers' Union, and the Hard-core Minority of SKP

Strength of trade unions are their membership. Collective agreements were the strongest means to recruit members and keep them in the union. The history of trade unions is often the history of demarcation conflicts and the rights to make collective agreements covering sectors, industries, occupations, or workplaces.

In Finland, the Construction Workers' Union and the Metal Workers' Union had many demarcation disputes about organizational boundaries and about rights to make collective agreements in the 1950s and 1960s. The Construction Workers' Union pressed for its own collective agreement in elevator installment works, even though collective agreement of elevator technicians in building sites belonged traditionally and according to the decisions of SAK to the Metal Workers' Union. Strike ensued. It was long, bitter, and unsuccessful. It started in May and lasted until October 1964.

In July, the leadership of SKP and its trade union section assessed that prospect of success were good. In September, the mood had changed. The analysis of the Communist leadership was more realistic. Danger of a totally lost struggle was imminent but the political committee of SKP decided against supporting strikes of other building workers. They thought that larger strikes could make things even worse. Damage control was on the agenda not enlargement of conflict for the purpose of political education of workers. After the lost battle strikers were—with good reasons—bitter.[27]

[27] The Labour Archives (*Työväen Arkisto*), Minutes to "Suomen Ammattiyhdistysten Keskusliiton työvaliokunta", April 20, May 14 and August 25, 1964; KA, Minutes to "SKP poliittinen toimikunta", July 16, and September 2 and 17, 1964; KA, SKP ay-jaosto Cb7, Minutes to "KK ay-jaoston tvk", August 18 and 31, and September 7 and 10, 1964; Helin, *Rakentajien liitto*, pp. 271–72; and Bergholm, *Sopimusyhteiskunnan synty II*, pp. 248–49.

Trade union representatives and leaders of the Construction Workers' Union were central figures in the unification process of the Finnish trade union movement in 1965–1969. They also took part in the overthrow of the dogmatic conservative leadership of SKP and supported reformers of the Communist party. Chairman of the Construction Workers' Union, Aarne Saarinen, was elected chairman of the Communist Party at the SKP Congress in January 1966. A manifestation of the central position of the Communist construction workers in the making of a more reformist and parliamentarian Communist Party in Finland.

Conservatives (Stalinists) formed a minority faction, and gradually the party split became institutionalized while the Stalinist minority faction grew more confident and united after the Warsaw Pact invasion of Czechoslovakia in 1968. However, decades of institutionalized factionalism inside Finnish Communism dwindled, when the Communist Party of Soviet Union made it clear to the majority and minority factions that a new breakaway party or expulsion of dissidents were not the way to solve problems in the SKP.[28]

In the General parliamentary election in March 1966, the Social Democratic Party (SDP) won many new seats, and the Left-wing parties obtained a majority in Parliament. SDP, the Centre Party of Finland (*Suomen Keskusta*), the Finnish People's Democratic League and the Workers' and Peasant's Social Democratic League (*Työväen ja Pienviljelijäin Sosialidemokraattinen Liitto*) (a breakaway party from SDP 1959) formed government, and the Communists entered the government for the first time since 1948. Nearly the same combination formed a new government after presidential elections in 1968, and the revisionist-wing of the SKP supported this co-operation.[29]

The Finnish currency (the markka) was devaluated dramatically in the fall of 1967. Wages, pensions, bank savings, and loans were secured quite strongly by index clauses. However, indexation clauses threatened to unleash rapid inflation or even inflation spiral after the big devaluation. In this situation, the indexation of bank loans caused uncertainty and problems in the building industry. Risk of unpredictable rise of interest rates

[28] Paastela, J. (1991) *The Finnish Communist Party in the Finnish Political System 1963–1982* (Tampere: University of Tampere), pp. 79–90; and Leppänen, V.-P. (1999) *Kivääri vai äänestyslippu? Suomen kommunistisen puolueen hajaannus 1964–1970* (Helsinki: Edita); and Bergholm, *Sopimusyhteiskunnan synty II*, pp. 249–367.

[29] Leppänen, *Kivääri vai äänestyslippu?*

postponed openings of new building sites. That was the main reason, why the SKP, the Communist leaders of Construction Workers' Union and leading members of the Communist group in SAK supported incomes policy agreement in the spring of 1968. The agreement dismantled indexation of wages, bank savings, and loans. However, a minority faction did not share the interpretation of the situation and criticized heavily the incomes policy agreement and the Communist leaders who supported it.[30]

The minority faction was quite aggressive in the Construction Workers' Union. A three-year agreement concluded in 1966, and participation in the making of incomes policy agreements in 1968 and 1969, were serious mistakes from the perspective of the dogmatic minority faction of SKP. Fiercely disloyal Communists were a rarity and came as a surprise for the Communist majority in the Construction Workers' Union. Members of this faction attacked union leadership with the same vocabulary of accusations they previously leveled against the Social Democratic leaders of SAK. Charges of betrayal, of class collaboration and surrender to Social Democrat leadership of SAK, were thrown against Communist trade union leaders. Already in May 1966, Paavo Koskinen, trade union secretary of SKP, blamed building worker activists belonging to the minority faction of SKP for abandoning democratic centralism. This accusation of rejection of core organizational principles of communism and apostasy showed how severe contradictions were among Communists.[31]

In Finnish historiography, there is a strong perception that the Ambassador of Soviet Union, Aleksei Beljakov, tried to agitate for large revolutionary strike action in the autumn of 1970 and winter 1970–1971. In this framework, major industrial conflicts in the metal and building industry were caused by Soviet involvement in Finnish industrial relations. Another interpretation of the metal workers' strike is political power struggle between Social Democrats and Communists in the trade union

[30] Bergholm, *Sopimusyhteiskunnan synty II*, pp. 401–23.

[31] KA, SKP ay-jaosto Cb7, Minutes to "Pöytäkirja SKP:n KK:n ammatillisen jaoston työvaliokunnan ja Rakennustyöläisten liiton puoluejaoston yhteisestä kokouksesta", May 3, 1966; Helin, *Rakentajien liitto*, pp. 303–08; and Bergholm, *Sopimusyhteiskunnan synty II*, pp. 413–23.

movement. Here interpretation is less dramatic, but more accurate and realistic.[32]

Communists had proposed targeted and partial strike action when the Social Democrats pushed through in Metal Workers' Union a decision of an all-out strike. The Construction Workers' Union avoided such costly and inefficient strikes because the Communist had majority in all official bodies. Not even this time, the idea of a revolutionary general strike was on the agenda in the Construction Workers' Union. Already in December 1970, the political committee of SKP decided in favor of a limited partial strike. The strike started on March 10 and the employers' partial lockout six day later. Parties reached an agreement on April 5, 1971. Both sides claimed victory, but the employers were more disappointed than workers about the outcome.[33]

In 1971–1972, the Bricklayers' Union merged with the Construction Workers' Union. The fusion was part of a larger restructuring of the Finnish trade union movement from 1969 to 1978. Without severe political pressure and tough guidance from SAK, the unification would not have happened. Craft pride of skilled bricklayers was the main problem in this partially and temporarily painful process. Also, the minority faction of SKP opposed the fusion.[34]

After heavy conflict in 1971, strike funds of the Construction Workers' Union were empty. Still, the union rejected centralized agreements negotiated between SAK and the employers' central organizations in 1972. With short local warning strikes, the union accelerated negotiations without any cost to union funds. The Construction Workers' Union had planned to put plumbers in the front line against employers. According to the plan, other branches could get the same terms in their collective agreements as the plumbers. However, this plan did not work very well because the employers retorted to more aggressive and larger lockout threats. The threat worked and the union avoided a bigger conflict, while the vanguard

[32] Suomi, J. (1996) *Taistelu puolueettomuudesta. Urho Kekkonen 1968–1972* (Keuruu: Otava), pp. 409–523; Ketola, E. (2007) *Suomen Metallityöväen Liitto 1960–1983*, (Keuruu: Otava), pp. 236–328; and Korkeaoja, J. (2009) *Punainen metalli. Kommunistit ja kansandemokraatit Suomen Metallityöväen Liitossa 1899–1983* (Keuruu: Metallin vasemmisto), pp. 176–200.

[33] KA, Minutes to "SKP poliittinen toimikunta", December 30, 1970, and January 20, 1971; and Bergholm, *Kohti tasa-arvoa*, pp. 231–33.

[34] Ibid., pp. 61–64.

of plumbers obtained so few concessions in their collective agreement that they were truly dissatisfied.[35]

In April 1973, the Labor Court ruled in favor of the Construction Workers' Union. Employers tried to introduce changes into collective agreement that would overrule the favorable interpretation of collective agreement made by the court. This made negotiations difficult, and the Construction Workers' Union used punctual and partial strikes to make employers more compromise prone. Short walkouts of painters, bricklayers, carpenters, and others—often one group after another—created chaos on building sites, whereas the employers' organizations in the building industry formed a united lockout-front against the partial strike strategy.

The lockout started on 23 May and ended on June 17, 1973, and this time employers were on the offensive and the union on the defensive. In the end of the day, the employers dropped their demands for substantial changes in the agreement. The compromise felt like a victory for the union leadership but hostile and belligerent criticism from a minority faction made the victory very bitter indeed. The Communist caucus of the Construction Workers' Union and members of the Communist Party had lots of dirty laundry to wash after the conflict. Members of the majority faction of SKP felt that both Social Democrats and members of the minority faction of SKP had sabotaged negotiations with their disloyal behavior.[36]

The Construction Workers' Union was brave and active when health and safety of its members were at stake. Boycott of poisonous paints started in 1972. This boycott and later boycotts of other toxic materials were successful, even though employers and their organizations protested strongly. The activism had no party-political connotations. It

[35] KA, Minutes to "SKP poliittinen toimikunta", April 28, and May 3, 9 and 17, 1972; Helin, *Rakentajien liitto*, pp. 347–48; and Bergholm, *Kohti tasa-arvoa*, pp. 260–63.

[36] KA, Minutes to "SKP poliittinen toimikunta", May 23 and 30, June 13, and October 17 and 31, 1973, Appendix (*Liite*) 1/20.10.73: "Helsingin ja Uudenmaan Rakennusalan kommunistit Kommunistinen Puolue ry Poliittiselle toimikunnalle", November 2, 1973; KA, SKP:n Ay-jaosto, He43, *Rakennusliitto*, "Rakennusalan puoluekomitea SKP:n poliittiselle toimikunnalle", Devember 19, 1973; KA, SKP:n Ay-jaosto, He44, *Rakennusliitto*, "Rakennusalan työehtosopimuskamppailu v. 1973", August 10, 1973"; Helin, *Rakentajien liitto*, pp. 348–49; and Bergholm, *Kohti tasa-arvoa*, pp. 309–11.

was common cause among building workers in the 1970s. Even all kinds of Communists stood united in these actions.[37]

In the early 1970s, industrial conflicts reached new peaks in Finland (see Chapter 12). This was not only due to the Communists' revolutionary zeal or stubbornness, or ideas of revolutionary education via strike participation. Even in the 1970s, collective bargaining goals and strike strategy of the Finnish Construction Workers' Union show how pragmatic and parsimonious Communists could be, when they had power and the responsibility of a trade union. It is also obvious, that resistance and the willingness of Finnish employers to take joint actions was stronger, when their negotiation partner was a Communist-dominated trade union. The defeat of the Communist strike movement in 1949, the downfall of the plumbers' strike in 1950, and later experiences showed that there were good reasons for the Construction Workers' Union to be cautious and alert: Communist trade union leadership had to avoid class struggle romanticism.[38]

Conclusions

This chapter analyzes the interaction between two trade unions with Communist leadership and the Finnish Communist Party. We get a rather mixed picture. The Construction Workers' Union and the Bricklayers' Union did reluctantly participate in the strike wave of 1949. After that they are much more cautious. The Construction Workers' Union was willing and able to resort to strike action, but the leadership was pragmatic, calculating and used when possible partial strike tactics in the 1950s, 1960s, and 1970s. These tactics of targeted strikes put minimum burden to members and finances of the union. The analysis of Pauli Kettunen of the Finnish trade union movement between the World Wars applies quite well even after World War II. Communist leadership internalized the responsibility to safeguard resources, to create stability, and to secure the future of their trade union.

[37] Helin, *Rakentajien liitto*, pp. 350–51; and Bergholm, *Kohti tasa-arvoa*, pp. 157–59.

[38] For example, the united front of employer organisations defeated the strike of the Rubber and Leather Workers' Union (*Kumi- ja Nahkatyöväen Liitto*) in 1977, because the leadership of the union was in the hands of minority faction of the SKP (Bergholm, *Kohti tasa-arvoa*, pp. 500–01).

References

Archives

The National Archives of Finland (*Kansallisarkisto*): Finnish Security Intelligence Service's archive (*Suojelupoliisin arkisto*).

People's Archives (*Kansan Arkisto*, KA): The Finnish Communist Party (*Suomen Kommunistisen Puolueen*, SKP).

The Labour Archives (*Työväen Arkisto*): The Central Organisation of Finnish Trade Unions (*Suomen Ammattiliittojen Keskusjärjestö*, SAK).

Literature

Bergholm, T. (1988) *Kovaa peliä kuljetusalalla I. Kuljetusalan ammattiyhdistystoiminta vuoteen 1924* (Helsinki: Auto- ja kuljetusalan Työntekijäliitto AKT).

Bergholm T. (1997) *Ammattiliiton nousu ja tuho. Kuljetusalan ammattiyhdistystoiminta ja työmarkkinasuhteiden murros 1944–1949* (Helsinki: Suomen Historiallinen Seura and Työministeriö).

Bergholm. T. (1997) *Kovaa peliä kuljetusalalla II. Kuljetusalan ammattiyhdistystoiminta vuosina 1925–1960* (Turenki: Auto- ja kuljetusalan Työntekijäliitto).

Bergholm, T. (1998) 'Uho, vastuuntunto ja hapuilu—SKP, palkkaliikkeet ja lakot 1944–1947' in Saarela, T., Krekola, J., Parikka, R. and Suoranta, A. (eds.) *Aave vai haave* (Saarijärvi: Työväen historian ja perinteen tutkimuksen seura), pp. 203–36.

Bergholm, T. (2005) *Sopimusyhteiskunnan synty I. Työehtosopimusten läpimurrosta yleislakkoon. Suomen Ammattiyhdistysten Keskusliitto 1944-1956* (Keuruu: Otava).

Bergholm, T. (2007) *Sopimusyhteiskunnan synty II. Hajaannuksesta tulopolitiikkaan. Suomen Ammattiyhdistysten Keskusliitto 1956-1969* (Keuruu: Otava).

Bergholm, T. (2012) *Kohti tasa-arvoa. Tulopolitiikan aika I, Suomen Ammattiliittojen Keskusjärjestö 1969-1977* (Keuruu: Otava).

Bergholm, T. (2016) *A History of the SAK* (Helsinki: SAK).

Bergholm, T. (2020) *Kiihkeä Koivisto. Nuoruus, sota, onni 1923-1959* (Keuruu: Otava).

Bergholm, T. and Jonker-Hoffrén, P. (2012) 'Farewell to the communist strike hypothesis?—The diversity of striking in Finland between 1971–1990' in van der Velden, S., Varela, R. and Simões do Paço, A. (eds.) *Strikes and Social Conflict. Towards a Global History* (Lisbon: International Association Strikes and Social Conflict), pp. 401–13.

Hakalehto, I. (1966) *Suomen kommunistinen puolue ja sen vaikutus poliittiseen ja ammatilliseen työväenliikkeeseen 1918-1928* (Helsinki: WSOY).

Hamark, J. (2014) *Ports, dock workers and labour market conflicts* (Gothenburg: University of Gothenburg).

Helin, J. (1998) *Rakentajien liitto. Rakennusalan työläisten järjestötoiminta Suomessa 1880-luvulta vuoteen 1995* (Jyväskylä: Rakennusliitto ry).

Hyman R. (1977) *Strikes* (London: Fontana/Collins).

Ketola, E. (2007) *Suomen Metallityöväen Liitto 1960-1983* (Keuruu: Otava).

Kettunen, P. (1986) *Poliittinen liike ja sosiaalinen kollektiivisuus. Tutkimus sosialidemokratiasta ja ammattiyhdistysliikkeestä Suomessa 1918-1930* (Jyväskylä: SHS).

Korkeaoja, J. (2009) *Punainen metalli. Kommunistit ja kansandemokraatit Suomen Metallityöväen Liitossa 1899-1983* (Keuruu: Metallin vasemmisto).

Leppänen, V.-P. (1999) *Kivääri vai äänestyslippu? Suomen kommunistisen puolueen hajaannus 1964-1970* (Helsinki: Edita).

Mattila, M. (1992) *Työriitojen sovittelun historia* (Helsinki: Työministeriö).

Paastela, J. (1991) *The Finnish Communist Party in the Finnish Political System 1963-1982* (Tampere: University of Tampere).

Rentola, K. (1994) *Kenen joukoissa seisot? Suomalainen kommunismi ja sota 1937-1945* (Juva: WSOY).

Schönhoven, K. (1980) *Expansion und Konzentration. Studien zur Entwicklung der Freien Gewerkschaften im Wilhelminischen Deutschland 1890-1914* (Stuttgart: Verlag Klett-Cotta).

Suomi, J. (1996) *Taistelu puolueettomuudesta. Urho Kekkonen 1968-1972* (Keuruu: Otava).

CHAPTER 10

The Peak Strike Period in Finland, 1970–1980: Wildcat Strikes and Income Politics

Tapio Bergholm

In 1978, Colin Crouch and Allessandro Pizzorno edited a two-volume research project *The Resurgence of Class Conflict in Western Europe since 1968*. Volume I include articles about measurement of industrial conflicts and national studies. The second volume contains comparative studies of different aspect of the strike wave in Western Europe.[1]

What is astonishing from a Finnish point of view, is that the 'resurgence' in many countries was so short and miniscule compared to local

[1] Crouch, C. and Pizzorno, A. (eds.) (1978) *The Resurgence of Class Conflict in Western Europe Since 1968. Vol. 1: National Studies* (New York: Holmes & Meier Publishers); and Crouch, C. and Pizzorno, A. (1978) *The Resurgence of Class Conflict in Western Europe Since 1968. Vol. 2: Comparative Analyses* (New York: Holmes & Meier Publisher).

T. Bergholm (✉)
University of Eastern Finland, Joensuu, Finland
e-mail: tapio.bergholm@uef.fi

© The Author(s), under exclusive license to Springer Nature Switzerland AG 2023

J. Jørgensen and F. Mikkelsen (eds.), *Trade Union Activism in the Nordic Countries since 1900*, Palgrave Studies in the History of Social Movements, https://doi.org/10.1007/978-3-031-08987-9_10

Table 10.1 Differences between Finnish practice and OECD-model concerning strike calculations in 1976

	Finnish practice	*OECD-model*
Number of industrial conflicts	3,282	717
Number of involved	513,000	289,000
Working days lost	1,326,000	1,220,000

Source Työtaistelut 1976 (1977) (Helsinki: Tilastokeskus), p. 3

and large-scale national industrial conflicts in Finland in the years 1970–1980. According to Crouch's calculations, Finland was second after Italy during the years 1970–1975, measured by the number of lost working days per thousand workers.[2] Steen Scheuer put Finland in fourth place after Spain, Italy, and the UK by calculating average working days lost per 1000 employees, 1970–1979.[3]

Statistics Finland which produces the official strike statistics based on information from both employers and trade unions, and from the news media (in which they report the length, participant per day, total number of workdays lost, cause and outcome of conflict). Before 1971, only strikes, mass resignations, lockouts, mass dismissals, and boycotts, when workers immediately left their workplace, were included in the statistics. After 1971, the scope of recorded industrial disputes was enlarged quite considerably. The officials started to count smaller strikes, lockouts, boycotts, refusals to work overtime, go-slow, and other forms of collective action used by workers and employers.

The OECD has proposed that only industrial conflict with a minimum of ten participants and at least hundred working days lost should be included in the statistics. The OECD-model has changed the inventories of the number of strikes and the number of participants but only to a limited extent the number of working days lost (see Table 10.1).[4]

[2] Crouch, C. (1996) *Industrial Relations and State Traditions* (Oxford: Clarendon Press), p. 255.

[3] Scheuer, S. (2006) 'A Novel Calculus? Institutional Change, Globalization and Industrial Conflict in Europe, *European Journal of Industrial Relations*, 12, 2, pp. 143–64, p. 152.

[4] Työtaistelut 1975 (1976) (Helsinki: Tilastokeskus), pp. 1, 3.

This chapter is based on the official strike statistics, the history of employers' organizations, and the history of trade unions as well as industrial relations studies. The reason for starting the analysis in 1970 is that the European strike wave came late to Finland, and it did not manifest itself until the early 1970s. Industrial conflicts in Finland have been driven by strikes, to such an extent that it is possible to discuss industrial disputes and strikes at the same time. The largest single category is straightforward strikes, and the second largest type is sympathy strikes, while important lockouts were often part of major national strikes.

Finnish industrial unrest in 1970s was peculiar (Fig. 10.1). It started later compared to France and Italy. France had peak years in 1968 and Italy in 1969.[5] In Finland the picture is mixed, because between 1970 and 1980 there were four peak years: 1971, 1973, 1976, and 1977. There was great variation of days lost from one year to the next. When you look at working days lost in Finland, it is hard to find a proper strike wave in this decade. Surprisingly, employers resorted to lockout in 1973, when the lockout was considered an odd instrument of the past.[6]

Arguments for a correlation between strikes and economic cycles do not apply in Finland. Economic boom years 1974–1975 was not matched by a corresponding increase in the number of working days lost, and the number of strikes was highest in 1976, when the Finnish economy went into recession. The third largest number of days lost occurred in 1977, when unemployment did rise to new heights due to zero growth of gross national product during the years 1975–1977. Extensive unemployment can explain the small number of days lost in 1978 and 1979, but not the number of strikes and lost working days in 1980. Seen in a Nordic perspective, the number of strikes and the number of working days lost, 1970–1980, was much higher in Finland compared to the other Nordic countries as shown in Table 10.2. In other words, Finland was at that time the strike champion of the Nordic countries.[7] The greatest peculiarity of Finnish industrial relations during these years was the odd combination

[5] Shalev, M. (1968) 'Lies, Damned Lies and Strike Statistics: the Measurement of Trends in Industrial Conflict' in Crouch and Pizzorno, *The Resurgence of Class Conflict*, p. 15.

[6] Mansner, M. (1990) *Suomalaista yhteiskuntaa rakenta massa. Suomen Työnantajain Keskusliitto 1956–1982* (Jyväskylä: Teollisuuden kustannus Oy), pp. 178–85.

[7] Ibid., pp. 159–85.

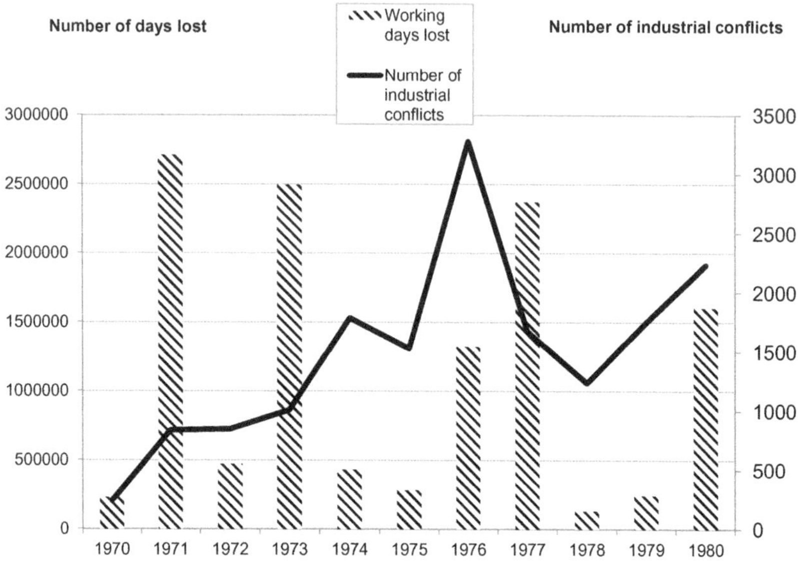

Fig. 10.1 Industrial conflicts in Finland, 1970–1980 (number of industrial conflicts and number of working days lost) (*Source* Statistics Finland)

of encompassing incomes policy agreements and strong local and national strike activity as will appear from the following pages.

Unstable Industrial Relations After the Second World War

From the beginning of the twentieth century, national collective agreements regulated industrial relations in Denmark, Norway, and Sweden, but in Finland national collective agreements became common only after 1945. In the other Nordic countries, the trade union movement constituted a significant power base in the 1920s and 1930s. In Finland, on the other hand, the trade union movement was socially sidetracked from 1918 until the Winter War against the Soviet Union in 1939 (see Chapter 2 in this book).

The Confederation of Finnish Trade Unions (*Suomen Ammattiyhdistysten Keskusliitto*, SAK) received an influx of new members after the war. In 1947, SAK had over 340,000 members. However, the organizational

Table 10.2 Number of working days lost in the Nordic countries, 1967–1980 (in 1,000s)

Year	*Denmark*	*Finland*	*Norway*	*Sweden*
1967	10	321	5	0.4
1968	34	282	14	1
1969	56	161	22	112
1970	102	233	47	156
1971	21	2,711	9	839
1972	22	473	12	11
1973	3,901	2,497	11	12
1974	184	435	318	58
1975	100	284	12	366
1976	210	1,326	138	25
1977	230	2,375	25	87
1978	129	132	63	37
1979	173	243	7	29
1980	187	1,606	104	4,479

Source Kauppinen, T. and Alasoini, T. (1985) *Työelämän suhteet. Aikasarjoja 1907–84* (Helsinki: Työelämän suhteiden neuvottelukunta), pp. 131–32)

basis of the trade union movement was not stable. Membership fell to 240,000 in 1953, and exhausting conflicts between the Communists and the Social Democrats weakened SAK already in the late 1940s and early 1950s.[8]

The confederation of white-collar unions, Confederation of Intellectual Employment (*Henkisen Työn Keskusliitto*, HTK), grew after war, too. In 1956, it had nearly 100,000 members and took a new name: the Federation of Clerical Employees' and Civil Servants' Organisations (*Toimihenkilö- ja Virkamiesjärjestöjen Keskusliitto*, TVK). The Finnish Confederation of Technical Salaried Employees (*Suomen Teknisten Toimihenkilöjärjestöjen Keskusliitto*, STTK) started in 1946. The Confederation of Unions for Academic Professionals (*Akateeminen valtuuskunta*, AKAVA) began in 1950. The explosive growth of the trade union movement also caused the employers to organize. In 1945, the foundation

[8] Bergholm, T. (2005) *Sopimusyhteiskunnan synty I. Työehtosopimusten läpimurrosta yleislakkoon. Suomen Ammattiyhdistysten Keskusliitto 1944–1956* (Keuruu: Otava).

of the Business Employers' Confederation (*Liiketyönantajain keskusliitto*, LTK) caused a split, which divided the employers' organizations in Finland along different lines from those in the other Nordic countries.[9]

In the autumn of 1949, the Communist Party tried to destabilize the Social Democratic minority government by a strike wave that was crushed by the government and the Social Democratic leadership of SAK.[10] A bigger strike movement occurred in 1950, when trade unions, led by the Social Democrats, tried to push through wage rises. These attrition conflicts gave unions tolerable collective agreements.[11]

From 1956, the Finnish parliament no longer maintained the price and wage control system, and after some rapid price increases SAK organized a general strike in March 1956. Approximately 400,000 workers went on strike for 19 days, even though SAK had about 270,000 members at that time. SAK enforced its claims, but price increases quickly offset all benefits.[12]

After the General Strike in 1956, even the Social Democrats started infighting, and SAK split into three parts: Those unions which stayed in SAK, those unions that joined breakaway peak organizations, and those which left SAK but stayed independent. However, SAK reunified between 1964 and 1969, and despite multiple twists and problems, the reunification process was unstoppable once it had got under way.[13]

The SAK congress in 1966 made considerable changes in the rules of the confederation. The new rules increased the independence of trade unions. Unions affiliated to SAK gained greater autonomy and freedom in collective bargaining and strike decisions. At an extraordinary congress in June 1969, SAK transferred even more powers from the central organization to the affiliated unions, and the name changed to Central Organization of the Finnish Trade Unions (*Suomen Ammattiliittojen Keskusjärjestö*) but kept the acronym SAK.[14]

[9] Bergholm, T. (2016) *A History of the SAK* (Helsinki: SAK), pp. 36–37.

[10] Bergholm, T. (1997) *Ammattiliiton nousu ja tuho. Kuljetusalan ammattiyhdistystoiminta ja työmarkkinasuhteiden murros 1944–1949* (Helsinki: Suomen Historiallinen Seura and Työministeriö); and Bergholm, *Sopimusyhteiskunnan synty I*.

[11] Ibid., pp. 256–57, 277–304.

[12] Ibid., pp. 454–506.

[13] Bergholm, T. (2007) *Sopimusyhteiskunnan synty II. Hajaannuksesta tulopolitiikkaan. Suomen Ammattiyhdistysten Keskusliitto 1956–1969* (Keuruu: Otava).

[14] Bergholm, *A History of the SAK*, pp. 59–62.

After 1969, union membership figures exploded. Finnish trade unions duplicated their combined membership first in 1958–1968 and again in 1968–1978, which meant that Finnish trade unions achieved the same organizational strength as the Nordic sister organizations in the 1970s. In 1958, union density was only about 30%, but had reached 77% in 1978.[15]

Strength of Workers and Unions

The Finnish state pushed for stability in labor market relations after the devaluation of the Finnish currency in the autumn of 1967. The state, the employers' organizations, and most trade union confederations agreed on incomes policy measures, and two years later the parties signed another incomes policy agreement. These encompassing agreements concerning social and economic policy were followed by fewer industrial conflicts in Finland 1968–1969, when strikes spread in other European countries.[16]

Devaluation in 1967 enlarged real wage difference between Finland and Sweden further and speeded up immigration to Sweden but labor shortages in Finland. Labor scarcity gave workers more power in personal wage negotiations and in connection with collective bargaining in 1971–1974. The tradition of unstable industrial relations was revitalized and opened for a renewed combination of national and local activism.[17]

However, the immigration of young Finnish workers to Sweden was not a one-way route. Some workers came back, and some worked in Sweden only during holiday seasons. The experience of better pay, cleaner and healthier workplaces, and strong trade union in Sweden put new grievances on the table, when workers returned to Finland. The possibility to leave the country and emigrate to Sweden and experiences with Swedish trade unions and workplaces empowered Finnish workers vis-à-vis Finnish employers.[18]

[15] Yli-Pietilä, P. (1990) *Työelämän suhteet: Aikasarjoja 1907–88* (Helsinki: Työministeriö), pp. 57–58, 60–61.

[16] Bergholm, T. (2012) *Kohti tasa-arvoa. Tulopolitiikan aika I, Suomen Ammattiliittojen Keskusjärjestö 1969–1977* (Keuruu: Otava), pp. 171–83, 208–09.

[17] Ibid., pp. 211–15, 405–13.

[18] Ibid., pp. 176, 211–13; and Vuorio, P. and Kvarnström, B. (2011) Koverharin raudan- ja teräksentekijöiden historia 1961–*2011* (Hanko: Koverharin Metallityöntekijäin ammattiosasto).

Due to variation of the coverage of comprehensive incomes policy agreements and the length of national collective agreements, the number of workers affected and working days lost fluctuated considerably. Incomes policy agreements created tensions, because wage drift was often substantial in industrial occupations, but weak or non-existing in public and private sector services. Incomes policy agreements set boundaries for those unions, which tried to rise their wages at the expense of other unions. The reason why the unions exceeded the wage agreements was that they resorted to previously more favorable wage structures and the rapid wage development in other sectors.

Peaks of Industrial Conflict, 1970–1980

The diversity of Finnish strike pattern was obvious in 1970, which was a peaceful year. A national strike in bus traffic was the largest conflict, while the building industry could muster the largest number of lost working days.[19] In 1971, the biggest industrial conflict took place in the metal industry in. About 65,000 workers were involved and around 2.3 million working days lost. Other important strikes and lockouts hit the construction sector.[20] The Finnish Secret Police, leaders of the employers' organizations and a majority of Finnish politicians, were anxious and even afraid that the Communist led strike movement would grow and develop into a full-scale rebellion even revolution.[21]

From this perspective, it was counterintuitive that the Communists in the Metal Workers' Union (*Metallityöväen Liitto*) and in the Construction Workers' Union (*Rakennustyöläisten Liitto*) tried to limit the scope of industrial strike activity. It was the Social Democratic leadership of the Metal Workers' Union who decided, against the Communist minority, to call an overall strike. The construction workers' partial strike was aimed

[19] Työnseisaukset vuonna 1970 (1971) (Helsinki: Tilastokeskus), p. 1.

[20] Työtaistelut 1971 (1972) (Helsinki: Tilastokeskus), p. 2.

[21] Suomi, J. (1996) *Taistelu puolueettomuudesta. Urho Kekkonen 1968–1972* (Keuruu: Otava), pp. 409–523; Ketola, E. (2007) *Suomen Metallityöväen Liitto 1960–1983*, (Keuruu: Otava), pp. 236–328; and Korkeaoja, J. (2009) *Punainen metalli. Kommunistit ja kansandemokraatit Suomen Metallityöväen Liitossa 1899–1983*, (Keuruu: Metallin vasemmisto), pp. 176–200.

only at the largest and most influential employers. As countermeasure the employers' association expanded the conflict with a major lockout.[22]

The year 1972 was rather peaceful with unions organizing strikes in road transport and rubber industries. Also, sales personnel in the state's alcohol monopoly shops, journalists, and schoolteachers went on strike. Most strikes were wildcat strikes. Statistics Finland reported that only one in a hundred had formal authorization from national trade union. Metalworkers and building workers were most keen to organize short walk-out and sit-in strikes.[23]

Dockers in the Northern ports protested against collective agreement, which enhanced technological change in port operations and diminished the demand for labor force. These wildcat strikes had a political aspect, too. The leaders of the transport workers union were Social Democratic, whereas the organizers of strikes were from the hard-core minority faction of the Finnish Communist Party. Employment offices cannot send unemployed to workplaces involved in (official) strikes, but during the wildcat dock strike in 1972, employment offices supported strike breaking organized jointly by the Finnish Transport Workers Union (*Auto- ja Kuljetusalan Työntekijäliitto*) and the Stevedoring Employers Union.[24]

The largest industrial conflict in 1973 was in building sites.[25] The Labour Court ruled in favor of the Construction Workers' Union in April. Employers were in the offensive and demanded changes of the agreement. The union used punctual and partial and short strikes to make employers more compromise prone. Short walkouts of only one occupation in row created chaos at building sites. The employers' organizations in the building industry formed a united lockout-front against the partial strike strategy but in the end of the day, the employers dropped their demands.[26]

[22] Bergholm, *Kohti tasa-arvoa*, pp. 209–33.

[23] Työtaistelut 1972 (1973) (Helsinki: Tilastokeskus), p. 2.

[24] Bergholm, T. (2000) *Kovaa peliä kuljetusalalla III. Kuljetusalan ammattiyhdistystoiminta vuosina 1960–1990* (Keuruu: Otava), pp. 350–61.

[25] Työtaistelut 1973 (1974) (Helsinki: Tilastokeskus), p. 2.

[26] People's Archives (*Kansan Arkisto*, KA), Minutes to "Suomen Kommunistisen Puolueen poliittinen toimikunta", May 23 and 30, and June 13, 1973; KA, SKP:n Ay-jaosto, He44, *Rakennusliitto*, "Rakennusalan työehtosopimuskamppailu v. 1973", August 10, 1973; Helin, J. (1998) *Rakentajien liitto. Rakennusalan työläisten järjestötoiminta*

Blue-collar workers often dominated strike statistics, but in Finland the picture is different. Here salaried employees participated in national industrial conflicts in many sectors and in large numbers. Thus, in 1973, salaried employees in the banking sector and technical white-collar employees launched some successful nationwide strikes.[27] Strikes in the metal industry and the combined lockouts and strikes in the construction sector in 1971 and 1973 were prolonged trials of strength that only served to emphasize the fact that the advent of the age of comprehensive incomes policy agreements had not brought peaceful co-existence to industrial relations.

Strike mobilization increased in Western Europe in the late 1960s and early 1970s, and some of the activities were linked to the rapid growth of leftist revolutionary groups among students. In Finland, too, the students turned toward the labor movement. For example, in the early 1970s, strikers in the metal industry and in the building trade got free medical attention from students who were acting as locums in medical services.[28]

In 1974–1975, encompassing incomes agreements were synonymous with some quiet years. On the other hand, wage drift was strongest during these years. Labor scarcity and local strikes created an upward wage spiral in export industries, but great dissatisfaction in sectors with less strong wage drift. And for the first time, Statistics Finland reported that salaried employees organized wildcat strikes too. Official and wildcat strikes of salaried employees accounted for 25% of working days lost in industrial disputes in 1975.[29]

After two peaceful years, industrial strife reached a new peak in 1976. National strikes of food workers, police, telephone fitters, and dock workers participated in this year's turbulent labor market. A police strike underscores how multifaceted the engagement in industrial conflicts were. It is hard to imagine that Communist infiltration in the police

Suomessa 1880-luvulta vuoteen 1995, (Jyväskylä: Rakennusliitto ry), pp. 348–49; and Bergholm, *Kohti tasa-arvoa*, pp. 309–11.

[27] Työtaistelut (1973, p. 2).

[28] Bergholm, *Kohti tasa-arvoa*, pp. 209–11.

[29] Työtaistelut 1974 (1975) (Helsinki: Tilastokeskus), p. 1; Työtaistelut (1975, p. 1); Työtaistelut 1976 (1977) (Helsinki: Tilastokeskus), p. 3; and Bergholm, *Kohti tasa-arvoa*, pp. 325–57, 403–13.

union caused this strike, when most of the members were conservative right-wing pillars of the existing order.[30]

The strike profile in 1977 was different. The number of strikes fell, while the number of affected workers and the amount working days lost increased significantly. Almost 744,000 workers and employees were on strike. This meant that about 35% of the labor force participated in industrial conflicts this year. It was a new Finnish record. Large-scale national strikes were organized in the transport industry, in the shoe industry, and in the hotel and restaurant branch. It was home market industries, which lagged in the wage competition with export industries, where wage growth had been significant in previous years.[31]

The employers' response was strong and organized in the shoe industry. The employers' confederation gave permission to the employers in the leather industry to organize a sympathy lockout to weaken the strike capacity of the Leather and Rubber Workers' Union (*Kumi- ja Nahkatyöväen Liitto*) whose leaders belonged to the hard-core minority faction of the Finnish Communist Party. The lockout, therefore, seems to be politically motivated. Due to the employers concentrated action the fruits of this nine-week-long strike were meager.[32]

In 1975–1977, economic growth was near zero in Finland, and unemployment figures were very high in 1978. Consequently, trade unions did not organize strikes in 1978–1979, and the number of working days lost plummeted.[33] However, in 1980, industrial peace was over. This time it was lumberjacks, drivers of timber harvest machines, mariners, officers of the merchant fleet, and office employees in industry who went on strike. Office employees instigated the biggest strikes; and employers were surprised, when "office girls" went on strike too. All these national strikes lasted more than one month.[34]

[30] Työtaistelut (1976, pp. 1, 3); and Mansner, *Suomalaista yhteiskuntaa rakenta massa*, p. 185.

[31] Työtaistelut (1977, pp. 1–2).

[32] Bergholm, *Kohti tasa-arvoa*, pp. 500–01.

[33] Työtaistelut 1978 (1979) (Helsinki: Tilastokeskus), p. 5; and Työtaistelut 1979 (1980) (Helsinki: Tilastokeskus), pp. 5–6.

[34] Työtaistelut 1980 (1981) (Helsinki: Tilastokeskus), pp. 5–6; and Bergholm, *Kohti tasa-arvoa*, pp. 185–88.

Wildcat Strikes as Part of Local Bargaining

During periods of recession in 1967 and 1977–1979, the national bank of Finland corrected for the comparative weakness of Finnish industry by lowering the value of the Finnish currency. The country's economy was characterized by cycles of devaluation followed by economic upswing in the export industry. This again, led to a growth in imports, inflation, a new recession, and another devaluation. The lack of stable industrial relations helped to aggravating this problematic circle and fostered a true strike wave spearheaded by local wildcat strikes in the 1970s,[35] which could also draw support from a strengthened trade union movement and the newly consolidated position of shop stewards.

The employers found it difficult to negotiate and come to terms with a strong trade union movement at the workplace. Wildcat strikes concentrated in sectors where the work force was male: in the harbors, in the building sites, in the metal and paper plants. In these branches, short industrial actions at the local level became the norm. More mixed gender composition was in food industry, where short wildcat strikes happened in the early 1970s.[36]

Sections of the Construction Workers' Union organized boycott of poisonous paints. It started in 1972. This boycott and later boycotts of other toxic materials were successful, even though employers and their organizations protested strongly. There were local strikes in other sectors to solve health and safety issues. The Finnish Transport Workers' Union organized a one-day stoppage in March 1973, to ensure that parliament enacted tighter working time regulations for road transport drivers. The Labour Court decided that this kind of political demonstration was not a violation of breach against the industrial peace obligations.[37]

[35] Pekkarinen, J. and Vartiainen, J. (1993) *Suomen talouspolitiikan pitkä linja* (Porvoo: WSOY), pp. 244–59.

[36] Työtaistelut (1972, p. 2); Työtaistelut (1973, p. 2); Työtaistelut (1974, p. 1); Työtaistelut (1975, p. 1); Työtaistelut (1976, p. 1); Työtaistelut (1977, p. 1); and Bergholm, *Kohti tasa-arvoa*.

[37] Helin, J. (1998) *Rakentajien liitto*, pp. 350–31; Bergholm, *Kovaa peliä kuljetusalalla III*, pp. 412–20; and Bergholm, *Kohti tasa-arvoa*, pp. 157–59.

Conclusion

Michael Biggs has analyzed the American strike wave of 1886 as interaction between employers, trade unions, and political authorities.[38] It is a fruitful approach that can be applied to Finnish experiences in the years 1970–1980. State, employer organizations, and trade union confederations tried to enhance industrial peace and economic growth supporting encompassing incomes policy. These actors were only partially successful seen in light of the events of 1970–1980, when strike level reached new heights. Greatest peculiarity of Finnish industrial conflict, during these years, was the combination of encompassing incomes policy agreements and strong local strike activity, and national industrial conflicts with substantial number of working days lost. Finland was at that time the strike champion of the Nordic countries.

Political explanations have dominated the discussion in the media and the scientific literature. This is very problematic, because Finnish strikers came from various occupations, from different sectors, and from all political persuasions. There were strikes of hard-core Communist dockers in 1972 as well as right-wing police officers in 1976. Blue-collar workers and white-collar employees went on strike. The number of strikes increased when support for left-wing parties—especially the Communist Party—had started to decline in general elections. The fluctuating character of industrial disputes as well as the high legitimacy of striking was a persistent part of Finnish industrial relations in the 1970s.

References

Archives

People's Archives (*Kansan Arkisto*, KA):
The Finnish Communist Party (*Suomen Kommunistisen Puolueen*, SKP).

Literature

Bergholm T. (1997) *Ammattiliiton nousu ja tuho. Kuljetusalan ammattiyhdistystoiminta ja työmarkkinasuhteiden murros 1944–1949* (Helsinki: Suomen Historiallinen Seura and Työministeriö).

[38] Biggs, M. (2002) 'Strikes as Sequences of Interaction. The American Strike Wave of 1886', *Social Science History*, 26, 3, pp. 583–617.

Bergholm, T. (2000) *Kovaa peliä kuljetusalalla III. Kuljetusalan ammattiyhdistystoiminta vuosina 1960–1990* (Keuruu: Otava).
Bergholm, T. (2005) *Sopimusyhteiskunnan synty I. Työehtosopimusten läpimurrosta yleislakkoon. Suomen Ammattiyhdistysten Keskusliitto 1944–1956* (Keuruu: Otava).
Bergholm, T. (2007) *Sopimusyhteiskunnan synty II. Hajaannuksesta tulopolitiikkaan. Suomen Ammattiyhdistysten Keskusliitto 1956–1969* (Keuruu: Otava)
Bergholm, T. (2012) *Kohti tasa-arvoa. Tulopolitiikan aika I, Suomen Ammattiliittojen Keskusjärjestö 1969–1977* (Keuruu: Otava).
Bergholm, T. (2016) *A History of the SAK* (Helsinki: SAK).
Biggs, M. (2002) 'Strikes as Sequences of Interaction. The American Strike Wave of 1886', *Social Science History*, 26, 3, pp. 583–617.
Crouch, C. (1996) *Industrial Relations and State Traditions* (Oxford: Clarendon Press)
Crouch, C. and Pizzorno, A. (eds.) (1978) *The Resurgence of Class Conflict in Western Europe Since 1968. Vol. 1: National Studies* (New York: Holmes & Meier Publishers)
Crouch, C. and Pizzorno, A. (1978) *The Resurgence of Class Conflict in Western Europe Since 1968. Vol. 2: Comparative Analyses* (New York: Holmes & Meier Publisher).
Helin, J. (1998) *Rakentajien liitto. Rakennusalan työläisten järjestötoiminta Suomessa 1880-luvulta vuoteen 1995* (Jyväskylä: Rakennusliitto ry).
Kauppinen, T. and Alasoini, T. (1985) *Työelämän suhteet. Aikasarjoja 1907-84* (Helsinki: Työelämän suhteiden neuvottelukunta).
Ketola, E. (2007) *Suomen Metallityöväen Liitto 1960–1983* (Keuruu: Otava).
Korkeaoja, J. (2009) *Punainen metalli. Kommunistit ja kansandemokraatit Suomen Metallityöväen Liitossa 1899–1983* (Keuruu: Metallin vasemmisto).
Mansner, M. (1990) *Suomalaista yhteiskuntaa rakenta massa. Suomen Työnantajain Keskusliitto 1956–1982* (Jyväskylä: Teollisuuden kustannus Oy).
Pekkarinen, J. and Vartiainen, J. (1993) *Suomen talouspolitiikan pitkä linja* (Porvoo: WSOY).
Scheuer, S. (2006) 'A Novel Calculus? institutional Change, Globalization and Industrial Conflict in Europe', *European Journal of Industrial Relations*, 12, 2, pp. 143–64.
Shalev, M. (1968) 'Lies, Damned Lies and Strike Statistics: the Measurement of Trends in Industrial Conflict' in Crouch, C. and Pizzorno, A. (eds.) *The Resurgence of Class Conflict in Western Europe Since 1968. Vol. 1: National Studies* (New York: Holmes & Meier Publishers), pp. 1–20.
Suomi, J. (1996) *Taistelu puolueettomuudesta. Urho Kekkonen 1968-1972* (Keuruu: Otava).
Työnseisaukset vuonna 1970 (1971) (Helsinki: Tilastokeskus).
Työtaistelut 1971 (1972) (Helsinki: Tilastokeskus).

Työtaistelut 1972 (1973) (Helsinki: Tilastokeskus).
Työtaistelut 1973 (1974) (Helsinki: Tilastokeskus).
Työtaistelut 1974 (1975) (Helsinki: Tilastokeskus).
Työtaistelut 1975 (1976) (Helsinki: Tilastokeskus).
Työtaistelut 1976 (1977) (Helsinki: Tilastokeskus).
Työtaistelut 1977 (1978) (Helsinki: Tilastokeskus).
Työtaistelut 1978 (1979) (Helsinki: Tilastokeskus).
Työtaistelut 1979 (1980) (Helsinki: Tilastokeskus).
Työtaistelut 1980 (1981) (Helsinki: Tilastokeskus).
Vuorio, P. and Kvarnström, B. (2011) *Koverharin raudan- ja teräksentekijöiden historia 1961–2011* (Hanko: Koverharin Metallityöntekijäin ammattiosasto).
Yli-Pietilä, P. (1990) *Työelämän suhteet: Aikasarjoja 1907–88* (Helsinki: Työministeriö).

CHAPTER 11

From Street Fighting years to Seizing the Agenda. Labor Militancy Challenging the Establishment in Norway, 1976–2010

Idar Helle

As in most Western Europe, the system of labour relations in Norway experienced wildcat strikes and social unrest during the 'Decade of 68' (1968–1978). The successive strike actions were highly local and hit individual business companies. At the same time, they were the result of radical political objectives on a centralist and nationwide basis. Besides hitting capital ownership through shutting down production lines, wildcat strikes were also organized as an open revolt against the hegemony of the Norwegian Confederation of Trade Unions (*Landsorganisasjonen i Norge*, LO) and the towering social democratic Labour Party (*Arbeiderpartiet*). In the turmoil peak year 1976, the non-legal strike actions were under heavy influence of a Maoist party, the Workers' Communist Party

I. Helle (✉)
De Facto, Oslo, Norway
e-mail: idar.helle@gmail.com

© The Author(s), under exclusive license to Springer Nature Switzerland AG 2023

J. Jørgensen and F. Mikkelsen (eds.), *Trade Union Activism in the Nordic Countries since 1900*, Palgrave Studies in the History of Social Movements, https://doi.org/10.1007/978-3-031-08987-9_11

(Marxist-Leninists) (*Arbeidernes Kommunistparti (marxist-leninistene)*, AKP(m-l)).[1]

The aim of this chapter is to explore certain aspects of labour militancy in Norway since 1976. My research hypothesis is that the 1980s were the years when the anti-establishment and leftist actors in the Norwegian trade union movement started a process of building semi-institutional networks that gained a wider audience. I call this practice 'power through agenda setting'. Although the cadres of the Maoist party and its collective actions remain at the center of the analysis, and has in fact remained influential until today, this study also tries to explore resource mobilization and local labour activism that were beyond the grasp of 'the Party'.

I focus in particular on two singular but interacting cases. The first is based on a study of highly organized working-class militancy in a local club affiliated to the Norwegian metal union federation, *Verkstedklubben Aker Verdal*, while the second case looks at the making of the radical rank and file *Trondheimskonferansen* in the end of the 1980s. Furthermore, I also try single out assets, aspects, and characteristics of the strategies of the challengers and anti-establishment segments of the Norwegian labour movement.[2] A key question here is to identify to what degree and how a concept of Maoist and Leninist-inspired 'class war at a local level' gradually transformed into agenda setting in the labour movement through negotiations and institution making.

Street Fighting Years

As Marcel van der Linden and Xavier Vigna observe, the great post-war industrial conflict cycle in Western Europe ended in the second half of the

[1] Helle, I. and Matos, T. (2018) 'Norway 1945–2015: Contention and Democracy' in Mikkelsen, F., Kjeldstadli, K. and Nyzell, S. (eds.) *Popular Struggle and Democracy in Scandinavia. 1700-Present* (London: Palgrave Macmillan), p. 248. The Maoist party AKP(m-l) was founded in 1973, after a four-year preparation period after the youth organization Socialist Youth League (*Sosialistisk Ungdomsforbund*) broke away from the Socialist People's Party in 1969 and added "(Marxist-Leninists)" to its name.

[2] See Hanssen, B.-E. (2021) *Dynamitt i borehullene. Trondheim Faglige Samorganisasjons historie 1870–2020* (Oslo: Pax Forlag), pp. 457–561; and Helle, I. (2009) *Utfordrerne. Verkstedklubben og arbeiderne på Aker Verdal 1969–2009* (Oslo: Forlaget Manifest).

1970s.[3] In Norway, 1976 should be considered as the 'climax of insubordination,' with several powerful strikes at the local level within different industrial branches and the transport sector.

Between 1975 and 1977, there were several militant and even violent strikes in Norway. Most of them occurred in the Oslo region. They stand out as an exception to the general impression of peaceful and highly legal labour relations in the post-war era. In all these rowdy wildcat actions young activists from the AKP(m-l) party or people close to the party were participating in and often initiating the events.

One such strike event was the highly mediatized dockers' strike in Oslo, January 1977.[4] Labour historian Jonas Bals describes the scene when the police force was ordered to remove the picket line in the harbor. The police observed without interfering while a 'voluntary worker' (strikebreaker) drove down one of the strikers which led to an escalation of the conflict. The police appeared determined to go after the supposed strike leader Jon Michelet. Lots of press photos of Michelet, a regular columnist in the AKP(m-l) newspaper The Class-Struggle (*Klassekampen*) and already a well-known author in Norway, were spread in the national press. This gave leeway to the claim that this was another strike led and controlled by the Maoists of AKP(m-l).

Clashes between striking workers and the police occurred in other places, too.[5] In October 1976, a group of Maoist activists took matters into their own hands in support of nine Pakistani workers who went on strike against their employers in the horticulture firm Norsk Champignon. The newspaper *Klassekampen* published a ranting poem against an individual worker in the company claiming he was a strikebreaker. Shortly after, three or four cars with militants went to this worker's family home 50 km north of Oslo. All windows in the house were smashed. Because the alleged strikebreaker also was member of the youth organization of the *Arbeiderpartiet*, the incident was seen as political rivalry. Even though

[3] van der Linden, M. (2003) 'The Aftermath of '1968': Interactions of Workers', Youth and Women's Movements' in van der Linden, M. (ed.) *Transnational Labour History. Explorations* (Aldershot: Ashgate Publishing), pp. 117–42; and Vigna, X. (2007) *L'Insubordination ouvrière dans les années 68. Essai d'histoire politique des usines* (Rennes: Presses Universitaires de Rennes).

[4] Bals, J. (2021) *Streik! En historie om strid, samhold og solidaritet* (Oslo: Res Publica), pp. 444–46.

[5] Bals, *Streik!*, pp. 423–28.

the AKP(m-l) denied any direct involvement in the window smashing, the episode has later become a signifier of Maoist labour activism out of proportion during the street fighting years of the mid-1970s. At the same time, there were also opponents of Maoist influence in the Norwegian labour unions. At the offshore construction yard of Aker Verdal in Trøndelag, unionized workers launched a ferocious resolution proposal to the annual club meeting of *Verkstedklubben* in 1977.

> What did folks do in the old times when the most precious they had, the livestock and the reindeer herd, were attacked by wolves? Obviously, they went hunting.
>
> What do we, the working people, do when the most precious we have, the union confederation, is attacked by AKP(m-l)? We as well must protect the organization and take counter measures.[6]

In addition to this infighting the Maoist party and part of the labour movement was becoming the primary focus of right-wing extremism. In the second half of the 1970s, there occurred several arsons and bombings targeting the October bookstores in the towns of Tromsø, Fredrikstad, Bergen, and Lillehammer. On May Day 1979 in Oslo, a militant with ties to the fascist organization, the Norwegian Front (*Norsk Front*), threw a bomb into the Maoist parade, seriously injuring one person. The motives of these attacks were xenophobia, but also anti-communist due to the extensive activities of the AKP(m-l) in these years.[7]

Social Democratic Labour Reforms

The second half of the 1970s marked the end of the classic social democratic era and its social reforms. Among them was the Work Environment Act (*Arbeidsmiljøloven*). After years of preparations through common learning, reports, and conferences by the union federations and the LO confederation, this important law act was passed in the last year of the parliamentary session when the Labour Party and the Socialist

[6] Helle, *Utfordrerne*, p. 74. Quotation from proposal of the A1 first and second shift department workers to the 1977 annual meeting of Verkstedklubben Aker Verdal.

[7] Nydal, K. (2007) *Sosialmoralsk engasjement og politisk aktivisme. Framveksten av en antirasistisk bevegelse i Norge 1975–1988*, unpublished PhD dissertation, Oslo University, pp. 89–90: and Helle and Matos, 'Norway 1945–2015', p. 268.

Left Party (*Sosialistisk Venstreparti*, SV) still enjoyed a left-wing majority. The Work Environment Act of 1977 focused on health and safety issues particularly for blue-collar workers. It also introduced regulations that strengthened the co-decision rights of workers and unions on these matters through work environment committees (*arbeidsmiljøutvalg*) and work environment officers (*verneombud*) at the local level.[8] There even appeared an exception to the general principle of management prerogatives (*styringsretten*), as work environment officers were given the right to bypass management decisions and impose a stop of work if she or he considered the work to be of 'immediate danger' due to health and safety reasons.

Another labour relations reform concerned 'economic democracy' and the question of workers' representation on executive boards and company assemblies. As Thomas Piketty has shown, the debates and reforms concerning workers representation were significantly more progressive and elaborated in Scandinavian and the German-speaking parts of Europe than elsewhere in these years.[9] In Norway, workers' representation on company boards was secured through legislation in 1972. Some years later, in 1980, a joint committee of LO and the Labour Party made a proposal to give workers and employees the same level of representation as capital ownership in private companies.[10] However, this ambitious plan was defeated by the LO and the Social Democratic leadership, at a time when the political winds were turning heavily to the right, i.e., toward neoliberalism.

A Regional Industrial Shift

In 1974, the sheer number of industrial workers in Norway reached its highest level ever with close to 400,000 employed in industrial branches and mining. This high level of industrial employment was almost maintained until the early 1980s. During this period, large parts of the industry in Western Europe were affected by growing unemployment. However,

[8] Bergh, T. (2009) *Kollektiv fornuft. LOs historie, Vol. 3: 1969–2009* (Oslo: Pax Forlag), pp. 137–41.

[9] Piketty, T. (2019) *Capital et idéologie* (Paris: Éditions du Seuil), pp. 567–95.

[10] Bergh, *Kollektiv fornuft*, pp. 143–44.

where Norway differed from its European trade partners, was the establishment of new industrial complexes, paralleled with continued output at already existing plants.

At the same time, a shift in regional industrial location took place. Central Eastern Norway (around the capital of Oslo) had constituted the core of industrialization during the last decade of the nineteenth century. Oslo, Østfold, and the coastal areas of Telemark were still industrial bastions alongside several smaller industrial communities in the deep fjords from Kvinesdal in the South to Kirkenes in the North. The main factor bringing about change was the production of platforms and installations for the expanding oil industry in the North Sea. It only took Rogaland and Hordaland on the west coast a few decades to establish themselves as the two strongest industrial counties in Norway.[11]

From around 1980, industrial employment in the eastern part of Norway fell dramatically. "Out of sight, out of mind": Among influential circles in the capital this development was perceived as the end of Norway as industrial nation. In Parliament and among academics at the universities, many did not comprehend the scope of the new oil industry, and it took a considerable amount of time before the urban elite in Oslo acknowledged that the shipyard and the metal unions at Aker Stord, Rosenberg in Stavanger and Aker Verdal were gaining positions as key actors.

Nord-Trøndelag, the county north of Trondheim, was a county with modest industrial development. In December of 1974, the leader of the metalworkers' union federation visited the local union section at Aker Verdal. He told the assembled trade unionists that, for the very first time, the federation now had more than 100,000 members. In Nord-Trøndelag alone, the membership had increased from 600 to 1,300 between 1970 and 1974. The numbers show clearly how weak the industrial employment base had been in the area, but also what effect the foundation of the Aker construction yard in Verdal had on the entire region.[12]

The rapid growth of workers at Aker Verdal is paramount to the understanding of the rough political confrontations taking place in the local union as the 1970s progressed. This construction yard and the entire emerging oil industry, onshore and offshore, went through a social and

[11] Helle, *Utfordrerne*, p. 44.

[12] Ibid., pp. 44–45.

political transition that had taken place in similar industrial communities on the European continent a few years earlier. A new trend among labour unions in Western Europe in 'the decade of 68' was the mobilization of youth, women, and immigrants who claimed a more prominent role in both strikes and union activism.[13] A local strike at Aker Verdal in 1973 should be seen as part of the European picture; it was led and initiated by young workers.

Retrospective debates on the development of labour unions and the working class during the 1970s often tend to focus on radical university students wishing to bring revolutionary and communist salvation to the workers. This rather amusing observation is not entirely wrong when it comes to AKP(m-l) and the Norwegian Maoists, but as an attempt to understand the wider picture it serves more as a caricature than accurate storytelling. Instead, we may look for similarities between young workers seizing initiative in the steelworks in Northern Italy, car factories in Köln and Stuttgart and the offshore construction yard at Aker Verdal. Social and structural explanations of political radicalization as a European trend will probably make more sense than a perception of a Norwegian exceptionalism.[14]

In this context, I have chosen to profile the local union club, *Verkstedklubben Aker Verdal*, as a showcase to illustrate vital characteristics of working-class empowerment and union militancy in Norway. The leadership of Verkstedklubben and its members truly challenged and expanded the boundaries of the Norwegian system of labour relations. As one veteran worker and former union official put it in 2009: "We have influenced and contributed to making this a good workplace."[15]

Ideological Disarray

The close ally of the Norwegian labour movement, the Labour Party, was in power for another four years until 1981. However, already in 1977–78 one could grasp the end of the social democratic political order. The single most influential event that changed the political picture was the

[13] van der Linden, 'The Aftermath of '1968'', pp. 117–23.

[14] Helle, *Utfordrerne*, p. 45.

[15] Based on interview with Kåre Gaasvik (Ibid., p. 234).

reversal of the Keynesian counter-cycle approach to economic policy.[16] Highly aware of the forthcoming petroleum incomes from the North Sea, the government of Odvar Nordli (the Labour Party) had stayed on a Keynesian inspired course after the 'oil shock' and the energy crisis of 1973–74. This counter-cycle economic policy continued to support the welfare state and it subsidized shipyards, the metal industry, and the mining sector, which to a substantial degree was owned by the state.[17]

Because the economic slump did not improve as expected, the Labour Party saw no other choice than to tighten public spending and cut off the subsidies to industrial sectors that had been strongholds of the labour movement and the Labour Party for several decades. This meant that already in 1978, well in advance of the Thatcher era in the UK, and four years before the austerity turn of the social democracy in Sweden, Norway had in fact taken a substantial step in the direction of financial cutbacks.

As the decades after 1980 were to be marked by political neoliberalism and shareholder value capitalism, both the Labour Party and its main left-wing challenger the Maoists affiliated to AKP(m-l) went into deep crises. A sudden lack of self-confidence among social democrats became apparent after the international demise of economic Keynesianism.[18] It resulted in an intensified power struggle at the top of the party and a more market friendly approach to economic policies. The internal contradictions also caused a widening gap between party leadership and layers of organized workers.

In the years around 1980, the Labour Party lost ground among workers and in many local labour unions. At the offshore construction yard of Aker Verdal, there was a strong but disputed social democratic leadership in *Verkstedklubben* between 1974 and 1982. When Bjørn Aarstad quitted as club chairman in 1980, it soon became clear that the leadership had depended more on his personal qualities and will to fight than any dedicated social democratic union delegate. The ongoing nationwide industrial crisis and the ideological disarray of the Labour

[16] Furre, B. (1991) *Vårt hundreår. Norsk historie 1905–1990* (Oslo: Det Norske Samlaget), pp. 383–94.

[17] Lie, E. (2012) *Norsk økonomisk politikk etter 1905* (Oslo: Universitetsforlaget), pp. 123–34.

[18] Kjeldstadli, K. and Helle, I. (2016) 'Social Democracy in Norway' in Schmidt, I. (ed.) *The Three Worlds of Social Democracy. A Global View* (London: Pluto Press), pp. 46–67, p. 56.

Party opened the gates to a left-wing political challenger. Thus, when Stein Aamdal, a well-known union militant and member of the Maoist AKP(m-l), took over in 1982, it was regarded as highly provocative to the labour movement leadership. For many years, *Verkstedklubben Aker Verdal* and its local leadership were cut off from any influence inside the metal workers' union federation and the LO confederation. In the long struggle to avoid outsourcing of the janitors at Aker Verdal 1986–1988, the union headquarters in Oslo even counteracted and hindered *Verkstedklubben* in its effort to defend the interests of their janitor members. Ultimately, it was only when the Aker Verdal CEO and the management of the Aker offshore corporation tried to remove Stein Aamdal as club chairman, in full public and through an outdoor speech to the workers in 1997, that the union federation took action to defend the right of *Verkstedklubben* to elect its leadership independently and free from management involvement.[19]

By that time, the AKP(m-l) party line and the Maoist movement's ultimate goal of a socialist revolution in Norway were long gone and off the table. Compared to their European 'sister movements', the Maoist movement in Norway was quite strong in the 1970s. By 1978–1979, however, there were internal signs that the party apparatus was worn out having used exceptionally amounts of human resources on strikes and strike support movements, and on the daily newspaper *Klassekampen*.[20] The Maoist party swore to a very hard and exaggerated internal security policy that brought militants and cadres to the brink of exasperation. Around 1980 a severe party crisis emerged, where different factions of the party stood up against the highly centralized leadership.[21] There also came a split in the so-called Diamond Gang, the inner circle of the party leadership.

[19] Helle, *Utfordrerne*, pp. 99–172.

[20] A small note on the *Klassekampen* is required. The daily newspaper has kept its name since the foundation in 1969. The paper is no longer affiliated to the Maoist cause nor any political party. However, *Klassekampen* has maintained a strong position on the Norwegian 'broad left.' It is in 2022 one of the ten largest newspapers in Norway with almost 50,000 printed and digital copies sold daily.

[21] Skjeseth, A. (2011) *Sykle på vatnet. Historia om Klassekampen* (Oslo: Samlaget), pp. 60–80; and Brekke, B. (2015) *Tron Øgrim. Det revolusjonære fyrverkeri* (Oslo: Aschehoug), pp. 164–216.

A non-intentional effect of the Norwegian Maoist party crisis was more autonomy to the union rank-and-file. Some of them were organizationally and politically gifted and, by this time quite experienced. They gained substantial ground in the unions during and after the 'party crisis' and they took control as shop stewards and union representatives in factories, construction yards, and shipyards as well as transport and logistics and even some public services. For instance, in 1990, party members or former party members of AKP(m-l) were in control of almost all the larger and established industrial union clubs in Rogaland, the vastly industrialized county in the southwestern part of Norway.

Unemployment and Closing Bell

Already under the conservative government of Kåre Willoch (Høyre) 1981–86, unemployment came back as an element in Norway. In small towns and rural districts where employment and local community were built around one big factory or pit, the fight for economic survival could be intense. In places like Tyssedal (aluminum smelter) on the west coast, or in the small mining towns of Sulitjelma and Kirkenes up north, union militancy shocked both management and the LO leadership. The will to fight and the capacity to act and mobilize made it possible to delay the closure of a plant for years. Most of these battles to preserve jobs were eventually lost. In these campaigns, there were typically a few AKP(m-l) party members who played crucial roles as union activists but also had the capacity to mobilize and educate workers.[22] So, if the party model and the party crisis might tell a story of elitism, hierarchy, and lack of internal democracy, the Maoist influence in the labour unions is also a story of working-class empowerment.

Also at Aker Verdal, the very existence of the offshore construction yard was threatened in the early 1980s. *Verkstedklubben* and the local management refused, however, to leave the fate of the construction site to the unpredictable market for offshore supplies. In February 1982, the community of Verdal stood behind a full-day general strike to avoid closure of the construction yard, which employed more than 1,000 workers. On several occasions during the 1980s and 1990s, unions

[22] Bals, *Streik!*, pp. 415–52.

tried to avoid downsizing and local unemployment. From 1983, *Verkstedklubben* took part in the innovative industrial union campaign "Yes to work" (see below). The largest actions taken against downsizing in the offshore supply industry were the nationwide campaign in 1999. Shop stewards and union representatives in the three leading Norwegian offshore supply corporations Aker, Kværner, and Umoe aligned with the seven municipalities along the Norwegian coastline where the construction yards were located. Together the industrial unions and the municipalities launched a political campaign and lobbying against the government and the parliamentarians to ensure new contracts to the offshore supply industry. At Aker Verdal, the management and the *Verkstedklubben* succeeded in raising public funding for vocational training and increased multi-disciplinarity among the workers.[23]

The most serious challenge to the Norwegian state apparatus and the system of labour relations in these years was triggered by 'the rebellion of the oil workers.'[24] In the offshore oil and gas industry, there was an intense labour versus capital struggle over unusual profits. Considering the strategic economic importance of the sector, the turmoil of these years brought anxiety to new heights in government circles. Wildcat strikes on the platforms reached its peaks in 1978, 1986, and the last time in 1990.[25] After the defeat of the rebellious independent union, The Federation of Oilworkers (*Oljearbeidernes Fellessammenslutning*), the revolt of the oil workers gradually faded away. The use of arbitrary wage regulation has been instrumental and effective in the authorities handling of wage struggles in Norway in the entire period. In the single year of 2012, no less than three strike movements were stopped by the government's use of arbitrary wage regulation.

1986: Industrial Capital and a Moment of Hubris

In 1986, the executive board of the Norwegian Employers' Confederation (*Norsk Arbeidsgiverforening*, NAF) found it was the right time to go on the offensive against the LO and the union federations in the private

[23] Helle, *Utfordrerne*, pp. 196–213.

[24] Ryggvik, H. and Smith-Solbakken, M. (1997) *Norsk oljehistorie. Blod, svette og olje* (Oslo: Ad Notam Gyldendal), pp. 232–70.

[25] Ibid., pp. 433–48.

sector. With neoliberalism on the rise, the employers decided on a big lock-out against the unions in LO when wage negotiations fell apart. This confrontational strategy turned out to be a great mistake. The NAF had to give up the lock-out and accept most of LO's demands after only one week of industrial conflict. The impact of the defeat made the employers' organization collapse. What followed was a complete restructuring of the new organization, the Confederation of Norwegian Enterprise (*Næringslivets hovedorganisasjon*, NHO), two years later. Considering it is better with a relatively strong compared to a weak social partner, the LO patiently awaited and helped the employers to get on their feet in the following years. The triumph of organized labour and LO in 1986 probably had long-term consequences for labour relations in Norway. Because LO demonstrated a stronger conflict capacity than organized capital, the employers had to act more leniently during the times of capitalist restructuring compared to employers in neighboring European countries.[26]

Fixing an Alternative Agenda: The Rise of the Trondheim Conference

When the nationwide Maoist cadres finally reached union positions that assured local and corporate power, the wildcat strategies from the 1970s were firmly left behind. Instead, they started to raise a union based and nationwide resistance to the market reforms of the Labour Party and the leadership of the LO.

The first signs of organized resistance, and quite apart from the street clashes with the police in the previous decade, were the campaign 'Yes to work' in 1983, and the conference 'Work for all' in the southern town of Kristiansand in 1986. The latter initiative came, among others, from the shop stewards of the Falconbridge nickel works, which raises above the center of the town. The conference aimed to articulate new union policies as an alternative to the allegedly right turn of the social democrats framed by such contemporary quotes from the Labour Party deputy Einar

[26] Bieler, A. and Morton, A. D. (2018) *Global Capitalism, Global War, Global Crisis* (Cambridge: Cambridge University Press), pp. 77–156.

Førde, "We have to get rid of all accusations that we are opposed to the market."[27]

The union activists at the 'Work for all' conference, still with the AKP(m-l) cadres at its core, considered that economic liberalism, inevitably, would lead to de-industrialization in several branches, unemployment, a weakened union movement, and increasing class inequalities in Norway.[28] This analysis drew substantial support from the negative shift of the Norwegian economy 1986–93. The economic shift started suddenly, with the collapse of the oil prices in the spring of 1986. The conservative Willoch resigned and Gro Harlem Brundtland (the Labour Party) took over as prime minister. To reduce the national trade deficit, the Brundtland government introduced austerity through a combination of monetary, financial, and labour policy measures. In 1988, for the first time since the German occupation during the Second World War, a temporary law act was introduced to freeze wages and deny all forms of industrial action for two years. Unemployment increased and reached a level around seven percent, which is considered very high by Norwegian standards.[29]

There was a neoliberal moon rising in these years. Fighting against market reforms under Prime Minister Brundtland and her ideological successor Jens Stoltenberg, the union activists behind the 'Work for all' conference came together again to create an alternative political agenda. In 1988, the next conference took place in Trondheim with 120 participants gathering at Bakke bydelshus, a community location. One of the organizers, Rolv Rynning Hanssen of the local union of municipality workers (*Fagforbundet*) and the local section of LO in Trondheim, was warned that he could be excluded because of 'fractionism' by his union federation.[30] The warning from the Big Brass in Oslo never led to any such organizational sanctions. In the upcoming next decade, the national union leadership in Oslo had to learn to live with the policy proposals and agenda making coming from the annually Trondheim conference.

[27] Hanssen, *Dynamitt i borehullene*, p. 467. The quote is from Einar Førde's speech to the national conference of the Labour Party in 1987.

[28] Ibid., pp. 464–69.

[29] Kjeldstadli and Helle, 'Social Democracy in Norway', p. 56.

[30] Hanssen, *Dynamitt i borehullene*, p. 470.

The intention was that the conference should be an annual recurring event, next time in Oslo. However, due to pressure from the mighty union federations and the LO confederation, the local organizers and the local transport workers union had to give up this attempt; Oslo as conference location was simply 'too close to the corridors of power.' From 1989, the conference was permanently placed in Trondheim. That year the conference paroles were "*In support of a free and independent union movement*" and "*Unity based on class struggle.*"[31]

Trondheim is Norway's third largest city and located between the more populated south and the long distances of the high north. By 2010, the Trondheim Conference was well established as an important national union event. People attending the conference came from the private and public sector, and from union federations also outside the LO confederation. Politically their sympathies were split between the Labour Party and the two parties of the Left, the Socialist Left (*Sosialistisk Venstreparti*) and the Red (*Rødt*)—partly founded by AKP in 2007.[32]

The Unions and the European Single Market

Around 1990, the issue of European economic integration was resumed in the political debate and in the labour movement.[33] In 1992, Norway signed the European Area Agreement (*EØS-avtalen*) and became part of the EU single market two years later, whereas the voters in a referendum rejected membership of the European Union in November 1994. The local section of LO in Trondheim and many local unions put forward demands that turned against the free movement of labour of the single market. Some of the local LO sections later became prominent as part of the 'permanent opposition' inside the union federations and the LO confederation. This was especially the case in larger cities like LO in Trondheim and LO in Oslo. Thus, a review of the contemporary history of LO in Oslo shows that the local LO section has been active on several battlegrounds inside the labour movement: on the EU and single market issues, on the demand for regular job contracts, on questions of

[31] Ibid., p. 475.

[32] AKP(m-l) changed its name to AKP in 1990.

[33] Norway voted 'no' to membership in the European Community (EC) by referendum first time in September 1972.

the environment and jobs, and on raising a debate on strategic labour issues.[34]

During Jens Stoltenberg's (the Labour Party) three-party government 2005–13 with the Center Party and the Socialist Left, Norwegian union militants managed to put considerable pressure on the government to limit the impacts of the freedom of movement for goods, services, people, and capital guaranteed by the European Economic Area (EEA) Agreement.[35] After the EU enlargement to include East European members in 2004, and the following influx of cheap labour, the Stoltenberg government had to strengthen labour market regulations to maintain support for the EEA agreement in the labour movement. Gradually, the LO confederation engaged in policies to avoid social dumping and growing income inequality. To a high degree, this engagement was the result of the active resistance against the EEA in many local unions and several of the union federations in LO.[36]

Between 1976 and 2010, the development of European labour unions and a Norwegian local industrial union like *Verkstedklubben Aker Verdal* went in opposite directions. In the mid-1970s, a good guess would be that you could find the highest wages, the strongest unions, and the most elaborated industrial democracy in Europe in West Germany and the most powerful local unions of IG Metall in the car industry surrounding the city of Stuttgart in Baden-Würtemberg.[37] In 2010, very few shop stewards in Norway would look to organized labour in Germany or continental Europa to find inspirations and examples to follow. In certain countries like France, Belgium, and Italy the union movement remained capable of mobilizing massive social protests until the financial crisis 2008–2011. Nevertheless, labour unionism in the EU and Europe

[34] See: Bernhardsen, A. (ed.) (2020) *LO i Oslo 100 år* (Oslo: LO i Oslo).

[35] Ullmann, B. (2020) 'Oslo Samorg/LO i Oslo og EEC-/EF-/EU/EØS-kamp' in Bernhardsen, *LO i Oslo*, pp. 82–91.

[36] In 2012 LO and the two largest union federations *Fagforbundet* and *Fellesforbundet* defied the decision of the Labour Party and the 'red-green' government to adopt the EU temporary agency work directive through the EEA.

[37] For more on the strength of IG Metall and trade unions in Baden-Württemberg, see the description of Lohnramentarifvertrag II of 1973 in Hyman, R. (2001) *Understanding European Trade Unionism. Between Market, Class and Society* (London: Sage Publications), pp. 125–26.

has gradually lost power vis à vis the employers, the state, and political institutions.

In Norway, the labour unions have enjoyed certain structural conditions for opposing neoliberalism and organized capital. The absence of long-term high unemployment since the early 1990s is one key point. Nationwide collective agreements and law regulation have not been rolled back in favor of corporate desire for flexibility and de-regulation. Besides, the fatal lock-out in 1986 was a reminder to organized capital what strength and cohesion unions could mobilize if necessary.

Then, in the decade 2000–2010, the developments of Norwegian and Western European labour relations looked more similar. The opening of the EU and EEA labour market to the new EU member states had considerable effects. The Aker Verdal construction yard, like other companies, hired several hundred East European skilled workers just as wages and work conditions at Aker Verdal and manual workers in the private sector became more dependent on EU legislation such as the service directive and the temporary workers' directive.[38]

The Challengers: A Conclusive Remark

In the post-war era, the economic sphere in Norway has been characterized by a stable system of industrial relations. The main social partners, LO and NHO, and the two dominant political parties, the Labour Party and the conservative *Høyre*, have been the four essential guardians watching over a business model that brings social peace to the world of work and steady amounts of profits and added value to capitalist ownership, and to the petroleum fund of the Norwegian state. Over a period of close to 40 years (1976–2010), there was a high-level consensus on market reforms and ever closer integration with the EU single market between the 'Big Four'.

During these four decades, capitalist restructuring and labour market reforms have certainly changed industrial relations but were also met with strong opposition. Both at the local level, as in the case of labour militancy at the *Verkstedklubben* at Aker Verdal, and at the national level through labour mobilization and campaigning that forged the Trondheim Conference into a prominent arena of working-class politics. On certain

[38] Helle, *Utfordrerne*, pp. 238–39.

occasions, the union militancy and the broader ranges of the labour union movement have been able to defeat one or several of the advocates of market reforms and restructuring. This was the case with the lock-out fiasco in 1986, and to an even greater extent when a majority of the population and the organized working classes defied the leadership of the 'Big Four' and voted 'no' to join the EU in 1994.

Crucial to the maintenance and strength of union militancy was the ability to challenge political and economic power. Again and again, *Verkstedklubben Aker Verdal* challenged the social democratic leadership of the union movement, and the local shop stewards were also willing to go against the management of the Aker corporation if this seemed necessary to secure jobs and the future of the construction yard. At the Trondheim Conference, the local section of LO in Trondheim and a broader network of union activists also acted as challengers, when they spearheaded an alternative agenda for labour issues and union policies, from the second half of the 1980s and the following decades.

References

Bals, J. (2021) *Streik! En historie om strid, samhold og solidaritet* (Oslo: Res Publica).

Bergh, T. (2009) *Kollektiv fornuft. LOs historie, Vol. 3: 1969–2009* (Oslo: Pax Forlag).

Bernhardsen, A. (ed.) (2020) *LO i Oslo 100 år* (Oslo: LO i Oslo).

Bieler, A. and Morton, A. D. (2018) *Global Capitalism, Global War, Global Crisis* (Cambridge: Cambridge University Press).

Brekke, B. (2015) *Tron Øgrim. Det revolusjonære fyrverkeri* (Oslo: Aschehoug).

Furre, B. (1991) *Vårt hundreår. Norsk historie 1905–1990* (Oslo: Det Norske Samlaget).

Hanssen, B.-E. (2021) *Dynamitt i borehullene. Trondheim Faglige Samorganisasjons historie 1870–2020* (Oslo: Pax Forlag).

Helle, I. (2009) *Utfordrerne. Verkstedklubben og arbeiderne på Aker Verdal 1969-2009* (Oslo: Forlaget Manifest).

Helle, I. and Matos, T. (2018) 'Norway 1945–2015: Contention and Democracy', in Mikkelsen, F., Kjeldstadli. K and Nyzell, S. (eds.) *Popular Struggle and Democracy in Scandinavia. 1700–Present* (London: Palgrave Macmillan), pp. 245–75.

Hyman, R. (2001) *Understanding European Trade Unionism. Between Market, Class and Society* (London: Sage Publications).

Kjeldstadli, K. and Helle, I. (2016) 'Social Democracy in Norway' in Schmidt, I. (ed.) *The Three Worlds of Social Democracy. A Global View* (London: Pluto Press), pp. 46–67.

Lie, E. (2012) *Norsk økonomisk politikk etter 1905* (Oslo: Universitetsforlaget).

Nydal, K. (2007) *Sosialmoralsk engasjement og politisk aktivisme. Framveksten av en antirasistisk bevegelse i Norge 1975–1988*, unpublished PhD dissertation, University of Oslo.

Piketty, T. (2019) *Capital et idéologie* (Paris: Éditions du Seuil).

Ryggvik, H. and Smith-Solbakken, M. (1997) *Norsk oljehistorie. Blod, svette og olje* (Oslo: Ad Notam Gyldendal).

Skjeseth, A. (2011) *Sykle på vatnet. Historia om Klassekampen* (Oslo: Samlaget).

Ullmann, B. (2020) 'Oslo Samorg/LO i Oslo og EEC-/EF-/EU/EØS-kamp' in Bernhardsen, A. (ed.) *LO i Oslo 100 år* (Oslo: LO i Oslo), pp. 82–91.

van der Linden, M. (2003) 'The Aftermath of '1968': Interactions of Workers', Youth and Women's Movements' in van der Linden, M. (ed.) *Transnational Labour History. Explorations* (Aldershot: Ashgate Publishing), pp. 117–42.

Vigna, X. (2007) *L'Insubordination ouvrière dans les années 68. Essai d'histoire politique des usines* (Rennes: Presses Universitaires de Rennes).

CHAPTER 12

Reaching Out. Oslo Construction Workers and Migrant Workers, 2004–2014

Knut Kjeldstadli

Insiders facing outsiders, old timers facing newcomers, is a general phenomenon. Trade unions' encounters with new recruits to the working class have taken place since their early days. This article offers an analysis of one such situation—how the construction workers of Oslo, Norway met migrant workers, primarily from around 2004 until today. As the construction industry is the focal point concerning labor migration, this study also offers some general insights.[1]

In 2004 and then again in 2007, the European Union expanded with several new countries in Eastern Europe. Norway is not an EU member but cooperates with EU in European Economic Area (EEA). Thus the

[1] A draft version of this text was original written in 2014 as part of a programme on transnational trade unionism at Centre of Advanced Studies in Oslo. I thank the other members of the team—Andreas Bieler, Roland Erne, Darragh Golden, Idar Helle, Tiago Matos and Sabina Stan.

K. Kjeldstadli (✉)
University of Oslo, Oslo, Norway
e-mail: knut.kjeldstadli@iakh.uio.no

© The Author(s), under exclusive license to Springer Nature Switzerland AG 2023

J. Jørgensen and F. Mikkelsen (eds.), *Trade Union Activism in the Nordic Countries since 1900*, Palgrave Studies in the History of Social Movements, https://doi.org/10.1007/978-3-031-08987-9_12

"four freedoms", including movement of people, have been implemented also in Norway.[2] A transitory system, where the worker had to present a work contract with "Norwegian wages" and full-time employment was a prerequisite for a residence permit of residence, was dismantled in May 2009, for Romania and Bulgaria in 2012. Also, Norway had its share of *Polonia,* the Polish name for those more than two million Poles abroad. The Poles came in great numbers, at the beginning of 2010 registered Polish migrants were 50,000, as compared to 30,000 Swedes or the 17,000 born in Pakistan. From Lithuania came 10,000. In addition, there were Polish workers on a temporary stay, ca. 10,000 in 2010, and an uncertain number of posted workers with Polish firms operating in Norway.[3] The transitory regulations did not affect these workers.

In particular, the Polish men worked in the construction industry. For the labor migrants, the first interest was to accumulate an amount of money in a limited time. Even if they earned less than the Norwegians, the wage was the double of what they earned in Poland.[4] If he intended to stay for a longer period, his interest might change to become like the resident population. Working for low wages and coping under the Norwegian price level proved hard. In some degree, the migrants were able to get into segments of the labor market with secure and well-paid work. Among the Polish construction workers 15% had a permanent job in 2006; in 2010 c. 20%.[5]

For the resident workers, be it Norwegian or former immigrants, labor migrants represented a possible downward pressure on wages and work conditions. "Social dumping" became a well-known phenomenon. The danger of producing an underclass was real. A survey from Oslo 2006

[2] Friberg, J. H. and Tyldum, G. (eds.) (2007) *Polonia i Oslo. En studie av arbeids- og levekår blandt polakker i hovedstadsområdet* (Oslo: Fafo); and Friberg, J. H. (2013) *The Polish Worker in Norway. Emerging Patterns of Migration, Employment and Incorporation after EU's Eastern Enlargement. PhD Dissertation* (Oslo: Fafo).

[3] Friberg, J. H. (2010) 'Working Conditions for Polish Construction Workers and Domestic Cleaners in Oslo: Segmentation, Inclusion and the Role of Policy' in Black, R., Engbersen, G., Okólski, M. and Pantîru, C. (eds.) *A Continent Moving West? EU enlargement and labour migration from Central and Eastern Europe* (Amsterdam: Amsterdam University Press), p. 11.

[4] Friberg and Tyldum, *Polonia i Oslo.*

[5] Friberg, *The Polish worker.*

showed that many worked illegally; on third did not pay taxes neither in Norway, nor in Poland.[6]

The conflicts were sharpened as the tendency went for the "normal worker" or "standard worker" with a permanent employment toward increasing the share of temporarily employed, a category that oscillated due to shifting demand. Some entrepreneurs and some of the big temporary work agencies offered permanent employment and tariff agreement. Several varieties of firms existed. At the other end of the scale, there were bizarre and also criminal firms. Despite of these differences, the "normal" construction worker was on his way to become someone who was not employed in the firm where they actually worked.

Rinus Penninx' and Judith Roosblad's by now classical triad of union dilemmas consist of the stance on immigration, should it be restrictive or more liberal; whether to organize labor migrants in the same union or not; and finally, whether to treat all workers alike, or accept that differential treatment is needed in order to reach a de facto equality.[7]

This article then deals with a local union in Oslo, Norway—the Construction Workers' Union. The building workers offer instructive insights in choices a union has to make. With respect to the three dilemmas, this union accepted migration and immigration as a fact. According to one spokesman (Informant 3) "the task for the unions was to organize those who were here, not decide who ought to be here". Furthermore, they actively chose a positive stance on organizing migrant workers: "We are a union for workers in Norway, not only for Norwegian workers".[8] Having chosen this "open" strategy, they faced the third dilemma, to what extent migrants should be met with special treatment or not. This study offers some insight into a union trying to mobilize immigrants and representing the interests of newcomers. *What did the union do to reach out? How far has it succeed? Is there a conflict between the resources spent on immigrants and the traditional "core tasks" of the union? Does*

[6] Friberg and Tyldum, *Polonia i Oslo.*

[7] Penninx, R. and Roosblad, J. (eds.) (2000) *Trade Unions, Immigration, and Immigrants in Europe 1960–1993. A Comparative Study of the Attitudes and Actions of Trade Unions in Seven West European Countries* (New York: Berghahn Books).

[8] For the learning processes leading to this stance, see: Kjeldstadli, K. (2015) 'A Closed Nation or an Open Working Class? When do Unions Opt for including Labor Migrant?' in Bieler, A. et al. (eds.) *Labour and Transnational Action in Times of Crisis* (London: Rowman & Littlefield).

the general type of political strategy of the union steer its approach toward newcomers?

The approach here is actor orientated, aiming at identifying micro mechanisms. Without understanding the minutiae of quotidian organizing, one does not understand the unions' choice of strategies. The material for this article consists of interviews with Norwegian and some Nordic unionists. This approach may be justly reproached for being union centered; ideally a relational approach also including the experiences of the migrant workers should have been chosen. There is also a possible bias in the material, being produced by people belonging more or less to the same circles; the statements are not really truly independent of one another. Yet this has the benefit of rendering their more or less unanimous version; understanding the "group think", the collective opinion, is an aim.

Types of Unionism, Phases of Mobilization

A common typology in trade union studies distinguish between *business unionism*, *political unionism* bent on cooperation with political parties, governments and authorities and *social* or *social movement unionism*.[9] These distinctions must be understood as prototypical, not as categorical.

Business unionism bets on cooperation with capital and employers, hooking up with the presumably strongest corporations, hoping to be part of a winning team in international competition. This may be a house union, but these have been rare in Norway. Political unionism is bent on cooperation with political parties and governmental authorities, demanding legislation and support to help further their case. The dominant strand in the Norwegian Confederation of Trade Unions (*Landsorganisasjonen i Norge*, LO) may be identified as political unionism, due to LO's long affiliation to primarily the social democratic labor party.

As an ideal type a social movement union shows several characteristics: It understands the world in conflict terms. It is activist. It thinks in lasting strategic alliances. It reaches out to other movements and organizations. It tries to include people who are at the margin of being wage earners, like unemployed or self-employed. It transcends the workplace into the local community. And finally—and most pertinent when it comes to this

[9] Ibid.

union and the migrants—it tries to address the lives of people, at work, but also their lives as dwellers, consumers and sometimes clients. Being backed by the unions helps them to find their way through a convoluted social benefit system.

Each of these prototypical union strategies was based on specific kind of power resource, to use the term of Eric Olin Wright.[10] Business unionism has *structural* power as a premise, i.e., power rising from occupying a certain place on the process of production. Where workers' know-how is necessary, employers are willing to share if the company makes it in the market competition. Political unionism draws on a resource we may call "*alliance* power". Finally social unionism has *associational* power as its base. The Construction Workers' Union had traits from all three types. Yet the practice of the Construction workers' union came closest to the model of social unionism or community unionism.[11]

The union's relations to migrants went through three *phases*—which may be dubbed foothold, breakthrough, and precarious stabilization. The first goal was simply—or not so simple—to make contact and establish a foothold within various nationality groups. The second phase was the breakthrough, when migrants came rapidly and in huge numbers to get help and to unionize. In the third phase, the goal was to stabilize the situation, keep the new recruits in the union, and in a way normalize them as "members", not as "migrants". This process of stabilization was not a once and for all effort. It has had to be repeated over and over, as there has been a huge rotation of members. One possible scenario is a growing fatigue among the unionist, which might lead to a new fourth phase and change of strategy, concentration on "core tasks".

In all three or maybe four phases, obstacles to unionization had to be overcome. Hindrances are often explained by pointing to traits connected to the actors—in this case to the migrants' national cultural background and their experience. Such an approach should not be totally dismissed. Yet this article argues in another direction, by expanding on the theory of the "workers' collective" by Norwegian sociologist Sverre Lysgaard (1961): The pertinent question is the degree of (in)stability and

[10] Wright, E. O. (2000) 'Working-Class Power, Capitalist-Class Interests, and Class Compromise', *American Journal of Sociology*, 105, 4, pp. 957–1002, p. 962.

[11] Waterman, P. (2004) 'Adventures of Emancipatory Labour Strategy as the New Global Movement Challenges International Unionism', *Journal of World-Systems Research*, 10, 1, pp. 217–53.

(un)predictability in the employment relation—a variable dictated by the organization of capital, the kind of firm in case.

Social Unionism—Foothold and Breakthrough

In the initial phase from 2004 onward, several practical measures had to be taken. The union had to make itself accessible. The most important approach was "good, old" agitation, going from one building site to another, trying to get in contact with the workers. Norwegian law gives organization representatives a legal right to enter the sites. Informant 1, from the Plumbers' Union, says that 98% of the site managers have been ok. Organizers are seldom physically hindered doing their job. Yet most have experienced situations where employers or their representatives have threatened to use violence, at the site (Informants 1, 5, 7). They often go to the dwelling barracks, hand out their call cards and encourage workers to call later when they are not at work. Small "clandestine" brochures on rights and wages, on how much people are entitled to, are handed out.

The triggering event for this development was almost accidental. A couple of Poles visited the union's offices. By chance, the Polish wife of the leader of the union at the time was present. She had the necessary qualities. Her presence was a most fortunate fact, "a Godsend", one trade unionist said (Informant 4). She was hired as translator, but came to function also as a broker, bridge builder and translator in the broader cultural sense. She asked the visitors: "Could they find more people to take along for a chat?" The first goal, recruiting 10, 20, 30 as a foothold, was reached. Then these pioneers became gate openers. By and by Polish language was used also in other contexts, in articles in the union's members' magazine and homepage.

After this initial opening, the second phase came like a veritable torrent. The union office held "Polish nights" twice a week with an intense activity. Rooms and corridors were teeming with people. "It was like the medical emergency room on a Friday night" (Informant 5). The union officials helped people to get their rights and to settle disputes with employers. They took on the job as social workers. At one time they handled 200 cases simultaneously, often small but time-consuming cases. In the start they helped with a broad range of problems not pertaining to work, any question the migrant might have: "Where could one buy tram tickets?" "How do I get back my car after it had been towed away because of wrong parking?" The workload was staggering.

By and by the unionists sought to draw the line between cases that were a task for professional social workers and those that were work related. For instance, they did not engage themselves in housing, unless the employer was responsible for quarters. Until 2010 the union organized teaching of Norwegian. This task they finally chose to leave to schools and organizations, as this was resource consuming and somewhat at the margin of classical trade union activities. According to a union officer, Informant 5, the cases they tried to solve comprised wages, vacation money, payment for overtime and workers who were sacked. They also helped and represented migrants vis-a-vis Norwegian authorities—the tax collectors, The Norwegian Directorate of Immigration (*Utlendingsdirektoratet*) and The Norwegian Labour and Welfare Administration (*Arbeids- og velferdsforvaltningen*).

In a way, the union in the years to come de facto became the kind of immigrant center it itself had proposed to LO. The idea was to meet the needs both of labor migrants and people *sans papiers*. The suggestion was backed at the 2013 LO conference but has been implemented rather hesitatingly by the secretariat. The need for information and practical advice, the social unionism dimension should not be underestimated. Yet the trade union officials felt that this was not and should not constitute the bulk of union activity (Informant 7).

According to an organizational worker (Informant 3): "The heart of a trade union is to stay together in a wage struggle". Therefore, the argumentative appeal vis-a-vis migrants changed over time, still within a social unionism horizon. As said, from 2004 to ca. 2009 the unions pursued individual cases also for immigrants who were not members of the union. This was a way to win trust and standing, to obtain an entry into the migrant milieus. There was not full agreement on this; not everybody in the union wanted to be that forthcoming. By and by they changed the message and demanded that migrants had to be or had to be willing to become organized, in order to get assistance. So initially the argument ran: "Join and you shall get help to secure a proper wage", an appeal to the immediate interest of the migrant. Then the argumentative line changed: "It is not the task of the unions to *help* you; the task is to build solidarity". Now the union was presented as an entity also including the migrant, the defense of interests rested on the collective: "Join the union and you are secured an agreement and wage earners' rights".

The union has had reasonable successes in their outreach. Now, reliable data on the level of unionization are few. It is hard to tell how many percent of East European building workers that have been union members. They are a minority. In 2006, 14% of Polish construction workers were unionized, among those working in a Norwegian based temporary work agency 20%. To call this a success rests on the role immigrants have come to play in the union. Estimates of the percentage of Poles as members in the union range from 22 to 40%, the total number of foreigners are said to be 50% (Informants 1, 4, 7).[12]

The transition of the Oslo Construction Workers' Union toward becoming a service center for migrant workers manifested itself in the efforts to use Polish nationals as staff and representatives. The nationwide United Federation of Trade Unions (*Fellesforbundet*) was initially skeptical as to the level of knowledge of unions and the competence of these people but realized that this worked well. After the initial rounds, the union tried to support Polish workers to become local shop stewards and union officials. During a strike in the branch in 2010 Polish workers came to the meetings, participated in the strike committee and in eight agitation "strike teams" that visited building sites to get colleagues to join the strike. In the county of Telemark some, if not very many, immigrants have been union representatives (Informant 8).

Another indicator of success is the number (85%) of Polish work migrants in an opinion poll saying they were content with the efforts of the union.[13] Finally, in an opinion poll in 2006 a clear majority of Polish workers named the union, when asked which Norwegian institution they trusted most.[14]

Stabilization—The Tricky Third Phase

So, from a phase of opening the door there has been a phase with the door wide open. Then came the third phase where the goal was so to speak to keep people indoors, to stabilize, consolidate and normalize the work migrants' relations to the unions. This has proved to be a challenge.

[12] Rodal, A. B. (2013) *Fagforeninger uten grenser—en studie av norske fagforeningers inkludering av utenlandske arbeidstakere i bygingsbransjen*, unpublished master's thesis, University of Bergen, p. 49.

[13] *IMDi-rapport 9-2007: Integreringskart 2007. Arbeidsinnvandring—en kunnskapsstatus* (Oslo: Integrerings—og mangfoldsdirektoratet).

[14] *IMDi-rapport 7-2007. Integreringsbarometeret 2006. Om befolkningens holdninger til integrerings—og mangfoldsspørgsmål* (Oslo: Integrerings—og mangfoldsdirektoratet).

First there is the problem of mobility, the cross draught among members. Some, Norwegians as well as Poles, have gone "the full round": From being ignorant about the union, to see it as an office for social welfare services to becoming a member and then to quit. To unionize, people is costly in terms of manpower, time and money. Therefore, one cannot recruit people only on the basis of a limited personal case, if this means they are leaving after the case is solved. From 2013 the union demanded membership before they took on individual cases for securing what was due to a person (Informant 4).

There have been difficulties simply in collecting the membership fees. Some members have disappeared, probably to the home country. Some have entered the black market. Some have changed their addresses without telling the union office. Some have been "secret" members collecting their mail at the union office. In rare cases, one has accepted that members have not paid the fees; but such a practice could easily spread to too many cases and be hard to overcome.

The second hindrance against leaving the "emergency aid" stage was the costs involved in solving the cases. "We worked our asses off", an organizer commented (Informant 5). So, there was a persistent dilemma on how much time and energy they could put in working with the "weak", "peripheral" sections of the work force; it was necessary to keep on to the "core", the "strong" workers (Informant 1). So far, the unions have kept to the concept of core tasks, defined as cartel for sellers of the commodity of labor power. So far, an idea about community unionism has not emerged to the extent that they have redefined what is the core.

A third problem in what they hoped to be a phase of consolidation has been a lack of union training among the bulk of the migrants. There was a need for a basic education on the unions. Efforts have been made, but it has been difficult to get into a more permanent mode. So, the union is still striving to establish itself in a stabilized field. Informant 7:

> The last couple of years a certain tiredness has developed in the unions, after the enthusiasm in the first phase. The transition to a stabilized period took place too seldom. The organization "burned cadres like coal", both the office workers and the organizers on the construction sites. One had to put a lot of strength into this to make its succeed. Sometimes the right

person was present in the right situation, but then it could fray, also in firms one imagined to be stable, such as Adecco or Jobzone.[15]

As stated, there was a tension between spending resources on temporary workers, often hard to reach and other tasks of the union. The union not only had to link to Polish members; it was necessary also to anchor this policy among Norwegian members. Semi-racist comments may be heard.[16] Yet, the unionists adamantly claim that protests against the general line and against the resources spent on immigrants have been few. Any vicious xenophobia has not surfaced. Although many members probably have voted for the right populist Party of Progress, they either did not bother or saw the necessity also in order to secure their own position in the labor market. No conflict episodes such as in Denmark and England have appeared (Informant 3). Trade unionists have claimed that derogatory statements about Poles are fewer among trade unionized workers. Although the evidence is somewhat anecdotal, it seems that unions function as a "political workshop" and a guardian (Informant 7),

So, there were interwoven learning processes—among the union leadership, among the migrants and finally among Norwegian rank and file union members.

Political Unionism—Collaborating with the State Authorities

The Norwegian authorities have represented both an ally, and opponent and a problematic cooperation partner. The unions have asked for and to a high degree also obtained various measures against social dumping. The red-green alliance in government, dominated by the Social Democrats (2005 to 2013) did deliver in these matters. It promoted three action plans, escalating from 2006 to 2008 and 2013. Each one came as a result of learning that the previous measures were too timid. The significance of a government that has been basically positive to these union demands should be underlined.

[15] Big temporary work agencies, where unionization came early.

[16] Stang, G. C. (2008) *Kortvarig ansettelse—langvarig læring? En studie av sammenhengen mellom arbeidsinnvandring, organisasjonsendring og læring i to utvalgte entreprenørbedrifter*, unpublished master's thesis University of Oslo, p. 13.

In other matters, such as the implementation of the EU Service Directive and the Directive on Temporary Work Agencies from 2008, the Red-Green government went against union wishes, triggering a series of demonstrations against the government in 2011–2013. So, the positive assessment of how politicians have catered to union needs is not unison. Some say politicians have not looked seriously into tenders, meaning that price is prioritized, while competence and quality are overlooked: "Politicians have done nil; they have not been engaged in the issue". Some even suggest a best buddy corruption is involved (Informant 8).

Relations to various authorities have been necessary—to the tax collectors' office, to the Norwegian Labour and Welfare Administration, Labour Inspection Authority (*Arbeidstilsynet*) and Norwegian Directorate of Immigration. Partly they pursued individual cases, as mentioned. Partly they had to rely on authorities when they came across cases of abuse of workers. And the unions have asked for an increase in staff, for instance, at the Labour Inspection Authority.

There is a dilemma involved: On the one side, the unions had to cooperate with the authorities. On the other hand, they have not seen themselves as "a reserve police for foreign labor power" (Informant 2) or as "the prolonged control apparatus of the state", which enforced rules that might lead to workers being sent out of the country (Informants 2 and 6). They focused on contact, not on control. The unionists did not want to be part of scenes such as this:

In the end of August 2006, 38 building workers employed in Baltic Construction Service were thrown out of the construction site by a police force of 17. They were ransacked, tested for alcohol and driven to Oslo in a bus with police escort and let out at the Estonian embassy. They went outdoors in Oslo one night, some of them two nights, without food or money, before they got home.[17]

One should not send a man out of the country simply because he is poor, they argued. A man should be able to come with one problem without being reported and turned in for another matter. Not only was this morally wrong and against class solidarity, but it also destroyed the trust they needed to reach out to migrants.

[17] Skjærvø, K. (2008) *Byggenæringa må ta ansvar—solidaransvar. Hvitbok om solidaransvar for lønn i byggenæringa* (Oslo: Oslofjordkonferansen).

Business Unionism—Collaborating with Factions of Capital

Pursuing a strategy of social or political unionism does not preclude elements of business unionism. The premise is that employers do not form a homogenous and unified bloc. What is rational for capital particularly in a longer time span, may go against the immediate interests of factions and individual firms. There have not been identical positions between the Federation of Norwegian Construction Industries (*Byggenæringens Landsforbund*, BNL), and the member firms; for instance, when it comes to training of apprentices. There have also been tensions between the big entrepreneurs and master craftsmen, for instance, on the issue of joint responsibilities. Likewise, BNL and Confederation of Norwegian Enterprise (*Næringslivets Hovedorganisasjon*, NHO) have disagreed on the use of the *ergo omnes* clause, and the Service Directive. BNL wants a clause to protect the use of skilled workers, while NHO is against as it is seen as breech of EU directive.

These inner divisions of capital have led the union to side with some factions. The union has taken a kind of "total capital" perspective—what is best for the totality in the longer run. They have chosen a de facto class cooperation with the "serious" firms as opposed to the "unserious" (Informant 8). One may also say that they side with "productive" capital as opposed to financial or speculative capital and claiming to represent a greater rationality than the firms.

Contained in this approach a set of arguments have been developed. Along with a class point of view, the unionists have framed issues within a kind of "productivism", a "unions' production ideology": A construction site is "one big central of communication" (Informant 7). At a construction site, many trades and work groups must be coordinated, to make a working production plan. There is also the building contractor, the architect and project planners. Effective communication, coordination involved contact with all involved groups and good logistics. The old hands in the branch knew how to fit these factors together, without too much control from above. Now, according to Informant 7: "Norwegian entrepreneurs no longer have a distinct production model". There is an NHO ideology about concentration on core tasks; leading to fewer employed and more workers outsourced, a small core and a growing periphery in the work force. As the number of permanently employed are drastically reduced, one cannot any more rely on their knowledge. There is a real problem with orders being transmitted and understood. The firms are left with a coordination problem and rising transaction costs.

Added to this is a more radical specialization. Before one reckoned that a carpenter journeyman knew enough to put up a villa. Now the division of labor has gone much farther. One worker knows how to make the fundament; another how to lay roof tiles, etc.—exacerbating the coordination problem.

There is a notion about Norwegian workers being independent in the daily work; they did not need to be told how to perform a task. Skilled Norwegian work teams traditionally had an inherent motive power, they were "self-propelling". The entrepreneur did not need to control. The unionists see this as a contrast to the new migrants and claim: "New workers had another work culture, used to being led. If they were told to work from A to B, they stop at B, whereas Norwegians would ask what C is and go on" (Informant 6 and 8). According to a Polish HR-leader in Adecco Norway, asking questions is a signal that you do not trust the leader. There has existed a notion about a Polish culture subservient and instilled on hard work without questions. But as pointed out by sociologist Jon Horgen Friberg, this submissive attitude was not cultural, but social, due more to a weak bargaining position and fear of losing the job.[18]

The notion about a less productive work culture among immigrants may remind of biased, even racist notions about the low ability and productivity of foreign workers.[19] Yet this is not a fair characteristic of the union point of view; differences are not seen as inherent, but as shaped by circumstances.

Into this insistence on skill, etc., is also woven an argument against low wages. These are criticized not only from the point of view of wage earners' class interest, but also from the "unionist total capital rationality": Low wages meant a weaker inducement to technological innovation. The wages have been so low in the construction sector that a movement toward more primitive techniques and lower productivity has taken place.

[18] Friberg, J. H. (2012) 'Culture at Work: Polish Migrants in the Ethnic Division of Labour on Norwegian Construction Sites', *Ethnic and Racial Studies*, 35, 11.

[19] Kay, T. (2014) 'Economic Interests Versus Organizational Culture: Explaining Variation in the Emergence in Labor Transnationalism'. Paper presented at workshop "Labour and Transnational Action in Times of Crisis: From Case Studies to Theory", 27–28 February 2014, Centre for Advanced Study, Oslo.

Workers have had to carry drywalls up several stories instead of using cranes. Spades and picks were being used instead of excavators to dig out sites. While the firms had been accustomed to buy premade concrete, several had resorted to mix cement at the construction site.

These trends also led to destruction of the institution of apprenticeship, causing a general lack of skilled workers. Here, the contradiction between the single firms and the branch as a whole is evident. Some firms think employing apprentices weaken their competitive position, as apprentices are not fully productive in their first years. Some undergo drastic oscillations in the work force, making it easier to hire workers temporarily than to take on apprentices (Informant 1). Among those coming from abroad many lack certificate of completion. Or even, if they are highly competent in their own trade the skills differ from those in demand in Norway. BNL has wanted to train foreign workers to obtain the formal and real skills. The member firms have not been interested. The unions worry that taking on migrant workers may bare the access for local apprentices.

According to Informant 6 employers have no general perspective; they think too much in single projects. Therefore, it has been difficult to implement a policy for language training and development of competence of workers, etc. And thus, the branch of construction undermines itself. Informant 5 comments: "The reorganization was said to lead to a hyper-productive business, while it really led to degeneration and decline".

The "productivist" demands of the unions are: "serious" firms—documented, for instance, by certified accountants, management with real and formally documented competence, permanent employment of huge proportion of work force, more skilled workers and an active program for apprentices. In addition, they want tariff agreements, and regional safety representatives, aimed particularly at conditions in small and medium, sized firms.[20]

Although BNL shares many of these analyses, so far, the union have not been able to change the practice of the builders in any great degree.

[20] *Fagbladet. Fellesforbundet Telemark*, 1, 2011.

Challenges to Unionization: Nationality or Instability and Unpredictability?

So far, we have concentrated on factors leading to the open union-stance, and also to its relative success. There were also factors pulling in another direction.

Direct threats and violence were seldom directed against union officers. But in some degree—not verified how much—threats did play a role in internal disciplining in nationality groups. Still there is reason to believe that these obstacles so far have only played a role in some segments of the labor market.

Nationality was relevant in the sense that previous experience with unions differed. Cultures, history and collective experience did play a role, and according to the Norwegian unionists there were significant differences due to national background.

The Poles—or their parents—had some experience from *Solidarność*, although this was conceived more as a political association than a trade union. Still, they interpreted the situation through other lenses than the Norwegians. As an example: There were some episodes in one big entrepreneurial firm, where workers had been deducted too much in income tax. The union wanted to get this right by contacting the tax collectors' office, but the Poles saw no point in this as "everybody knows that you never get anything back from the state". Many saw the unions more or less a branch of the authorities. Or they suspected unionists to be Mafiosi—simply because they were seen talking to employers (Informant 8).

Thus, Poles could work against union policies. For instance, it was claimed that Poles operated with several agreements on wages—one version was shown to the authorities, another was the real one, to be used when they were paid in Poland. However, when the initial break-through for unionization finally came, in the multinational Adecco, they came "in torrents", as "fire in dry grass".

Balts proved harder to organize; the first heat came in 2005, and the necessary agitation work was slow and difficult. The Norwegians thought Balts had no idea about a union. They had a general anti-collectivist, individualist attitude, thinking "that you are strong by standing alone" (Informant 3). They quoted one Balt: "In 1991 we stood together [i.e., making a human chain as part of the revolution]. Today, we stand apart". According to Informant 7 "the reason is that they have lost both during state socialism and during market liberalism. They have gone from not having responsibility for themselves to only being occupied with themselves". Every second Latvian and Lithuanian wants to establish themselves as small independent business owners, the Norwegians claim (Informants 4, 5, 7). Many still see the unions as either an organ of the company, a lawyer's office or a part of the authorities, the police and the tax collectors. In addition, Baltic employers hostile to unions had a grip on their workers. Yet Lithuanians have come to the union, after the first serious effort to organize in 2007; they have come to see that the union solves cases.

Relatively recently Kosovars have come, establishing themselves in the painting segment. Not being an EU member, many have been brought on the so-called specialist quota. According to Norwegian unionists Kosovars are clannish, not only in a metaphorical way, but as part of a clan society with proper Mafia.[21] To some extent Kosovars hire workers from other nationalities such as Rumanians, who often were paid in cash in small sums, with no papers and no way to control actual wages. They are afraid of their own leaders, gang bosses and spies for the firm in the barracks and are notoriously difficult to reach out to.

Now, although such images may be strongly colored by prejudices or generalizations, there may be a core of truth in these national stereotypes. This is simply based on the assumption that people are affected by and learn from their environment, and that differences in historical trajectories are real. Individuals coming from non-unionized circles are less liable to join than those who learnt about unions with their "mother's milk". The effect on previous experience is corroborated by examples from the organizing among the first generation of East European workers in US in the early twentieth century.[22]

Nationality, language, etc., also created everyday obstacles to forming one unified workers' collective. There have been tendencies toward ethnic or national niches within the industry. The nationality of owners and workers have changed from one sub-branch to another. Among painters are many Albanians and Kosovars. Masons, tilers and also steel fixers are

[21] The newspaper *Aftenposten* in 2014 ran a series of articles documenting work life criminality. Kosovars were not the only group; also, Norwegians and other nationalities were involved.

[22] Milkman, R. (ed.) (2000) *Organizing Immigrants. The Challenge for Unions in Contemporary California* (Ithaca: Cornell University Press), p. 4.

Polish. Balts are active in construction with concrete. Plumbers mostly work in Norwegian firms (Informant 1). Firms organized work teams according to nationality, maybe with one Norwegian speaking crew boss. And when they do work at the same workplace, workers sat in national groups during lunch breaks.[23]

Yet immigrant workers did participate. In his classic on "the workers' collective" Norwegian sociologist Sverre Lysgaard states that three conditions must be met in order to form a collective among subaltern workers: A similarity between workers produces common interests and makes it possible to identify with one another. A spatial proximity allows them to transact with one another and realize these interests. And finally, they must have a common problem interpretation, a shared subjective understanding that work is laden with problems. Workplace organization along national lines was a challenge both to identification, interaction and a common problem definition. However, the experiences from the building scene point to another explanatory factor that seems to trump nationality—namely the kind of employment relationship. Also, migrants learn. When people stay on, as has been the case with many Poles, they gradually adopt the prevalent attitudes in the new environment. Polish workers who have been in Norway for a while and who intend to stay on, change their orientation. Instead of working very hard in intense periods they "ration" their work power. Instead of wanting to go home to the family, they bring their family to Norway. This adds to stability.[24] And being stable and having a longer time horizon the rationality changes: Union come to be seen as guarantees of security. Those with a permanent position in a firm most are open to unionization; the temporarily employed are hard to reach (Informant 5).

So, in addition to Lysgaard's conditions we should add a fourth condition, a minimum of stability over time.[25] Stability or fluency may be guided by workers' own preferences, but more so by the hiring policy of capital, of the firm in case. Migrant workers employed at a Norwegian entrepreneur differed from temporary agency workers or posted workers.

[23] Stang, *Kortvarig ansettelse*, p. 100.

[24] In 2008 60% of Polish work migrants imagined that they would be living in Norway in five years (*IMDi-rapport 1-2008: Vi blir... Om arbeidsinnvandring fra Polen og Baltikum* (Oslo: Integrerings—og mangfoldsdirektoratet)).

[25] Kjeldstadli, K. (1989) *Jerntid. Fabrikksystem og arbeidere ved Christiania Spigerverk fra om lag 1890 to 1940* (Oslo: Pax forlag), p. 104.

This crucial importance of the employment relationship should be heavily emphasized. This includes the length of stay in the country, the length of the employment period and the time perspective—immediate or farther into the future. For the worker predictability matters.

Now, the most important force steering the employment relationship is the way capital has chosen to organize, both judicially and practically. The kind of working class and the kind of workers' response to their situation are governed by their opponent. The organizational forms of capital have a strong impact on the composition of working class. Although workers *do* have agency, their actions tend to be more reactive than pro-active vis-à-vis capital. An effort to understand workers' and unions' rationality should therefore include a grip on the organization of the capitalist firm. The differentiating and decisive dimensions may be dichotomized as shown in Table 12.1.

Such characteristics should be seen as extremes on a scale, as prototypes more than definite categories. The variables listed vertically may be linked, but not necessarily so. For instance, big temporary work agencies have opted for having their own permanent staff and agreed to tariff agreements. "Permanent" is maybe an embellishing term; although workers are employed in a work agency this is not obliged to secure them employment, and they are not paid while waiting for a job. In 2011 and 2012, 50% of the workers were hired, 25% were employed by the main contractor and 25% with subcontractors (Informant 4).

Competitive pressure may blur the dividing line between "serious" and other behavior. Yet, there are real, not only ideological-rhetorical

Table 12.1 Characteristics of the capitalist firm

Entrepreneurs, builder	*Temporary work agencies*
Production, selling products	Finance, selling labour
Main contractor	Subcontractor
Big size	Medium, small
Financially sound	Marginal
Bureaucratic, professional	Personal, "rough" leadership
"Serious"	"Unserious", bordering on criminal
Effects for workers:	
Permanent employment	Temporary
Security	Insecurity

differences. In the years after 2004, there were hundreds of temporary work agencies, much too many and much too unserious. Existing firms in other branches changed into this field, so there were businesses which dealt in "import of horse semen, mobile games and hiring labor power" or "espresso machines, accounting and hiring workers" (Informant 5). There was a firm dedicated to "coastal and ocean fisheries" operating as a builder in the county of Telemark in the south. Another entrepreneur was called "Writing itch", a third offered psychiatric services (Informant 8). According to one union official "everyone" ran such agencies, the firms found Poles, hired them to employers and dumped the wages. Most of the bizarre firms disappeared in the financial crisis from 2008.

How may we summarize the impact of type of capital on workers' class formation? Now, the first alternative of the two mentioned in the dichotomies above—considerable size, stability, permanent employment, bureaucratic administration, productive capital, entrepreneur orientation, economic surplus, good profits, seriousness and orderliness—usually dispose for a long-time perspective for immigrant workers. Hence, they increase the probability for forming collectives and for formal unionizing. These dimensions may be summarized under the caption "Fordism".

A post-Fordist regime has dissolved these traits making for stability. Disappearance of regulation leaves temporarily employed wage earners more vulnerable. Raising issues may mean that they risk not getting more jobs. "People get so damned cowed. It is a bloody unhealthy system". The insecurity has created "scared workers" (Informants 5, 7). There has also been a global competitive pressure to cut costs, for instance, by greater "flexibility" with the number of employees fluctuating according to company needs. Beverly Silver writes: As a result of these transformations, once-stable working classes have been replaced by "networks of temporary and cursory relationships with subcontractors and temporary help agencies". The result is a structurally disaggregated and disorganized working class prone more to a "politics of resentment" than to "traditional working-class unions and leftist politics".[26]

[26] Silver, B. J. (2003) *Forces of Labor. Workers' Movements and Globalization since 1870* (Cambridge: Cambridge University Press), p. 5, quoting: Jenkins, J. C. and Leicht, K. (1997) 'Class Analysis and Social Movements: A Critique and Reformulation' in Hall, J. R. (ed.) *Reworking Class* (Ithaca: Cornell University Press), pp. 369–97.

What's at Stake?

Union organizer (Informant 5) comments:

> The future may be difficult. Each year people say, "it can't get worse." Nothing points towards improvements. Criminality, trafficking, more workers outside the well-ordered work life. All this is on the way now.

It is obvious that there is a lot at stake in this situation—the issue is whether organized labor can exert power over work life in the future. The ability of the Construction Workers' Union to influence the development of the construction business may be seen as test case. On one hand, this union is exemplary and probably one of the best placed to keep on organizing newcomers—while the industry is highly instructive with regard to hindrances. The battle is a possible forerunner. The outcome may play a role—within Norway and also to the development for building workers in northern Europe. If this union does not make it, several that are worse situated, may also fail.

The challenges are obvious. A "disaggregated and disorganized" (Silver) class means erosion of conditions for developing informal collectives (Lysgaard) and unions. Still the situation is open ended—it is not given which kind of unionism shall prevail.

Choosing the *political* strategy means that the unions will have access to what we have called an "alliance power resource". In exchange for delivering union members' votes, a party pays back by backing the demands of unions. Coming to the *business* unionism the building workers still have their structural power resource (Olin Wright), based on the entrepreneurs' dependency on the workers' knowledge of production. This is depending on the employers' choices. If these do not follow the proclaimed policy of BNL, the classical building workers' skill may be devalued to naught. And erosion of structural power shall by and by threaten associational power.

Associational power (Olin Wright) is an important component in any social movement unionism. So far, the Oslo Construction Workers' Union has considerable clout. As we have seen there is a feeling that resources are being spent for organizing migrants, perhaps to excess. But the tasks connected to labor migrants shall not disappear in any foreseeable future. And if they are not met, unions shall lose their basis. So maybe there are two alternatives: Union breakdown or taking on the challenges of the long march of unionization. In the words of an organizer among the US United Brotherhood of Carpenters, facing a similar choice:

> Immigrants are positive and negative for unions [...] But if we keep them out, like the union has been doing, they become a double negative [...] If we go after them, it can revitalize us [...] give us purpose.[27]

References

Archives

Private archive of Knut Kjeldstadli, Interviews 2012:
Informant 1: Boye Ullmann
Informant 2: Roy Pedersen
Informant 3: Kjell Skjærvø
Informant 4: Petter Vellesen
Informant 5: Odd Magnar Solbakken
Informant 6: Steinar Krogstad
Informant 7: Jonas Bals
Informant 8: Arne Hagen

Serials

Fagbladet. Fellesforbundet Telemark

Reference Literature

Friberg, J. H. & Tyldum, G. (Eds.). (2007) *Polonia i Oslo. En studie av arbeids— og levekår blandt polakker i hovedstadsområdet*. Fafo.

Friberg, J. H. (2010) 'Working Conditions for Polish Construction Workers and Domestic Cleaners in Oslo: Segmentation, Inclusion and the Role of Policy' in Black, R., Engbersen, G., Okólski, M. and Pantîru, C. (eds.) *A Continent Moving West? EU Enlargement and Labour Migration from Central and Eastern Europe* (Amsterdam: Amsterdam University Press).

[27] Nissen, B. and Grenier, G. (2001) 'Union Responses to Mass Immigration: The Case of Miami, USA' in Waterman, P. and Wills, J. (eds.) *Place, Space and the New Labour Internationalisms* (Oxford: Blackwell), p. 275.

Friberg, J. H. (2012) Culture at Work: Polish Migrants in the Ethnic Division of Labour on Norwegian Construction Sites. *Ethnic and Racial Studies, 35*, 11.

Friberg, J. H. (2013) *The Polish Worker in Norway. Emerging Patterns of Migration, Employment and Incorporation after EU's Eastern Enlargement. PhD Dissertation*. Fafo.

IMDi-rapport 7–2007. Integreringsbarometeret. (2006) *Om befolkningens holdninger til integrerings—og mangfoldsspørgsmål*. Integrerings—og mangfoldsdirektoratet.

IMDi-rapport 9–2007: Integreringskart. (2007) *Arbeidsinnvandring—en kunnskapsstatus*. Integrerings—og mangfoldsdirektoratet.

IMDi-rapport 1–2008: Vi blir... Om arbeidsinnvandring fra Polen og Baltikum (Oslo: Integrerings—og mangfoldsdirektoratet).

Jenkins, J. C. & Leicht, K. (1997) Class Analysis and Social Movements: A Critique and Reformulation. In J. R. Hall (Ed.), *Reworking Class* (pp. 369–397). Cornell University Press.

Kay, T. (2014) 'Economic Interests Versus Organizational Culture: Explaining Variation in the Emergence in Labor Transnationalism'. Paper presented at workshop "Labour and Transnational Action in Times of Crisis: From Case Studies to Theory", 27–28 February 2014, Centre for Advanced Study, Oslo.

Kjeldstadli, K. (1989) *Jerntid. Fabrikksystem og arbeidere ved Christiania Spigerverk fra om lag 1890 to 1940*. Pax forlag.

Kjeldstadli, K. (2015) 'A Closed Nation or an Open Working Class? When do Unions Opt for including Labor Migrant?' in Bieler, A. et al. (eds.) *Labour and Transnational Action in Times of Crisis* (London: Rowman & Littlefield).

Lysgaard, S. (1961) *Arbeiderkollektivet. En studie i de underordnedes sosiologi*. Universitetsforlaget.

Milkman, R. (Ed.). (2000) *Organizing Immigrants. The Challenge for Unions in Contemporary California*. Cornell University Press.

Nissen, B. & Grenier, G. (2001) 'Union Responses to Mass Immigration: The Case of Miami, USA' in Waterman, P. and Wills, J. (eds.) *Place, Space and the New Labour Internationalisms* (Oxford: Blackwell).

Penninx, R. & Roosblad, J. (Eds.). (2000) *Trade Unions, Immigration, and Immigrants in Europe 1960–1993. A Comparative Study of the Attitudes and Actions of Trade Unions in Seven West European Countries*. Berghahn Books.

Rodal, A. B. (2013) *Fagforeninger uten grenser—en studie av norske fagforeningers inkludering av utenlandske arbeidstakere i bygingsbransjen*, unpublished master's thesis, University of Bergen.

Silver, B. J. (2003) *Forces of Labor. Workers' Movements and Globalization since 1870*. Cambridge University Press.

Skjærvø, K. (2008) *Byggenæringa må ta ansvar—solidaransvar. Hvitbok om solidaransvar for lønn i byggenæringa*. Oslofjordkonferansen.

Stang, G. C. (2008) *Kortvarig ansettelsese—langvarig læring? En studie av sammenhengen mellom arbeidsinnvandring, organisasjonsendring og læring i to utvalgte entrprenørbedrifter*, unpublished master's thesis University of Oslo.

Waterman, P. (2004) Adventures of Emancipatory Labour Strategy as the New Global Movement Challenges International Unionism. *Journal of World-Systems Research, 10*(1), 217–253.

Wright, E. O. (2000) Working-Class Power, Capitalist-Class Interests, and Class Compromise. *American Journal of Sociology, 105*(4), 957–1002.

CHAPTER 13

Trade Unions' Protest Cycles in Sweden, 1980–2020

Jenny Jansson and Katrin Uba

Much has been written about the Swedish trade union movement and the corporatist system during the "golden age" of social democracy.[1] During the post-war period, Swedish industrial relations were predominantly described as peaceful. However, starting in the 1970s, industrial relations became more conflict-prone in Sweden. The subsequent decades featured many industrial actions, mostly strikes and lockouts and several

[1] Öberg, P. (1994) *Särintresse och allmäninteresse: Korporatismens ansikte* (Uppsala: Acta Universitatis Upsaliensis); Öberg, P., Svensson, T., Christiansen, P. M., Nørgaard, A. S., Rommetvedt, H. and Thesen, G. (2011) 'Disrupted Exchange and Declining Corporatism: Government Authority and Interest Group Capability in Scandinavia', *Government and Opposition*, 46, 3, pp. 365–91; and Rothstein, B. (1992) *Den korporativa staten* (Stockholm: Nordstedts).

J. Jansson (✉) · K. Uba
Uppsala University, Uppsala, Sweden
e-mail: jenny.jansson@statsvet.uu.se

K. Uba
e-mail: katrin.uba@statsvet.uu.se

© The Author(s), under exclusive license to Springer Nature Switzerland AG 2023

J. Jørgensen and F. Mikkelsen (eds.), *Trade Union Activism in the Nordic Countries since 1900*, Palgrave Studies in the History of Social Movements, https://doi.org/10.1007/978-3-031-08987-9_13

reorganizations of the wage-bargaining system. After the mid-1990s, the "peacefulness" returned, and work stoppages became rare in Sweden.[2] These changes are not unique to Sweden or the Nordic countries: strikes and lockouts have decreased across Europe.

However, strikes are only one form of protest that unions can use to mobilize their members, affect politics and engage in public debate. Trade unions' various protest activities have been of great interest to researchers. Concerned about the unions' loss of influence, John Kelly suggested in his seminal work from 1998 that trade unions needed to learn from and increase their cooperation with social movements to revitalize themselves.[3] Although prior research has demonstrated that unions engage in various forms of protests and learn from other social movements,[4] the literature lacks a systematic investigation of unions' broader protest repertoire. Instead, emerging literature often covers a short time period or a specific trade union. For instance, studies have reported on diverse protests taking place during the living-wage campaigns in the UK, of union mobilizations on social media and of various protest strategies occurring during the recent economic crisis.[5] Symbolic actions such as May Day demonstrations have also been examined.[6] Still, in the light

[2] Thörnqvist, C. (1994) *Arbetarna lämnar fabrikken: Strejkrörelser i Sverige under efterkrigstiden, deras bakgrund, förlopp och följder* (Gothenburg: Historiska institutionen). Thörnqvist, C. (2007) 'From Blue-Collar Wildcats in the 1970s to Public Sector Resistance at the Turn of a new Millennium' in van der Velden, S., Dribbusch, H., Lyddon, D. and Vandaele, K. (eds.) *Strikes Around the world, 1968–2005. Case-Studies of 15 Countries* (Amsterdam: Aksant), pp. 321–38.

[3] Kelly, J. E. (1998) *Rethinking Industrial Relations: Mobilization, Collectivism and Long Waves* (New York: Routledge).

[4] Tarrow, S. (1993) 'Cycles of Collective Action: Between Moments of Madness and the Repertoire of Contention', *Social Science History*, 17, 2, pp. 281–307.

[5] Psimitis, M. (2011) 'The Protest Cycle of Spring 2010 in Greece', *Social Movement Studies*, 10, 2, pp. 191–97; Peterson, A., Wahlström, M. and Wennerhag, M. (2015) 'European Anti-Austerity Protests—Beyond "Old" and "New" Social Movements?', *Acta Sociologica*, 58, 4, pp. 293–310; Rüdig, W. and Karyotis, G. (2013) 'Who Protests in Greece? Mass Opposition to Austerity', *British Journal of Political Science*, 44, 3, pp. 487–513; and Peterson, A., Thörn, H. and Wahlström, M. (2018) 'Sweden 1950–2015: Contentious Politics and Social Movements Between Confrontation and Conditioned Cooperation' in Mikkelsen, F., Kjeldstadli, K. and Nyzell, S. (eds.) *Popular Struggle and Democracy in Scandinavia, 1700–Present* (London: Palgrave Macmillan), pp. 377–432.

[6] Peterson, A., Wahlström, M., Wennerhag, M., Christancho, C. and Sabucedo, M. (2012) 'May Day Demonstrations in Five European Countries', *Mobilisation: An International Quarterly*, 17, 3, pp. 281–300.

of globally declining strike levels, it is necessary to ask whether other forms of protests are also deteriorating, or whether these other forms are actually replacing the strikes. Scholars studying industrial conflicts in Canada, the US and the UK have suggested that, when one form of contentious action (e.g., strikes) decreases, other protest activities (e.g., go slow, demonstrations or petitioning) may increase.[7] In other words, a *displacement process takes place*. This chapter investigates whether and how this displacement process functions in Sweden by analyzing the Swedish trade unions' protest repertoire from 1980 to 2020. This period was chosen for two reasons: first, it covers essential changes in Swedish industrial relations; and second, detailed protest event data is available from 1980 to 2020. A long-term perspective makes it possible to study how trade unions react to changing political and economic contexts and how they adapt their protest repertoire accordingly. Hence, our analysis will cover the changed opportunity structures for strikes and explore whether decreasing strikes have impacted the innovation of the Swedish trade unions' protest repertoire.

This chapter is structured as follows: we start by presenting our theoretical framework for examining labor protests and by providing details about the material used in the empirical analysis. Next, we provide an overview of the changing industrial regime in Sweden from 1980 to 2020 and describe the decreasing strike levels. We then describe the trade unions' protest cycles and examine whether displacement has taken place—first by analyzing protest frequency over time and then by discussing the claims made by unions while protesting.

Theoretical Framework and Description of the Data

Determining why work stoppages occur has been a common research topic among industrial relation scholars. According to historians and sociologists, the likelihood of industrial actions taking place is related to the relative balance of power resources between the labor market parties, where power resources are usually defined as union density, access to the

[7] Kelly, J. (2015) 'Conflict: Trends and Forms of Collective Action', *Employee Relations*, 37, 6, pp. 720–32.

government and access to financial means (i.e., strike funds).[8] Scholars seeking economic explanations of industrial action, on the other hand, have looked into structural conditions, highlighting how work stoppages relate to the business cycle and arguing that economic prosperity tends to increase the number of conflicts.[9] Judging from these studies, the globalization of the economy and the weakening of organized labor (in terms of both union density and the propensity for labor parties to win elections) have changed the opportunity structures for unions to use strikes. However, even if strike opportunities have changed, the conflict between employers and unions has not disappeared. Instead, we suggest that this conflict is likely to be expressed through new collective or individual forms of protest.[10]

Changing protest repertoires are often linked to changes in the opportunity structures for using certain protest forms. Most social movement scholars argue that movements use different protest activities simultaneously, while also learning from each other and responding to shifting political opportunity structures (POS).[11] Alterations in POS or institutional rules of the game change the power discrepancies between involved parties—including the state, trade unions and employers—and thereby change the perceived costs and expected outcomes of collective action. When strikes become "routinised" and ineffective for achieving

[8] Gall, G. and Hebdon, R. (2008) 'Conflict at Work' in Blyton, P., Bacon, N., Fiorito, J. and Heery, E. (eds.) *The SAGE Handbook of Industrial Relations* (London: Sage), pp. 588–605; Shorter, E. and Tilly, C. (1974) *Strikes in France, 1830–1968* (London: Cambridge University Press); van der Velden, S., Dribbusch, H., Lyddon, D. and Vandaele, K. (eds.) (2007) *Strikes Around the World, 1968–2005. Case-Studies of 15 Countries* (Amsterdam: Aksant); and Molinder, J., Karlsson, T. and Enflo, K. (2022) 'Social Democracy and the Decline of Strikes', *Explorations in Economic History*, 83, 101420.

[9] Franzosi, R. (1989) 'One Hundred Years of Strike Statistics: Methodological and Theoretical Issues in Quantitative Strike Research', *ILR Review*, 42, 3, pp. 348–62.

[10] Sapsford, D. and Turnbull, P. (1994) 'Strikes and Industrial Conflict in Britain's Docks: Balloons or Icebergs?', *Oxford Bulletin of Economics and Statistics*, 56, 3, pp. 249–65.

[11] Tarrow, S. (1994) *Power in Movement: Social Movements, Collective Action and Politics* (Cambridge: Cambridge University Press); and Kitschelt, H. P. (1986) 'Political Opportunity Structures and Political Protest: Anti-Nuclear Movements in Four Democracies', *British Journal of Political Science*, 16, 1, pp. 57–85.

the unions' goals, changing the unions' protest repertoire via institutionalization or radicalization might be expected.[12] Such a development would involve shifting the unions' repertoire of contention.

Although studies on the displacement of different protest forms have reported incoherent empirical support in the UK,[13] there are good reasons to examine whether unions have replaced strikes with other forms of action in Sweden. First, Sweden and the UK belong to different industrial relation regimes.[14] Although several changes took place in Swedish industrial relations during the 1980s and 1990s, which constrained unions' opportunities to strike, the general character of the regime did not change. Second, Sweden has a comparably higher union density than the UK. Even though the union density has decreased over time, it remains at about 70% in Sweden.[15] Hence, trade unions are likely to have the resources and incentives to shift tactics and engage in other forms of protest action.

We examine displacement in two ways. First, like Kelly (2015), we expect that the suppression of opportunities for strikes and the subsequent decline in the number of strikes would increase the *number* of other forms of protest mobilized by trade unions.[16] Second, according to the social movement research on tactical innovations, movements may not only replace one form of action with another but also choose other ways of being innovative when opportunity structures change.[17] In their work on social movements' tactics in the US, Wang and Soule (2016) analyze protest event data and demonstrate how social movements innovate by changing the *claims* and not necessarily the strategies of

[12] Koopmans, R. (1995) 'The Dynamics of Protest Waves' in Kriesi, H., Koopmans, R., Duyvendak, J. W. and Giugni, M. G. (eds.) *New Social Movements in Western Europe: A Comparative Analysis* (Minneapolis: University of Minnesota Press), pp. 111–44.

[13] Kelly, 'Conflict'; and Gall, G. and Kirk, E. (2018) 'Striking Out in a New Direction? Strikes and the Displacement Thesis', *Capital & Class*, 42, 2, pp. 195–203.

[14] Pontusson, J. (2005) *Inequality and Prosperity* (Ithaca/London: Cornell University Press).

[15] Kjellberg, A. (2021) 'Parternas organisaionsgrad och kollektivavtalens utbredning' in *Avtalsrörelsen och lönebildningen 2020* (Stockholm: Medlingsinstitutet), pp. 233–39.

[16] Kelly, 'Conflict'.

[17] McAdam, D. (1983) 'Tactical Innovation and the Pace of Insurgency', *American Sociological Review*, 48, 6, pp. 735–54; and Wang, D. J. and Soule, S. A. (2016) 'Tactical Innovation in Social Movements: The Effects of Peripheral and Multi-Issue Protest', *American Sociological Review*, 81, 3, pp. 517–48.

protests. Following this result, we expect that the decline of strikes would encourage unions to express conventional strike claims (i.e., increased wages) through other forms of protests. Thus, even if other forms of protest (e.g., demonstrations) do not increase when strikes decline, the unions could still shift their claims to adapt to declining shifts. Consequently, the proportion of strike claims expressed through other forms of action would increase over time. In the analysis, we describe the changing frequency of protests that are not strikes and analyze which claims are expressed via these diverse forms of protests.

To examine Swedish unions' protest repertoire and analyze whether any form of displacement of protest activities has occurred, we use official statistics about work stoppages from the Swedish National Mediation Office (*Medlingsinstitutet*) and Statistics Sweden. This data is complemented with protest event data from the Swedish Protest Database (SPD). The database is constructed from reports of protest events in prominent geographically representative Swedish newspapers (e.g., *Dagens Nyheter*, *Uppsala Nya Tidning* and *Göteborgs Posten*). We focus only on protests that were predominantly mobilized by trade unions—that is, events that, according to the newspapers, were organized by trade unions or whose protest participants primarily came from trade unions. Although newspapers provide useful information about protest events, such reports are sometimes imprecise regarding the actors involved. For instance, the media may report on protest events without mentioning specific trade unions by name, instead describing the protest participants as "workers" or as members of some particular profession such as teachers, construction workers or nurses. Such cases have been collapsed into a separate category in the analysis.[18] The investigation is done at the aggregate level, focusing primarily on annual data—counting the number of strikes or other forms

[18] The SPD includes events that are defined as follows: a collective action is one in which individuals collectively (three or more people) make a claim or express a grievance for collective outcomes, such as on behalf of some group (social movement, interest group, etc.) or social category (e.g., the poor, pupils, or a neighborhood). We have excluded purely individual grievances, hate crimes, and public displays of anger that do not have a clear claim (e.g., football riots). We have included an act performed by one person if it aims at a collective outcome (e.g., hunger strike or self-immolation in the name of some group), as well as collective acts that refer to an individual who represents some social category (e.g., a demonstration against the expulsion of asylum seekers from Sweden). If a letter in the newspaper (i.e., a letter to the editor [*insändare*] or debate article) was written by an organization or by three or more people, then we have included it; otherwise, not. While regular protest event analysis excludes celebrative events, we have

of protest per year or analyzing the proportions of different claims (e.g., wages, collective agreements) expressed via various protests annually.

Changes in the Swedish Industrial Relations Regime and the Decline of Strikes

The centralized bargaining system, which started in the 1950s, was still in force in the early 1980s. As described in Chapter 2 of this book, wage bargaining in Sweden was centralized to the peak organizations of the trade union movement and the employers' organizations during 1952–1983. As a result, the wages across sectors were negotiated by just a handful of men from the Trade Union Confederation (*Landsorganisationen*, LO) and the Swedish Employers' Confederation (*Svenska Arbetsgivareföreningen*, SAF). However, in the 1970s, certain signs indicated that this system was no longer worked smoothly. The number of strikes—especially unofficial strikes—rose tremendously during the 1970s, and these conflictual relations continued during the 1980s.[19] Dissatisfaction with the way in which wage bargaining was carried out was exceptionally high among the employers in the industrial sector. Not having the decision-making power in wage bargaining had been a price worth paying in earlier decades, when inflation was controlled through the centralized system, but was no longer worthwhile in the 1980s. Eventually, the Swedish Engineering Employers' Association (*Verkstadsföreningen*) refused to be part of the centralized wage bargaining in 1983. By offering the Metal Workers' Union a generous wage agreement, the Swedish Engineering Employers' Association convinced the Metal Workers' Union to leave the centralized system. Criticism within LO was harsh.[20] Wage formation during the remainder of the 1980s was complex due to the overheated Swedish economy, as illustrated by the high number of official (legal) and unofficial (illegal) strikes during

included the 1st of May manifestation, as these events are of great importance for trade unions.

[19] Thörnqvist, *Arbetarna lämnar fabrikken*.

[20] Öberg, A. D. and Öberg, T. (2015) *Ledartröja eller tvångströja? Den svenske lönebildningens ansikten eller berättelsen om hur vi hamnade här* (Stockholm: Premiss), pp. 43f.; Edin, P.-O., Hägg, L. and Jonsson, B. (2012) *Så tänkte vi på LO – och så tänker vi nu* (Stockholm: Hjalmarson & Högberg), pp. 160–61, 174; and *TT Nyhetsbyrån* (TT), January 28, 1983: "SAF-LO".

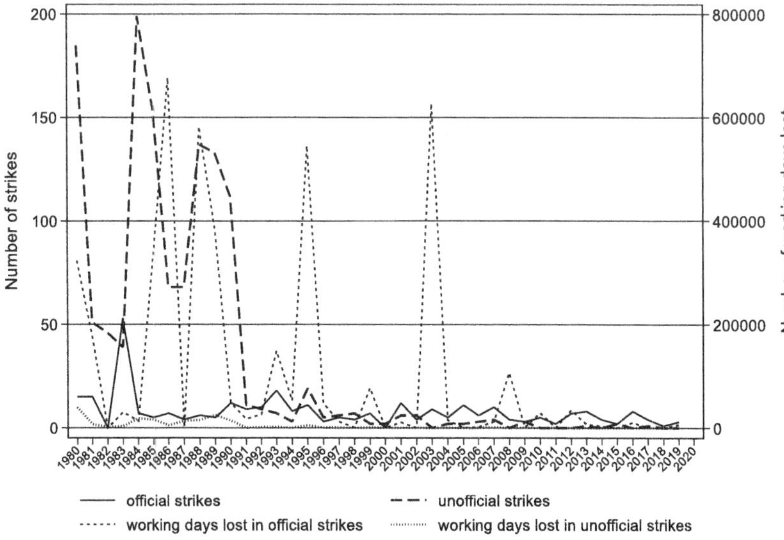

Fig. 13.1 Number of official and unofficial strikes (right axis) and working days lost in legal and illegal strikes (left axis) in Sweden, 1980–2020 (*Source* Medlingsinstitutet)

that period (Fig. 13.1). The number of unofficial strikes outnumbered the legal ones. Among the official work stoppages, there were several comprehensive conflicts in the public sector during that decade.

There has been a sharp decline in unofficial strikes since 1991,[21] which may be related to several crucial political and economic changes that altered unions' opportunities to strike. First, the 1990s was a period in which both recentralization and decentralization of wage bargaining occurred. The decade began with one of the most profound economic crises modern Sweden has gone through. Because of the crisis, the government intervened in the wage-formation process and appointed the so-called Rehnberg Commission to design collective agreements for the entire labor market. It was important for all economic sectors to be included in the negotiation process and to agree to the same length for the new collective agreements, thereby creating a period of labor market

[21] Thörnqvist, 'From Blue-Collar Wildcats'.

peace.[22] The Rehnberg agreements were signed in 1991 and lasted until March 1993.

Second, the corporatist system was dismantled in 1991, which critically changed the trade unions' opportunities to impact the political process. In an attempt to diminish the powers of the union movement, the Swedish Employers' Organization (*Svenska Arbetsgivarföreningen*) decided to withdraw all of its representatives from governmental agencies, which forced the unions to do the same.[23] This change gave the labor market parties less influence over the implementation of policies while simultaneously granting the unions a more independent role in regard to the state. Hence, while the change decreased the unions' formal political influence, their increased autonomy may have opened up opportunities for the unions to develop new protest activities.

Third, the center-right government, which formed after the elections of 1991, modified Sweden's strike legislation. In an attempt to address all unofficial strikes and adapt the legislation to the changed economic conditions, the government changed the so-called 200 SEK rule. This rule had been established in 1927, when the parliament adopted the law of collective agreement. It declared that any person going on an unofficial strike should pay a 200 Swedish krona (SEK) fine. At that time, the fine was roughly equivalent to a monthly wage for an industrial worker. Although wages had increased since 1927, the penalty had remained the same. Two arguments were used by the proponents for changing the fine: first, 200 SEK no longer correspond to a worker's monthly wage; and second, in order for the fine to have a deterrent effect, it should be related to the eventual damage of the strike. Thus, the fine was set to 2000 SEK.[24] Even though this fine was far from an industrial worker's monthly wage, the reform made it 10 times more expensive to start

[22] Larsson, R. (2006) 'Ett systemskifte i medlingsverksamheten' in Egerö, A.-M. and Nyström, B. (eds.) *Hundra år av medling i Sverige* (Stockholm: Medlingsinstitutet), pp. 67–95; Öberg and Öberg, *Ledartröja eller tvångströja?*, pp. 52–53; and Nycander, S. (2008) *Makten över arbetsmarknaden: ett perspektiv på Sveriges 1900-tal* (Stockholm: SNS Förlag), pp. 206–210.

[23] Svensson, T. and Oberg, P. (2002) "Labour Market Organisations' Participation in Swedish Public Policy-Making', *Scandinavian Political Studies*, 25, 4, pp. 295–315; and Johansson, J. (2000) *SAF och den svenska modellen. EN studie av uppbrottet från förvaltningskorporatismen 1982–91* (Uppsala: Acta Universitatis Upsaliensis).

[24] Ericson, B. and Eriksson, K. (2020) *Stridsåtgärder i arbetstvister* (Stockholm: Norsteds Juridik), p. 25.

an illegal strike, thereby diminishing the opportunities for strikes. Consequently, as shown in Fig. 13.1: Number of unofficial strikes (shown as a dashed line) decreased radically after 1991.

The two wage-bargaining rounds that followed the Rehnberg agreements (1991–1993) involved some significant conflicts. As shown in Fig. 13.1, the number of working days that were lost due to official strikes increased in 1993 and 1995. In particular, the negotiations in 1995 were complex and resulted in strikes in most sectors. The bargaining rounds signaled that the stabilization agreements from the Rehnberg Commission had not affected the wage-bargaining system in the way the government had wished. Before the next comprehensive negotiation round, which would occur in 1998 for most sectors, the trade unions and employers in the industrial sector agreed to change the wage-bargaining procedure. The labor market parties feared that, if the wage bargaining proceeded as it had in 1995, the conflicts would start a new spiral of inflation and the government would intervene. Moreover, high inflation tended to create unemployment in some sectors (e.g., industry) but not necessarily in other sectors. Thus, the parties in the industrial sector were particularly keen to make changes. The unions in the industrial sector initiated a dialogue to change the wage-bargaining system and invited the employers to negotiate via an op-ed article in the leading daily newspaper *Dagens Nyheter*.[25]

The parties reached an agreement in 1997, which included institutionalized coordination of wage bargaining in the industrial sector. An Economic Council for Industry (ECI) consisting of experts was founded to be in charge of analyzing the economic situation for Swedish industry. In addition, an impartial chair with far-reaching authority was established that would lead the wage bargaining. The agreement also included a rule that negotiations should start three months before the old agreement runs out, giving the parties more time to solve the eventual disagreements. As means of industrial conflict could only be used once an agreement had ended, the prolonged negotiation period allowed parties to reach an agreement before any use of strikes or lockouts became possible.[26] The new system also allowed the industrial sector to start wage bargaining

[25] *Dagens Nyheter* (DN), June 1, 1996: "Låga löneökningar vårt ansvar".

[26] Elvander, N. (2002) 'The New Swedish Regime for Collective Bargaining and Conflict Resolution: A Comparative Perspective', *European Journal of Industrial Relations*, 8, 2, pp. 197–216.

Table 13.1 Average annual number of strikes and working days lost (WDL)

	Before the increase in fines (1980–1991)		*Before the Industrial Agreement (1992–1996)*		*After the Industrial Agreement (1997–2020)*	
	Number	*WDL*	*Number*	*WDL*	*Number*	*WDL*
Official strikes	11.5	215,294.5	10.0	164,060.0	5.4	41,550.7
Unofficial strikes	100.3	13,166.8	8.6	1,878.2	2.0	234.7
All strikes	111.7	228,461.3	18.6	165,938.2	7.4	41,785.4

Source and *Note* Medlingsinstitutet. Authors' calculations based on official statistics from Medlingsinstitutet

and thereby set a threshold for a wage increase that was sustainable for the Swedish economy. A norm was established in which all other sectors followed this threshold (or "mark"), implying that the wage increase in the industry delimited the wage increases in other sectors.

In addition to the Industrial Agreement of 1997, the government strengthened the mediation institutions during the latter half of the 1990s. The Arbitration Office, which had existed in Sweden since 1906, was reorganized into the National Mediation Office. This new agency was given more authority than the old one to intervene in the wage-bargaining process. In the event of industrial action, mediation became mandatory.[27]

The changes in the "200 SEK" rule (1992) and the informal institutional change of collective bargaining that was established in the Industrial Agreement (1997) constitute the two most significant changes that constrained unions' opportunities to strike. The increased fine and the new bargaining norms strongly encouraged the labor market parties to lower the level of conflict. Table 13.1 shows how these changes align with the decline in strikes in terms of the total number of strikes and the number of working days lost. Before 1992, 112 strikes occurred per year on average. This number dropped to 19 strikes from 1992 to 1997. After the Industrial Agreement, the average number dropped even further, to seven strikes per year. The average number of working days lost due to strikes show a similar decline.

[27] Egerö and Nyström, *Hundra år av medling*.

Although wage bargaining has been relatively peaceful since the Industrial Agreement, the unions that organize low-income earners—particularly unions in the sheltered sector and public sector unions—are not satisfied with the system. The norm in which the industrial sector "sets the mark" for the maximum wage increase that other sectors are expected to follow makes it very difficult to decrease wage gaps between sectors (rather, it preserves wage gaps). The system also challenges the coordination between the different LO-affiliated unions, which has been a cornerstone for the labor movement in pursuing a solidaristic wage policy. Historically, the coordination between all the LO unions was a precondition for putting pressure on employers to raise the wages of those who earned the least. After the Industrial Agreement, however, the loyalties of the unions in the industrial sector became torn between the unions in the sector and the LO. In 2010, the Paper Mill Workers' Union left the Industrial Agreement, claiming that solidarity with fellow workers was more important than solidarity with the other unions in the sector.[28] Still, the Swedish "labor quiescence" continued. Not even the Great Recession of 2008–2010 significantly increased the number of strikes. The latter is probably related to the fact that most trade unions had signed a three-year collective agreement in 2007 and were therefore bound by a peace obligation until 2010. However, few unofficial strikes followed the economic crisis, and the number of strikes did not increase after 2010, which signals a deeply established labor market peace. Another major crisis—namely, the global health crisis due to the COVID-19 pandemic—has similarly not been accompanied by labor unrest: first, the planned wage bargaining for 2020 was postponed; then, when it finally started in the autumn of 2020, no working days were lost due to industrial conflict.[29]

In sum, the opportunities to strike have become more constrained over time, but the reasons for trade unions to mobilize—which include wages, working conditions and the implementation of collective agreements—have not disappeared. The globalization of the economy has led to rationalizations in most sectors, increased unemployment, increased precariousness and an increased wage gap in Sweden.[30] Thus, labor

[28] Öberg and Öberg, *Ledartröja eller tvångströja?*, p. 121.

[29] *Avtalsrörelsen och lönebildningen 2020*, pp. 40ff.

[30] Håkansson, P. and Nilsson, A. (2019) 'Getting a Job When Times Are Bad: Recruitment Practices in Sweden Before, During and After the Great Recession', *Scandinavian*

discontent has not decreased during the period. Therefore, it would not be surprising if unions were to look for other ways to express their claims.

Examining Displacement: Have Other Protest Activities Replaced Strikes?

Having mapped the overall strike pattern and the changed opportunity structures for striking, we now turn to the unions' mobilization of other forms of protests. Before discussing the eventual displacement process, we explain how we selected the examined protest events. The SPD has information on about 4,299 protests (including strikes) directly or indirectly related to trade unions. The first category (i.e., protests directly related to trade unions) refers to events that were—according to the newspapers—clearly mobilized by one or more Swedish trade unions. The second (i.e., protests indirectly related to trade unions) refers to protests for which the newspapers did not mention the union but claimed that the event was mobilized by workers or representatives of specific professions (e.g., teachers, doctors, or nurses). The protests that were directly and indirectly related to trade unions make up about 23% of all the protests registered in the dataset. Since we are interested in protest activities other than strikes, we have excluded the strikes reported in the media. Consequently, the analysis below focuses on 3,542 protests. About 64% of those events were directly mobilized by trade unions, while 36% were indirectly mobilized.

It is essential to note that most of these protests were peaceful, non-disruptive events, often taking the form of public statements in newspapers. No less than 57% of the unions' protests were letters or debate articles in various newspapers. These statements expressed diverse claims, including support for Polish workers and their strikes in the 1980s,[31] teachers' mobilization for improved working conditions,[32] opposition against the government's privatization plans[33] and a call for an improved

Economic History Review, 67, 2, pp. 132–53; and Lindberg, I. and Bengtsson, E. (2013) *Den sänkta löneandelen: orsaker, konsekvenser och handlingsalternativ* (Stockholm: Premiss).

31 *Uppsala Nya Tidning*, August 30, 1980: "Stöduttalande för Polenstrejk".

32 *Uppsala Nya Tidning*, May 21, 1981: "Lärare satsar på arbetsmiljön".

33 DN, October 1, 1987: "Kommunalarbetare mot privatisering".

Table 13.2 Protest activities during 1980–2020 that were directly and indirectly related to trade unions (in %)

	1980–1989	*1990–1999*	*2000–2011*	*2012–2020*	*Total (N)*
Letters, debate articles	62	54	55	54	57 (2,027)
Petitions	7	8	7	12	8 (269)
Boycotts	3	7	7	0	5 (172)
Demonstrations	14	20	17	22	17 (607)
Other actions	14	12	13	12	13 (467)
Total	100 (1,276)	100 (897)	100 (1,076)	100 (293)	100 (3,542)

Source Swedish Protest Dataset

social security system,[34] to mention just a few. There are also letters making claims about collective bargaining rounds.[35]

While the proportion of letters and debate articles declines somewhat during the early 2000s (Table 13.2), this does not mean that the unions are opting to use other forms of protest activity. Instead, it is likely that many of these protests have moved to social media channels (i.e., Twitter, Facebook, YouTube) and are therefore not covered by our dataset. Uba and Jansson (2021) have shown that many of the unions' election-related campaigns are run via social media, for example.[36] It is debatable whether letters to the editor and op-eds are protest events, as they do not disrupt public life. However, they are forms of collective claim-making, and trade unions compete with other interest groups and civil society organizations for the attention of the public and the politicians. Thus, we still argue that letter writing forms an essential part of unions' public claim-making.

The second most used type of protest activity (17% of all union protests) involves more contentious or disruptive actions, such as demonstrations, manifestations, marches and picketing. Or data shows that the proportion of these actions has varied over time, ranging from a low 6% in 1984 to a high 47% in 2012. Among other unions' protest activities, we find petitions (8%), boycotts and blockages (5%), and other forms

[34] *Västerbottens Kuriren*, October 1, 1993: "Socialförsäkring".

[35] *Uppsala Nya Tidning*, March 30, 1985: "Bort med tassarna från avtalsrörelsen"; and *Uppsala Nya Tidning*, September 11, 2002: "Pilotfack kräver kollektivavtal".

[36] Uba, K. and Jansson, J. (2021) 'Political Campaigns on YouTube: Trade Unions' Mobilisation in Europe', *New Technology, Work and Employment*, 36, 2, pp. 240–60.

of protests such as legal actions, actions involving civil disobedience and some symbolic display of discontent (13%). These different forms constitute a relatively small share of the unions' overall protest events, although some have mobilized a significant part of the population. One of the largest petitions was against having waiting days in the sickness insurance that was introduced in the 1990s during the economic crisis. This petition involved about half a million signatures.[37] Another large petition mobilized a quarter of a million signatures in protest against the changes in the unemployment benefit system in 2006.[38] Even though these petitions did not achieve their goals and the government was unresponsive to the unions' demands, collecting such a large number of signatures demonstrates the mobilization potential of the Swedish trade unions.

One of the most significant blockages was mobilized in September 1999, when the ongoing collective bargaining between the Electricians' Union and the Swedish Installation Federation broke down. Instead of starting a strike, the Electricians' Union initiated a blockage involving about 20 000 electricians.[39] In addition to other protest activities, the Swedish unions have opted for legal action on occasion. For instance, unions have turned to the Parliamentary Ombudsman (JO)[40] and the Labor Court[41] to protest against the government. Another legal tactic is to turn to international organizations, such as the International Labour Organisation, for help and support.[42] Finally, other less frequently used forms of protest involve symbolic actions such as a "calling-in-sick" protest against poor working conditions,[43] or interrupting traffic.[44] The category of "other protests" in Table 13.2 refers to meetings with politicians or employers that involved clearly expressed verbal protests. These

[37] DN, May 25, 1992: "Massiv protest".

[38] DN, December 15, 2006: "LO-medlemmar trappar upp protester mot nya a-kassan".

[39] DN, September 23, 1999: "Elektrikerblockad återupptas"; and *Göteborgs-Posten*, September 13, 1999:"Facklig rivalitet bakom el-tvist".

[40] TT, November 11, 1993: "Polisen JO-anmäld för bevakningen av demonstration 6 november".

[41] *Sydsvenskan*, May 23, 2002: "Seko stämmer staten".

[42] *Uppsala Nya Tidning*, February 27, 1993: "TCO anmäler regeringen".

[43] DN, September 27, 1988: "Fångvårdare trötta på arbetsförhållanden, Stannar hemma i protest"; and DN, March 23, 1987: "Massjukskrivning bland tekniker. Flygtrafik ställdes in".

[44] DN, March 14, 2000: "Ny taxiaktion orsakade trafikproblem".

events were often used to present a petition or protest letter with specific claims.

In sum, unions have used various protest activities during the period examined. For our aims, the pattern of protest frequency and how this relates to the declining number of strikes over time is key in detecting the eventual displacement process. Hence, Fig. 13.2 demonstrates the number of strikes (official and unofficial), the number of unions' protests and the number of demonstrations that were directly or indirectly mobilized by trade unions.

In general, a decline is visible in the annual number of protests mobilized by unions during the last 40 years. The trend follows the typical patterns of protest cycles: there are years in which unions have protested a great deal, followed by years in which the mobilization was lower. However, this empirical description of protest events does not support the argument that unions have compensated for fewer strikes by using other protest strategies.

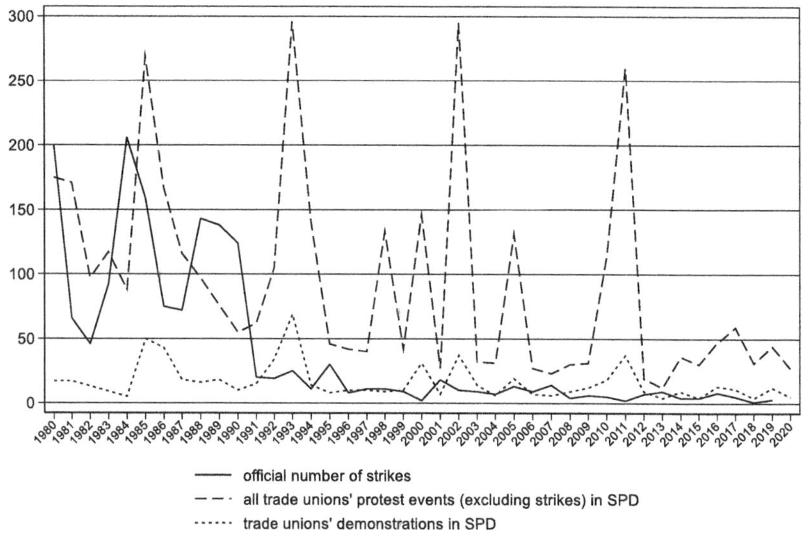

Fig. 13.2 Annual number of strikes, protests in general and demonstrations (*Source* Swedish Protest Dataset)

Since a large share of unions' protests consists of letter writing (57%), there are theoretical reasons to disentangle the trends of different forms of protest. While the previous studies on unions' shifting protest activities have focused on very trade-union-specific forms of protests such as "going slow", we look here at the most typical forms of street protest: demonstrations, manifestations, picketing and rallies. Scholarly discussions on unions needing to learn from social movements to revitalize always reference the more visible and contentious forms of action. Hence, the most obvious form of protest activity is not writing debate articles or letters but mobilizing on the streets.

The frequency of demonstrations does not decline as rapidly as the number of strikes. Despite a number of "peak years", the annual number of union demonstrations remains relatively stable. Some of the peaks deserve a closer look. In 1993, the largest demonstration and several smaller ones were related to the high level of unemployment. For example, in December, in the midst of the economic crisis, a total of 30,000 people gathered in Stockholm to protest against the government's unemployment policies. The event was organized by LO and TCO, and LO even arranged transportation to Stockholm from all over the country.[45] Smaller demonstrations mobilized that were also related to the economic crisis, criticizing how the government handled the situation.[46]

The peak around 2002, as shown in Fig. 13.2, is due to one of the largest demonstrations in Sweden against privatization in the healthcare sector. The Municipal Workers' Union mobilized the demonstration.[47] The Metal Workers' Union mobilized another large demonstration against the US owners of a factory in Motala who had decided to close the factory.[48] The last peak, in 2011, involved many smaller demonstrations against cuts in the healthcare sector[49] and a more extensive demonstration against the loss of jobs at Volvo.[50] Thus, at least some parts of these demonstrations were related to the Great Recession. Still, taking the numbers in total, unions did not mobilize protests associated with the

[45] TT, December 15, 1993: "30 000 demonstrerade mot regeringen".

[46] TT, November 25: "Byggettan hoppas på Dennispaketet".

[47] *Sydsvenskan*, February 1, 2002: "Fritt fram för anbud på vård".

[48] TT, April 9, 2002: "Förbittrad Motalaprotest mot USA-ägare".

[49] *Sydsvenskan*, September 18, 2011: "Manifestation för bättre vård".

[50] TT, November 2, 2011: "Anställd: Skönt med uppbackning".

Table 13.3 Annual average number of demonstrations during 1980–2020

	Before the increase in fines (1980–1991)	*Before the Industrial Agreement (1992–1996)*	*After the Industrial Agreement (1997–2020)*
Demonstrations	16.9	25.4	11.5
All other protests	98.6	94.0	53.4

Source Swedish Protest Dataset, N=3542

economic crisis that started in 2008 to the same degree as they protested in the 1990s.

Regardless of the peaks, it is not possible to directly say that unions opted for demonstrations to a more considerable extent when strikes declined. A comparison of the annual average numbers (Tables 13.1 and 13.3) of demonstrations reveals that the number of demonstrations is undoubtedly higher than the number of strikes for both periods since 1992. But the trend does not demonstrate an apparent displacement effect. It could be argued that, when unions mobilize many strikes, they also mobilize other forms of protests; thus, when strikes decline, so do other forms of protest. On the other hand, the annual average number of other protests has not fallen as rapidly as the number of strikes. There was even a slight increase in the number of demonstrations for 1992–1996, which could be related to the "200 SEK" rule (i.e., the suddenly increased cost of unofficial strikes), indicating that demonstrations replaced unofficial strikes. However, the overall annual number of protests has declined since the 1980s. Therefore, it is difficult to identify a robust displacement effect.

Have Protest Events Shifted Focus Toward Wage Claims?

The second way in which we examine displacement is to focus on the claims expressed through unions' protest actions. While strikes are usually about collective agreements and salary-related issues, the claims stated by the unions through other forms of protests vary (see Table 13.4). Claims about labor issues are still the most frequent ones. The second most important issue around which unions have mobilized protests is related to the government's school and educational policies. Unsurprisingly, unions have mobilized protests about themes such as changes in the social insurances, including how benefits are calculated, who is covered by benefits and how long a person is entitled to gain these benefits. Other essential issues are neoliberal reforms and privatization, which are related to cutbacks in the welfare state.

According to the research on displacement, we would expect that, when unions strike less often, protests on issues that are usually a reason to start a strike (e.g., wages, working conditions and collective agreements) should increase. An examination of the content of protest claims over time indicates that the proportion of protests related to wages, salaries and collective agreement has increased slightly (Fig. 13.3). Thus, even though unions are not replacing strikes with a greater number of other protests, a larger proportion of their other protest actions focus on wages, working conditions and collective agreements. Thus, the trend indicates that the Swedish unions are channeling their discontent regarding these issues from strikes into other forms of protest. The trend is evident when looking at demonstrations that were directly mobilized by unions. Out of all the demonstrations during 1980–1991, the average proportion of events related to wages and collective agreement was 11%. This increased to 18% during 1997–2020. This trend indicates that the constrained opportunity structures for striking have not been directly translated

Table 13.4 Most common issues raised by trade unions' protests (excluding strikes)

Claims	*Demonstrations (%)*	*All unions' protests (%)*
Labour issues (salary, working conditions)	43	35
School, education	13	15
Healthcare, sickness benefits	9	11
Neoliberalism, privatization	4	4
The welfare state in general	4	3
Infrastructure (housing, roads)	2	3
Unemployment	2	1
Other (pensions, taxes, immigration)	23	29
Total	100% (669)	100% (3787)

Source Swedish Protest Dataset

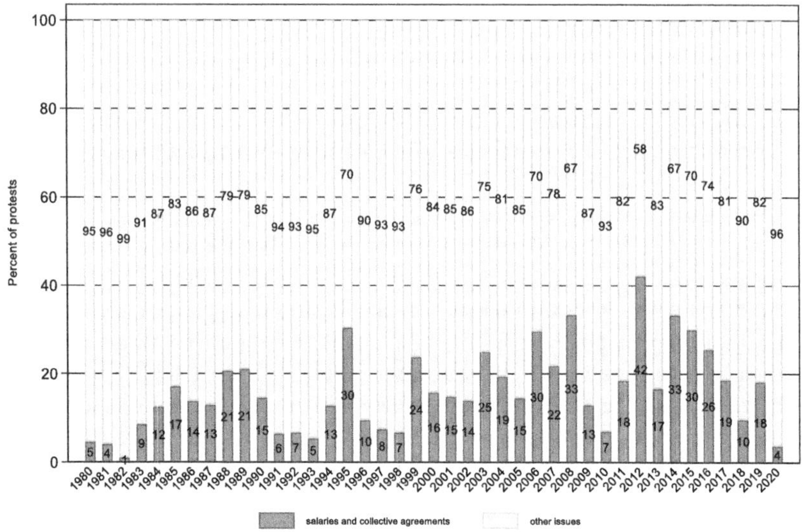

Fig. 13.3 Proportion of unions' protests focusing on wages and collective bargaining (*Source* Swedish Protest Dataset)

into new protest activities or an increased number of demonstrations. However, the trend does illustrate a certain shift in unions' claim-making patterns: claims that were previously expressed through strikes are now aired through demonstrations.

Conclusions

Trade unions have always used a broad repertoire of contentious activities that go beyond strikes. The protests against the law on collective agreements in 1928, in which the so-called peace obligation was manifested in legislation, remains one of the largest protest events mobilized by the unions in Sweden. The unions have used several different forms of protests, including demonstrations, petitions, letters to the government and letters in newspapers.[51] Whether or not protests have replaced strikes is a contested issue. In our analysis, we demonstrate that, in line with

[51] Casparsson, R. (1951) *LO under fem årtionden 1924–47*, Vol. II (Stockholm: Tiden Förlag), pp. 107–39.

results from the UK,[52] the number of protests has not increased as the number of strikes decreased. However, over time, unions' protests have come to be about wage-related issues—issues that usually beget strikes. In particular, demonstrations organized by unions increasingly express claims about wages. This trend indicates that a form of (weak) displacement has taken place in Sweden.

Between 1980 and 2020, Swedish industrial relations went through extraordinary changes, due to both the government's interference and changes in wage-bargaining institutions. These limited unions' opportunities for striking and should have increased the incentive for unions to replace strikes with other contentious activities. Perhaps the changed opportunity structures for strikes also apply to other forms of protests? One of the most important changes to the industrial relations system was the Industrial Agreement, which involves, roughly speaking, self-imposed discipline. These norms likely cover more than just strikes in terms of abstaining from the use of contentious actions. The well-established routines in the collective bargaining system probably make it difficult for unions to protest employers: all the parties know that they will soon meet around the negotiation table again. Engaging in street protests against employers affects the negotiation climate and, with an impartial chair running the bargaining and a strict timetable, it is likely that these procedures act as a constraint on unions. Moreover, the well-established routines in the collective bargaining system allow unions to address their claims in a non-disruptive manner and delegitimize contention. Given that protest actions such as demonstrations or letter writing usually put less pressure on employers than strikes, the expected efficacy and impact of these forms of protests are lower than those of strikes. In this context, it may not be surprising that unions are not opting for contentious activities. However, such apparent passivity can make unions appear less relevant to both their members and the general public.

References

Serials

Dagens Nyheter (DN)
Göteborgs-Posten

[52] Kelly, 'Conflict'; and Gall and Kirk, 'Striking Out in a New Direction?'.

Sydsvenskan
TT Nyhetsbyrån (TT)
Uppsala Nya Tidning
Västerbottens Kuriren

Literature

Avtalsrörelsen och lönebildningen 2020 (2021) (Stockholm: Medlingsinstitutet)

Casparsson, R. (1951) *LO under fem årtionden 1924–47*, Vol. II (Stockholm: Tiden Förlag).

Edin, P.-O., Hägg, L. and Jonsson, B. (2012) *Så tänkte vi på LO – och så tänker vi nu* (Stockholm: Hjalmarson & Högberg).

Egerö, A.-M. and Nyström, B. (2006) *Hundra år av medling i Sverige. Jubileumsskrift: historik, analys och fremtidsvisioner* (Stockholm: Medlingsinstitutet).

Elvander, N. (2002) 'The New Swedish Regime for Collective Bargaining and Conflict Resolution: A Comparative Perspective', *European Journal of Industrial Relations*, 8, 2, pp. 197–216.

Ericson, B. and Eriksson, K. (2020) *Stridsåtgärder i arbetstvister* (Stockholm: Norsteds Juridik).

Franzosi, R. (1989) 'One Hundred Years of Strike Statistics: Methodological and Theoretical Issues in Quantitative Strike Research', *ILR Review*, 42, 3, pp. 348–62.

Gall, G. and Hebdon, R. (2008) 'Conflict at Work' in Blyton, P., Bacon, N., Fiorito, J. and Heery, E. (eds.) *The SAGE Handbook of Industrial Relations* (London: Sage), pp. 588–605.

Gall, G. and Kirk, E. (2018) 'Striking Out in a New Direction? Strikes and the Displacement Thesis', *Capital & Class*, 42, 2, pp. 195–203.

Håkansson, P. and Nilsson, A. (2019) 'Getting a Job When Times Are Bad: Recruitment Practices in Sweden Before, During and After the Great Recession', *Scandinavian Economic History Review*, 67, 2, pp. 132–53.

Johansson, J. (2000) *SAF och den svenska modellen. EN studie av uppbrottet från förvaltningskorporatismen 1982–91* (Uppsala: Acta Universitatis Upsaliensis).

Kelly, J. (2015) 'Conflict: Trends and Forms of Collective Action', *Employee Relations*, 37, 6, pp. 720–32.

Kelly, J. E. (1998) *Rethinking Industrial Relations: Mobilization, Collectivism and Long Waves* (New York: Routledge).

Kitschelt, H. P. (1986) 'Political Opportunity Structures and Political Protest: Anti-Nuclear Movements in Four Democracies', *British Journal of Political Science*, 16, 1, pp. 57–85.

Kjellberg, A. (2021) 'Parternas organisaionsgrad och kollektivavtalens utbredning' in *Avtalsrörelsen och lönebildningen 2020* (Stockholm: Medlingsinstitutet), pp. 233–39.

Koopmans, R. (1995) 'The Dynamics of Protest Waves' in Kriesi, H., Koopmans, R., Duyvendak, J. W. and Giugni, M. G. (eds.) *New Social Movements in Western Europe: A Comparative Analysis* (Minneapolis: University of Minnesota Press), pp. 111–44.

Larsson, R. (2006) 'Ett systemskifte i medlingsverksamheten' in Egerö, A.-M. and Nyström, B. (eds.) *Hundra år av medling i Sverige* (Stockholm: Medlingsinstitutet), pp. 67–95.

Lindberg, I. and Bengtsson, E. (2013) *Den sänkta löneandelen: orsaker, konsekvenser och handlingsalternativ* (Stockholm: Premiss).

McAdam, D. (1983) 'Tactical Innovation and the Pace of Insurgency', *American Sociological Review*, 48, 6, pp. 735–54.

Molinder, J., Karlsson, T. and Enflo, K. (2022) 'Social Democracy and the Decline of Strikes', *Explorations in Economic History*, 83, 101420.

Nycander, S. (2008) *Makten över arbetsmarknaden: ett perspektiv på Sveriges 1900-tal* (Stockholm: SNS Förlag).

Peterson, A., Thörn, H. and Wahlström, M. (2018) 'Sweden 1950–2015: Contentious Politics and Social Movements Between Confrontation and Conditioned Cooperation' in Mikkelsen, F., Kjeldstadli, K. and Nyzell, S. (eds.) *Popular Struggle and Democracy in Scandinavia, 1700–Present* (London: Palgrave Macmillan), pp. 377–432.

Peterson, A., Wahlström, M. and Wennerhag, M. (2015) 'European Anti-Austerity Protests—Beyond "Old" and "New" Social Movements?', *Acta Sociologica*, 58, 4, pp. 293–310.

Peterson, A., Wahlström, M., Wennerhag, M., Christancho, C. and Sabucedo, M. (2012) 'May Day Demonstrations in Five European Countries', *Mobilisation: An International Quarterly*, 17, 3, pp. 281–300.

Pontusson, J. (2005) *Inequality and Prosperity* (Ithaca/London: Cornell University Press).

Psimitis, M. (2011) 'The Protest Cycle of Spring 2010 in Greece', *Social Movement Studies*, 10, 2, pp. 191–97.

Rothstein, B. (1992) *Den korporativa staten* (Stockholm: Nordstedts).

Rüdig, W. and Karyotis, G. (2013) 'Who Protests in Greece? Mass Opposition to Austerity', *British Journal of Political Science*, 44, 3, pp. 487–513.

Sapsford, D. and Turnbull, P. (1994) 'Strikes and Industrial Conflict in Britain's Docks: Balloons or Icebergs?', *Oxford Bulletin of Economics and Statistics*, 56, 3, pp. 249–65.

Shorter, E. and Tilly, C. (1974) *Strikes in France, 1830–1968* (London: Cambridge University Press).

Svensson, T. and Oberg, P. (2002) "Labour Market Organisations' Participation in Swedish Public Policy-Making', *Scandinavian Political Studies*, 25, 4, pp. 295–315.

Tarrow, S. (1993) 'Cycles of Collective Action: Between Moments of Madness and the Repertoire of Contention', *Social Science History*, 17, 2, pp. 281–307.

Tarrow, S. (1994) *Power in Movement: Social Movements, Collective Action and Politics* (Cambridge: Cambridge University Press).

Thörnqvist, C. (1994) *Arbetarna lämnar fabrikken: Strejkrörelser i Sverige under efterkrigstiden, deras bakgrund, förlopp och följder* (Gothenburg: Historiska institutionen).

Thörnqvist, C. (2007) 'From Blue-Collar Wildcats in the 1970s to Public Sector Resistance at the Turn of a New Millennium' in van der Velden, S., Dribbusch, H., Lyddon, D. and Vandaele, K. (eds.) *Strikes Around the World, 1968–2005. Case-Studies of 15 Countries* (Amsterdam: Aksant), pp. 321–38.

Uba, K. and Jansson, J. (2021) 'Political Campaigns on YouTube: Trade Unions' Mobilisation in Europe', *New Technology, Work and Employment*, 36, 2, pp. 240–60.

van der Velden, S., Dribbusch, H., Lyddon, D. and Vandaele, K. (eds.) (2007) *Strikes Around the World, 1968–2005. Case-Studies of 15 Countries* (Amsterdam: Aksant).

Wang, D. J. and Soule, S. A. (2016) 'Tactical Innovation in Social Movements: The Effects of Peripheral and Multi-Issue Protest', *American Sociological Review*, 81, 3, pp. 517–48.

Öberg, A. D. and Öberg, T. (2015) *Ledartröja eller tvångströja? Den svenske lönebildningens ansikten eller berättelsen om hur vi hamnade här* (Stockholm: Premiss).

Öberg, P. (1994) *Särintresse och allmäninteresse: Korporatismens ansikte* (Uppsala: Acta Universitatis Upsaliensis).

Öberg, P., Svensson, T., Christiansen, P. M., Nørgaard, A. S., Rommetvedt, H. and Thesen, G. (2011) 'Disrupted Exchange and Declining Corporatism: Government Authority and Interest Group Capability in Scandinavia', *Government and Opposition*, 46, 3, pp. 365–91.

PART III

Comparative Perspective

CHAPTER 14

Lockouts in Scandinavia, c. 1900–1938

Jesper Hamark

Quantitative research on labor conflicts is almost exclusively based on statistics that amalgamate strikes and lockouts. In other words, no distinction is made between tools used by two different social categories, namely employees and employers. This situation is among other things caused by unwillingness of national statistical bureaus to make the distinction. Since lockouts are relatively few, they tend to drown in an ocean of strikes. This fact has been used as an argument against the study of lockouts proper. Because they are so few, we can ignore them.[1] Nonetheless, during the last couple of decades, some quantitative research on lockouts proper

[1] Hamark, J. (2022) 'Strikes and Lockouts: The Need To Separate Labour Conflicts', *Economic and Industrial Democracy*, online October 19.

J. Hamark (✉)
University of Gothenburg, Gothenburg, Sweden
e-mail: jesper.hamark@gu.se

© The Author(s), under exclusive license to Springer Nature Switzerland AG 2023

J. Jørgensen and F. Mikkelsen (eds.), *Trade Union Activism in the Nordic Countries since 1900*, Palgrave Studies in the History of Social Movements, https://doi.org/10.1007/978-3-031-08987-9_14

has been done.[2] As far as known, the only cross-country study on lockouts is Chris Briggs' on Australia and New Zealand.[3] This chapter aligns with the slowly growing interest in lockouts and especially with Briggs' cross-country approach.

The remainder of the chapter is arranged as follows: The next section discusses material and methods used to build time series on strikes and lockouts for Denmark, Norway, and Sweden. The following section then shows some empirical results, including a quantitative comparison with The Netherlands. The consecutive section considers the characteristics of the Scandinavian lockout, to what purposes it was used, and some of its preconditions. Preconditions are the topic also in the following section, in which Scandinavian lockouts are contrasted with American strikebreaking. Finally, a conclusion ends the chapter.[4]

[2] LeRoy, M. (1996) 'Lockouts Involving Replacement Workers: An Empirical Public Policy Analysis and Proposal to Balance Economic Weapons Under the NLRA', *Washington University Law Review*, 74, 4, pp. 981–1059; van der Velden, S. (2000) *Stakingen in Nederland: Arbeidersstrijd 1830–1995* (Amsterdam: IISH); Briggs, C. (2004) 'The Return of the Lockout in Australia: A Profile of Lockouts Since the Decentralisation of Bargaining', *Australian Bulletin of Labour*, 30, 2, pp. 101–12; Shyam Sundar, K. R. (2004) 'Lockouts in India, 1961–2001', *Economic and Political Weekly*, 39, 39, pp. 4377–85; Briggs, C. (2005) 'Lockout Law in Comparative Perspective: Corporatism, Pluralism and Neo-liberalism', *International Journal of Comparative Labour Law and Industrial Relations*, 21, 3, pp. 481–502; van der Velden, S. (2006) 'Lockouts in The Netherlands: Why Statistics on Labour Disputes Must Discriminate Between Strikes and Lockouts, and Why New Statistics Need to Be Compiled', *Historical Social Research/Historische Sozialforschung*, 31, 4, pp. 341–62; Cooper, R., Ellem, B., Briggs, C. and van den Broek, D (2009) 'Antiunionism, Employer Strategy, and the Australian State, 1965–2005', *Labour Studies Journal*, 34, 3, pp. 339–62; Briskin, L. (2016) 'The Employer Offensive: Antiunionism and Lockouts', in Marín Corbera, M., Domènech Sampere, X. and Martínez i Muntada, R. (eds). *III International Conference Strikes and Social Conflicts: Combined Historical Approaches to Conflict* (Barcelona: CEFID-UAB), pp. 191–208; and Hamark, J. (2018) 'From Peak to Trough: Swedish Strikes and Lockouts in the First Half of the Twentieth Century', *Workers of the World: International Journal on Strikes and Social Conflict*, 1, 9, pp. 137–66.

[3] Briggs, C. (2005) 'Strikes and Lockouts in the Antipodes: Neo-liberal Convergence in Australia and New Zealand', *New Zealand Journal of Employment Relations*, 30, 3, pp. 1–15.

[4] The research for this chapter was financially supported by Stiftelsen Anna Ahrenbergs Fond för vetenskapliga m.fl. ändamål. I am grateful to Flemming Mikkelsen and Tobias Karlsson for valuable comments on earlier drafts.

Material and Methods

The source material is the official statistics produced in the three countries,[5] complemented by figures from the Norwegian Confederation of Trade Unions (*Arbeidernes Faglige Landsorganisasjon*, AFL, later *Landsorganisasjonen i Norge*).

There are always difficulties involved in trying to quantify strike and lockout activity. For instance, solid time series require that definitions and level of ambition in collecting data do not change and that thresholds and other rules for exclusion stay the same. Often, these requirements are not fulfilled even within a single country. And if we cross borders, things get worse. Renowned expert Michael Shalev once wrote: "each of the problem-areas in strike measurement [...] in the context of a single country are amplified almost beyond redemption in an internationally comparative context."[6] Shalev made a strong case against the habit of comparing across countries in *levels* (*trends*, he argued, often worked well), but from a Scandinavian perspective also somewhat excessive. I believe the statistics in Denmark, Norway, and Sweden are uniform enough to allow comparison in levels between the countries, given that we limit ourselves to the study of the number of workers involved in conflicts.

The concept of strike and lockout activity can be operationalized in different ways, four of which are standard: frequency, duration, involvement, and volume. In this particular context, I prefer involvement. *Frequency* is acknowledged to be the least suitable in comparative studies.[7] *Duration*—as it is commonly measured—is conceptually

[5] For a review, see: Mikkelsen, F. (1992) *Arbejdskonflikter i Skandinavien 1848–1980* (Odense: Odense Universitetsforlag).

[6] Shalev, M. (1978) 'Appendix II: Problems of Strike Measurement' in Crouch, C and Pizzorno, A (eds.) *The Resurgence of Class Conflict in Western Europe Since 1968. Vol. 1: National Studies* (London: Palgrave Macmillan), pp. 321–34, p. 325.

[7] Edwards, P. K. (1983) 'The Pattern of Collective Industrial Action' in Bain, S (ed.) *Industrial Relations in Britain* (Oxford: Blackwell), pp. 209–34, pp. 210–11; Wallace, J. and O'Sullivan, M. (2006) 'Contemporary Strike Trends Since 1980: Peering Through the Wrong End of a Telescope' in Morley, M., Gunnigle, P. and Collings, D. G. (eds.) *Global Industrial Relations* (London: Routledge), pp. 273–91, p. 275; and Lyddon, D. (2007) 'Strike Statistics and the Problems of International Comparison' in van der Velden, S., Dribbusch, H., Lyddon, D. and Vandaele, K. (eds.) *Strikes Around the World, 1968–2005: Case-Studies of 15 Countries* (Amsterdam: Aksant), pp. 24–39, pp. 28–29.

problematic.[8] *Volume* is the most frequently used measurement in cross-country settings.[9] To some extent, however, the Scandinavian countries did not follow the same estimation methods (e.g., neither Denmark nor Norway included indirectly involved workers in their volume estimations, but Sweden did).[10] *Involvement*, finally, was defined as workers directly involved in a conflict in all three countries. It means that only strikers and locked out workers were accounted for, excluding those workers being laid off as a result of the conflict.[11] At least three different methods have been used to estimate the number of workers involved in a conflict,[12] but the bureaus in Denmark, Norway, and Sweden made the same choice:

[8] Edwards, P. K. (1981) *Strikes in the United States 1881–1974* (Oxford: Blackwell), pp. 316–20.

[9] Dribbusch, H. and Vandaele, K. (2007) 'Comprehending Divergence in Strike Activity. Employers' Offensives, Government Interventions and Union Responses' in van der Velden, Dribbusch, Lyddon and Vandaele, *Strikes Around the World*, p. 367.

[10] *Arbetsinställelser under åren 1903–1907 jämte öfversikt af arbetsinställelser under åren 1859–1902 samt den s.k. politiska storstrejken år 1902* (1909) (Stockholm: Kommerskollegii afdelning för arbetsstatistik), p. 12; 'Statistique des greves et des lock-outs' (1920) *Annuaire international de statistique*, 6, p. 135 (published by *L'office permanent de l'institut international de statistique*); 'Strejker og lockouter i Danmark 1926–30' (1931) *Statistiske Meddelelser*, 4, 88, 5, p. 12; *Methods of Compiling Statistics of Industrial Disputes* (1926) (Geneva: International Labour Office), p. 41; and Woodbury, R. M. (1949) 'The Incidence of Industrial Disputes', *International Labour Review*, 60, 5, pp. 451–66, pp. 452–53. The most comprehensive inter-war overview of sources and methods across countries was published *by L'office permanent de l'institut international de statistique. L'office* sent out questionnaires to 24 countries, including the Scandinavian. The inquiry is of value for the present purpose since the Danish and Swedish bureaus answered some questions they did not address in their own publications. Unfortunately, Norway did not respond at all. Many of the results presented by *L'office* were reproduced by the International Labour Office in 1926.

[11] The proportion of workers indirectly involved differed across countries. In Denmark (1926–1930) and Czechoslovakia (1930–1934), it constituted 6% of total involvement, in Hungary (1932–1936) 13%, and in the UK (1929–1944) 17% ('Strejker og lockouter i Danmark 1926–1930', p. 12; and Woodbury, 'The Incidence of Industrial Disputes', p. 455).

[12] For illustrative examples of the different methods, see: 'Strejker og lockouter i Danmark 1897–1899' (1901) *Statistiske Meddelelser*, 4, 8, 4, pp. 34–35. See also: Lyddon, 'Strike Statistics', p. 31.

to count the maximum number of workers involved in a given period, normally a week.[13]

In addition, a few general aspects make Scandinavian conflict statistics suitable for comparisons. The bureaus in Denmark and Sweden made several changes regarding which variables they presented, and Statistics Denmark published its data in an astonishingly confusing way. Yet, in both countries, methods of compilation and calculation stayed the same over the years. The official statistics in Norway are consistent only for the period 1922–1938, but fortunately the union confederation used the same method of collecting data from 1909 to 1938.[14] No thresholds were applied.[15] The bureaus thought all conflicts should be accounted for—at least in principle.[16] While the Norwegian AFL was not explicit on this point, its individual conflict reports include conflicts with a single striker and with a handful of conflict days.[17]

There were also weaknesses. The Scandinavian bureaus often excluded political strikes, as well as many strikes occurring in the politically turbulent period 1917–1919, from their published figures.[18] The exclusion was never thoroughly discussed, leaving the impression of ad hocery. In many cases, it would be possible to add political strikes to the official figures. Yet I have refrained from doing so, in order to use the same

[13] 'Strejker og lockouter i Danmark 1897–1899', pp. 15, 34–35; *Arbetsinställelser under åren 1903–1907*, p. 12; *Methods of Compiling Statistics*, p. 37; and 'Industrial Disputes' (1933) *International Labour Review*, 28, 1, pp. 92–99, pp. 93–96.

[14] Mikkelsen, *Arbejdskonflikter i Skandinavien*, pp. 426–28, 447–48; and Hamark, J. (2014) *Ports, Dock Workers and Labour Market Conflicts* (Gothenburg: University of Gothenburg), pp. 158–59.

[15] According to Ross, A. M. and Hartman, P. T. (1960) *Changing Patterns of Industrial Conflict* (New York: Wiley), p. 185, Statistics Denmark (*Danmarks Statistik*) reported conflicts only within the realm of the Danish Employers' Confederation, and only those with at least 100 conflict days. But thresholds were not introduced before 1946 (Mikkelsen, *Arbejdskonflikter i Skandinavien*, p. 428).

[16] 'Strejker og lockouter i Danmark 1897–1899', p. 14; *Statistisk aarbog for kongeriget Norge 1906* (1906) (Kristiania: Det Statistiske Centralbureau), pp. 73–75; and *Arbetsinställelser under åren 1903–1907*, p. 11.

[17] See, e.g., *Beretning. Arbeidernes Faglige Landsorganisasjon*, 1909, pp. 154–59.

[18] 'Strejker og Lockouter i Danmark 1916–20' (1922), *Statistiske Meddelelser*, 4, 66, 2, pp. 10–11; Mikkelsen, *Arbejdskonflikter*, p. 224; and Hamark, *Ports, Dock Workers*, pp. 160–61.

conflict data as previous researchers. Trade unions were used as important sources in all three countries. Naturally, the unions kept better track of their members than of the non-unionized labor force. It means the contribution to conflict activity by non-union members—be it as strikers or locked out workers—is underestimated. From a comparative perspective, it is comforting that the problem was basically the same all over Scandinavia.[19]

A serious deficiency is that Statistics Norway did not distinguish between strikes and lockouts. I have addressed the problem by using the total involvement given by Statistics Norway combined with the relative shares of strikers and locked out workers given by AFL (see Appendix for an elaboration). It means, however, that the Norwegian series does not begin until 1909, because only then AFL produced high-quality statistics.

Scandinavian Lockout Statistics

Figure 14.1 and Table 14.1 show the development of strikes and lockouts—including mixed conflicts[20] in the Swedish case—over four decades.

As mentioned, generally lockouts are few in relation to strikes. This is consistent with the inherent logic of the employment relationship, in which the employer usually can alter conditions of work without taking industrial action whereas employees cannot.[21] Involvement tells a very different story. In relative terms, Denmark was *the* lockout country. The number of workers involved in lockouts by far exceeded the number of strikers, in both the 1920s and 1930s. But also in Norway and Sweden locked out workers made up a substantial share of total involvement.

A Quantitative Comparison: Scandinavia vs The Netherlands

There is a lack of quantitative data which Scandinavian lockouts can be judged against. To my knowledge only one country, the pre-World War II Netherlands, meets the standards. I have merged the data on Scandinavian strikes and lockouts 1900–1938 with the corresponding series for

[19] 'Strejker og lockouter i Danmark 1897–1899', p. 18; *Statistisk aarbog for kongeriget Norge 1906*, p. 74; and *Arbetsinställelser under åren 1903–1907*, p. 21.

[20] Mainly when a lockout follows a strike or vice versa.

[21] Hyman, R. (1989) *Strikes* (London: Palgrave Macmillan).

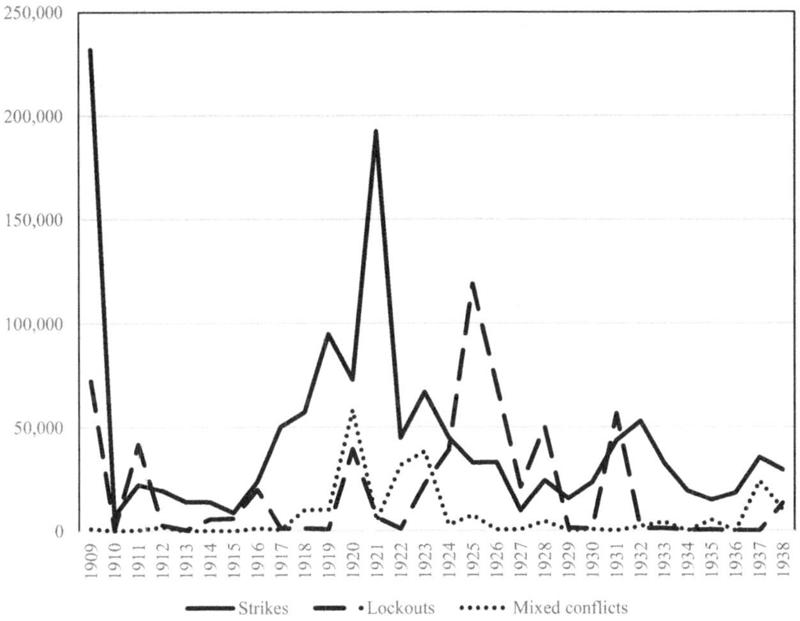

Fig. 14.1 Number of workers involved in conflicts. Scandinavia, 1909–1938 (*Sources Statistisk Aarbog. Danmarks Statistik*, 1912–1946; Norges Offisielle Statistikk, 1906–1939 [consult Mikkelsen, *Arbejdskonflikter*, pp. 445–47, for a full account of the different series]; *Beretning. Arbeidernes Faglige Landsorganisasjon*, 1909–1938; and *Arbetsinställelser och kollektivavtal samt förlikningsmännens verksamhet m.m.* [1938] [Stockholm: Socialstyrelsen])

Table 14.1 Number of workers involved in conflicts, Denmark, Norway, and Sweden, 1900–1938

Period	*Denmark*		*Norway*		*Sweden*		
	Strikes	*Lockouts*	*Strikes*	*Lockouts*	*Strikes*	*Lockouts*	*Mixed*
1900–1909[a]	51,777	45,682	n/a	n/a	300,218	82,921	70,887
1910–1919	90,281	27,083	90,371	54,530	221,503	26,150	25,345
1920–1929	82,557	155,854	259,130	117,905	279,096	253,984	150,505
1930–1938	24,372	105,178	93,555	61,315	176,791	13,765	47,327

Sources and *Note* See Fig. 14.1. [a]Denmark, 1897–1909 and Sweden 1903–1909. Norway, with data only for 1909, is excluded

The Netherlands and standardized using labor force figures.[22] Norway and Sweden had relatively high involvement in conflicts, and Denmark and The Netherlands relatively low. The finding is in line with earlier research.[23] But this is only half of the story—the other half cannot be told by studies on labor conflicts in aggregation.

Denmark had the highest rate of locked out workers of all four countries. (And, by inference, very few strikers.) The ratio of locked out workers in Denmark to The Netherlands was substantial, 6:1. It implies that Scandinavian (and especially Danish) and Dutch capitalists chose differently how to combat unions and strikes. Thus, at least in relation to The Netherlands, Scandinavia was a lockout region. But what were the characteristics of the Scandinavian lockout? And to what purposes was it used?

The Scandinavian Sympathy Lockout

Danish Employers Lead the Way

The 1870s was the breakthrough for the strike in Denmark[24]—and in Scandinavia, as the Danes were well ahead of their northern neighbors in most socio-economic aspects. The demands of the strikers concerned wages, working hours, the right to join unions, and all kinds of workplace rules. The execution of strikes varied too. Often work was stopped spontaneously, without much consideration or organization. Far more effective, however, was the planned method of targeting one or a few employers at a time. With a limited number of union members on strike at a given time, it was relatively easy to get financial support from members still at work. When the first employer was defeated, workers moved on to the

[22] Bairoch, P. (1969) *La Population active et sa structure* (Bruxelles: Centre d'économie politique (de l') Université libre de Bruxelles); and van der Velden, *Stakingen in Nederland*.

[23] Shorter, E. and Tilly, C. (1974) *Strikes in France, 1830–1968* (London: Cambridge University Press); and Korpi, W. and Shalev, M. (1980) 'Strikes, Power, and Politics in the Western Nations, 1900–1976', *Political Power and Social Theory*, 1, pp. 301–34.

[24] Knudsen, K. (1999) *Arbejdskonflikternes historie i Danmark: Arbejdskampe og arbejderbevægelse 1870–1940* (Copenhagen: SFAH), pp. 39–54; and Knudsen, K. (2000) 'Storlockout og Septemberforlig 1899' in Ibsen, F. and Scheuer, S. (eds.) *Septemberforliget og det 21. århundrede: historiske perspektiver og fremtidens dilemmaer* (Copenhagen: Jurist- og Økonomforbundets Forlag), pp. 77–88.

next. And the next—and by that time the *threat* of striking was often enough.

The Danish Employers' Confederation (*Dansk Arbejdsgiverforening*, DA) found a countermeasure. When 350 Jutland carpenters went on strike in 1899, DA responded by locking out every unionized carpenter in Denmark.[25] Shortly afterward, the lockout was extended to the entire construction sector and parts of the metal industry. 25,000 organized Danes were locked out for three months. Measured as conflict days in relation to population, there was no equivalent conflict in any other country. The world had seen the first massive sympathy lockout.

By extending the conflict to companies that were not initially involved—and thereby locking out a very large number of union members—the unions' strike funds quickly drained. In the short run, it was costly to lock out workers *en masse* in sympathy with the strike-affected companies. In the long run, there was a lot to gain. The mass lockout of 1899 aimed to discipline the trade union movement by sending the message: We have a method of fighting your guerrilla tactics. If you strike at single workplaces, we extend the conflict to all of them. And we empty your strike funds.

The lockout ended with the so-called September Compromise (*Septemberforliget*). Unions were recognized as the workers' representatives, with the right to bargain collectively on their behalf. In return, unions acknowledged managerial prerogatives. The compromise also established rules that obstructed local strikes. Both the Danish method of struggle and the agreement following the lockout became models for employers' confederations throughout Scandinavia.

Union Recognition. Swedish Employers Follow Suit

The recognition of the Danish trade unions in 1899 is worth stressing. At the same time in Sweden, battles for the right to join unions were still raging. The employers fought organizational efforts with blacklisting, dismissals, and evictions. But there was a turnaround in the early years of the new century.[26] More and more employers started to question the

[25] Mikkelsen, *Arbejdskonflikter i Skandinavien*, pp. 51–56; and Knudsen, 'Storlockout og Septemberforlig'.

[26] Casparsson, R. (1951) *LO under fem årtionden, Vol. 1: 1898–1923* (Stockholm: Tiden); Schiller, B. (1967) *Storstrejken 1909: förhistoria och orsaker* (Göteborg: Elander);

actions taken against unionization. The costs of these battles included not only the immediate loss of production but also lingering hostility between workers and management. The idea of negotiating with a socialist trade union instead of talking directly to the individual employee was certainly disgusting in principle. But to avoid the many conflicts, perhaps it was time to accept the union as such, instead focusing on how to minimize its harmful effects. Soon Swedish employers drew the same conclusion as their Danish counterparts had already done: The unions were too strong to be crushed, but they could be tamed.

In 1906 erupted what became known as the "eight minor conflicts"—all within the Swedish Employers' Confederation's (*Svenska Arbetsgivareföreningen*, SAF) bargaining domain and all concerning managerial rights.[27] The conflicts were answered by SAF with threats of a lockout that would shut down half of Sweden's manufacturing industry. The Swedish Trade Union Confederation (*Landsorganisationen*, LO) averted the lockout by forcing individual unions to end the eight minor conflicts and by signing the so-called December Compromise (*Decemberkompromissen*) with SAF. The compromise established the right of employers to lead and distribute work, as well as to freely hire and fire workers. SAF, for its part, promised to respect the right of association. Now, also Swedish employers had shown how small, single conflicts were to be dealt with: with the threat of a full-scale lockout with the aim of emptying LO's and the national unions' strike funds.

The Preferred Choice: A Social Democratic, Centralized Opponent

The Swedish general strike of 1909—which was preceded by extensive lockouts—ended in defeat for labor. After the strike, SAF's chairman Hjalmar von Sydow remarked that employers could easily have crushed the unions. Whether this was a correct assessment can be discussed, but von Sydow's motivation why SAF *did not want* to destroy the unions is illuminating: the effectiveness of lockouts rested on LO's existence.[28]

and Swenson, P. A. (2002) *Capitalists Against Markets: The Making of Labor Markets and Welfare States in the United States and Sweden* (New York: Oxford University Press).

[27] Schiller, *Storstrejken 1909*.

[28] von Sydow, H. (1913) *Riktlinier för Svenska arbetsgifvareföreningens verksamhet under gångna och kommande år* (Stockholm: Svenska arbetsgivareföreningen); and Swenson, *Capitalists Against Markets*, p. 84.

Without a centralized trade union movement, there was no one to punish when individual unions obstructed. The alternative to LO was syndicalist unions, which not only refused to recognize the peace obligation of collective agreements but also lacked centralized funds. Nothing could be worse than syndicalist unions, according to SAF. The view that a social democratic trade union movement was better than any realistic alternative was shared by the Norwegian Employers' Confederation (*Norsk Arbeidgiverforening*, NAF).[29]

Recession Lockouts

From 1920 onwards, the Scandinavian mass lockout was mainly used to push down wages in recessions. The 1931 Norwegian lockout in the midst of depression is typical in this respect, deviating only in its enormous scope with 55,000 workers locked out for five months.[30] The prolonged conflict forced AFL to take large loans, while employers suffered less: As the economic activity was lower than usual already when the conflict started, the costs of forgone production were lower too. Lockouts work best in recessions.

The Lockout as a Collective Action Problem

Any lockout that extends beyond the individual workplace or company requires coordination. This raises the issue of collective action in industrial relations.[31] Imagine an industry-wide lockout targeting high wages. If the lockout is successful, all employers in the industry benefit. At the same time, individual companies have strong incentives not to cooperate but rather to take a free ride, by continuing to produce and letting the other companies carry the burden. Free riders, "lockout breakers" in this case, jeopardize the collective effort of employers.

[29] Mikkelsen, *Arbejdskonflikter i Skandinavien*, p. 238.

[30] Pedersen T. (1977) 'Tariffoppgjøret 1931. Fagorganisasjonen og storlockouten', *Tidsskrift for arbeiderbevegelsens historie*, 1, pp. 119–43; Mikkelsen, *Arbejdskonflikter i Skandinavien*, pp. 233–38.

[31] Bowman, J. R. (1998) 'Achieving Capitalist Solidarity: Collective Action Among Norwegian Employers', *Politics & Society*, 26, 3, pp. 303–36; and Kelly, J. (2012) *Rethinking Industrial Relations: Mobilisation, Collectivism and Long Waves* (New York: Routledge).

Under what circumstances were employers and their associations able to overcome the problem of free riding? In Sweden, lockouts were generally indiscriminate: All workers within the affected branch were targeted, including "innocent", non-unionized workers. The reason spells solidarity. It was considered unfair that firms with non-unionized labor should be allowed to continue production; all employers should carry the burden of the lockout.[32] Interestingly, in Denmark, lockouts mainly seem to have targeted unionized workers only.[33] Only future research could tell how Denmark—the lockout country par excellence—could overcome free riding.

Political scientist John Bowman, examining Norway in the twentieth century, showed how employers were reluctant to participate in sympathy lockouts, especially "in sectors with high fixed costs, in sectors experiencing strong demand, and in sectors in which low levels of employer organisation expose cooperators to competitive incursions by free-riding competitors."[34] Furthermore, since sympathy lockouts are built on the idea of reciprocity, in some cases even companies that benefited from a particular lockout were reluctant, knowing they had to pay back at a later stage. While Bowman clearly pointed out the impediments, a troubling fact remains. However serious the obstacles to Norwegian capitalist collective action were, massive sympathy lockouts did occur, and their occurrence needs to be explained.

Scandinavian Lockouts Versus American Strikebreaking

Lack of proper quantitative data in countries outside Scandinavia does not exclude the possibility to put the mass lockout in international perspective. A qualitative comparison with the USA illuminates both preconditions and effects of the lockout.

Scandinavian and American employers had a choice when facing growing labor organization and militancy in the form of strikes: to replace strikers with workers from the outside or to enlarge conflicts using massive lockouts. And employers chose differently. In a comparison between the

[32] Swenson, *Capitalists Against Markets*, pp. 75–76.

[33] Hamark, 'Strikes and Lockouts'.

[34] Bowman, 'Achieving Capitalist Solidarity', p. 322.

industrial relations systems in the USA and Sweden—the basic argument applies to Scandinavia as a whole—political scientist Peter Swenson concluded: "Lockouts were to Swedish developments what strikebreaking and blacklisting was to American ones."[35] Whereas no comparative quantitative data could back the statement, Swenson is most likely correct. Various studies show the extensive use of strike-breakers, spies, armed guards, and paramilitary groups in the US labor market.[36] Of course, blacklisting occurred also in Norway, in Sweden labor conflicts led to lethal outcomes in both 1908 and 1931, and Danish strikers were recurrently replaced by strike-breakers (*skruebrækkere*). But overall, American and Scandinavian employers chose different strategies. Why?

Swenson suggested that where the supply of labor was relatively scarce, strikebreaking would be difficult to pursue and hence lockouts would be more prominent. But this could hardly explain the difference between the USA and Scandinavia. In fact, the relative scarcity of American labor is considered important in explaining the high wages in the nineteenth-century US economy.[37] Arguably, the European migration 1850–1910—including large streams from Norway and Sweden—equalized the relative labor supply between the regions. The decisive difference was the enormous American labor supply in *absolute* terms, in combination with railroads. In the USA, there were always enough underemployed or unemployed *somewhere*, and with the railway, it became possible to transport them quickly over long distances to break strikes.[38]

The difference in labor supply also had a qualitative component. The Scandinavian countries were distinguished by the relative absence of linguistic and ethnic cleavages. It facilitated the emergence of purely class-based organizations. (The fact that the Scandinavian labor movement was

[35] Swenson, *Capitalists Against Markets*, p. 73.

[36] Gitelman, H. M. (1973) 'Perspectives on American Industrial Violence', *The Business History Review*, 47, 1, pp. 1–23; Norwood, S. H. (2002) *Strikebreaking and Intimidation: Mercenaries and Masculinity in Twentieth Century America* (Chapel Hill: University of North Carolina Press); Smith, R. M. (2003) *From Blackjacks to Briefcases: A History of Commercialized Strikebreaking and Unionbusting in the United States* (Athens: Ohio University Press); and Tuttle, W. M. (1969) 'Labor Conflict and Racial Violence: The Black Worker in Chicago, 1894–1919', *Labor History*, 10, 3, pp. 408–32.

[37] Habakkuk, H. J. (1962) *American and British Technology in the Nineteenth Century: The Search for Labour-Saving Inventions* (Cambridge: Cambridge University Press).

[38] Norwood, *Strikebreaking and Intimidation*, p. 78.

divided by gender is less important in this context, as women were subordinate to men in *all* countries.) Also, as sociologist Walter Korpi points out, the Reformation wiped out Catholicism.[39] In Europe, at the turn of the last century, the Catholic Church would become one of organized labor's toughest opponents. Still, even among white Protestants, there were ways to separate one group from another. The employers did—as did workers themselves. The action taken by Gothenburg dockworkers at the end of the nineteenth century illustrates the point. The local union—which had won preferential rights to work for its members—tried to limit the supply of labor. Unable to use skin color, religion, language, or nationality as a differentiator, they used the city's perimeter: Boys from the countryside were not allowed to be union members.[40] But it was, after all, impossible to ignite the same hatred between Danes born in Aalborg and Roskilde as between Americans with different skin colors.

The American labor movement was dominated by white workers, and until the 1930s, Afro-Americans were referred to as "the scab race".[41] The conditions for black strikebreaking were exceptionally good. Blacks were excluded from industrial work in most northern states until the end of the 1910s, and in many professions, the ban lasted even longer. Afro-Americans seldom had union experience; the rate of unionization was generally low in the South, and they often worked in agriculture where unions barely existed. In addition, actions taken by white unions had the unintentional though predictable effect of boosting strikebreaking even further. For instance, in 1900, eight of the national unions excluded blacks from membership. The reasons given for the apartheid policy were that competition threatened the living standard of white workers and that white customers detested blacks.[42] Against this background, it is hardly surprising that black workers became "a formidable strikebreaking force,"

[39] Korpi, W. (1986) 'Den svenska arbetarrörelsens förutsättningar och strategier', *Arbetarhistoria*, 37–38, 1–2, p. 39.

[40] Björklund, A. (1984) *Hamnens arbetare: En etnologisk undersökning av stuveriarbetet i Göteborg* (Stockholm: Nordiska museet), pp. 20–23.

[41] Norwood, *Strikebreaking and Intimidation*, p. 78.

[42] Green, J. (1998) *The World of the Worker: Labor in Twentieth-Century America* (Urbana: University of Illinois Press), pp. 46–47; and Norwood, *Strikebreaking and Intimidation*, p. 79.

as historian Stephen Norwood puts it.[43] Nor is it surprising that black leaders encouraged strikebreaking to gain access to industrial jobs.

There are more aspects to the divergent labor market regimes in the USA and Scandinavia than quantitative and qualitative differences in the supply of labor. Mass lockouts presuppose centralism, i.e., that employers as a collective have power over individual employers. Conditions were worse in the United States. With a land area twelve times larger than Scandinavia as a whole—and with a continuous and rapid influx of new companies—it was difficult to get the coordination required.[44]

The Atlantic was the demarcation line of another industrial relations-aspect: extensive use of violence. In general, both the federal state and the states in the USA were more employer-accommodating than in Scandinavia. Strikebreaking almost always led to bitter conflicts, and therefore, it was necessary to protect the strike-breakers physically. Protection was offered by the police and the military or by union busting firms like Pinkerton.

That strikebreaking—and the violence following it—was a nearby solution in the USA could partly be attributed to the so-called frontier culture. "The whole history of the American frontier is a narrative of taking what was there to be taken," historian Joe Frantz wrote.[45] Violence was an everyday aspect of life in the Wild West, just like it became in strikebreaking. A recurrent theme in the press was that the professional strike-breaker reincarnated the vigilante of the frontier. The culture of violence penetrated every pore of society, and experts of violence became natural authorities. US streetcar strikes were particularly violent affairs in the first decades of the twentieth century, one of the bloodiest occurred in St Louis in 1900. During an interview with the legendary gunfighter Frank James, *St. Louis Dispatch* found it appropriate to ask how Mr James would have handled the bloody conflict, had he been Missouri's governor.[46]

Also, the Scandinavian compromises at the turn of the last century—enforced by mass lockouts—in themselves fostered "orderly" relations, at

[43] Ibid., p. 78.

[44] Swenson, *Capitalists Against Markets*, p. 78.

[45] Frantz, J. B. (1969) 'The Frontier Tradition: An Invitation to Violence' in Graham, H. D. and Gurr, T. R. (eds.) *Violence in America: Historical and Comparative Perspectives* (New York: Bantam), pp. 101–19, p. 102.

[46] Norwood, *Strikebreaking and Intimidation*, p. 47.

least compared to the US labor market. The workers got their unions, and the employers got their managerial rights. A similar exchange has never been made in the USA. *Fortune Magazine* once noted that most American employers "greet the prospect of unionization with the enthusiasm that medieval Europeans reserved for an outbreak of the Black Death."[47] This was true for the period discussed here, as well as today.[48]

Conclusion

Scandinavian lockout activity in relation to total conflict activity was substantial from around 1900 until World War II. In relative terms, Danish employers used the lockout most extensively. In comparison with The Netherlands—the only country where statistics allow comparison—Scandinavia was a lockout region. Mass lockouts, including credible threats of mass lockouts, were a means to enforce managerial control. In the interwar years, mass lockouts were primarily used to cut wages during recessions. Mass or sympathy lockouts required employer associations strong enough to exercise power over individual companies. The creation of employer associations was a token of the strength of labor, and the Scandinavian lockout was not used with the aim of wiping out unions. On the contrary, its success depended on the presence of a reasonably strong union confederation with centralized strike funds.

How Scandinavian employers dealt with the problem of collective action is still not understood: the Norwegians locked out in sympathy despite various obstacles. And while the Swedes addressed free riding in a way that makes theoretical sense, the Danes did the opposite—and made it work in practice.

Over the years, several distinguished scholars have argued that the statistical separation of strikes and lockouts is meaningless or even harmful.[49] *Meaningless* because the effect is the same (stoppage of work) and because the distinction provides no indication of where the "war guilt

[47] Logan, J. (2006) 'The Union Avoidance Industry in the United States', *British Journal of Industrial Relations*, 44, 4, p. 669.

[48] For example, Logan, J. (2021) 'Crushing Unions, by Any Means Necessary: How Amazon's Blistering Anti-union Campaign Won in Bessemer, Alabama', *New Labor Forum*, 30, 3, pp. 38–45.

[49] Hamark, 'Strikes and Lockouts'.

lies," and is "based on the notion of responsibility, which is an inadequate basis for statistical definitions." *Harmful*—to workers—because most conflicts are strikes, and if this fact shows up in official statistics, workers would be blamed for industrial disorder.

In Denmark, 1920–1929, 65% of all workers involved in conflicts were locked out. It does not tell us which side should be blamed for industrial disorder. The figure does not reveal that Danish employers were the guilty party to a larger extent than employers elsewhere in the world. What it does say, however, is that Danish employers made extensive use of the lockout. Employers in other countries—such as the USA—leaned on strike-breakers.

The comparison demonstrates that employers across the world chose differently how to combat wage increases or to defend managerial prerogatives. The aims of employers differed too, from disciplining the unions to crushing them. What factors affected their choices need to be studied more. A reasonable start is to separate strikes and lockouts, to make one of employers' main weapons visible.

Appendix: Norwegian Conflict Statistics

To make Norway comparable to Denmark and Sweden, I have been forced to manipulate the statistics. Statistics Norway did not distinguish between strikes and lockouts, except for the period 1922–1925. But AFL did. When the union confederation in 1909 hired a new secretary in charge of the statistical gathering, the foundation was laid for a comprehensive labor conflict statistics.[50] From that year on, every booklet offered summary tables on strikes and lockouts on frequency, involvement and volume, and individual conflict reports with information on branch, character, duration, workers involved, whether the parties were organized or not, the immediate reason for—as well the result of—the conflict, etc. Importantly, the AFL method of collecting conflicts was the same until 1938, the last pre-war year for which the confederation produced statistics. Therefore, I use the AFL time series on strikes and lockouts, 1909–1938.

[50] This and the following two paragraphs are based on Mikkelsen, *Arbejdskonflikter i Skandinavien*, pp. 448–49. See also: *Beretning. Arbeidernes Faglige Landsorganisasjon*, 1909, especially p. 117.

As pointed out by Flemming Mikkelsen, the year-by-year correlation is high between AFL's and Statistics Norway's figures on total conflict involvement ($r = 0.98$). Nonetheless, Statistics Norway systematically gave higher figures than AFL. One reason is that AFL focused on unionized workers, whereas Statistics Norway registered more non-unionized workers.

My solution is to use the proportions of strikes and lockouts as given by AFL and scale them up according to Statistics Norway's conflict figures. Apart from the fact that there is reason to believe that the aggregated figures of Statistics Norway are better than AFL's, the method has the advantage of adding knowledge to existing one. My estimated figures on strikes and lockouts are compatible with conflict data already used by other researchers.

Imagine that total involvement in year X is 10,000 according to Statistics Norway and 8,000 according to AFL; that is, Statistics Norway reports 25% higher involvement. Equivalently, 10,000 divided by 8,000 equals 1.25. Further, assume that AFL reports 5,000 strikers and 3,000 locked out workers. These figures are then multiplied by the quotient, 1.25, yielding new, scaled-up values of 6,250 and 3,750, respectively—the sum of which equals 10,000. The steps are repeated for each year (each year has its own quotient).

The Norwegian official statistics before 1922 are of poorer quality than 1922 onwards.[51] The pre-1922 data are definitely good enough to detect trends in involvement. Further analysis is needed to determine whether the data also allow comparisons in levels. A pragmatic—if not very principled—argument for comparing in levels also prior to 1922, is that other scholars have done so before.[52]

[51] Mikkelsen, *Arbejdskonflikter i Skandinavien*; and Hamark J. (2023 [Forthcoming]) 'Scandinavian Strikes and Lockouts, c. 1900–1939. Material, Methods and Empirical Findings for Denmark, Norway and Sweden', *Göteborg Papers in Economic History*.

[52] Ross and Hartman, *Changing Patterns*; Shorter and Tilly, *Strikes in France*; and Korpi and Shalev, 'Strikes, Power, and Politics'.

References

Serials

Beretning. Arbeidernes Faglige Landsorganisasjon (https://www.arbark.no/Digitale_dokumenter_beretninger_LO.htm), retrieved April 28, 2022.

Statistisk Aarbog. Danmarks Statistik

Literature

Arbetsinställelser och kollektivavtal samt förlikningsmännens verksamhet m.m. (1938) (Stockholm: Socialstyrelsen).

Arbetsinställelser under åren 1903–1907 jämte öfversikt af arbetsinställelser under åren 1859–1902 samt den s.k. politiska storstrejken år 1902 (1909) (Stockholm: Kommerskollegii afdelning för arbetsstatistik).

Bairoch, P. (1969) *La Population active et sa structure* (Bruxelles: Centre d'économie politique (de l') Université libre de Bruxelles).

Björklund, A. (1984) *Hamnens arbetare: En etnologisk undersökning av stuveriarbetet i Göteborg* (Stockholm: Nordiska museet).

Bowman, J. R. (1998) 'Achieving Capitalist Solidarity: Collective Action Among Norwegian Employers', *Politics & Society*, 26, 3, pp. 303–36.

Briggs, C. (2004) 'The Return of the Lockout in Australia: A Profile of Lockouts Since the Decentralisation of Bargaining', *Australian Bulletin of Labour*, 30, 2, pp. 101–12.

Briggs, C. (2005) 'Lockout Law in Comparative Perspective: Corporatism, Pluralism and Neo-liberalism', *International Journal of Comparative Labour Law and Industrial Relations*, 21, 3, pp. 481–502.

Briggs, C. (2005) 'Strikes and Lockouts in the Antipodes: Neo-liberal Convergence in Australia and New Zealand', *New Zealand Journal of Employment Relations*, 30, 3, pp. 1–15.

Briskin, L. (2016) 'The Employer Offensive: Anti-unionism and Lockouts' in Marín Corbera, M., Domènech Sampere, X. and Martínez i Muntada, R. (eds). *III International Conference Strikes and Social Conflicts: Combined Historical Approaches to Conflict* (Barcelona: CEFID-UAB), pp. 191–208.

Casparsson, R. (1951) *LO under fem årtionden, Vol. 1: 1898–1923* (Stockholm: Tiden).

Cooper, R., Ellem, B., Briggs C. and van den Broek D (2009) 'Antiunionism, Employer Strategy, and the Australian State, 1965–2005', *Labour Studies Journal*, 34, 3, pp. 339–62.

Dribbusch, H. and Vandaele, K. (2007) 'Comprehending Divergence in Strike Activity. Employers' Offensives, Government Interventions and Union Responses' in van der Velden, S., Dribbusch, H., Lyddon, D. and Vandaele,

K. (eds.) *Strikes Around the World, 1968–2005: Case-Studies of 15 Countries* (Amsterdam: Aksant), pp. 366–81.

Edwards, P. K. (1981) *Strikes in the United States 1881–1974* (Oxford: Blackwell).

Edwards, P. K. (1983) 'The Pattern of Collective Industrial Action' in Bain, S (ed.) *Industrial Relations in Britain* (Oxford: Blackwell), pp. 209–34.

Frantz, J. B. (1969) 'The Frontier Tradition: An Invitation to Violence' in Graham, H. D. and Gurr, T. R. (eds.) *Violence in America: Historical and Comparative Perspectives* (New York: Bantam), pp. 101–19.

Gitelman, H. M. (1973) 'Perspectives on American Industrial Violence', *The Business History Review*, 47, 1, pp. 1–23.

Green, J. (1998) *The World of the Worker: Labor in Twentieth-Century America* (Urbana: University of Illinois Press).

Habakkuk, H. J. (1962) *American and British Technology in the Nineteenth Century: The Search for Labour-Saving Inventions* (Cambridge: Cambridge University Press).

Hamark, J. (2014) *Ports, Dock Workers and Labour Market Conflicts* (Gothenburg: University of Gothenburg).

Hamark, J. (2018) 'From Peak to Trough: Swedish Strikes and Lockouts in the First Half of the Twentieth Century', *Workers of the World: International Journal on Strikes and Social Conflict*, 1, 9, pp. 137–66.

Hamark, J. (2022) 'Strikes and Lockouts: The Need to Separate Labour Conflicts', *Economic and Industrial Democracy, 43*, 4, pp. 1891–1910.

Hamark, J. (2023 [Forthcoming]) 'Scandinavian Strikes and Lockouts, c. 1900–1939. Material, Methods and Empirical Findings for Denmark, Norway and Sweden', *Göteborg Papers in Economic History.*

Hyman R. (1989) *Strikes* (London: Palgrave Macmillan).

'Industrial Disputes' (1933) *International Labour Review*, 28, 1, pp. 92–99.

Kelly, J. (2012) *Rethinking Industrial Relations: Mobilisation, Collectivism and Long Waves* (New York: Routledge).

Knudsen, K. (1999) *Arbejdskonflikternes historie i Danmark: Arbejdskampe og arbejderbevægelse 1870–1940* (Copenhagen: SFAH).

Knudsen, K. (2000) 'Storlockout og Septemberforlig 1899' in Ibsen, F. and Scheuer, S. (eds.) *Septemberforliget og det 21. århundrede: historiske perspektiver og fremtidens dilemmaer* (Copenhagen: Jurist- og Økonomforbundets Forlag), pp. 77–88.

Korpi, W. (1986) 'Den svenska arbetarrörelsens förutsättningar och strategier', *Arbetarhistoria*, 37–38, 1–2, pp. 36–43.

Korpi, W. and Shalev, M. (1980) 'Strikes, Power, and Politics in the Western Nations, 1900–1976', *Political Power and Social Theory*, 1, pp. 301–34.

LeRoy, M. (1996) 'Lockouts Involving Replacement Workers: An Empirical Public Policy Analysis and Proposal to Balance Economic Weapons Under the NLRA', *Washington University Law Review*, 74, 4, pp. 981–1059.

'Statistique des greves et des lock-outs' (1920) *Annuaire international de statistique*, 6, pp. 127–47.

Logan, J. (2006) 'The Union Avoidance Industry in the United States', *British Journal of Industrial Relations*, 44, 4, pp. 651–75.

Logan, J. (2021) 'Crushing Unions, by Any Means Necessary: How Amazon's Blistering Anti-union Campaign Won in Bessemer, Alabama', *New Labor Forum*, 30, 3, pp. 38–45.

Lyddon, D. (2007) 'Strike Statistics and the Problems of International Comparison' in van der Velden, S., Dribbusch, H., Lyddon, D. and Vandaele, K. (eds.) *Strikes Around the World, 1968–2005: Case-Studies of 15 Countries* (Amsterdam: Aksant), pp. 24–39.

Methods of Compiling Statistics of Industrial Disputes (1926) (Geneva: International Labour Office).

Mikkelsen F. (1992) *Arbejdskonflikter i Skandinavien 1848–1980* (Odense: Odense Universitetsforlag).

Norwood, S. H. (2002) *Strikebreaking and Intimidation: Mercenaries and Masculinity in Twentieth Century America* (Chapel Hill: University of North Carolina Press).

Pedersen, T. (1977) 'Tariffoppgjøret 1931. Fagorganisasjonen og storlockouten', *Tidsskrift for arbeiderbevegelsens historie*, 1, pp. 119–43.

Ross, A. M. and Hartman, P. T. (1960) *Changing Patterns of Industrial Conflict* (New York: Wiley).

Schiller, B. (1967) *Storstrejken 1909: förhistoria och orsaker* (Göteborg: Elander).

Shalev, M. (1978) 'Appendix II: Problems of Strike Measurement' in Crouch, C. and Pizzorno, A. (eds.) *The Resurgence of Class Conflict in Western Europe Since 1968. Vol. 1: National Studies* (London: Palgrave Macmillan), pp. 321–34.

Shorter, E. and Tilly, C. (1974) *Strikes in France, 1830–1968* (London: Cambridge University Press).

Shyam Sundar, K. R. (2004) 'Lockouts in India, 1961–2001', *Economic and Political Weekly*, 39, 39, pp. 4377–85.

Smith, R. M. (2003) *From Blackjacks to Briefcases: A History of Commercialized Strikebreaking and Unionbusting in the United States* (Athens: Ohio University Press).

Statistisk aarbog for kongeriget Norge 1906 (1906) (Kristiania: Det Statistiske Centralbureau).

'Strejker og Lockouter i Danmark 1897–1899' (1901) *Statistiske Meddelelser*, 4, 8, 4.

'Strejker og Lockouter i Danmark 1916–20' (1922) *Statistiske Meddelelser*, 4, 66, 2.

'Strejker og Lockouter i Danmark 1926–30' (1931) *Statistiske Meddelelser*, 4, 88, 5.

Swenson, P. A. (2002) *Capitalists Against Markets: The Making of Labor Markets and Welfare States in the United States and Sweden* (New York: Oxford University Press).

Tuttle, W. M. (1969) 'Labor Conflict and Racial Violence: The Black Worker in Chicago, 1894–1919', *Labor History*, 10, 3, pp. 408–32.

van der Velden, S. (2000) *Stakingen in Nederland: Arbeidersstrijd 1830–1995* (Amsterdam: IISH).

van der Velden, S. (2006) 'Lockouts in The Netherlands: Why Statistics on Labour Disputes Must Discriminate Between Strikes and Lockouts, and Why New Statistics Need to Be Compiled', *Historical Social Research/Historische Sozialforschung*, 31, 4, pp. 341–62.

von Sydow, H. (1913) *Riktlinier för Svenska arbetsgifvareföreningens verksamhet under gångna och kommande år* (Stockholm: Svenska arbetsgivareföreningen).

Wallace, J. and O'Sullivan, M. (2006) 'Contemporary Strike Trends Since 1980: Peering Through the Wrong End of a Telescope' in Morley, M., Gunnigle, P. and Collings, D.G. (eds.) *Global Industrial Relations* (London: Routledge), pp. 223–46.

Woodbury, R. M. (1949) 'The Incidence of Industrial Disputes', *International Labour Review*, 5, pp. 451–66.

CHAPTER 15

Wildcat Strikes Between 1960 and 1973: A German-Danish Comparison

Peter Birke

On May 15, 1968, the largest strike in the history of the twentieth century began in France.[1] It was, at least in its first phase, a "wild-cat" strike, not organized by the unions. Three aspects played a central role. First, "new" workers, people who had entered the labor market in the 1960s, and groups that were structurally disadvantaged in the labor market, played an important role. Second, at least some of the actions were explicitly critical against institutional points of reference, be it by the trade unions, social-democratic government, or the Communist Party.

[1] Seidman, M. (2004) *The Imaginary Revolution: Parisian Students and Workers in 1968* (London: Berghan), cf. Gehrke, B. and Horn, G. R. (eds.) (2018) *1968 und die Arbeiter in Europa. Studien zum 'proletarischen Mai' in Europa* (Hamburg: VSA), Introduction.

The original version of this chapter was revised: Incorrect author name has been updated. The correction to this chapter is available at https://doi.org/10.1007/978-3-031-08987-9_18

P. Birke (✉)
University of Göttingen, Göttingen, Germany
e-mail: peter.birke@uni-goettingen.de

© The Author(s), under exclusive license to Springer Nature Switzerland AG 2023, corrected publication 2023

J. Jørgensen and F. Mikkelsen (eds.), *Trade Union Activism in the Nordic Countries since 1900*, Palgrave Studies in the History of Social Movements, https://doi.org/10.1007/978-3-031-08987-9_15

And third, the wildcat strikes were a kind of hinge between the labor movement and the youth movement, and thus, they illustrate the connection between labor struggles and social movements to which the editors of this volume refer in the introduction. In the following, I will show that all three features can be found in labor struggles outside France, and not at least in the Federal Republic of Germany (FRG) and in Denmark, although these countries were at the time considered as prototypes of social partnership and "peaceful" relations at the labor market.[2] In the first section of this text, I focus on the development of the three aforementioned aspects in the time before 1968, while in the second section I look at "1968" as a period of upsurge, which is defined here as lasting from ca. 1967 to 1973.

Labor Struggles Before 1968

Wildcat strikes may take different forms in different regulatory contexts. Here, the definition is simply "industrial disputes that are not organized by the unions." It should be noted, however, that such forms of action are not legally protected in both countries, and neither in Denmark nor in Germany was there an individual right to strike. Wildcats had been and still are seen as a violation of individual employment contracts and of the collective peace obligations laid down in bargaining agreements. However, for the period under discussion, sanctions were mostly absent, as the labor market position of those affected was by and large favorable. And this takes us to another point: Wildcat strikes in the 1960s did largely imply an active stance of the workers, as they tried to change power relations at the rank-and-file level to their favor. Thus, it seems to be biased to follow the mainstream of historical research on labor struggles at this point: Periods of intensification of wildcat strikes should ultimately not be perceived solely as *reactions to* social dislocations.[3] It seems to be important to adopt a *reverse perspective* when looking at single strike movements, but also in terms of strike conjunctures. While labor struggles prior to 1968 took place in the context of the Cold War, which certainly contributed to their containment, they took place as well in the context of a sustained economic boom, which meant that workers often had a good

[2] This perspective is also developed here: Birke, P. (2007) *Wilde Streiks im Wirtschaftswunder. Arbeitskämpfe und soziale Bewegungen in der Bundesrepublik und Dänemark, 1950–1973* (Frankfurt a.M./New York: Campus).

[3] Frings, C. (2009) 'Die Ungleichzeitigkeiten der „globalen Revolution". 1968 im Weltsystem' in Birke, P., Hüttner, B. and Oy, G. (eds.) *Alte Linke – Neue Linke. Die sozialen Kämpfe der 1968er Jahre in der Diskussion* (Berlin: Dietz), pp. 49–66.

bargaining position. Given this ambivalence, an increasing quantitative importance of the wildcat strikes from the end of the 1960s onwards[4] can hardly be explained by their geopolitical and economic framework alone. It therefore makes sense not to view the wildcat strikes before and after 1968 solely as a reaction to or expression of crises. In the following, we will also look at more independent moments of social change, in which a massive social recomposition of the working class and the associated *potential* redefinition of the social division of labor are expressed.

Denmark: Wildcat Strikes During the Economic Boom

In the last two years of the 1950s, "one of the most striking periods of expansion in modern economic history" took place in Denmark.[5] Gross national product grew by an average of 5.3% per year between 1957 and 1965, surpassed among Western industrialized countries only by Italy (5.5%) and the FRG (5.4%). One of the key features of the boom was the rapid expansion of modern industry as well as industrial agriculture. In this context, not only the economy changed, but also lifestyles, forms of consumption, and everyday life. A core element of industrial expansion, in addition to investment-friendly policies and the simultaneous securing of demand through wage increases and the welfare state, was the mobilization of labor. As south of Flensburg, this took the form of a reconfiguration of labor markets, characterized by the mobilization of resources from internal migration. Agricultural workers, and around 1960 increasingly small, self-employed farmers, continued to be transformed into industrial workers. About 70% of these new workers were initially employed as unskilled.[6] Between 1957 and 1970, moreover, the registered labor force participation rate of women increased significantly, with an above-average rise in the proportion of married women.[7] The bulk of these women was employed for longer periods in the growing public

[4] Birke, *Wilde Streiks*, pp. 55, 73, 111, 130, 160, 193, 219.

[5] Hansen, S. A. (1977) *Økonomisk vækst i Danmark, Vol. 2: 1914–1975* (Copenhagen: Universitetsforlaget i København), p. 177, also in the following.

[6] Andersen, S. A. (1997) *Arbejderkultur i velfærdssamfundet* (Copenhagen: SFAH), p. 102.

[7] The labor force participation rate of women over 16 increased from about 35% (1955) to 50% (1965). However, the figures are somewhat distorted by the registration of informal work, cf. Borchorst, A. and Siim, B. (1986) *Kvinder i velfærdsstaten.*

sector and in the service sector. At the same time, women workers in the industry formed a precariously employed and underpaid stratum as well.

How did these new workers appear in the strike movements of the 1950s and 1960s? And what significance had wildcat strikes within this development? In the early 1950s, wildcats played only a marginal role in Denmark. After the struggles against the German occupation, in which strikes had played a very important role in 1943 and 1944, as well as attempts to shift the parameters of the political reorganization after 1945 in the direction of socialist politics, a depoliticization and repression of labor struggles had taken place. A strike against the dismissal of a worker who had refused the demand for extra work at the Philips company on the island of Amager off Copenhagen first broke this relative calm in 1954.[8] The five-week labor dispute stood as a symbol of the struggle of (often female) workers in a state-of-the-art electrical plant with Taylorist management principles and repetitive part-time work. Two years later, a mass strike was directed against the mechanism of "wage restraint" embedded in the logic of Keynesianism, which the government considered a prerequisite for enabling the expansion of the welfare state. The strikers reacted against an intervention of a social-democratic government in the industrial bargaining round.[9] At its peak, over 200,000 people demonstrated outside the seat of government in Copenhagen. In the sustained containment of the unrest thereafter, the geopolitical situation played a crucial role. The suppression of the workers' uprising in Hungary denounced the Danish CP, which again had been an important organizing factor for the mass strike. At the same time, the expansion of the welfare state (including the establishment of the People's Pension [*Folkepension*]) illustrated a "trade-off" between a "stability" of wages and state compensation.

Conflicts in the factories did not intensify again until the end of the decade. Between September 10, 1958, and December 1, 1960, no fewer than 261 wildcat strikes were recorded.[10] In August 1960, observers

Mellem moderskab og lønarbejde gennem 100 år (Aalborg: Aalborg Universitetsforlag), pp. 105–07.

[8] Loft, S. and Høj, J. (1954) *Philips-strejken* (Copenhagen).

[9] Larsen, S. B. (1977) *Kommunisterne og arbejderklassen. Danmarks kommunistiske Partis rolle i dansk arbejderbevægelse - en politisk biografi* (Copenhagen: Tiderne Skifter), p. 56.

[10] *Socialdemokratiske Noter* (SN), No. 10, July 1960, pp. 930–35.

spoke of the wildcat strikes as a "summer fashion" that had seemed to the public like a "natural social disaster." They were also difficult to pin down, they said, because "the focus was quite obviously on the individual workplace."[11] The problem of classifying the strikes was certainly also contributed to by the fact that they were often led by workers who had had previously played no visible role in labor struggles.[12] Many of the actions were directed against the wage framework defined in the 1958/59 bargaining round in the face of increased inflation. While skilled workers had the right to company-based wage re-negotiations, contracts for unskilled blue-collar workers in most cases excluded such negotiations. Thus, the strike wave reacted to the widening wage gap and in doing so translated the women's movement's demand for "equal pay for equal work" into labor unrest.

In the spring of 1960, for example, a conflict escalated at a rubber and galoshes factory in Køge, triggered by the fact that, as production increased, the 650 men working at the factory were granted wage increases that were denied to the 540 women.[13] In the immediate aftermath of the strike in Køge, many wildcat strikes were counted, often led by women workers, but also generally in the low-wage sector. One example was the breweries. There, women's work was traditionally seasonal: overtime in the summer contrasted with unemployment in the winter.[14] In the 1950s, women were marginalized, employed largely on a piecework basis, especially in the bottling halls and as cleaners. They were disadvantaged in terms of wages, but also in terms of sick pay and vacation. This was cemented by a separate union organization, which, however, could at the same time become the starting point for an

[11] Petersen, C. H. (1979) 'Sommerens mode: ulovlige strejker' in Petersen, C. H. (ed.) *Fra klassekampens slagmark i Norden* (Aarhus: Modtryk), pp. 208–12.

[12] Thus began the wildcat strikes in the provincial slaughterhouses, where, in view of the renewed tightening of the pace of work in late summer, there were so-called *slomo actions*, that is, the nationwide coordinated lowering of the pace of work (Grelle, H. and Knudsen, K. [1995] *Gris på kniven. Slagteriarbejdernes arbejde og organisering i 100 år* [Copenhagen: SFAH], p. 108).

[13] Rostgård, M. (1979) *Det danske socialdemokrati efter 1945. En gennemgang af socialdemokratiets økonomiske politik 1945–1963*, unpublished master's thesis, Aarhus University, p. 79.

[14] Assens, J., Hansen, A. E., Jensen B. B. and Nielsen, M. (1993) *De slukkede vores tørst - og gjorde livet lidt rødere: Bryggeriarbejdernes forbund, DBBMF 1898–1990* (Copenhagen: SFAH), pp. 106–09.

independent articulation of "women's demands."[15] Already since mid-March 1960, the leftist-oriented clubs and associations of male brewery workers in Copenhagen had been demanding immediate wage increases of 20 crowns a week.[16] After a short wildcat strike, they pushed through these demands. The fact that women and provincial workers were left empty-handed did not seem to be their problem.[17] Female employees in breweries in Helsingør and Aalborg reacted with a wildcat for one day and in Aarhus for three days in early June 1960. On June 2, female workers in Copenhagen followed suit, also demanding the same wage increase as the men.[18] On June 3, 1,500 female workers demonstrated in front of the labor court against the fines imposed there due to their "unlawful action."[19] They also refused to resume work as ordered by the court. In the end, the wage increase achieved through the strikes was limited. Women's wages were still more than a third lower than men's. But the importance of being publically visible as active and capable of acting couldn't be denied.

Various groups of employees inspired each other with their strikes. Everywhere, the demand for a *linear wage increase* was now being formulated: From June 8 to 16, 1960, unskilled shipyard and metal workers in Copenhagen and Aarhus, milk suppliers in Herning, bus drivers in Aarhus, and workers at three dairies in Copenhagen went on strike.[20] On June 15, the brewery workers resumed work after their demands were met.[21] New strikes began almost daily in late summer, but the generalized labor unrest that had gripped Danish industry took the unions by surprise. A means of getting the "wildfire" under control did not seem to be at hand, also in view of the employers' refusal to start collective bargaining ahead of time. Intervention in the strike wave was also hampered by the fact that the wildcats were hardly coordinated. Hearsay and media coverage of the labor unrest were certainly of greater importance than the organized left-wing of the trade unions. Only in the case of the warehouse

[15] Ibid., p. 106.

[16] Ibid., pp. 109f.

[17] Rostgård, *Det danske socialdemokrati*, p. 77.

[18] Cf. Assens et al., *De slukkede vores tørst*, pp. 110–15.

[19] Christensen, C. O. (1961) *Den faste Voldgiftsrets Kendelser* (Copenhagen), p. 24.

[20] *SN*, 10, 1960, p. 933.

[21] Assens et al., *De slukkede vores tørst*, p. 111.

workers,[22] the dockworkers, and the seamen,[23] it is possible to speak of a certain sectoral coordination. Finally, on September 12 and 13, an industrial action by 3,000 postal workers, in Copenhagen, caused a public stir. The strike, which was joined by postal workers in Aarhus and Odense on September 13, protested against the hiring of temporary workers to undermine an overtime boycott.[24] The background to the boycott, in turn, was the demand for linear wage increases, just as in industry. The postal workers, whose wages were, in a certain contrast to their status as civil servants, far below average, finally succeeded in their demand. It was the first significant strike in the public sector in Denmark's postwar history. From October onward, the strike wave ebbed, primarily because most strikes were successful or, from late summer onward, the threat of work stoppages alone often brought about wage increases. In the three years after 1960, Danish collective bargaining and labor policy was not insignificantly determined by the shock that the loss of control by the institutional labor market parties, visible in the "summer strikes," had caused: Many of its features remind, as we will see later, of those that characterize the struggles around 1968.

The strike wave of 1960 was also reflected in the collective bargaining round of the following year. The unions of unskilled and semi-skilled workers demanded an increase in the minimum wage. While the dispute in the metal industry was quickly settled,[25] a strike by transport workers, who had been relatively poorly paid up to that point, lasted almost four weeks and paralyzed large parts of the Danish economy. In mid-May 1961, it was finally settled by record wage increases[26]—this, too, was not only a "natural" result of the booming economy, but also, and above all, of the strike wave of 1960. It was not until the collective bargaining round of 1963 that the broad workplace unrest vanished again. The freezing of wages and prices in the government's "Holistic Solution" (*Helhedsløsningen*) and the associated suspension of collective bargaining were accompanied by a massive expansion of the welfare state. Not only

[22] Rostgård, *Det danske socialdemokrati*, p. 83, and *SN*, 10, 1960, p. 333.

[23] Rostgård, *Det danske socialdemokrati*, p. 83.

[24] *SN*, 12, September 1960, p. 1082.

[25] Cf. *SN*, 8, May 1961, p. 656.

[26] Mikkelsen, F. (1992) *Arbejdskonflikter i Skandinavien 1848–1980* (Odense: Odense Universitetsforlag), p. 328.

regarding the history of labor disputes, it is important to keep in mind that the "most developed form of a planned income policy" in international comparison,[27] just like the "golden age" of the welfare state, was also a *reaction to* a new quality of local labor unrest. After 1964, apart from a major but largely unsuccessful labor dispute in the breweries in 1965, which was part of a collective bargaining round, conflicts again took a more localized and invisible form, though their scope was at any time greater than that of the early 1950s.

Germany: Cold War and "Localization"

A "localization" of the struggle over working conditions with a simultaneous centralization of collective bargaining policy was a general phenomenon in northwestern Europe, but in the FRG this dualism was particularly pronounced. That the FRG was a Cold War borderland played an important role in this context. In the two German states, the system conflict was played out particularly drastically. The policies of the West German trade unions, like those of the oppositional and since 1956 illegalized Communist Party, reproduced the cold war within the factories.[28] Significantly more than in other Western European countries, strike action and especially wildcat strikes were subject to the suspicion of "communist infiltration." Based on this, strikers often experienced defeats when their actions took on a more public character and employers and media articulated anti-communist resentments. Thus, labor struggles in the Federal Republic took on the character of hardly conspicuous actions, visible only locally and invisible outside the factory. Consequently, an illegal "second negotiation" was established in many companies under the conditions of the economic boom, which until the mid-1960s resulted in "unofficial" wages being far above the collectively agreed, especially in the metal industry and at the steel mills.[29] Given full employment after 1960, short, and "invisible," wildcat strikes were indeed relatively promising.

[27] Flanagan, R. J. and Ulman, L. (1971) *Wage Restraint. A Study of Incomes Policy in Western Europe* (Los Angeles: University of California Press), p. 130.

[28] Cf. Kalbitz, R. (1978) 'Gewerkschaftsausschlüsse in den 50er Jahren' in Jacobi, O., Müller-Jentsch, W. and Schmidt, E. (eds.) *Gewerkschaftspolitik in der Krise* (Berlin: Rotbuch Verlag), pp. 159–75.

[29] Cf. Birke, *Wilde Streiks*, pp. 106–11.

Such rank-and-file wage policies caused considerable nervousness within the Trade Unions, especially in light of the fact that they contradicted a strongly centralized collective bargaining policy, which reached its peak around 1960 with the agreements on the reduction of working hours negotiated between the central bodies of the metalworkers' union and the employer's organization.[30] Between late summer 1959 and the beginning of 1960, a large number of workplace disputes occurred that the IG Metall's official paper spoke of a "strike wave unprecedented in the history of the Federal Republic of Germany," a diction that seems far exaggerated in view of the figures actually ascertained, but which illustrates the perception as a problematic development.[31] Throughout the 1960s, this perception remained, especially since it was accompanied by a declining level of union membership.

At the same time, like in Denmark, the social composition of the strikers changed around 1960. In the early 1960s, many work stoppages were carried out by the so-called guest workers—for example, in February 1962 in several mines in the Ruhr coalfield or in the winter of 1962/63 among the assembly line workers at VW in Wolfsburg.[32] In addition to protests against working conditions on the assembly line, the focus here was on the miserable housing conditions. Unlike the workers with German passports, migrants had to expect a harsh reaction even in the case of local and selective strikes: It was not uncommon for the affected companies to call the police and have alleged strike leaders deported. In addition, the archives for the period around 1962 contain several strikes by unskilled female industrial workers against wage discrimination. In this context, both employers and unions underestimated the readiness and willingness of women to fight for their rights. While wildcats otherwise mostly had been of short duration, women's strikes around 1960 could be extremely protracted due to the idea of employers to "sit them out."[33]

The recession of 1966/67 changed the pattern of wildcat strikes in the FRG. However, social differentiation within the working class retained an important role: an only slight general increase in unemployment to an

[30] Schroeder, W. (2000) 'Industrielle Beziehungen' in Schildt, A., Siegfried, D. and Lammers, K. C. (eds.) *Dynamische Zeiten: Die 60er Jahre in beiden deutschen Gesellschaften* (Hamburg: Hans Christians Verlag), pp. 494–99.

[31] *Metall*, No. 25, 1959, p. 2.

[32] Birke, *Wilde Streiks*, pp. 133–36.

[33] Ibid., pp. 137–39.

annual average of 2.1% in 1967 obscures the fact that at the beginning of the recession, precariously employed workers, above all migrants, had to pack their things first.[34] In a second step, all company-based achievements were attacked. In this situation, the unions' collective bargaining policy entered a crisis. The SPD's entry into the Grand Coalition at the end of 1966 and its participation tri-partial bargaining (*Konzertierte Aktion*) since the spring of 1967 committed the unions to wage restraint; and they were hardly in a position to ward off the ongoing attacks on effective wages. An increase in the share of wildcat strikes in labor disputes during the recession thus also reflected the powerlessness of the unions. Particularly in the course of 1967, wildcat strikes increased massively: The annual report of IG Metall for the period from 1965 to 1967 speaks of 300,000 participants in such actions.[35] The beginning of the nationwide wave of protests was a wildcat strike at the printing press manufacturer Faber und Schleicher in Offenbach in December 1966,[36] where workers demanded that an authoritarian supervisor would be removed. In addition, there were protests against extensive overtime work, like at the ILO plants in Pinneberg near Hamburg in September 1967.[37] In his work on the history of wildcat strikes at Hanomag in Hanover and Hoesch AG in Dortmund, Klaus-Peter Surkemper showed that the continuity of informal networks, their links to the local public, and the position of shop stewards and works councils were crucial prerequisites for the emergence of strike movements at the end of the 1960s.[38]

In both countries studied, wildcat strikes before 1968 had some characteristic features. First, they were decentralized in form, which is also reflected by the demands. They were often based on conflicts over increasing workloads or authority in the workplace, whereas the most central demand was for equal wages for equal work. This, in turn, is also

[34] Cf. Mandel, E. (1969) *Die deutsche Wirtschaftskrise. Lehren der Rezession 1966/67* (Frankfurt a.M.: Suhrkamp).

[35] *Geschäftsbericht 1968* (1969) (Frankfurt a.M.: IG Metall), pp. 132–33.

[36] Steinhaus, K. (1975) *Streiks in der Bundesrepublik 1966–1974* (Frankfurt a.M.: Institut für Marxistische Studien und Forschungen), pp. 33–35.

[37] Schulenburg, L. (ed.) (1998) *Das Leben ändern, die Welt, verändern! 1968, Dokumente und Berichte*, (Hamburg: Nautilus), pp. 92–95.

[38] Surkemper, K.-P. (1981) *Inoffizielle Streiks, informelle Systeme und betriebliche Gegenmacht: Eine empirische Untersuchung ausgewählter inoffizieller Streiks*, doctoral dissertation, Technische Universität Hannover, Vol. 1.

the central aspect that enabled a "diffusion" of labor struggles between different groups of workers.

Labor Unrest Around 1968

In historical research, it still often appears that the main actors of the social movements around 1968 were the middle-class academics and their children. This view has been criticized time and again, whereas the point here is not to say that class and/or labor struggles produced the decisive dynamic of the revolts. They were, however, especially in connection with other social movements, an important aspect of "1968," while the strike waves around this year also changed the labor struggles themselves.

Wildcat Strikes and New Trade Union Policy in Denmark

Three movements appeared on the stage of May 1968 in Denmark[39]: the new youth movement; second, the movement against the Vietnam War; and a left-wing, oppositional trade union movement. The least mentioned experienced a comeback when labor disputes broke out among telephone operators and steersmen in the maritime sector. Then at that time newly inaugurated right-wing government's attempt to stop both strikes led the B&W shipyard union clubs to call for a demonstration in front of the Parliament on May 24, 1968, on the occasion of the third reading of the law. While the unions warned against action during working hours, 100,000 workers in Copenhagen participated in the strike and about 30,000 demonstrated in front of the *Folketing*.[40] About 5,000 people demonstrated in Aarhus, and strikes were held at the shipyards in Helsingør and Odense. For the first time in more than ten years, left-wing activists had successfully called for political protests independently of the official trade union structures.

The initially almost non-existent reference between the various segments of the social movements was subsequently established not least on the basis of the wildcat strikes. A small foreshadowing was offered in November 1968 by the blockade of a printing plant in the Vesterbro

[39] On the Danish "1968s": Warring, A. (2008) 'Around 1968. Danish Historiography', *Scandinavian Journal of History*, 33, 4, pp. 353–65.

[40] *Beretning 1968* (1969) (Copenhagen: Landsorganisation i Danmark), p. 22.

district of Copenhagen.[41] In addition, the winter of 1968/69 saw several strikes in sectors with a tradition of wildcat strikes: slaughterhouses, tobacco processing, and large shipyards.[42] In February and March 1969, however, the industrial bargaining round went relatively smoothly. Most union members were in favor of only slightly improved contracts; solely female-dominated federations protested, once again, against the abandonment of gender equality in wages. However, workplace struggles gained more visibility in the months to follow, since economic stagnation had been replaced by an economic upswing. Companies' bargaining leverage effectively increased, but the polarization of wages and incomes also intensified. Rising inflation even caused many employees to lose in real wages. In addition, another aspect attracted the attention of the rebelling students: As in the educational institutions, some of the protests by workers were directed against a democratic deficit at work as within the unions. For example, a weeklong strike by SAS aircraft mechanics in the spring of 1969 was not only about wage conditions, but also explicitly uttered criticism about the politics of the works council and the trade unions.[43]

But it was not until the second half of 1969 that this constellation condensed into a wave of strikes. As in Germany, traditionally strongly unionized groups of employees laid down their tools in the first place. From July to September 1969, the metal employers' association alone counted 65 wildcat strikes. Many skilled workers of that time considered wildcats to be more effective than even the "renegotiation" legalized in their collective agreements. However, because many employers agreed to the strikers' demands in view of the full order books, strikes by skilled workers were already decreasing in September, while unskilled and semi-skilled workers were increasingly going on strike.[44] Demands for wage inflation compensation were supplemented by protests against

[41] Arbejdermuseet & Arbejderbevægelsens Bibliotek og Arkiv (ABA), Dansk Typograf-Forbund, Københavns Afdeling, Archive no. 564, Box 49: Collection Blockade Brdr. Hilfling Petersen, November 9, 1968.

[42] ABA, Dansk Typograf-Forbund, Archive no. 597, Box 44: Collection on wildcat strikes.

[43] Meidell, B. (1972) *En undersøgelse af lønarbejdernes muligheder for myndiggørelse* (Copenhagen: Kollektivets Publikationsgruppe), p. 16.

[44] Groth, M. V. (1979) *Strejker i Danmark 1969–1972. En empirisk analyse* (Copenhagen: Nyt fra samfundsvidenskaberne), p. 102.

poor working conditions. Symptomatic in this regard was an incident at the electrical manufacturer Thrige-Titan, where women employed in mass production resisted wage discrimination as well as harassing working conditions on the assembly line and arbitrary dismissals in a series of wildcat strikes.[45]

In the fall of 1969, Danish labor parties remained relatively marginal in the movement. It was not until the end of the year that some trade union officials close to the Communist Party tried to influence and unite the local actions: a group of the party's trade union officials demanded a general wage increase of one crown per hour—and an immediate replacement of the bourgeois government. At first, however, none of the wildcat strikes referred to these demands. It was not until three months after the demand was launched that 818 members of the male brewery workers' union went on strike, albeit unsuccessfully, in support. Then, after the Christmas vacations, a spectacular occupation of the premises of the Shipowners' Association by the traditionally left-wing Seamen's Union occurred, during which a wage increase of one Danish krone was made.[46] Only when, after some hesitation, workers at the B&W shipyard in Copenhagen also took up that demand in a strike, did some 40 further actions take place between January 22 and 30, 1970.[47] On January 29, 1970, shop stewards from all the major shipyards met and called for a one-day, nationwide strike on February 2. About 40,000 people, or 10% of the industrial workers, took part in the subsequent actions: 7,000 on Funen, 3,500 in Aalborg, and 3,000 in Aarhus, and almost all the rest in Copenhagen.[48] Essential to the story of the "One Crown Strikes," however, given a relatively moderate participation, was probably rather

[45] During these strikes, women workers detained a director in his office for a few minutes, which was perceived as the arrival of a new kind of "militancy" (Danish National Business Archives (*Erhvervsarkivet*), Dansk Arbejdsgiverforening, Archive no. 1090, Box 85, 1969/II: Investigation of the labor situation at TT in Odense and Aalborg.

[46] ABA, Landsorganisation i Danmarks arbejdsret (LO), Archive no. 800, Journal no. 6,764: Interview with P.M. Hansen, Jan. 5, 1970.

[47] Jespersen, K. (1972) 'Strejkebevægelsen i Danmark i 69/70. En uensartet arbejderklasse – udviklet kapitalisme og småborgerlighed', *Socialistisk politik*, 5, pp. 3–42.

[48] ABA, LO, 800, 6,764. Following the industrial action, the shipyard owners attempted to remove from their positions the activist shop stewards whom they held responsible for the movement, triggering another protest strike lasting several days and a demonstration by some 20,000 workers outside the employers' headquarters in Copenhagen.

the communication that developed on its basis with other social movements. Thus, a meeting of a "worker-student committee" took place during the strike at Copenhagen University, in which about 200 people participated. A wildcat strike at the Schaub and Co. slaughterhouse in Nyborg on Funen between November 17 and December 8, 1970, became thereafter one of several starting points for an investigative work by an "industrial medicine group" founded by students at the Aarhus University, which studied the health consequences of piecework.[49] The strike also became the trigger for the establishment of an independent and inter-firm committee to support wildcat strikes. The *Arbejdersolidaritet* association provided a model for similar initiatives that were partially effective in the 1970s/1980s.

The health consequences of Taylorism, assembly line production, and piecework, which became public through the students' research work, were scrutinized by the young academics and step by step within the left-liberal nationwide media as well. Mediated through the cooperation of various groups of strikers, students, and left trade union associations, these studies contributed to a selectively articulated break with modernist and functionalist conceptions of wage labor.[50]

Another example of a new, but effective collaboration between workers and social movements was the campaign for "equal pay for equal work," which resumed around 1970 under the impact of the new women's movement. In this sphere, criticism of the male-dominated union's politics in bargaining rounds and public, and spectacular actions by the new-feminist Red Stockings (*Rødstrømperne*), led to a new focus on wildcat strikes, for example, the industrial action by female crane operators at the shipyards in mid-1970.[51] However, the action that drew the most interest from feminists was that of the woman workers at the Royal Porcelain Factory, which, in the winter of 1972/73, challenged the internal gender division of labor as a whole with its piecework conditions.[52] In the run-up

[49] Studenterfrontens arbejdsmedicingruppe (1971) *Malerrapporten. En foreløbig rapport om sundhedsfarerne i malerfaget* (Aarhus: Studenterrådet – Aarhus Universitet); and Studenterfrontens slagterigruppe (1971) *Slagterirapport. Slagterier, stramninger og strejker* (Aarhus: Studenterfronten – Århus Universitet).

[50] Birke, *Wilde Streiks*, pp. 309–15.

[51] *Fagbladet*, 16, 1970, p. 471.

[52] Thygesen, E. (ed.) (1974) *Erfaringer fra en arbejdskamp. Plattekonflikten på Den kgl. Porcelainsfabrik 1972–73* (Copenhagen: Tiderne Skifter). In 1976, the same group of

to the collective bargaining round of 1973, this labor struggle triggered a solidarity that can probably only be compared with the Philips strike of 1954—and similarly benefited from ***subvertising***: the women's actions addressed "The flip side of the Christmas plate," a porcelain Christmas ornament popular in Denmark at the time.

The 1973 round of collective bargaining then triggered the largest legal strike in Danish postwar history. It was also the last labor dispute in which fundamental social landmarks were set. The outcome was the implementation of the eight-hour day and the five-day week, an increase in vacation to four weeks and the abolition of "women's wages," which was enshrined in law two years later.[53] The following strikes were already under the sign of the political and economic crisis: In 1973, a bourgeois minority government gained power and imposed a harsh austerity policy. In May 1974, several hundred thousand people went on strike and protested against this, an event that was seen as the reason for the fall of the government as well as a signal that strikes would by no means lose their significance in the crisis.[54]

From the Septemberstreiks *to the Crisis*

In Germany, strike movements took a very similar course: In May 1968, coinciding with the height of the protests at the universities and against the emergency laws, employers and unions agreed on a contract in which relatively small wage increases were framed by a post-crisis policy of "secure employment." The year after, wildcat strikes once again began in the steel industry of North Rhine-Westphalia, whose workers had fallen behind the metal industry in terms of wages during the renewed boom and had to fear shrinking wages due to inflation.[55] From September 2 to 19, 1969, the strike wave spread to companies in the coal and steel industry following a both spectacular and successful action at three

women workers struck again against low "women" wages (Sønderriis, E. [1975] 'Der går aldrig skår i en paptallerken. Samtale', *Politisk Revy*, 293, pp. 7–8).

[53] Hansen, A. E. (1998) 'LO 1960–1980' in Grelle, H. (ed.) *I takt med tiden. LOs historie 1960–1997*, Vol. 2 (Copenhagen: Forlaget Fremad), pp. 14–95, p. 65.

[54] See: Mikkelsen, *Arbejdskonflikter*, pp. 331f.

[55] *Die Septemberstreiks 1969* (1969) (Frankfurt a.M.: Institut für Marxistische Studien und Forschungen); and Schmidt, E. (1972) *Ordnungsfaktor oder Gegenmacht. Die politische Rolle der Gewerkschaften* (Frankfurt a.M.: Suhrkamp), pp. 202–302.

Hoesch AG plants in Dortmund. In all, at least 140,000 people went on strike, although some strikes in the public sector and in metalworking are often overlooked in the literature and not counted.[56] The movement's demands focused on a linear increase in wages of between 30 and 70 Pfennig, which corresponded to an increase of between about 5 and 15%, depending on the wage group. IG Metall and the miner's union IG Bergbau und Energie, which had been taken completely by surprise by the strike, tried to regain control by bringing forward collective bargaining. For a short time in the following years, some of the trade unions (notably the chemical worker's union) decentralized their collective bargaining policies and raised record wage demands, albeit based on percentage wage increases. In the fall of 1970, after a wave of warning strikes in the metal industry and the steel sector, the scale of which exceeded that of the *Septemberstreiks*, IG Metall achieved wage increases of over 10%.[57] However, the momentum that developed in the wake of the September strikes paid off handsomely for the unions. In the early 1970s, union density began to rise again in almost all unions for the first time in decades.

Also similar to Denmark, the wildcat strikes became the basis for stronger cooperation with the new youth movement and the new social movements. The process of rapprochement was by no means uncomplicated, because among the strikers a positive reference to the young, new left, and especially the student movement was by no means self-evident. But there was a relatively positive public reception of some of the strikes, which was linked to the weakening of the East–West conflict. And the strike wave took place in the immediate run-up to the elections to the German *Bundestag*, which also reduced anti-communist attacks.[58] Thus, the September strikes could become the trigger for "non-tariff" wage improvements for about eight million employees. However, counterreactions were not equally weak where more was at stake. This applies to the strike in five Dortmund mines, where, among other things, the demand for an increase in the basic wage from about 600 to 1,000 DM was formulated, above all with regard to two labor disputes of migrant

[56] Cf. Birke, *Wilde Streiks*, p. 249.

[57] Birke, *Wilde Strikes*, pp. 300–06.

[58] Schmidt, *Ordnungsfaktor oder Gegenmacht*, pp. 156–59.

workers in the metalworking industry.[59] At Hella in Lippstadt, the explicit issue was the abolition of the lower wage groups in which the migrant women workers had been placed. At Ehrenreich in Oberkassel, the dispute concerned the piece rates for assembly line workers. Both strikes ended quickly, with the intervention of the police (Hella) or with the help of a massive mobilization of xenophobic resentment (Ehrenreich). However, both actions pointed to a potential that was to become more significant after 1969: The September strikes' demands for fixed incomes opened a field in which the hitherto completely separate local tradition of migrant struggles over working, housing, and living conditions could relate to the demands of a general movement.

The year 1971 then marked the beginning of a counteroffensive by the employers. A legal strike in the metalworking industry of North Baden-North Württemberg, which lasted from October 18 to December 15, 1971, was met with a mass lockout by the employers' association *Gesamtmetall*.[60] There were 145,000 strikers and up to 360,000 lockouted workers. After having made far-reaching concessions in 1970, the metal employers now rejected an arbitration proposal that provided for a relatively small wage increase of 7.5%, given continuous high inflation. The CDU's attempt to topple the Brandt government in April 1972 was seen within a section of the workforce as a consequence of the new hard-line approach of the employers, and it triggered a small wave of protest strikes. From April 25 to 27, 1972, a total of about 100,000 workers, mainly in large companies, went on strike against the vote of no confidence. Ironically, it was precisely the context of the small victory of the social-liberal coalition that prompted the unions to abandon their comparatively offensive wage policy of the previous two years. In the course of 1972, IG Metall again declared its willingness to accept a state-set "wage framework" in support of the "stabilization policy." This triggered a renewed wave of wildcat strikes over the year, which lasted not only for a few weeks, but until late summer 1973.

In January 1973, IG Metall signed collective agreements for the 4.3 million metalworking employees in the various districts, each providing

[59] *Die Septemberstreiks 1969*, pp. 124–30.

[60] Meyer, R. (1977) *Streik und Aussperrung in der Metallindustrie. Analyse der Streikbewegung in Nordwürttemberg-Nordbaden 1971* (Marburg: Arbeiterbewegung und Gesellschaftswissenschaft).

for a wage increase of 8.5%.[61] In the steel industry, a linear increase of 46 Pfennig was agreed at the same time, corresponding on average to the wage increase in metal processing. Dissatisfaction with these agreements was nevertheless unmistakable, particularly in the steel sector. In the ballot, only 26% of members voted in favor of the result, which nevertheless was accepted in accordance with the union's rules. The wave of strikes that followed had a basis in employee dissatisfaction with the rollback in collective bargaining policy. In addition to a wildcat strike at Hoesch related to criticism of the union's policy, employees of a lock factory in Velbert, for example, stopped work for two weeks in February 1973, and at the end of February/beginning of March the sectional rolling mill workers at Mannesmann in Duisburg-Huckingen. In both cases, the demand was for an improvement in working conditions. In April, the VW Group went on strike again for the first time in almost ten years, partly because it had tried to cancel a bonus.[62] In May, the wildcat strikes intensified in the Mannheim area, where at least 29 factories went on strike only that month, mainly in engineering companies and automotive suppliers, but also in the chemical industry.[63]

In the same month, IG Metall negotiated a special payment with the iron and steel employers' association, which on the one hand led to a reduction in the conflicts in the steel industry, and on the other hand to a wave of strikes in the metalworking industry. In June and July 1973, work stoppages occurred in over 60 plants. The strike wave reached its peak in August 1973, with over 100 companies on strike and around 80,000 strikers: In the second half of August, strikes were held at Ford in Cologne, Pierburg in Neuss, and Opel in Bochum, among others. In September, there were still almost 80 companies on strike, including now also parts of the public sector in Hanover. In October, miners at Saarbergwerke again went on strike. Their action, largely unsuccessful as in 1969, marked the end of the strike wave. Overall, the scale of the wildcat strikes had exceeded that of 1969, with around 275,000 participants in

[61] Express (eds.) (1974) *Spontane Streiks 1973. Krise der Gewerkschaftspolitik* (Offenbach a.M.: Verlag Zweitausend).

[62] Höhne, G. (1974) *Wir gehen vorn! Erfahrungsbericht über die Arbeitskämpfe bei Mannesmann* (Berlin: Rotbuch Verlag).

[63] Wieser, H. (ed.) (1973) *Jahrbuch zum Klassenkampf 1973: Sozialistische Initiativen im kapitalistischen Deutschland* (Berlin: Rotbuch Verlag), pp. 48–72.

335 companies. Compared with the *Septemberstreiks*, in which the workforces of only 69 companies took part, it was noticeable that the number of small and medium-sized companies on strike was significantly higher.

More importantly, working conditions of assembly line workers came under practical criticism. The named labor dispute at Ford in Cologne in August 1973 is probably the best-known case in point.[64] It was ignited by the dismissal of several hundred migrant workers who had returned late from their summer vacation. In addition, there was a linear wage demand of one DM/hour. And finally, the long-standing demand for additional breaks on the assembly lines was raised. During the wildcat, the plant was occupied predominantly by migrant workers, while there was a growing rejection of the strike by the predominantly German skilled workers. In the end, Ford was recaptured in cooperation between supervisors and the police. Despite the defeat of the strikers, this conflict unleashed a lasting public impact. However, the reaction of the press, like the spectacular appeal of Chancellor Brandt, who called for "moderation" during the Ford strike in a televised "speech to the nation," was primarily characterized by a rejection of the alleged "riots." The fact that, according to a survey, over 90% of those questioned had heard of the strike was probably also due to racist headlines in the tabloid press, which spoke in large letters of "Turkish terror in Cologne." However, even beyond Ford, a significant part of the strike wave of 1973 was about migrant issues. And not all these struggles ended in defeat: Wildcat strikes by predominantly migrant women in the electrical industry, for example, following the example of the actions at Hella in Lippstadt in 1969, once again attacked the so-called light-wage groups, achieved the support of the public and especially of the new women's movement. The struggle at the auto supplier Pierburg in Neuss succeeded in enforcing the principle of formal wage equality a few years before this was also confirmed in the collective agreement.

While IG Metall supported the women's strikes in some cases, it was much more hostile to most of the other "wildcat" actions in 1973

[64] Gruppe Arbeiterkampf (1973) *Streik bei Ford in Köln* (München: Trikont); Bojadžijev, M. (2002) 'Antirassistischer Widerstand von Migrantinnen und Migranten in der Bundesrepublik: Fragen der Geschichtsschreibung', *1999. Zeitschrift für Sozialgeschichte des 20. und 21. Jahrhunderts,* 1, pp. 125–52. Cf. Goeke, S. (2020) *„Wir sind alle Fremdarbeiter!" Gewerkschaften, migrantische Kämpfe und soziale Bewegungen in Westdeutschland 1960–1980* (Paderborn: Schöningh).

than it had been in 1969. This was also related to the fact that in 1973 a left-wing trade union opposition had gained importance in some plants.[65] Groups like the *GOG* (Gruppe oppositioneller Gewerkschafter, later: Gewerkschafter ohne Grenzen (group of oppositional unon activists at Opel, Bochum)) at Opel in Bochum, the *Plakatgruppe* at Daimler, or the *Kölner Fordarbeiter* threatened established hierarchies in works councils and shop stewards' bodies, while the migrant workers mostly had their own networks, independent of the German left. Not only in IG Metall, but also in other individual trade unions such as DRUPA (Industriegewerkschaft Druck und Papier (Printing and Paper Industry Workers Union)) or IG Chemie (Union of Workers in the Chemical Industry), a massive wave of repression against the left-wing began around 1973, which ultimately reached the scale of the anti-communist purges of the 1950s.[66] Nevertheless, the leftist influence in the 1973 strikes must not be overestimated. And it was ultimately also pushed back by an integration of some of their demands, initially perceived as "exotic," in "official" collective bargaining, as became clear, for example, in view of the enforcement of extra-breaks for workers at the assembly line in North Württemberg-North Baden in the late fall of 1973.

On the eve of the crisis, the culture of wildcat strikes had emerged more clearly than before in all its differentiation and diversity: It was not just male skilled workers with German passports who were involved, but a wide variety of groups of workers, each of whom associated a specific, local meaning with their actions. The publication of the concerns directed against assembly line work, etc., had a liberating moment, as did the criticism of the gendered and ethnicized company hierarchy. Indirectly, and without overestimating their intervention, this differentiation and individualization linked the wildcat strikes to other contemporary protest movements that located themselves beyond the sphere of wage labor.

Summary

The labor struggles in the FRG and Denmark are indicators of a transformation in the priorities of strikers during the period of the economic

[65] Birke, *Wilde Streiks*, pp. 21–22.

[66] Erd, R. (1978) 'Gewerkschaftsausschlüsse in den 70er Jahren' in Jacobi, O., Müller-Jentsch, W. and Schmidt, E. (eds.) *Gewerkschaftspolitik in der Krise* (Berlin: Rotbuch Verlag), pp. 166–75.

miracle from about 1955 to 1973. This change in priorities brought to light needs of workers that still seem quite topical today: shorter working hours, less work compression, equal pay for equal work, and good and healthy jobs. What is special about some of these demands is that they can by no means only be enforced at the factory. For example, gender equality is ultimately determined by the way, in which social reproduction is organized in society. In this respect, strike movements of the late 1960s more and more open converged into "political" struggles in a narrow sense, which at the same time pointed far beyond the local perspective and condensed into mass actions in both countries at the end of the 1960s. At the same time, the comparison shows that these dynamics must be understood independently of state policies (strike bans, but also expansion of the welfare state) and even existed relatively independently of a more or less pronounced militancy of the unions. However, the dispersed, decentered character of these labor struggles is by no means unconnected with state regulation and union bargaining policy, which repeatedly react to them, take up the demands, reinterpret them, etc. To this day, disputes at the workplace have remained the material around which the question of a reorganization of trade union strategies and perspectives for action in the direction of a "social movement unionism" is concerned.[67]

References

Archives

The Workers Museum & The Labour Movement's Library and Archive (*Arbejdermuseet & Arbejderbevægelsens Bibliotek og Arkiv, ABA*):
Dansk Typograf-Forbund, Archive no. 44.
Dansk Typograf-Forbund, Københavns Afdeling, Archive no. 564.
Landsorganisation i Danmarks arbejdsret (LO), Archive no. 800.
Danish National Business Archives (*Erhvervsarkivet*):
Dansk Arbejdsgiverforening, Archive no. 1090.

Serials

Fagbladet

[67] Waterman, P. (1993) 'Social-Movement Unionism: A New Union Model for a New World Order?', *Review*, 16, 3, pp. 245–78.

Metall
Socialdemokratiske Noter

Literature

Andersen, S. A. (1997) *Arbejderkultur i velfærdssamfundet* (Copenhagen: SFAH).

Assens, J., Hansen, A. E., Jensen B. B. and Nielsen, M. (1993) *De slukkede vores tørst - og gjorde livet lidt rødere: Bryggeriarbejdernes forbund, DBBMF 1898–1990* (Copenhagen, SFAH).

Beretning 1968 (1969) (Copenhagen: Landsorganisationen i Danmark).

Birke, P. (2007) *Wilde Streiks im Wirtschaftswunder. Arbeitskämpfe und soziale Bewegungen in der Bundesrepublik und Dänemark, 1950–1973* (Frankfurt a.M./New York: Campus).

Bojadžijev, M. (2002) 'Antirassistischer Widerstand von Migrantinnen und Migranten in der Bundesrepublik: Fragen der Geschichtsschreibung', *1999. Zeitschrift für Sozialgeschichte des 20. und 21. Jahrhunderts*, 1, pp. 125–52.

Borchorst, A. and Siim, B. (1986) *Kvinder i velfærdsstaten. Mellem moderskab og lønarbejde gennem 100 år* (Aalborg: Aalborg Universitetsforlag).

Christensen, C. O. (1961) *Den faste Voldgiftsrets Kendelser* (Copenhagen).

Die Septemberstreiks 1969 (1969) (Frankfurt a.M.: Institut für Marxistische Studien und Forschungen).

Flanagan, R. J. and Ulman, L. (1971) *Wage Restraint. A Study of Incomes Policy in Western Europe* (Los Angeles: University of California Press).

Erd, R. (1978) 'Gewerkschaftsausschlüsse in den 70er Jahren' in Jacobi, O., Müller-Jentsch, W. and Schmidt, E. (eds.) *Gewerkschaftspolitik in der Krise* (Berlin: Rotbuch Verlag), pp. 166–75.

Express (eds.) (1974) *Spontane Streiks 1973. Krise der Gewerkschaftspolitik* (Offenbach a.M.: Verlag Zweitausend).

Frings, C. (2009) 'Die Ungleichzeitigkeiten der „globalen Revolution". 1968 im Weltsystem' in Birke, P., Bernd Hüttner, B. and Oy, G. (eds.) *Alte Linke – Neue Linke. Die sozialen Kämpfe der 1968er Jahre in der Diskussion* (Berlin: Dietz), pp. 49–66.

Gehrke, B. and Horn, G. R. (eds.) (2018) *1968 und die Arbeiter in Europa. Studien zum 'proletarischen Mai' in Europa* (Hamburg: VSA).

Geschäftsbericht 1968 (1969) (Frankfurt a.M.: IG Metall).

Goeke. S. (2020) *„Wir sind alle Fremdarbeiter!" Gewerkschaften, migrantische Kämpfe und soziale Bewegungen in Westdeutschland 1960–1980* (Paderborn: Schöningh).

Grelle, H. and Knudsen, K (1995) *Gris på kniven. Slagteriarbejdernes arbejde og organisering i 100 år* (Copenhagen: SFAH).

Groth, M. V. (1979) *Strejker i Danmark 1969–1972. En empirisk analyse* (Copenhagen: Nyt fra samfundsvidenskaberne).

Gruppe Arbeiterkampf (1973) *Streik bei Ford in Köln* (München: Trikont).

Hansen, A. E. (1998) 'LO 1960–1980' in Grelle, H. (ed.) *I takt med tiden. LOs historie 1960–1997*, Vol. 2 (Copenhagen: Forlaget Fremad), pp. 14–95.

Hansen, S. A. (1977) *Økonomisk vækst i Danmark, Vol. 2: 1914–1975* (Copenhagen: Universitetsforlaget i København).

Höhne, G. (1974) *Wir gehen vorn! Erfahrungsbericht über die Arbeitskämpfe bei Mannesmann* (Berlin: Rotbuch Verlag).

Jespersen, K. (1972) 'Strejkebevægelsen i Danmark i 69/70. En uensartet arbejderklasse – udviklet kapitalisme og småborgerlighed', *Socialistisk politik*, 5, pp. 3–42.

Kalbitz, R. (1978) 'Gewerkschaftsausschlüsse in den 50er Jahren' in Jacobi, O., Müller-Jentsch, W. and Schmidt, E. (eds.) *Gewerkschaftspolitik in der Krise* (Berlin: Rotbuch Verlag), pp. 159–75.

Larsen, S. B. (1977) *Kommunisterne og arbejderklassen. Danmarks kommunistiske Partis rolle i dansk arbejderbevægelse - en politisk biografi* (Copenhagen: Tiderne Skifter).

Loft, S. and Høj, J. (1954) *Philips-strejken* (Copenhagen).

Mandel, E. (1969) *Die deutsche Wirtschaftskrise. Lehren der Rezession 1966/67* (Frankfurt a.M.: Suhrkamp).

Meidell, B. (1972) *En undersøgelse af lønarbejdernes muligheder for myndiggørelse* (Copenhagen: Kollektivets Publikationsgruppe).

Meyer, R. (1977) *Streik und Aussperrung in der Metallindustrie. Analyse der Streikbewegung in Nordwürttemberg-Nordbaden 1971* (Marburg: Arbeiterbewegung und Gesellschaftswissenschaft).

Mikkelsen, F. (1992) *Arbejdskonflikter i Skandinavien 1848–1980* (Odense: Odense Universitetsforlag).

Petersen, C. H. (1979) 'Sommerens mode: ulovlige strejker' in Petersen, C. H. (ed.) *Fra klassekampens slagmark i Norden* (Aarhus: Modtryk), pp. 208–12.

Rostgård, M. (1979) *Det danske socialdemokrati efter 1945. En gennemgang af socialdemokratiets økonomiske politik 1945–1963*, unpublished master's thesis, Aarhus University.

Schmidt, E. (1972) *Ordnungsfaktor oder Gegenmacht. Die politische Rolle der Gewerkschaften* (Frankfurt a.M.: Suhrkamp).

Schroeder, W. (2000) 'Industrielle Beziehungen' in Schildt, A., Siegfreid, D. and Lammers, K. C. (eds.) *Dynamische Zeiten: Die 60er Jahre in beiden deutschen Gesellschaften* (Hamburg: Hans Christians Verlag), pp. 494–99.

Schulenburg, L. (ed.) (1998) *Das Leben ändern, die Welt, verändern! 1968, Dokumente und Berichte* (Hamburg: Nautilus).

Seidman, M. (2004) *The Imaginary Revolution: Parisian Students and Workers in 1968* (London: Berghan).

Silver, B. (2004) *Forces of Labor. Worker's Movements and Globalization Since 1870* (Cambridge: Cambridge University Press).

Sønderriis, E. (1975) 'Der går aldrig skår i en paptallerken. Samtale', *Politisk Revy*, 293, pp. 7–8.

Steinhaus, K. (1975) *Streiks in der Bundesrepublik 1966–1974* (Frankfurt a.M.: Institut für Marxistische Studien und Forschungen).

Studenterfrontens arbejdsmedicingruppe (1971) *Malerrapporten. En foreløbig rapport om sundhedsfarerne i malerfaget* (Aarhus: Studenterrådet – Aarhus Universitet).

Studenterfrontens slagterigruppe (1971) *Slagterirapport. Slagterier, stramninger og strejker* (Aarhus: Studenterfronten – Århus Universitet).

Surkemper, K.-P. (1981) *Inoffizielle Streiks, informelle Systeme und betriebliche Gegenmacht: Eine empirische Untersuchung ausgewählter inoffizieller Streiks*, doctoral dissertation, Technische Universität Hannover.

Thygesen, E. (ed.) (1974) *Erfaringer fra en arbejdskamp. Plattekonflikten på Den kgl. Porcelainsfabrik 1972–73* (Copenhagen: Tiderne Skifter).

Warring, A. (2008) 'Around 1968. Danish Historiography', *Scandinavian Journal of History*, 33, 4, pp. 353–65

Waterman, P. (1993) 'Social-Movement Unionism: A New Union Model for a New World Order?', *Review*, 16, 3, pp. 245–78.

Wieser, H. (ed.) (1973) *Jahrbuch zum Klassenkampf 1973: Sozialistische Initiativen im kapitalistischen Deutschland* (Berlin: Rotbuch Verlag).

CHAPTER 16

Developing Public Sector Trade Unionism in Scandinavia: From Noble Civil Servants to Militant Wage Earners

Laust Høgedahl

Developing the Frameworks for Collective Bargaining—The Private Sector Beginning

In Scandinavia, trade unionism originates in the private sectors. It all started with the industrial breakthrough in the 1860s, which led to profit-oriented companies coming into competition with each other and the formation of a market for the purchase and sale of labor.[1] The immediate consequent was an insecure existence for the workers in the form of unemployment and pressure on wages. The response of the new

[1] Webb, S. and Webb, B. (1897) *Industrial Democracy* (London: Longmans), see introduction of this volume.

L. Høgedahl (✉)
Aalborg University, Aalborg, Denmark
e-mail: hogedahl@dps.aau.dk

© The Author(s), under exclusive license to Springer Nature Switzerland AG 2023

J. Jørgensen and F. Mikkelsen (eds.), *Trade Union Activism in the Nordic Countries since 1900*, Palgrave Studies in the History of Social Movements, https://doi.org/10.1007/978-3-031-08987-9_16

working class was the formation of trade unions that were to withstand the pressure of the capitalists.[2] In Denmark, Louis Pio became the first Danish chairman of Karl Marx's International in 1871, which in 1878 was formally separated into a trade union, and a political part, which later became the movement of the Danish Confederation of Trade Unions (*Landsorganisationen i Danmark*, LO) and the Social Democratic Party.[3] Louis Pio and the emerging trade union movement were strongly inspired by the trade union struggle that took place in many European countries, where industrial development had gone further than in Denmark, especially France. The goal for the dawning labor movement was very clear: a wage to live on and a shorter working time than the approximately 60 hours per week, which the workers at that time had to deliver to the employers. However, the trade union movement was sluggish in the beginning, when employers in large numbers fired organized workers. The economic crisis of the 1880s also claimed the lives of many trade unions. But the 1890s became in many ways the hay days for the Danish trade union movement with the formation of many local unions, nationwide unions, the interdisciplinary joint organizations in the big cities, and the final creation of the central organization the Danish Federation of Trade Unions (*De samvirkende Fagforbund*, DsF, later LO, and since 2019 the Danish Trade Union Confederation (*Fagbevægelsens Hovedorganisation*) in 1898. The trade union movement quickly learned how a systematic use of the strike weapon could be an effective means of securing better wages and reduced working hours from the capital owners, who had a monopoly on private property and distribution rights over machines and other equipment.

The trade union movement launched a new strategy, in which it took one employer/business owner at a time and went on strike for better pay and reduced working hours by demanding a collective agreement. The workers involved in the industrial conflict were supported by a collective strike fund so that they could keep wages during the conflict. The strategy and thus the strike weapon were so effective that Danish employers felt compelled to organize into employers' associations, which in time also became nationwide. The employers also followed the

[2] Ibsen, F. and Jørgensen, H. (1979) *Fagbevægelse og stat*, Vol. I–II (Copenhagen: Gyldendal).

[3] Knudsen, K. (2011) 'Faglig internationalisme før Anden Verdenskrig. Første del: Organisering af arbejdernes internationale solidaritet', *Arbejderhistorie*, 3, pp. 41–62.

same strategy as the trade union movement by centralizing the movement and by 1898 forming the central organization Danish Employers' and Masters' Confederation (*Dansk Arbejdsgiver- og Mesterforening*, later *Dansk Arbejdsgiverforening*).[4]

Now, the two 'industrialized armies' faced each other, and relations between them were still unclear: How should wages and working conditions be regulated, should market forces rule with its ups and downs, or should there be some form of collective regulation of wages and working conditions? One wing of the employers' association—the 'Iron Barons'—would defeat the nascent trade union movement, while another and more moderate wing—the masters of the construction sector—would embrace and pacify the trade union movement through regulations and a set of binding agreements on wages and working conditions, which was primarily to be used to reduce the possibility of strikes. Above all, the employers wanted to determine who was in charge in their own companies when it came to the right to manage and distribute the work.[5]

A small carpentry strike developed in 1899 into a major conflict. The strike resulted in a general lockout, as it was the entire employers' front that declared the entire trade union movement war. The major conflict was only ended after several mediations and a 100-day labor struggle. The result was the conclusion of the famous 'September Compromise of 1899', which must still be regarded as the 'Constitution of the Danish Labor Market', as the rules and principles laid down in the September Compromise still apply to today's labor market in Denmark both in the private sector and later in the public sector as they shall see later in this chapter. The Danish September Compromise of 1899 has also since become known as the world's first general agreement concluded by social partners.[6]

[4] Knudsen, K. (2009) 'Fagbevægelse og arbejdsgiverforeninger i Danmark 1857–1914', *Rubicon*, 17, 3, pp. 52–69; and Due, J., Madsen, J. S. and Jensen, C. S. (1999) 'Septemberforliget: Et strategisk valg' in Andreasen, M. L., Kristiansen, J. and Nielsen, R. (eds.) *Septemberforliget 100 år* (Copenhagen: Jurist- og Økonomforbundet), pp. 85–112.

[5] Ibsen and Jørgensen, *Fagbevægelse og stat*.

[6] Ibsen, F. (2014) 'Det fagretlige system' in Jørgensen, H. (ed.) *Arbejdsmarkedsregulering* (Copenhagen: Jurist- og Økonomforbundets Forlag).

The September Compromise of 1899 was a 'historic compromise',[7] where both parties had to give concessions to the other party. The trade unions were acknowledged as legitimate parties by the employers who also accepted collective agreements as a mean to regulate wages and working conditions. On the other hand, trade unions accepted the 'peace obligation' meaning that when a collective agreement is in effect it is propitiated to strike. Trade union also accepted the managerial right of the employers.[8]

We find similar developments in both Sweden and Norway. In *Sweden,* the peak organization for workers LO (*Landsorganisationen i Sverige*) was founded in 1898. Four years later, the Swedish Employers' Confederation (*Svenska Arbetsgivareföreningen*, SAF) was founded. As early as 1906, the parties reached the December Compromise. This was an important step toward mutual recognition and balancing of the power relationship between the parties. Here, the freedom of association and the right of management were enshrined, which was important for both the employer and the employee side. During an extensive strike in 1909, the SAF drafted an actual general agreement, but the LO rejected, and the conflict led to a major defeat on the part of the workers. The Swedish labor market experienced a number of conflicts in the following years. The 1920s and 1930s were full of industrial conflict in Sweden. This gave rise to a strong political desire for future conflicts to be regulated due to the damaging effects.[9]

In 1932, the Social Democrats took over the government in Sweden. Among the Social Democrats, there was also a widespread perception that a forced law on the duty of peace would be an option, which, however, was never actualized. The political focus on resolving labor disputes through law led to LO and SAF meeting for negotiations in 1938, which was the first time since 1909. The result was the so-called Saltsjöbad Agreement (*Saltsjöbadsavtalet*)—the first Swedish general agreement and

[7] Due, J., Madsen, J. S. and Jensen, C. S. (1993). *Den danske model: En historisk sociologisk analyse af det kollektive aftalesystem* (Copenhagen: Jurist -og Økonomforbundets Forlag); and Ibsen and Jørgensen, *Fagbevægelse og stat.*

[8] Galenson, W. (1952) *The Danish System of Labor Relations* (Cambridge: Harvard University Press).

[9] Lundh, C. (2002) *Spelets regler. Institutioner och lönebildning på den svenska arbetsmarknaden 1850–2000* (Stockholm: SNS Förlag).

the basis for what would later be called as 'the Swedish model'.[10] The agreement narrowed the gap between legal and interest disputes, peace obligations and bargaining norms and procedures. In addition, the agreement also answered regulated questions about third-party law and 'socially dangerous' conflicts or conflicts that threaten socially important functions. Thus, legislation or norms for this were made superfluous,[11] and the Saltsjöbad Agreement therefore regulated far more matters than the Danish September Compromise.

In *Norway* in 1902, the Norwegian LO (*Landsorganisasjonen i Norge*) and the Norwegian Employers' Confederation entered into an agreement on the arrangement of conciliation boards and arbitral tribunals for the treatment of disputes between employers and workers.[12] This agreement was in fact the first major agreement in Norway, but the agreement was terminated in 1905 after disagreements between the parties. The Treaty of 1907 or the Iron Agreement was the first Norwegian agreement with so-called general provisions, i.e., general provisions or rules which regulated the relationship between the social partners, and which were formulated with the Danish September Compromise of 1899 and the Swedish Iron Agreement of 1906 as role models.[13] The agreement had the character of a general agreement, but only regulated matters for the iron industry. In the years after, the Norwegian labor market continued to experience major conflicts in the form of both strikes and lockouts. Following a labor dispute in the paperwork industry in 1907, the Norwegian parliament (*Stortinget*) asked the government to introduce a bill on forced arbitration as a means of ending ongoing labor disputes. However, the social partners were not enthusiastic about the prospect of a law on forced arbitration, and the compromise between the government and the parties was the establishment of a commission led by Supreme Court Judge

[10] Elvander, N. (2002) 'The New Swedish Regime for Collective Bargaining and Conflict Resolution: A Comparative Perspective', *European Journal of Industrial Relations*, 8, 2, pp. 197–216; and Elvander, N. (2003) Two Labour Market Regimes in Sweden. A Comparison Between the Saltsjöbaden Agreement of 1938 and the Industrial Agreement of 1997, *Industrielle Beziehungen/The German Journal of Industrial Relations*, pp. 146–59.

[11] Elvander, N. (1988) *Den svenska modellen: Löneförhandlingar och inkomstpolitiik, 1982–1986* (Stockholm: Allmänna förlaget).

[12] Galenson, W. (1949) *Labor in Norway* (Cambridge: Harvard University Press).

[13] Hippe, J. and Berge Ø. (2014) *Den nordiske modellen mot 2013. Et nytt kapittel?* (Oslo: Fafo).

Solnørdal.[14] The commission's task was to investigate how labor disputes could be minimized and resolved in the best possible way. The commission's report came in 1909 and made a clear distinction between legal disputes and conflicts of interest.[15] The commission also emphasized the importance of the peace obligation once an agreement had been reached. However, the commission was divided on the issue of the use of arbitration: The social partners were not in favor of a model that included a compulsory arbitration in connection with conflicts of interest, i.e., upon conclusion or termination of an agreement, or when an agreement should be renewed.[16]

The Nordic model of collective bargaining, as described above, has been created in the private sectors in the formative years of 1870–1938 based on general agreements concluded by the social partners. However, this new model of labor market regulation did not have any immediate effect on the public sector based on a public servant system as described in the next section.

Reforming the Civil Servant Systems—The First Steps Toward Public Sector Unionism

We find several reasons why the general agreements in the private sectors did not have any immediate effects on the public sectors:

- The conflict system was not relevant in the public sector, as the strike and lockout weapon would not be politically acceptable. The salaries and working conditions of civil servants were/are politically determined regulated by law including rules on the employment, dismissal, posting, and retirement. There were also special duties associated with the employment of civil servants, e.g., on appropriate conduct 'decorum officiale'.

[14] Sundet, L. T. (2015) Arbeidstvistloven 100 år, *Arbeidsretten*, pp. 232–39.

[15] *Vårens vakreste eventyr …? Innstilling fra Utvalget for tarifforhandlingssystemet oppnevnt ved kongelig resolusjon 28. mai 1999. Avgitt til Kommunal- og regionaldepartementet 2. april 2001* (2001) (Oslo: NOU).

[16] Stokke, T. A. (2001) 'Medling i de nordiska länderna', *Arbetsmarknad & Arbetsliv*, 7, 2, pp. 97–112.

- The loyalty relationship between the individual public employee—the civil servant—and the employer—'the public sector' or state—was quite different from the loyalty between the employee and the employer in the private labor market. The loyalty of the public servant depended on lifelong employment and the prospect of a special privilege in relation to the private labor market—a good pension.
- Many civil servants were recruited from the bourgeoisie and thus the more affluent sections of society, who were not immediately positive toward trade unions and the use of the strike weapon and other 'militant' behavior.
- Most public employees engaged in administration, a field of work that traditionally did not support labor struggles.

In Denmark, the civil servant system dates to the second half of the nineteenth century, when central administration grew and was organized according to bureaucratic and hierarchical principles. In the period around the conclusion of the September Compromise in 1899, there were in the range of 100,000 public employees. Less than half of them were civil servants—the rest were freelancers who were paid and worked through contract terms in the form of regulations and the like.[17]

It is the expansion of Denmark's infrastructure (transport and communication network) at the end of the nineteenth century and the beginning of the twentieth century that really helps to create an increase in the number of public employees—and a new type of public employees, not only was part of the central administration, but also took care of many job functions around the country. These structural changes provided fertile ground for trade unionism among public employees. The first attempts to organize government employees in trade unions came in 1895 with the Provincial Post Officers' Trade Union (*Provinspostbudenes Fagforening*) and the Tram and Omnibus Officers' Organization (*Sporvejs- og Omnibusfunktionærernes Organisation*) as some of the first. Next came, i.e., the Danish Railway Union (*Dansk Jernbaneforbund*) in 1899, the Central Organisation of Danish Trade and Office Aid Associations (*Handels- og Kontormedhjælpernes Forbund i Danmark*) in 1900, the Danish Police

[17] Pedersen, D. (1997) *Forhandlet Forvaltning - en ny institutionel orden for den statslige løn- og personalepolitik*, PhD dissertation, Center for offentlig Organisation og Styring, Copenhagen.

Federation (*Dansk Politiforbund*) and the State Schools Teachers' Association (*Statsskolernes Lærerforening*) in 1902, and the Customs Officers' Association (*Toldbetjentforeningen*) in 1904. At the same time, many branches and local sections were set up under DsF.[18]

As far as the employer side is concerned, there was no central employer function in either the state or the municipality at the time around the September Compromise in 1899. The employer function was located at the individual workplace in, e.g., Railroads and Post, the municipality, which at the time numbered 1,300. Wage determination was unequivocally with the employers. The first bargaining rules were issued in 1903 in the Ministry of Public Works and later the Ministry of Transport. This gave state railway officials and workers access and right to form associations/unions, elect representatives, and negotiate with the management on official matters.[19] Central to these bargaining rules, however, was that when legislative changes were prepared regarding staff duties, rights, remuneration terms, and the like. The draft law and regulations were to be submitted to the relevant agency organizations for discussion.[20]

In 1908 came the first organized attempt to influence the wage law, which the Danish Parliament (*Folketinget*) usually dictated, and which set the framework for wage heights and wage relations. This led to an important organizational development with the formation of the Central Organization of State Officials I (*Statstjenestemændenes Centralorganisation I*) and the Central Organization of State Officials II (*Statstjenestemændenes Centralorganisation II*), which primarily organized member organizations within the large agencies. Popularly, these two central organizations were called the 'Silver Cords' and the 'Gold Cords', respectively, with the latter occupying the higher functionaries, while the former spoke of lower-ranking officials.[21] The 'Silver Cords' often worked outside, for example,

[18] Pedersen, D. (1999) *Det statslige aftalesystem. Fra central til lokal forhandling. 100-året for Septemberforliget – Et festskrift* (Copenhagen: Schultz Information).

[19] Due, J. J. and Madsen, J. S. (2015) 'Fra tjenestemænd til overenskomstansatte: en historisk analyse af konfliktformer i det offentlige aftalesystem', *Økonomi & Politik*, 89, 4, pp. 64–75, 93–94.

[20] Jørgensen, H. (2010) *Det offentlige forhandlings- og aftalesystem og uligelønnen: Historiske og aktuelle aspekter af de offentlige aftaleforhandlingers evne til at tilgodese ligelønskrav* (Aalborg: CARMA-Center for Arbejdsmarkedsforskning, Aalborg Universitet).

[21] Ibid.

in railway operations, while the 'Gold Cords' worked inside, for example, ministries and other parts of the administration.

In 1910, an executive order (D 880) was issued, which confirmed common rules of negotiation between ministries and organizations in Denmark. Until 1919, however, there was no obligation for employers in relation to entering negotiations with the trade unions. It was only a matter of 'judgment for the employer' whether in the specific situation it was 'useful' to have the acceptance of a trade union organization, or whether one wanted to make a unilateral decision without negotiation.[22] After 1910, civil servants were more strongly organized and given seats in a new pay commission, which in 1917 was set up by the government. The commission's task was to devise a simplification of the approximately 70 wage laws, which were current at the time, and which needed to be renewed on an ongoing basis. Next, it was the commission's task to consider how the wage determination could take place based on, among other things, the development in prices (due to inflation during the First World War) as well as equal pay between men and women (as a result of the Constitutional Amendment from 1915, where women were given the right to vote). The commission's work later became the foundation of the Civil Servants Act of 1919.[23] Here, the organizations' right to negotiate was enshrined in law still civil servants had no right to strike.

We find similar developments when we look to Norway and Sweden. In *Norway*, the general agreement and the Labour Disputes Act did not have immediate consequences for the public sector. The reason for this was that civil servants in the state in Norway dominated, and civil servants basically had no right to negotiate nor strike in Norway, as in Denmark. After a long period of pressure and a lawsuit against the state, the civil servants were granted the right to negotiate in 1933, but still without the conflict and access to the state conciliation institution. The right to negotiate for the Norwegian civil servants came, among other things, with inspiration from Denmark and Sweden.[24] In *Sweden*, the Saltsjöbad Agreement only

[22] Hoffmann, F. (1999) *Den danske model og den offentlige sektor. 100-året for Septemberforliget – Et festskrift* (Copenhagen: Schultz Information).

[23] Due, J. J. and Madsen, J. S. (2009) *Forligsmagere og forumshoppere: analyse af OK 2008 i den offentlige sektor* (Copenhagen: Jurist- og Økonomforbundets Forlag).

[24] Seip, Å. A. (1998) *Rett til å forhandle. En studie i statstjenestemennenes forhandlngsrett i Norge og Sverige 1910–1965* (Oslo: Fafo).

included parties the private sector. Civil servants in Sweden did not get the right to negotiate with the employer until 1937.[25]

Copying the Collective Bargaining Model

After the Second World War, the social democratic welfare state project took shape creating several new types of public sectors employees such as kinder garden personal, social, and health care workers. These new wage earner groups were primarily women performing part-time work.[26]

In *Denmark*, these new groups were employed on collective agreements and not as civil servants. In 1969, Civil Servant gained a formal right to negotiate, and by 1973, the Danish Labour Court and Conciliation Board were given the competency to the public sector.[27]

During the 1950s and 1960s, there had been similar a gradual transition in Sweden from law-based to negotiation-based wage formation in parallel with a centralization of negotiations in both municipalities and the state. In 1965, public employees were given right to negotiate with the associated possibility to legally use strikes. Officials without official responsibility already had rights in line with the rules applicable to the private sector, and mediation in some cases played a role for state and municipal employees with official responsibility. With the law in 1965, Sweden got the most extensive right to strike in the public sector compared to the remaining Scandinavian countries at that time.[28] The agreement from 1965 also meant organizational changes on both the employee and employer side. The state established the State Contracting Authority (*Statens avtalsverk*, SAV), which was to form a negotiating counterpart in the state's territory. In the beginning, there was uncertainty about how the new agreement system would work, and SAV, which

[25] Thörnquist, A. and Thörnqvist, C. (2018) 'Do Public Sector Industrial Relations Challenge the Swedish Model?', *Labor History*, 59, 1, pp. 87–104.

[26] Jacobsen, K. and Pedersen, D. (2010) *Kampen om den danske model: Da Sosu'erne rystede det etablerede system* (Copenhagen: Informations Forlag).

[27] Kristiansen, J. (2015) 'Konfliktret på det offentlige arbejdsmarked', *Økonomi & Politik*, 88, 4, pp. 51–63.

[28] Stokke, T. A. (1998) *Lønnsforhandlinger og konfliktløsning: Norge i et skandinavisk perspektiv* (Oslo: Fafo).

was formally established as an independent institution, was in practice managed by the Swedish government.[29]

In the late 1970s and 1980s, the Swedish economy began to show serious signs of crisis. At the same time, increased rivalry between private and public officials was built up.[30] The Swedish agreement system also experienced large wage slips and inflation problems. Although the Swedish model is largely based on a strong principle of freedom of the labor market and the parties, the negotiations were heavily politicized during the 1980s, especially in the public sector. The state tried to control wage developments through indirect influence on the agreement model. Among other things, the State was reserved in appointing mediation commissions, which resulted in a very short mediation period. The Swedish government thus used its responsibility for facilitating mediation to try to influence the outcome of the negotiations. This mixture of the state's double roles has since given rise to strong criticism both in the Swedish Parliament (*Riksdagen*) and especially among the workers' organizations. The dual role of the state as both legislator and employer was hotly debated.[31] The economic crisis in Sweden in the early 1990s put the private collective bargaining system in a deep crisis. This led to the Stabilization Agreement (later known as the Industry Agreement) negotiated under the so-called Rehnberg Commission, which, i.e., introduced more private mediation and restored the private sector agreement system.[32] The

[29] *Från politisering till professionell arbetsgivarroll Arbetsgivarpolitik i statlig sektor 1994–2014* (2014) (Stockholm: Arbetsgivarverket).

[30] Korpi, W. (1981) 'Sweden: Conflict, Power and Politics in Industrial Relations' in Doeringer, P. B., Gourevitch, P., Lange, P. and Martin, A. (eds.) *Industrial Relations in International Perspective* (London: Palgrave Macmillan), pp. 185–217.

[31] Bjuggren, C. M. and Johansson, D. (2009) 'Privat och offentlig sysselsättning i Sverige 1950–2005', *Ekonomisk Debatt*, 37, 1, pp. 41–53; and Fredriksson, P. and Topel, R. H. (2010) 'Wage Determination and Employment in Sweden Since the Early 1990s: Wage Formation in a New Setting' in Freeman, R. B., Swedenborg, B. and Topel, R. H. (eds.) *Reforming the Welfare State. Recovery and Beyond in Sweden* (Chicago: University of Chicago Press), pp. 83–126.

[32] Bergholm, T. and Bieler, A. (2013) 'Globalization and the Erosion of the Nordic Model: A Swedish-Finnish Comparison', *European Journal of Industrial Relations*, 19, 1, pp. 55–70; and Karlson, N. and Lindberg, H. (2008) *En ny svensk modell: Vägval på arbetsmarknaden: Sönderfall, omreglering, avreglering eller modernisering?* (Stockholm: Norstedts akademiska förlag).

Industry Agreement also had consequences for the public sector, which in 2000 adopted the private mediation system.[33]

After several strikes in *Norway* in the field of teaching in the 1950s, the Norwegian parliament passed the Service Disputes Act of 1958, in which the right to bargain in the state territory was continued, made reciprocal, and the civil servants were also covered under the state conciliation institution. However, the Service Disputes Act of 1958 differs from the Labour Disputes Act on several points. The Service Disputes Act contains, i.e., several requirements for the number of members to obtain the right to bargain. It had and still has consequences in practice; firstly, the requirement has meant that several smaller organizations have joined together in cartels to obtain the right to bargain, including the Civil Servants Cartel.[34]

The two laws, the Labour Disputes Act and the Service Disputes Act, thus indicate a formal separation between government employees and other employees in Norway. According to the Norwegian historian Åsmund Arup Seip, the state's employer function and political character have been crucial for the state's agreement and conflict resolution model to have developed differently from the rest of the Norwegian labor market. The employees in Norwegian municipalities are subject to the Labour Disputes Act together with the private labor market.[35]

In all the analysis of the development and creation of the public model of collective bargaining shows that Denmark, Sweden, and Norway have developed along several basic institutional commonalities, but that the countries have also developed interesting institutional trajectories. In all three Nordic countries, the parties in the private sector are the first to conclude general agreements.[36] However, all three countries within the same period gradually introduced or copied the collective bargaining model into the public sector. This is an incremental process and happens in parallel with the expansion of welfare states during the 1950s and

[33] Bengtsson, M. and Berglund, T. (2012) 'Den stora omvandlingen – Svensk arbetsmarknadspolitik under tre decennier', *Arbetsmarknad & Arbetsliv*, 18, 3, pp. 21–33; and Elvander, 'The New Swedish Regime'.

[34] *Vårens vakreste eventyr …?*

[35] Seip, Å. A. (2013) *Bruk av tvungen lønnsnemnd i Norge 1990–2012* (Oslo: Fafo).

[36] Stokke, T. A. and Seip, Å. A. (2008) 'Collective Dispute Resolution in the Public Sector: The Nordic Countries Compared', *Journal of Industrial Relations*, 50, 4, pp. 560–77.

1960s where many public employees are being employed as workers and not as civil servants. The collective bargaining model in the public sector is fully implemented in all three Nordic countries in the period 1966–1976, and therefore, public sector trade unionism is much younger compared to the private sectors.

It is also a Nordic common feature that the right to take industrial actions follows a principle of parallelism, i.e., that the parties have equal conflict weapons in the form of strikes, blockades for employees, and lock-outs/boycotts for employers, respectively. This basically applies to both the private sector and the public sector. With this, the Nordic countries differ from the other Western European countries, where the right to strike is often based solely on the national constitution and therefore the same parallelism does not exist in the weapons of conflict. However, there are certain restrictions on the use of conflict weapons in the public sector in all the Nordic countries. Consideration for third parties and society in general in connection with labor disputes plays a role in all the Nordic countries, but there are differences in how and which considerations are taken into account. In Denmark, there are rules for, e.g., emergency preparedness, but otherwise it is the government that can end a labor dispute based on an estimate of when the Danish economy is threatened or when the inconveniences for third parties are too great. This happened most recently in 2021 after a 71-day strike among nurses. In Norway, exemptions are negotiated regarding who can be exempted from conflict, and otherwise, legal intervention applies as a conclusion based on the same logic as in Denmark. In Sweden, the parties agree to set up commissions to assess when a conflict is 'socially dangerous' or threatens socially important functions.

Public Sector Trade Union Activism Today

It is clear that the public sector trade unionism is rather new compared to the private sector. We see a very similar institutional path in Denmark, Norway, and Sweden from 1966 to 1976 where the collective bargaining model from the private sectors is imported into the public sector. The civil servant system still exists but have largely been suppressed by employment regulated by collective agreements.

Table 16.1 Collective bargaining coverage public/private sector (in %)

	Public	*Private*	*Total (year)*
Denmark	100	74	83 (2019)
Norway	100	52	69 (2017)
Sweden	100	83	90 (2019)

Sources Høgedahl, L. (2020) 'The Danish Labour Market Model: Is the Bumblebee Still Flying?' in Christiansen, P. M., Elklit, J. and Nedergaard, P. (eds.) *The Oxford Handbook of Danish Politics* (Oxford: Oxford University Press), pp. 559–76; Nergaard, K. (2020) *Organisasjonsgrader, tariffavtaledekning og arbeidskonflikter 2017/2018* (Oslo: Fafo); and The Swedish National Mediation Office (*Medlingsinstitutet*)

Today around a third of all employed in Denmark, Sweden, and Norway are working in the public sector.[37] All three countries have a 100% collective bargaining coverage in the public sectors while the private sectors have areas not covered ranging from 52% in Norway to 83% in Sweden (cf. Table 16.1). It is important to note that Norway has a legal tradition in terms of extension mechanisms that extent collective bargaining agreements to the uncovered areas of the labor market by law.

Looking at the trade union density across the three Nordic countries, it is evident that the trade union density varies a lot across the public and private sectors. In Norway, the difference is 42 percentage points (cf. Table 16.2). The Nordic labor market model based on strong social partners and a wide collective bargaining coverage is more widespread in the public sector today compared to the private sectors. The high public sector trade union density is based on several factors.[38] First, a 100% collective bargaining coverage gives strong incitements for a trade union membership. A high collective bargaining coverage also means that most workplaces in the public sectors have shop stewards—an important recruiting tool for trade unions.[39] Second, the public sector consists of

[37] Høgedahl, L. and Jørgensen, H. (2017) 'Development in the Regulation of Wages and Working Conditions: The Employee Perspective', *Nordic Journal of Working Life Studies*, 7, 1, pp. 3–17.

[38] Høgedahl, L. (2014) *Fagforening på markedsvilkår: Markedsgørelse af den faglige organisering og nye vilkår for kollektiv handling på det danske arbejdsmarked* (Aalborg: Aalborg Universitetsforlag).

[39] Ibsen, F., Høgedahl, L. and Scheuer, S. (2011) *Kollektiv handling – faglig organisering og skift af fagforening* (Copenhagen: Samfundslitteratur).

Table 16.2 Trade union density public/private sectors (in %)

	Public	*Private*	*Total (year)*	*Difference (public – private)*
Denmark	80	64	67 (2019)	16
Norway	80	38	52 (2017)	42
Sweden	79	63	68 (2019)	16

Sources Høgedahl, 'The Danish Labour Market'; Nergaard, *Organisasjonsgrader, tariffavtaledekning*; and Medlingsinstitutet

large organizations that a stabile compared to the private sector were many companies open and close making organizing more costly and time-consuming. Finally, many public employees have a professional bachelor's degree such as nurses and schoolteachers. These professions or professionals often have strong trade unions based on their education.[40] Many of these professionals see their trade unions as a part of their professional identity and many become members while studying.[41]

It is also clear that the public sector has surpassed the private sector in terms of lost working days due to work stoppages. This is not a unique, Nordic development but can be traced to most European countries.[42] Yet the trend is rather clear in specially Denmark, but also Norway and to some degree Sweden. First, Sweden has a much lower number in terms of lost working days due to work stoppages. We might identify several reasons for this trend.[43] However, the primary reason seems to be connected to the fact that Sweden does not have direct democracy in terms of membership ballots involving rank-and-file members in the collective bargaining process. In Sweden, when a collective bargaining agreement has been concluded, the agreement will be approved or voted down by a competent representation in each trade union in most cases

[40] Clegg, H. A. (1976) *Trade Unionism Under Collective Bargaining: A Theory Based on Comparisons of six Countries* (Oxford: B. Blackwell); and Scheuer, S. (2006) 'A Novel Calculus? Institutional Change, Globalization and Industrial Conflict in Europe', *European Journal of Industrial Relations*, 12, 2, pp. 143–64.

[41] Høgedahl, *Fagforening på markedsvilkår*.

[42] Scheuer, S., Ibsen, F. and Høgedahl, L. (2016) 'Strikes in the Public Sector in Denmark—Assessing the Economic Gains and Losses of Collective Action', *Transfer: European Review of Labour and Research*, 22, 3, pp. 367–82.

[43] See: Høgedahl, L. (2019) *Den danske model i den offentlige sektor: Danmark i et nordisk perspektiv* (Copenhagen: Djøf Forlag).

the central board or an executive committee. In Denmark and Norway, the negotiated results must be approved by a membership ballot which increases the risk of industrial conflict.[44] It is also important to note that the wage settlement in Sweden is more decentralized compared to Denmark and Norway, especially in public sectors. This means that a larger share of the total salary is negotiated locally with no right to strike; hence, the risk of collective action is less pronounced. Norway is also the only country not operation the so-called Ghent system were trade unions control state subsided unemployment insurance funds.[45]

In Denmark, as mentioned, it is the public area that is leading the conflict in the period from 2008 to 2020, while the private area in recent years has experienced a historically low level of conflict (cf. Table 16.3). In Sweden, the public sector also accounts for most lost working days although at a much lower level. In 2008, it was the Swedish nurses who were on strike, which makes up more than half of the lost working days in the period 2008–2020 in Sweden (cf. Table 16.4). In Norway, the public sector is also leading the conflict statistics, with two major conflicts in 2010 and 2012. Table 16.3 shows that there is a difference in the frequency of conflict. In Norway, the collective agreements typically run for two years, but in the intervening period there are the so-called intermediate settlements, which are the hearth for many labor disputes in Norway.[46] Another significant difference between Norway and Denmark is found in the size of the labor disputes. In Denmark, there is a tendency for conflicts in the public sector to develop to be very extensive, where virtually all employees are either on strike or locked out (except for any emergency preparedness). In Norway, so-called point strikes have been the norm in the public sector since the 1980s and in the private sector since 1990. During a point strike, the selection of employees for conflict is limited. Typically, the employee organizations in Norway will start by taking approximately 10% of the employees. The conflict can thus be escalated over time by either expanding to other areas/workplaces or allowing

[44] Stokke, T. A. (2002) 'Conflict Regulation in the Nordic Countries', *Transfer: European Review of Labour and Research*, 8, 4, pp. 670–87; and Høgedahl, *Den danske model*.

[45] Nergaard, K. and Stokke, T. A. (2007) 'The Puzzles of Union Density in Norway', *Transfer: European Review of Labour and Research*, 13, 4, pp. 653–70.

[46] See: Stokke, T. A., Nergaard, K. and Evju, S. (2015) *Det kollektive arbeidslivet. Organisasjoner, tariffavtaler og lønnsoppgjør* (Oslo: Universitetsforlaget), p. 212.

Table 16.3 Lost working days per 1000 workers due to work stoppages, 2008–2020 (public and private sector) (in 1000s)

Year	*2008*	*2009*	*2010*	*2011*	*2012*	*2013*	*2014*	*2015*	*2016*	*2017*	*2018*	*2019*	*2020*	*Total*
DK	693	6	7	6	4	364	7	4	6	10	7	3	3	1120
N	25	0	199	0	139	4	56	10	63	3	9	8	51	567
S	24	0	7	0	8	2	1	0	2	1	0	1	NA	46

Sources and *Note* Statistics Denmark; Statistics Norway; and Medlingsinstitutet. Calculated by total number of lost working days/workforce*1000

Table 16.4 Lost working days per 1000 workers due to work stoppages, 2008–2020. Sectors (in 1000s)

	2008	*2009*	*2010*	*2011*	*2012*	*2013*	*2014*	*2015*	*2016*	*2017*	*2018*	*2019*	*2020*	*Total*
Denmark														
Public	655	1	1	0	0	351	0	0	0	0	1	0	0	1008
Private	16	6	10	8	6	6	8	4	15	10	6	3	3	79
Norway														
Public	23	–	163	–	127	–	52	0	6	3	1	4	0	370
Private	3	0	43	0	17	4	7	10	60	0	8	4	51	143

Sources and *Note* Statistics Denmark; Statistics Norway; and Medlingsinstitutet. Calculated by total number of lost working days/workforce*1000. Medlingsinstitutet does not show sector

more people to take part in the conflict in the areas already affected by the strike.

The use of point strikes in Norway has several causes. Firstly, legal intervention is the norm in Norway, which is why a large part of the labor struggle is about 'time' when a government intervenes.[47] In addition, the use of point strikes is also described as a strategy that has a longer strategic aim than just the collective agreement renewal in which the strike is carried out.[48] As public employers can rarely be affected financially in

[47] Stokke, T. A. and Thornqvist, C. (2001) 'Strikes and Collective Bargaining in the Nordic Countries', *European Journal of Industrial Relations*, 7, 3, pp. 245–67.

[48] Høgedahl, *Den danske model.*

a conflict, it is largely a matter of influencing public opinion and politicians.[49] The purpose of the point strike can therefore be to create broad public awareness of a matter or a case without the consequences for either the third party or the strike fund becoming very severe.[50] The gains from a point strike must thus not only be read in the immediate benefits and gains that it obtains in the current collective agreement renewal, but as part of a larger strategy, where the winning gains may be found at the next collective agreement renewal or 'intermediate settlement'.

A large part of the conflicts in Norway is largely due to dissatisfaction with the public being dependent on the private sector in terms of wage settlement. The strong public sector trade unions find this mechanism hampering for wage development in the public sector.

Although Sweden has a very low level of conflict, strikes are also seen here from time to time. In 2008, when Sweden has the highest number of lost working days per 1,000 employees in the period 2008–2020 (cf. Table 16.3), it was precisely the public area of the nurses that was in conflict. This strike can also be characterized as a point strike, as not all nurses were selected for conflict, but only about 10%.

In contrast to Sweden and Norway, Denmark has a tradition of major conflicts in the public sector (cf. Table 16.4). This form of conflict is primarily costly for both employees and their organizations, as they quickly get their war chests emptied, but also for third parties, who in the public sector are very dependent on public services. The relatively large conflicts in Denmark must also be seen in light of public employers' use of defensive and offensive lockout in response to a strike.

The review of the use of labor disputes in the public sector in the Nordic countries also shows that Denmark is the only country where public employers have used the lockout weapon offensively, i.e., that employers withdraw the conflict weapon only without prior notice or implementation of a strike. This happened in 2013 during the 5 weeks teacher lockout.[51] There are no precedents in the other Nordic countries.

[49] Hyman, R. (2008) 'The State in Industrial Relations', in Blyton, P., Bacon, N. and Fiorito, J. (eds.) *The SAGE Handbook of Industrial Relations* (London: Sage), pp. 258–83.

[50] Mikkelsen, F. (1998) 'Unions and New Shopfloor Strike Strategies and Learning Processes Among Public Employees', *Economic and Industrial Democracy*, 19, 3, pp. 505–38.

[51] For more, please see: Høgedahl, L. and Ibsen, F. (2015) 'Konfliktrettens anvendelighed i den offentlige sektor set i lyset af OK13', *Økonomi & Politik*, 88, 1; and

This also applies to the private sector, with one exception in Norway in 1986.[52] Another interesting difference is found in the use of the lockout weapon defensively, i.e., in response to an announced or launched strike. This lockout form has also been used in the public sector in Denmark, i.e., in 1981 and in 1995, and announced in 2008 and 2018. This lockout form has not previously been used in the public sector in the other Nordic countries. This is despite the fact that the opportunity is formally available. However, both Norway and Sweden have seen an increased use of defensive lockouts in the private sector over the past ten years.[53] Most recently, the dock workers at the port of Gothenburg were locked out in May 2017.

Concluding Remarks—From Noble Civil Servants to Militant Wage Earners

In this chapter, I have looked at public sector trade unionism in Norway, Sweden, and particularly Denmark. In the Nordic countries, industrial conflict is regulated by the general agreements concluded by the social partners with some supplement of law. In all of the Nordic countries, general agreements were first concluded in the private sectors. It is also very clear that trade unionism and activism were sparked in the private sectors. By the time the social partners in the private sectors concluded their general agreements, the civil servant employment was dominating in the public sectors. These employees had a very different relation to their employer counterparts and were much less militant. Their wages and working have traditionally been regulated by law and not by collective agreements. However, the development of the infrastructure, mainly railroad and telegraph in 1900s and 1910s, brought about a new type of public employees more favorable to trade union activism. Although all the Nordic countries saw civil servant reforms bringing a right to negotiate to some degree, it is not until 1950s and 1960s that a number of new types of public sectors employees are being employed as workers covered

Høgedahl, L. and Ibsen, F. (2017) 'New Terms for Collective Action in the Public Sector in Denmark: Lessons Learned from the Teacher Lock-Out in 2013', *Journal of Industrial Relations*, 59, 5, pp. 593–610.

[52] Stokke, Nergaard and Evju, *Det kollektive arbeidslivet*.

[53] Kjellberg, A. (2011) 'Storkonflikten 1980 och andra stora arbetskonflikter i Sverige', *Arbetarhistoria*, 35, 138–139, pp. 33–40.

by collective bargaining. From 1968 to 1978, Sweden, Denmark, and Norway import the collective bargaining model developed in the private sector to the public sector. Today, around a third of the workforce is public employed. This is a relatively large share compared to other countries due to the universal welfare states found in Scandinavia. However, like most other countries, we find that public employees today are better unionized in Scandinavia and have a 100% collective bargaining coverage. It is also clear that the public sector is leading in terms of labor unrest and thus accountable for most working days lost due to strikes and lockouts. The public employees have been transformed from noble civil servants to militant wage earners surpassing their private sector counterpart when it comes to labor unrest. This is the case for Denmark, Norway, and Sweden albeit the latter has a much lower number in terms of lost working days due to work stoppages compared to Norway—and specially Denmark. Equal pay has been the catalyst for many strikes in Norway, Sweden, and Denmark in recent years yet other issues have also sparked industrial conflict. In Norway, public employees have been dissatisfied by the wage settlement based on the industry. Public sector trade unions are better unionized and feel that they can gain better results not being tied to the private sector wage settlement. Denmark is the only country that has seen the use of the lockout weapon when teachers were lockout for five weeks in 2013. The collective bargaining model is still rather young in the public sectors in Denmark, Sweden, and Norway. Sweden and Norway have to some degree adjusted the collective bargaining model to better suit the public sector. This process has not been made in Denmark yet.

References

Avtalsrörelsen och lönebildningen 2020 (2021) (Stockholm: Medlingsinstitutet).

Bengtsson, M. and Berglund, T. (2012) 'Den stora omvandlingen – Svensk arbetsmarknadspolitik under tre decennier', *Arbetsmarknad & Arbetsliv*, 18, 3, pp. 21–33.

Bergholm, T. and Bieler, A. (2013) 'Globalization and the Erosion of the Nordic Model: A Swedish-Finnish Comparison', *European Journal of Industrial Relations*, 19, 1, pp. 55–70.

Bjuggren, C. M. and Johansson, D. (2009) 'Privat och offentlig sysselsättning i Sverige 1950–2005', *Ekonomisk Debatt*, 37, 1, pp. 41–53.

Clegg, H. A. (1976) *Trade Unionism Under Collective Bargaining: A Theory Based on Comparisons of Six Countries* (Oxford: B. Blackwell).

Due, J. J. and Madsen, J. S. (2009) *Forligsmagere og forumshoppere: analyse af OK 2008 i den offentlige sektor* (Copenhagen: Jurist- og Økonomforbundets Forlag).

Due, J. J. and Madsen, J. S. (2015) 'Fra tjenestemænd til overenskomstansatte: en historisk analyse af konfliktformer i det offentlige aftalesystem', *Økonomi & Politik*, 89, 4, pp. 64–75, 93–94.

Due, J., Madsen, J. S. and Jensen, C. S. (1993) *Den danske model: En historisk sociologisk analyse af det kollektive aftalesystem* (Copenhagen: Jurist-og Økonomforbundets Forlag).

Due, J., Madsen, J. S. and Jensen, C. S. (1999) 'Septemberforliget: Et strategisk valg' in Andreasen, M. L., Kristiansen, J. and Nielsen, R. (eds.) *Septemberforliget 100 år* (Copenhagen: Jurist- og Økonomforbundets Forlag), pp. 85–112.

Elvander, N. (1988) *Den svenska modellen: Löneförhandlingar och inkomstpolitiik, 1982-1986* (Stockholm: Allmänna förlaget).

Elvander, N. (2002) 'The New Swedish Regime for Collective Bargaining and Conflict Resolution: A Comparative Perspective', *European Journal of Industrial Relations*, 8, 2, pp. 197–216.

Elvander, N. (2003) 'Two Labour Market Regimes in Sweden. A Comparison Between the Saltsjöbaden Agreement of 1938 and the Industrial Agreement of 1997', *Industrielle Beziehungen/The German Journal of Industrial Relations*, pp. 146–59.

Från politisering till professionell arbetsgivarroll Arbetsgivarpolitik i statlig sektor 1994–2014 (2014) (Stockholm: Arbetsgivarverket).

Fredriksson, P. and Topel, R. H. (2010) 'Wage Determination and Employment in Sweden Since the Early 1990s: Wage Formation in a New Setting' in Freeman, R. B., Swedenborg, B. and Topel, R. H. (eds.) *Reforming the Welfare State. Recovery and Beyond in Sweden* (Chicago: University of Chicago Press), pp. 83–126.

Galenson, W. (1949) *Labor in Norway* (Cambridge: Harvard University Press).

Galenson, W. (1952) *The Danish System of Labor Relations* (Cambridge: Harvard University Press).

Hippe, J. and Berge Ø. (2014) *Den nordiske modellen mot 2013. Et nytt kapittel?* (Oslo: Fafo)

Hoffmann, F. (1999) *Den danske model og den offentlige sektor. 100-året for Septemberforliget – Et festskrift* (Copenhagen: Schultz Information).

Høgedahl, L. (2014) *Fagforening på markedsvilkår: Markedsgørelse af den faglige organisering og nye vilkår for kollektiv handling på det danske arbejdsmarked* (Aalborg: Aalborg Universitetsforlag).

Høgedahl, L. (2019) *Den danske model i den offentlige sektor: Danmark i et nordisk perspektiv* (Copenhagen: Djøf Forlag).

Høgedahl, L. (2020) 'The Danish Labour Market Model: Is the Bumblebee Still Flying?' in Christiansen, P. M., Elklit, J. and Nedergaard, P. (eds.) *The Oxford Handbook of Danish Politics* (Oxford: Oxford University Press), pp. 559–76.

Høgedahl, L. and Ibsen, F. (2015) 'Konfliktrettens anvendelighed i den offentlige sektor set i lyset af OK13', *Økonomi & Politik*, 88, 1.

Høgedahl, L. and Ibsen, F. (2017) 'New Terms for Collective Action in the Public Sector in Denmark: Lessons Learned from the Teacher Lock-Out in 2013', *Journal of Industrial Relations*, 59, 5, pp. 593–610.

Høgedahl, L. and Jørgensen, H. (2017) 'Development in the Regulation of Wages and Working Conditions: The Employee Perspective', *Nordic Journal of Working Life Studies*, 7, 1, pp. 3–17.

Hyman, R. (2008) 'The State in Industrial Relations' in Blyton, P., Bacon, N. and Fiorito, J. (eds.) *The SAGE Handbook of Industrial Relations* (London: Sage), pp. 258–283.

Ibsen, F. (2014) 'Det fagretlige system' in Jørgensen, H. (ed.) *Arbejdsmarkedsregulering* (Copenhagen: Jurist- og Økonomforbundets Forlag).

Ibsen, F. and Jørgensen, H. (1979) *Fagbevægelse og stat*, Vol. I–II (Copenhagen: Gyldendal).

Ibsen, F., Høgedahl, L. and Scheuer, S. (2011) *Kollektiv handling – faglig organisering og skift af fagforening* (Copenhagen: Samfundslitteratur).

Jacobsen, K. and Pedersen, D. (2010) *Kampen om den danske model: Da Sosu'erne rystede det etablerede system* (Copenhagen: Informations Forlag).

Jørgensen, H. (2010) *Det offentlige forhandlings- og aftalesystem og uligelønnen: Historiske og aktuelle aspekter af de offentlige aftaleforhandlingers evne til at tilgodese ligelønskrav* (Aalborg: CARMA-Center for Arbejdsmarkedsforskning, Aalborg Universitet)

Karlson, N. and Lindberg, H. (2008) *En ny svensk modell: Vägval på arbetsmarknaden: Sönderfall, omreglering, avreglering eller modernisering?* (Stockholm: Norstedts akademiska förlag).

Kjellberg, A. (2011) 'Storkonflikten 1980 och andra stora arbetskonflikter i Sverige', *Arbetarhistoria*, 35, 138–139, pp. 33–40.

Knudsen, K. (2009) 'Fagbevægelse og arbejdsgiverforeninger i Danmark 1857–1914', *Rubicon*, 17, 3, pp. 52–69.

Knudsen, K. (2011) 'Faglig internationalisme før Anden Verdenskrig. Første del: Organisering af arbejdernes internationale solidaritet', *Arbejderhistorie*, 3, pp. 41–62.

Korpi, W. (1981) 'Sweden: Conflict, Power and Politics in Industrial Relations' in Doeringer, P. B., Gourevitch, P., Lange, P. and Martin, A. (eds.) *Industrial Relations in International Perspective* (London: Palgrave Macmillan), pp. 185–217.

Kristiansen, J. (2015) 'Konfliktret på det offentlige arbejdsmarked', *Økonomi & Politik*, 88, 4, pp. 51–63.

Lundh, C. (2002) *Spelets regler. Institutioner och lönebildning på den svenska arbetsmarknaden 1850–2000* (Stockholm: SNS Förlag).
Mikkelsen, F. (1998) 'Unions and New Shopfloor Strike Strategies and Learning Processes Among Public Employees', *Economic and Industrial Democracy*, 19, 3, pp. 505–38.
Nergaard, K. (2020) *Organisasjonsgrader, tariffavtaledekning og arbeidskonflikter 2017/2018* (Oslo: Fafo).
Nergaard, K. and Stokke, T. A. (2007) 'The Puzzles of Union Density in Norway', *Transfer: European Review of Labour and Research*, 13, 4, pp. 653–70.
Pedersen, D. (1997) *Forhandlet Forvaltning - en ny institutionel orden for den statslige løn- og personalepolitik*, PhD dissertation, Center for offentlig Organisation og Styring, Copenhagen.
Pedersen, D. (1999) *Det statslige aftalesystem. Fra central til lokal forhandling. 100-året for Septemberforliget – Et festskrift* (Copenhagen: Schultz Information).
Scheuer, S. (2006) 'A Novel Calculus? Institutional Change, Globalization and Industrial Conflict in Europe', *European Journal of Industrial Relations*, 12, 2, pp. 143–64.
Scheuer, S., Ibsen, F. and Høgedahl, L. (2016) 'Strikes in the Public Sector in Denmark—Assessing the Economic Gains and Losses of Collective Action', *Transfer: European Review of Labour and Research*, 22, 3, pp. 367–82.
Seip, Å. A. (1998) *Rett til å forhandle. En studie i statstjenestemennenes forhandlngsrett i Norge og Sverige 1910–1965* (Oslo: Fafo).
Seip, Å. A. (2013) *Bruk av tvungen lønnsnemnd i Norge 1990–2012* (Oslo: Fafo).
Stokke, T. A. (1998) *Lønnsforhandlinger og konfliktløsning: Norge i et skandinavisk perspektiv* (Oslo: Fafo).
Stokke, T. A. (2001) 'Medling i de nordiska länderna', *Arbetsmarknad & Arbetsliv*, 7, 2, pp. 97–112.
Stokke, T. A. (2002) 'Conflict Regulation in the Nordic Countries', *Transfer: European Review of Labour and Research*, 8, 4, pp. 670–87.
Stokke, T. A. and Seip, Å. A. (2008) 'Collective Dispute Resolution in the Public Sector: The Nordic Countries Compared', *Journal of Industrial Relations*, 50, 4, pp. 560–77.
Stokke, T. A. and Thornqvist, C. (2001) 'Strikes and Collective Bargaining in the Nordic Countries', *European Journal of Industrial Relations*, 7, 3, pp. 245–67.
Stokke, T. A., Nergaard, K. and Evju, S. (2015) *Det kollektive arbeidslivet. Organisasjoner, tariffavtaler og lønnsoppgjør* (Oslo: Universitetsforlaget).
Sundet, L. T. (2015) 'Arbeidstvistloven 100 år', *Arbeidsretten*, pp. 232–39.

Thörnquist, A. and Thörnqvist, C. (2018) 'Do Public Sector Industrial Relations Challenge the Swedish Model?', *Labor History*, 59, 1, pp. 87–104.

Vårens vakreste eventyr …? Innstilling fra Utvalget for tarifforhandlingssystemet oppnevnt ved kongelig resolusjon 28. mai 1999. Avgitt til Kommunal- og regionaldepartementet 2. april 2001 (2001) (Oslo: NOU).

Webb, S. and Webb, B. (1897) *Industrial Democracy* (London: Longmans).

CHAPTER 17

Closing the Gender Pay Gap: Global Concepts, Local Negotiations in Iceland and Sweden, 1900–1985

Ragnheiður Kristjánsdóttir and Silke Neunsinger

In the late 1940s, the Nordic countries' trade union confederations were confronted with female trade union activists who demanded that during upcoming wage negotiations, the emphasis would be placed on higher wage increases for women than for men. While this unified claim for closing the gendered wage gap can be seen as the result of meetings of women trade unionists at the Nordic level, held since the end of the 1930s,[1] it can also be explained in terms of broader transnational

[1] Waldemarson, Y. (1998) *Mjukt till formen, hårt till innehållet. LO:s kvinnoråd 1947–1969* (Stockholm: Atlas), p. 92.

R. Kristjánsdóttir
University of Iceland, Reykjavík, Iceland
e-mail: ragnhk@hi.is

S. Neunsinger (✉)
Swedish Labour Movement Archives and Library & Department of Economic HistoryUppsala University, Stockholm & Uppsala, Sweden
e-mail: silke.neunsinger@arbark.se

© The Author(s), under exclusive license to Springer Nature Switzerland AG 2023

J. Jørgensen and F. Mikkelsen (eds.), *Trade Union Activism in the Nordic Countries since 1900*, Palgrave Studies in the History of Social Movements, https://doi.org/10.1007/978-3-031-08987-9_17

developments. In the wake of the First World War, wage equality was on the agenda of international institutions, most effectively the International Labour Organization (ILO). Indeed, it is important to consider the transnational context to understand the dynamics of the struggle for equal remuneration in the Nordic countries. Focusing on the equal pay struggles in two Nordic countries, Iceland, and Sweden, one of our aims is to illustrate this point. Using social movement theory as a point of reference, as well as previous research on the international aspect of the struggle for equal remuneration, we shall map out the interaction between the local and global from the turn of the twentieth century to the end of the United Nations Decade for Women in 1985.

Despite its crucial role in labor market relations and the development of economic citizenship, equal pay has not been a central topic for gender history in the Nordic countries which has primarily been concerned with issues such as women's political and social rights, and their labor force participation. The same can be said about labor history. Despite the large body of work on the Nordic labor market, the labor movement, and the welfare state, the struggle for equal remuneration has received relatively little attention.[2]

Women's trade union activism is a neglected aspect of Icelandic gender and labor history. While the pioneers of women's history during the 1980s and 1990s were interested in women's work and how the Women's Rights Association concerned itself with the rights of working women.[3] The most comprehensive survey on women's union work is to be found in a two-volume history of the Icelandic Confederation of Labour (*Alþýðusamband Íslands*, ASÍ), published in 2013[4], Moreover,

[2] See though: *Arbetarhistoria*, 3–4, 2016, pp. 159–60; and Sørensen, A. E. (2018) *Pæne pigers oprør. Ligestillingsprojekter i de kvindedominerede fagforbund 1985–2010* (Aarhus: Aarhus University Press) as well as the studies mentioned below. For an overview of the historiography of studies on the labor movement in the Nordic countries, see Hilson, M., Neunsinger, S., Vyff, I. and Kristjánsdóttir, R. (2017) 'Labour, Unions and Politics in the Nordic Countries c. 1700–2000: Introduction' in Hilson, M., Neunsinger, S. and Vyff, I. (eds.) *Labour, Unions and Politics Under the North Star: The Nordic Countries, 1700–2000* (New York: Berghahn Books), pp. 1–70.

[3] Erlendsdóttir, S. Th. (1993) *Veröld sem ég vil* (Reykjavík: KRFÍ), pp. 245–57; and Sigurðardóttir, A. (1985) *Vinna kvenna í 1100 ár* (Reykjavík: Kvennasögusafn).

[4] Ísleifsson, S. R. (2013) *Saga Alþýðusambands Íslands* (Reykjavík: Forlagið) I, pp. 85–100, 293–302, II, pp. 213–20. See also: Neunsinger, S. and Kristjánsdóttir, R. (forthcoming) 'A Global Turning Point for Equal Pay Struggles: International Women's

the politics of women's work is one of the central themes of a recent book about the lives and politics of Icelandic women voters 1916–2017.[5]

For Sweden, we have more in-depth research about equal pay struggles. These have shown how the struggle for equal pay was complicated by the labour movements' support for the principle that the state should not intervene in wage setting in the private sector, on the other hand. This explains why legislation in the private sector for a long time was not an option even though legislation concerning equal remuneration for teachers had been introduced in 1906 already. Despite the comparatively strong position of Swedish female trade unionists, their influence on the Swedish debate on equal remuneration remained for a long time relatively weak. It led to transnational alliances with female trade unionists in the Nordic countries and cross-class alliances in parliament to put pressure on parliament and the unions at home. Centralized wage negotiations were meaningful when equal pay became a substantial part of the collective agreements at the beginning of the 1960s. All studies refer to the importance of the ILO for permanently reminding about the importance of adopting the ILO convention and later implementing it and, at the same time, creating a real challenge for the Swedish labor market model of non-intervention in wage setting in the private sector.[6]

Year, 1975' in Pasolli, L. and Smith, J. (eds.) *Rethinking Feminist History and Theory. Reflections on Gender, Class and Labour* (Toronto: Toronto University Press).

[5] Halldórsdóttir, E. H., Tómasdóttir, K. S., Kristjánsdóttir, R. and Þorvaldsdóttir, Þ. H. (2020) *Konur sem kjósa. Aldarsaga* (Reykjavík: Sögufélag).

[6] Florin, C. (1987) *Kampen om katedern. Feminiserings- och professionaliseringsprocessen inom den svenska folkskolans lärarkår 1860–1906* (Stockholm: Almqvist & Wiksell), pp. 152–97; Irlinger, I. (1990) *TCO och kvinnorna: tidsperioden 1944–1974: studie av TCOs och SIFs arbetsmarknadspolitik och behandling av principen lika lön för lika arbete* (Uppsala: Almqvist & Wiksell); Hirdman, Y. (1998) *Med kluven tunga: LO och genusordningen* (Stockholm: Atlas); Waldemarson, *Mjukt till formen*; Waldemarson, Y. (2000) *Kvinnor och Klass - en paradoxal skapelseberättelse* (Stockholm: Stockholms universitet); and Svenéus, L. (2017) *Konsten att upprätthålla löneskillnader mellan kvinnor och män: en rättssociologisk studie av regler i lag och avtal om lika lön* (Lund: Department of Sociology of Law, Lund University).

Local Struggles, National Governments, and International Organizations

Sociologist Sidney Tarrow has studied the mechanisms and processes of recent transnational activism. His model has proven applicable in historical contexts. Tarrow is interested in understanding what happens with domestic grievances when they travel abroad and back home, and in which ways international organizations and activism abroad can be helpful in the struggle against domestic grievances.

Situating transnational activism in the triangular relationship between activists, states, and international organizations, Tarrow defines ***internationalization*** as entailing three interrelated trends: (i) an increasing horizontal density of relations across states, (ii) increased relations between government officials of different states, and (iii) the trend of increasing vertical links among nonstate actors on the subnational, national, and international level. Internationalization thus stimulates and creates formal and informal structures that invite transnational activism and facilitate the formation of networks of nonstate, state, and international actors.[7] The formation of the international labor movement and the ILO—an organization of state and non-state actors—are excellent examples of increased internationalization in the first half of the twentieth century. Tarrow counts the following six processes involved in the internationalization of grievances:

i. *Global framing*: mobilization of international symbols to frame domestic conflicts.
ii. *Internalization*: a response to foreign or international pressure within domestic politics.
iii. *Diffusion*: a transfer of claims from one site to another.
iv. *Scale shift*: coordination of collective action at a different level than where it began.
v. *Externalization*: vertical projection of domestic claims onto international institutions or foreign actors.

[7] Tarrow, S. (2010) *The New Transnational Activism* (Cambridge: Cambridge University Press), p. 19.

vi. *Transnational coalition formation*: Horizontal formation of common networks among actors from different countries with similar claims.[8]

Tarrow's model is useful when explaining why some of the struggles for equal remuneration were sent on global journeys, why some were more successful than others, and how they could become entangled. Further insights can be drawn from social movement theory formulated by Charles Tilly, Douglas McAdam, and Sidney Tarrow who have proposed that mobilization processes depend on the creation and use of:

i. *Political opportunities* can be static structures (e.g., legal frameworks, formal agreements, and declarations, collective bargaining) or changing political environments (e.g., new constitutions, decolonization, enfranchisement).
ii. *Mobilization structures* can be formal organizations (e.g., workers' and women's movements and women's committees in male-dominated organizations) and social networks of everyday life (e.g., at the workplace, or through a collective of women activists).
iii. *Interpreting and framing grievances* to convince the opponent within available cultural constants (e.g., women's specific rights to be protected as women workers and working mothers, or the later discourse on gender equality).
iv. The use of specific *repertoires of protest* can evolve from a response to changes in capitalism, state-building or other processes.[9]

As we will show, Iceland and Sweden are two Nordic countries characterized by various political and mobilization structures which created different alliances. In Sweden, female members of the blue-collar workers' unions had a comparatively strong position in the labor movement, due to their mobilization structures linked to the labor movement. This

[8] Tarrow, *The New Transnational Activism*, pp. 29ff.

[9] Tilly, C. (1978) *From Mobilization to Revolution* (Reading: Addison-Wesley); McAdam, D., McCarthy, J. D. and Zald, M. N. (eds.) (1996) *Comparative Perspectives on Social Movements, Political Opportunities, Mobilizing Structures, and Cultural Framings* (Cambridge: Cambridge University Press); Tarrow, S. (1998) *Power in Movement. Social Movements and Contentious Politics* (Cambridge: Cambridge University Press); and Tarrow, *The New Transnational Activism*, p. 23.

enabled labor feminists to use transnational alliances in the Nordic countries and the North-Western transatlantic region. In Iceland, however, women relied on alliances with the women's movement which also gave access to transnational alliances. Iceland and Sweden were affiliated with the same international organizations, namely the ILO and the United Nations (UN). We will show that despite different patterns of action in the triangular relationship between activists, the state and international bodies, they confirm a general periodization of equal pay struggles worldwide and show the importance of transnational entanglements for their outcome on the local and national level. We use the concepts of transnational activism and mobilization processes outlined above to discern the triangular relationship between transnational actors, the state and international institutions in the struggle for wage equality in Sweden and Iceland. We explain why and how political opportunities emerging locally, nationally, or internationally were transferred and used in protests and struggles for equal remuneration, as was the case in the late 1940s, when female trade unionists used the international and inter-Nordic momentum to exert concerted pressure on their national organizations.

Periodization of International Political Opportunity Structures c. 1870–1980s

By looking at previous research, the minutes of international congresses and meetings, as well as investigations carried out by international trade union organizations, women's organizations, the ILO, the League of Nations, and its successor, the UN, we get a rough periodization of the international political opportunity structures for equal pay struggles.[10]

[10] This periodization is based on: Neunsinger, S. (2018) 'The Unobtainable Magic of Numbers: Equal Remuneration, the ILO and the International Trade Union Movement 1950s–1980s' in Boris, E., Hoehtker, D. and Zimmerman, S. (eds.) *Women's ILO. Transnational Networks, Global Labour Standards, and Gender Equity, 1919 to Present* (Leiden/Boston: Brill), pp. 121–48; Neunsinger, S. and Warrier, M. V. S. (2020) 'Transnational Activism and Equal Remuneration in India During the Twentieth Century' in Bellucci, S. and Weiss, H. (eds.) *The Internationalisation of the Labor Question. Ideological Antagonism, Workers' Movements and the ILO Since 1919* (Cham: Palgrave Macmillan), pp. 329–50; and Neunsinger, S. (2019) 'Translocal Activism and the Implementation of Equal Remuneration for Men and Women. The Case of the South African Textile Industry, 1980–1987', *International Review of Social History*, 64, 1, pp. 37–72.

We propose that the development since 1870 can be divided into four phases—the first three of which are under discussion here.

The first phase, from the 1870s to the 1940s, shows a shift from domestic demands for equal remuneration to the international level. Feminist and working-class organizations brought the demand for equal remuneration to the international level.[11] As a result, it was included in the Treaty of Versailles and the constitution of the ILO in 1919. During this period demands for women workers were part of the discourse about special protective legislation for women workers and working mothers, e.g., the introduction of minimum wages for home-based workers.[12] The ILO constitution offered a radical definition of equal remuneration as it included the same rate for the same or comparable jobs and remained for a long time the broadest definition when it comes to the comparison of the value of work.

The second phase spans from the 1940s to the 1960s and sees the adoption of the principle of wage equality in various global agreements and conventions: the UN's Declaration of Human Rights in 1948, ILO Convention 100 on Equal remuneration adopted in 1951, and the European Community's Treaty of Rome in 1957. In this period, the discourse shifted toward equal rights for male and female workers.[13] However, the definition of equal remuneration in the UN Declaration of Human Rights and the Treaty of Rome referred to the same rate for the same job. It was thus narrower than the clause in the ILO constitution and Convention 100. Moreover, the UN Declaration of Human rights was broader in its protection as it took a stand against the discrimination of all individuals rather than specifying men and women.

The third phase starts in the 1960s and shows a shift from the global to the domestic level, where international agreements and conventions lead to the adoption of national legislation around the globe. In 1967,

[11] Wikander, U. (2006) *Feminism, familj och medborgarskap. Debatter på internationella kongresser om nattarbetsförbud för kvinnor 1889–1919* (Göteborg: Makadam).

[12] Boris, E. (2019) *Making the Woman Worker. Precarious Labor and the Fight for Global Standards, 1919–2019* (New York: Oxford University Press); and Zimmermann, S. (2021) *Frauenpolitik und Männergewerkschaft Internationale Geschlechterpolitik, IGB-Gewerkschafterinnen und die Arbeiter- und Frauenbewegungen der Zwischenkriegszeit* (Wien: Löcker Verlag), p. 232.

[13] Zimmermann, *Frauenpolitik und Männergewerkschaft*, pp. 232–233; Cobble, D. S. (2021) *For the Many. American Feminists and the Global Fight for Democratic Equality* (Princeton: Princeton University Press); and Boris, *Making the Woman Worker*.

the UN adopted the Declaration on the Elimination of Discrimination against Women (DEDAW), and the decision to dedicate 1975 and the following decade to women, engendered other international opportunity structures. In 1975, the International Labour Conference adopted the Declaration on Equality of Opportunity and Treatment for Women Workers,[14] and the EC adopted The Equal Pay Directive in the same year. In 1979 then, the UN adopted the Convention on the Elimination of Discrimination Against Women (CEDAW). During this entire period and especially from 1975 after the UN Women's conference in Mexico, national governments adopted new equal pay legislation or revised older equal pay legislation.[15] Equal remuneration became part of the human rights discourse and shifted toward the definition of the ILO with equal pay for the same or comparable work.

International Mobilization Structures Reaching Globally

International meetings, conferences, and various women's committees and organizations, were important *mobilization structures* for equal pay struggles from the beginning in Sweden and Iceland as elsewhere around the globe. Of course, it can be assumed that direct involvement had more impact. Still, we have examples of how reports from meetings abroad served as an inspiration to mobilize for equal remuneration at the local and national level without the direct personal or organizational links to the mobilization structures abroad.[16] While international mobilization structures grew to a genuinely global reach after the Second World

[14] Määttä, P. (2008) *The ILO Principle of Equal Pay and Its Implementation* (Tampere: Tampere University Press), p. 150; and *ILO, Record of Proceedings, ILC 60th Session, Geneva* (1975) (Geneva: ILO), p. 681.

[15] Neunsinger and Kristjánsdóttir, 'A Global Turning Point'.

[16] Neunsinger, 'The Unobtainable Magic of Numbers', p. 140; and *La grève des femmes de la Fabrique nationale d'armes de guerre de Herstal* (1966) (Brussels: FGTB, Centrale des Métallurgistes de Belgique). See also: Van Hemeldonck, M. (2006) 'De vrouwenstaking van Herstal (1966): in België startschot van het modern feminism, in Europa grondslag van het EU-gelijkheidsrecht', *Brood & Rozen,* 11, 1, pp. 45–51; Ravesloot, S. (2013) *Exchange of Good Practices on Gender Equality. Equal Pay Day, Estonia, 18–19 June 2013*, discussion paper, Belgium, for the European Commission; and Coenen, M. T. T. (1991) *La grève des femmes de la FN en 1966* (Brussels: De Boeck Supérieur).

War, the demand for equal remuneration had been discussed internationally since the second half of the nineteenth century. The centrality of the demand across the world can be illustrated by the fact that it was on the agenda of international women's congresses and international working-class congresses from their start.[17] Equal pay struggles generated multifarious transnational coalition building, including cross-class and cross-gender alliances. Thus, labor feminists of the International Federation of Trade Unions (IFTU), together with more conservative women's organizations such as the International Council of Women (ICW) had brought demands for equal pay to the debates about a labor charter to be part of the Treaty of Versailles in 1919.[18]

In the interwar period, the demand for equal remuneration was instrumental in the emergence of specific women's committees, organizations, and alliances concerned with the condition of women workers. Under pressure from these transnational women's coalitions, the ILO started its own women's committee in 1932, signalizing that the ILO recognized women workers, but as different from men, with special needs and demands as working women and mothers.[19] Women's conferences held during the interwar period, served as mobilization structures when putting women's wages, as well as minimum wages for home-based workers—at that time, a female-dominated group of workers—as one of the main items on their agendas.[20]

After the Second World War, additional women's committees emerged: the United Nations established the Commission on the Status of Women (CSW); the ILO Panel of Consultants on the Problem of Women Workers Questions replaced the ILO's Correspondence Committee on

[17] Wikander, *Feminism, familj och medborgarskap*.

[18] Zimmermann, *Frauenpolitik und Männergewerkschaften*, p. 232. The original 1919 *ILO Constitution* can be found online under Part XIII of the Treaty of Versailles or in *ILO, Official Bulletin* 1919–1920, 1, Chapter VI, 'Part XIII of the Treaty of Peace of Versailles,' pp. 332–345. See also: Määttä, *The ILO Principle*, pp. 88f.; Lubin, C. and Winslow, A. (1991) *Social Justice for Women: The International Labor Organization and Women* (Durham: Duke University Press), pp. 21–23; and Cobble, D. S. (2018) 'The Other ILO Founders: 1919 and Its Legacies,' in Boris, Hoehtker and Zimmerman, *Women's ILO*, pp. 27–49.

[19] Boris, *Making the Woman Worker*, pp. 35f.

[20] Zimmermann, *Frauenpolitik und Männergewerkschaft*, pp. 55, 235ff., 269f.; Boris, *Making the Woman Worker*; and Nilsson, M., Mazumdar, I. and Neunsinger, S. (eds.) (2021) *Home-Based Work and Home-Based Workers (1800–2021)* (Leiden/Boston: Brill).

Women's Work; the Joint Committee on Women Worker's Questions was formed by the International Trade Secretariats (ITS); and the International Confederation of Free Trade Unions (ICFTU). These women's committees produced several reports investigating wage discrimination among women workers in member states and organizations. The ICFTU women's committee collected the information and forwarded it to the ILO and the UN. International conferences and meetings were held to investigate possible ways to implement equal remuneration.[21]

Decolonization after the Second World War increased the number of women from the Global South in these international committees. By the 1970s, these women gained access to international mobilization structures (women's committees and conferences), and they brought back home the demand for economic and social equality. The impact was now, for the first time, truly global. Preparations for and decisions for the UN's International Women's Year of 1975 and the women's conference in Mexico City served as a new international mobilization structure that gave impulses for the ongoing equal pay struggles at the local and national level.[22]

Between the Shopfloor and the International Arena—Sweden and Iceland, 1900–1940

In 1919, Swedish labor feminists sent two identical petitions for equal remuneration for men and women to the congress of the Swedish Trade Union Confederation (*Landsorganisationen*, LO) and to the first IFTU congress in Bern.[23] In this way, they contributed to the labor charter that

[21] Neunsinger, 'The Unobtainable Magic of Numbers', p. 126.

[22] Olcott, J. (2017) *International Women's Year: The Greatest Consciousness Raising Event in History* (Oxford: Oxford University Press); Jain, D. (2005) *Women, Development and the UN. A Sixty-Year Quest for Equality and Justice* (Bloomington: Indiana University Press), p. 67; Pietilä, H. (2002) *Engendering the Global Agenda: The Story of Women and the United Nations* (Geneva: UN Non-Governmental Liaison Services), pp. 30–32; and Pietilä, H. and Vickers, J. (1990) *Making Women Matter: The Role of the United* Nations (London: Zed Books), pp. 75–76.

[23] Petition from Socialdemokratiska kvinnornas Centralstyrelse and Socialdemokratiska kvinnors samorganisation in Flood, H. (1939) *Den Socialdemokratiska kvinnorörelsen i Sverige* (Stockholm: Tiden), p. 136. On the debates about night work prohibition for women, see: Wikander, *Feminism, familj och medborgarskap*.

influenced the Versailles Treaty and the ILO constitution.[24] When equal remuneration was entirely dependent on agreements between the worker and the employer and collective agreements were still scarce, Swedish labor feminists fought to put equal remuneration on the agenda of trade unions and make them part of collective agreements. This externalization of demands to national agenda items and international standards was at that time of symbolic value as the real struggles were carried out on the shop floor. And as we will show, this externalization remained an exception.

In the early years, the labor movements in the Nordic countries were predominantly male organizations. Women had to create their mobilization structures, either with separate women's trade unions, through collaboration with women within political parties, or through women's organizations. In Sweden, several short-lived women's trade unions were established between 1870 and 1890.[25] In 1902, the Swedish Women's Trade union was founded, and to ensure representation, it paid for the costs to participate in the LO congress.[26] Coalition building with social democratic women was the key to organizing working women. This persistent form of separate organizing has been exceptional in international comparison.[27] The organization turned into a socialist women's organization in 1906. The members of these organizations were supported in their struggle for equal remuneration by male trade unionists who regarded unorganized women working for lower salaries at the workplace as unwelcome competition.[28] As soon as women gained access to the male-dominated Swedish labor movement, debates about equal remuneration became a standard topic on the agenda of the national congresses. In 1909, LO took the first formal decision in favor of equal remuneration.[29]

[24] Zimmermann, *Frauenpolitik und Männergewerkschaft*, pp. 231ff.

[25] Neunsinger, S. and Waldemarson Y. (2016) 'ILO och kampen för lika lön: en kort introduction till en lång historia', *Arbetarhistoria*, 3–4, pp. 6–10, p. 10.

[26] Flood, *Den Socialdemokratiska kvinnorörelsen*, pp. 35–36.

[27] Jonsson, P. and Neunsinger S. (2012) *Gendered Money: Financial Organization in Women's Movements, 1880–1933* (New York: Berghahn Books).

[28] Flood, *Den Socialdemokratiska kvinnorörelsen*, p. 24.

[29] Hirdman, *Med kluven tunga*, p. 10.

As mentioned above, the Icelandic labor movement provided few opportunities in the struggle for equal remuneration. Even though a woman had been elected to the first central committee of ASÍ in 1916, there was neither a separate women's organization within the confederation until 1932 nor a women's secretary. The first steps toward organizing working women were taken on behalf of the Women's Rights Association (*Kvenréttindafélag Íslands*, KRFÍ). In 1914, the association was instrumental in founding the first Icelandic women's union, *Framsókn* in Reykjavík. Similarly, in 1922, when women clerks (shop girls) organized in a union, it was on the initiative of KRFÍ. It was first in 1930 that ASÍ accepted a resolution on wage equality, and a half-hearted one at that since it stated that women and juveniles taking on the same work as men in hard labor, be paid the same as men. At a congress in 1936, ASÍ finally accepted a resolution on equal pay for men and women undertaking the same job. Significantly, this resolution had been proposed by Laufey Valdimarsdóttir, president of KRFÍ and active participant in the transnational women's rights movement.[30]

To see the demand for equal pay as part of the program of ASÍ was important, but the real struggles took place elsewhere. The confederation was formed by autonomous trade unions, each with complete freedom to act independently of the confederation. The shopfloor was the most important site of contention. Moreover, in the interwar years, many women workers were not unionized. Before the Second World War their negotiating position was generally much weaker than that of male workers.[31]

In Sweden, the struggle for equal pay took place on the shop floor during this time. A women's strike at a laundry in Stockholm in June 1903, organized by the women's trade union demanding at least the same pay as at other laundries, indicates the need to be paid the same wage

[30] Erlendsdóttir, *Veröld*, pp. 172, 245–48; and Ísleifsson, *Saga Alþýðusambands* I, pp. 51, 97–100.

[31] Ísleifsson, *Saga Alþýðusambands* I, 94. For survey of shop floor negotiations and strikes before 1940, see: Magnúsdóttir, Þ. (2002) *Þörfin knýr. Upphaf verkakvennahreyfingar á Íslandi* (Reykjavík).

in the same sector.[32] But differently from Iceland, where there were no collective agreements until after the Second World War,[33] the demand for equal remuneration was also handled in collective agreements in Sweden. The first collective agreements were made during the second half of the nineteenth century and until the end of the Second World War often the result of local negotiations. Early collective agreements codified wage differentials between men and women, but after the turn of the century, collective agreements could also include equal remuneration more explicitly.[34] They were not a guarantee for equal remuneration per se. Still, if they included equal remuneration for men and women or did not explicitly mention wage differentials between male and female workers they could be used as a political opportunity structure. The reason for this was the new legislation of 1928. After years of strikes and labor conflicts in the Swedish labor market, the Swedish parliament adopted laws on collective agreements and a labor court at the initiative of employers and conservative members of parliament.[35] The decisions of the labor court between the end of the 1920 and the 1940s show that unions brought cases of wage discrimination against women to the court because they broke against collective agreements.[36]

Due to the absence of legislation and general agreements on equal remuneration for blue-collar workers, wage equality was highly dependent on the content of collective agreements. The absence of different wage rates for men and women was sometimes interpreted as an intention toward wage equality. Still, in some cases the neutral agreements meant that employers could also decide about women's wage rates without negotiation with the unions, as women workers were not part of the collective agreement. One of these cases concerned women being paid

[32] Swedish Labour Movement Archives and Library (*Arbetarrörelsen arkiv och bibliotek*, ARAB), Kvinnornas fackförbund, Archive no. 2330, Box 2: "Flygblad Kvinnornas Fackförbund Strejk at Inedals Tvättinrättning, June 1, 1903". Thanks to Karin Wallmark for bringing this to our attention.

[33] See: Ísleifsson, *Saga Alþýðusambands* I, pp. 303–05.

[34] Svenéus, *Konsten att upprätthålla löneskillnader*, see court cases on equal remuneration.

[35] Lundh, C. (2010) *Spelets regler. Institutioner och lönebildning på den svenska arbetsmarknaden* (Stockholm: SNS), pp. 170ff.

[36] *Arbetsdomstolens domar*, 48, 1929; and Svenéus, *Konsten att upprätthålla löneskillnader*, pp. 86–89, 94.

less than men because women cleaned the inside of the bus and the men the outside. Unions were not generally acting in favor of women workers. In the case of the bus cleaners, the union went to court as the women workers were seen as cheaper competition for the same work.[37] It would take more time to turn collective agreements into a resource for women workers in Sweden for their struggle for wage equality.

1940s–1965: New Political Opportunities and Internalization

Writing in the journal of the Icelandic Women's Rights Association (KRFÍ) in 1955, Rannveig Þorsteinsdóttir, a woman activist, lawyer, and former MP, claimed that it was because of the unceasing struggle of international women's organizations that the UN and ILO had decided to embrace the issue of equal remuneration. Now it was up to women in each member country to prepare the ground for its ratification. Icelandic women should exert pressure within unions and political parties, on members of the parliament, government, and the general public. She claimed that wage equality was on its way, but it was up to women to secure that it would arrive sooner than later.[38] Rannveig referred to ILO's attempt to end global economic wage injustice against women, the 1951 adoption of Convention 100 on Equal Remuneration. Her article indicates trust in international agreements and conventions as an instrument for implementing equal remuneration. At the same time, her words illustrate how internationalism offered a framework, a set of focal points, and an opportunity structure for domestic struggles in the 1950s.

Similarly, in 1951, in an article referring to one of the many postwar investigations on equal remuneration, namely by the Swedish Labour Market Committee on Women (*Svenska arbetsmarknadens kvinnoutredning*), the conservative *Svensk tidskrift* drew attention to the influence of international debates about equal remuneration:

> The problems of women's work have gained in importance during recent years, on the one hand due to the international debate about the question

[37] *Arbetsdomstolens domar*, 84, 1945; and Svenéus, *Konsten att upprätthålla löneskillnader*, pp. 95, 99.

[38] Þorsteinsdóttir, R. (1955) 'Jöfn laun karla og kvenna fyrir jafnverðmæt störf', *19. Júní*, 5, 1, pp. 6–9.

of equal pay and the lack of female labor on the Swedish Labor market. The fact that this issue has been discussed internationally is the reason why it is taken up in this investigation, because the decision in Geneva will only take place during next summer's labor conference the issue has only been treated briefly, and even more so because the international decision will not automatically affect the Swedish decision.[39]

In the 1950s, the Nordic model of labor relations turned out to be an obstacle when it came to implementing the policies of the ILO. Thus, the social democratic governments in Denmark, Finland, Norway, and Sweden claimed their opposition to ratifying C100 because it went against the principle of keeping the state out of the wage setting between the social partners. During the discussions at the ILC in 1951, the Scandinavian employers stated their opposition on the same grounds. In the final voting, the Swedish worker's representative voted in favor of the ILO convention, the Swedish employer's representative was against it and the Swedish state representatives abstained from voting.[40]

In 1958, Iceland was the first Nordic country to ratify C100; Norway followed in 1959, Denmark in 1960, Sweden in 1962, and Finland in 1963. As regards Norway, Inger Bjørnhaug has explained the comparably early ratification against the resistance from the Norwegian government with the role of Konrad Nordahl, chair of the Norwegian LO and member of the board of the ILO who convinced the government to vote for a convention at the ILC.[41] And as we will show similar mechanisms were at work in Sweden. There was also a Nordic supranational actor intervening, the Nordic council, which is the formal body for the interparliamentary cooperation of the Nordic countries. The council recommended the ratification of ILO convention 100.[42]

[39] *Svensk Tidskrift*, December 31, 1951, pp. 122–24: "Kvinnolönefråga".

[40] Svenéus, *Konsten att upprätthålla löneskillnader*, pp. 109f.

[41] Bjørnhaug, I. (2016) 'Likelønn mellom marked, klasse og kjonn. Norsk LOs rolle i ratifiseringen og implementeringen av Den internasjonale arbeidsorganisajons likelønnskonvensjon', *Arbetarhistoria*, 3–4, pp. 36–46, p. 36.

[42] Irlinger, *TCO och kvinnorna*, p. 131.

The Synergy of Icelandic and International Opportunity Structures

During the Second World War, a women's union in the small town of Akranes in South-West Iceland had struck deals ensuring women working in fish processing the same wages as men doing the same jobs. And in 1946, mixed-gender union of workers in fish-net production made a wage agreement securing equal wages for men and women. This was the result of a six-week strike—led by a female leader of the union—and entailed a 62% wage increase for women while the rate of the men increased by 24%.[43] The examples illustrate that in the 1940s new political opportunities for wage equality had become available in Iceland. These changes were felt at all levels of scale, at the shop floor, and on the national level.

On the national level, the adoption of equal pay for the same jobs to the agenda of the Icelandic Confederation of Labour (ASÍ) coincided with an attempt to even out regional wage differences.[44] In 1949 the issue was brought to parliament when a social democratic MP and later president of ASÍ put forth a parliamentary bill for political, social, and economic equality between men and women including wage equality in the private and the public sector.[45] The bill was rejected, but in 1950, on the initiative of the abovementioned Rannveig Þorsteinsdóttir, parliament instigated an investigation on the legal status and working conditions of women.[46]

Wage equality had been introduced in 1919 legislation on school teachers and 1945 law on public servants, assigning men and women to the same wage categories.[47] In 1954, a new law on public servants clearly stated that women and men had equal rights to public office and to the same wages for the same jobs.[48] But there was still no legislation on wage equality in the private sector, and here we have a clear example of the

[43] Ísleifsson, *Saga Alþýðusambands* I, p. 294.

[44] Ibid., pp. 281–83.

[45] *Alþingistíðindi*, 1948 A, pp. 759–63.

[46] Ibid., 1949 A, pp. 366–67.

[47] Stjórnartíðindi, 1919 A, pp. 232–35; and Ibid., 1945 A, pp. 89–93.

[48] According to historian Sigríður Th. Erlendsdóttir this clause was put into the legislation on the initiative of the KRFÍ. See: Erlendsdóttir, S. Th. (1997) '"Til færri fiska metnar". Hlutur Kvenréttindafélags Íslands í kjarabaráttu kvenna 1920–1960' in Kress, H. and Traustadóttir, R. (eds.) *Íslenskar kvennarannsóknir* (Reykjavík: Rannsóknastofa í

impact of ILO C100. Ratification went relatively smoothly through the Icelandic legislature. In 1954, the Icelandic (all male) parliament agreed to take the necessary steps toward ratifying ILO Convention 100. Three years later, the parliament decided to ratify and implement Convention 100.[49] Iceland's ratification of C100 took force in February 1958. Hence, Iceland became the first of the Nordic countries to ratify C100.[50]

When discussing the implications of ILO C100, Icelandic women activists emphasized that the resolution alone would not solve inequality in the labor market. Implementation would be easier and only possible with the introduction of legislation to secure equal remuneration.[51] The parliamentary discussion addressed how the associations of employers and workers could be made responsible for implementing the convention. The representatives of the employers and some members of the labor movement had spoken against the legislation. But by the early 1960s—and following increased state intervention in labor disputes during the 1950s—a consensus was reached for legislation against wage discrimination. In 1961, this was followed up with a law on equal pay, the aim of which was to eliminate the gender pay gap in occupations where it appeared to have been particularly wide and persistent. The specified occupations were manual labor/unskilled jobs, factory work, and store and office work.[52]

International Opportunity Structures Challenge the Swedish Model of Labor Relations

The ratification process of ILO C100 in Sweden was far more complicated and took much longer than in the other Nordic countries. The main problem was not resistance to the principle of equal pay, but the

kvennafræðum), pp. 279–89, p. 286. For the legislation, see: *Stjórnartíðindi*, 1954 A, pp. 109–16.

49 For the proposed resolutions, see: *Alþingistíðindi*, 1953 A, pp. 856–58; and Ibid., 1956 A, pp. 356–63.

50 *ILO Ratifications of C100 – Equal Remuneration Convention, No. 100* (1951) (https://www.ilo.org/dyn/normlex/en/f?p=NORMLEXPUB:11300:0::NO:11300:P11300_INSTRUMENT_ID:312245:NO); latest retrieved November 13, 2018.

51 Helgadóttir, G. (1951) 'Sömu laun til karla og kvenna fyrir störf af sama verðmæti', *19. Júní*, 1, 1, pp. 19–20.

52 *Stjórnartíðindi*, 1961 A, p. 171.

rejection of any form of state or international intervention in the Swedish model of labor relations in the private sector. The discussion in Sweden was vivid, illustrated by the many investigations about wage discrimination against women. And the demand for equal remuneration was raised at every congress of the LO since 1941 and once a year in the Swedish parliament by women MPs. In addition, the ILO sent out reports and suggestions and asked for comments.[53]

A publication by the LO from 1942 had shown the blatant wage discrimination against female blue-collar workers, being paid two-thirds of male hourly wages.[54] This sparked the first investigation about equal remuneration carried out by LO, followed by many more investigations until equal pay legislation finally was adopted.[55]

At the same time, mobilization structures in the unions improved during this period partly due to the transnational alliance building with labor feminists from Denmark, Norway, and Finland. After returning home from a Nordic meeting Swedish labor feminists demanded the establishment of women's advisory boards for the national trade union confederation to handle the issue of equal remuneration.[56] In Norway the first women's committee was established in 1940, and Sweden followed in 1948.[57] In 1947 Sigrid Ekendahl had become the secretary of the LO with responsibility for the women's advisory board with a specific task to work on women's wages.[58] Moreover, in 1946 all female members of parliament sent in a petition demanding equal remuneration.[59]

[53] Hirdman, *Med kluven tunga*, pp. 37f.

[54] Wigforss, E. (ed.) (1942) *Kvinnorna på Arbetsmarknaden* (Stockholm: Tiden).

[55] Hirdman, *Med kluven tunga*, pp. 22f; and Svenéus, *Konsten att upprätthålla löneskillnader*, p. 118.

[56] Swedish TCO's women's committee was established in 1960 and became a permanent committee in 1962 (Irlinger, *TCO och kvinnorna*, p. 55).

[57] Bjørnhaug, 'Likelønn mellom marked', p. 40; and Waldemarson, 'Likalönen och det nordiska'.

[58] Neunsinger and Waldemarson, 'ILO och kampen'. See also: Florin, C. and Nilsson, B. (1999) '"Something in the Nature of a Bloodless Revolution…": How New Gender Relations Became Gender Equality Policy in Sweden in the Nineteen-Sixties and Seventies' in Torstendahl, R. (ed.) *State Policy and Gender System in the Two German States and Sweden 1945–1989* (Uppsala: Historiska institutionen) on the importance of LO:s kvinnoråd, p. 36.

[59] Irlinger, *TCO och kvinnorna*, pp. 67f. All female members of parliament demanded equal remuneration (*Riksdagens protkoll*, Första kammaren, 19, 1946, p. 67; Ibid., Andra

The main opposition against equal remuneration came from the employers' organization against the inclusion of equal remuneration in collective agreements. However, similar to the employers, the LO continued for some time to accept the argument that women were more costly workers due to their absenteeism and thus created a split between male and female workers. The Swedish white-collar trade union confederation (*Tjänstemännens Centralorganisation*, TCO) did not share this opinion and reacted against this argumentation throughout the after-war period. The LO repeatedly stressed the praxis of negotiating collective agreements without state intervention as an argument against legislation and ratification.[60] A closer look at ILO convention article 2 shows that collective agreements were accepted to implement equal remuneration.[61] The trade unions were interested in solving the problem and the post-war program of the LO on wages became crucial. The problem of wage dispersion between different groups of blue-collar workers, men and women, industrial and agricultural workers, other low-income sectors and various regions in Sweden, just like in Iceland, had been a growing problem since the 1930s. According to economic historian Christer Lundh, the spread of Fordism contributed to the standardization of wages and opened for the rate for the job principle in Sweden.[62] When LO economists Gösta Rehn and Rudolf Meidner developed what became known as solidary wage politics (*Solidarisk lönepolitik*) the rate for the job, or equal pay for work of equal value became central to the wage program of the LO. Instead of framing equal remuneration as a matter of gender equality it became part of a larger project on wage equality among blue-collar workers. The goal was to minimize wage dispersion among workers. Industrial male workers earned one-third more than female industrial workers and industrial workers also earned one-third more than agricultural workers. Trade unions from low-wage sectors, such as the clothing and the metal workers federations had long demanded the abolition of separate wage categories for women. At the 1951 year's congress of the LO no less than 5 motions concerning equal pay were on the agenda;

kammaren, 20, 1946, p. 108; *Motion i Första kammaren*, 62, 1946; and *Motion i Andra kammaren*, 124, 1946).

[60] Hirdman, *Med kluven tunga*, pp. 20–57; Svenéus, *Konsten att upprätthålla löneskillnader*, p. 119; Irlinger, *TCO och kvinnorna*, pp. 95, 100.

[61] *ILO Ratifications of* C100, Article 2.

[62] Lundh, *Spelets regler*, p. 228.

some of which were in favor of the legislation.[63] LO's post-world war wage program included three measures that were seen as a solution to the problem of wage dispersion regarding sectors, gender, and geography. The first measure was to implement the principle of equal remuneration for equal work gender neutral for all workers from different sectors. The second measure was to increase the mobility of labor. The third measure was unions pressuring enterprises to keep up wage levels, using taxation so non-profitable enterprises would close and increasing productivity in the low-wage sector through rationalizations.[64]

In addition to the moral pressure from the ILO with its permanent reminders to ratify the C100, the pressure from female members of parliament, and the ICFTU put moral pressure on the representatives of the Swedish confederations. LO's chairman, Arne Geijer, announced in 1957 that something needed to be done to discard the lower paid wage categories for women.[65] Similar to the Norwegian Konrad Nordahl, Geijer was a transnational activist and had become the chairman of the ICFTU in the same year. At that time the ICFTU had worked for the ratification of the ILO convention ever since it had been adopted. The international pressure on Geijer changed the picture. He admitted in 1958 that the non-action was due to the agreement with the employers' organization, but that Sweden now was one of the last countries in Western Europa that had not ratified the ILO convention and change was due. He also referred to the importance of the ongoing negotiations about a European free trade zone, demanding that members ratify the ILO convention.[66] In the end, external pressure from the ICFTU, the EEC and pressure from the Swedish Parliament, the TCO, the LO women's committee, the employer's organization, and the LO had to find a way that enabled the government to ratify the ILO convention. In 1960, during the central wage negotiations and under the threat of the ILO convention being ratified by the Swedish parliament, LO and SAF agreed to abolish the

[63] Hirdman, *Med kluven tunga*, pp. 45–46.

[64] Lundh, *Spelets regler*, pp. 195–203.

[65] Hirdman, *Med kluven tunga*, pp. 55–57; and Svenéus, *Konsten att upprätthålla löneskillnader*, p. 134.

[66] Hirdman, *Med kluven tunga*, p. 64; and Misgeld, K. (1997) *Den fackliga europavägen: LO, det internationella samarbetet och Europas enande 1945–1991* (Stockholm: Atlas), p. 77.

specific women's wages before 1965. This was a way of avoiding legislation.[67] Sigrid Ekendahl, who had also been a member of parliament earlier, was the first woman to be part of the central wage negotiations in Sweden in 1958 and played an essential role in this agreement. In 1963 Ekendahl became the chair of the Women's committee of the ICFTU.[68]

In Iceland, the optimistic aim of the 1961 legislation to eliminate the gender pay gap by the end of 1967 proved to be more difficult than expected. One problem was a strong tendency to rate jobs typically occupied by women lower than jobs typically occupied by men. This was also the case in Sweden. The elimination of the so-called women's wages, resulted in a recategorization of women's work into gender neutral categories, but women found their jobs in the lowest categories. This time the Swedish wage politics of solidarity helped the unions to bargain successfully about the low-wage funds in 1964 and 1969. Over time the wage gap between men's and women's wages decreased by up to 20%.[69]

1966–1985 Global Framing in Iceland and Sweden

On October 24, 1975, the United Nations Day, nine out of ten Icelandic women famously walked out of their homes and workplaces to demonstrate the value of their work. The United Nations International Women's Year (IWY) had brought together various factions of the women's movement—from the most radical to the more conservative—in deliberations about the status of women. The Women's Day Off, as the event was called, was planned by a women's committee formed by a wide range of Icelandic women's organizations to prepare events during IWY.

As we have argued elsewhere, the preparations and the outcome of IWY were significant to the globalizing women's struggles in general and the struggles for equal remuneration in particular.[70] At the beginning of the 1970s, the UN had initiated national reports on the status of women to prepare for international women's year in 1975. These

[67] Hirdman, *Med kluven tunga*, p. 63, and Svenéus, *Konsten att upprätthålla löneskillnader*, p. 134.

[68] Neunsinger, S. 'Sigrid Hildur Elvira Ekendahl', *Svenskt kvinnobiografiskt lexikon* (www.skbl.se/sv/artikel/SigridEkendahl); retrieved February 2, 2022.

[69] Hirdman, *Med kluven tunga*, pp. 304ff.

[70] Neunsinger and Kristjánsdóttir, 'A Global Turning Point'.

reports become important national mobilization structures for the implementation of equal remuneration. India is an important example where the report of the Commission on the Status of Women led to changes in national legislation with new political opportunity structures on the national level and international political opportunity structures are used more widely.[71]

The Icelandic government introduced a law on equality between women and men. That decision is directly linked with the UN international year of women. The *travaux preparatoires* of the bill, introduced in the spring of 1976, directly refere to the UN's objectives for the women's decade. Moreover, one of the principal authors was, Guðrún Erlendsdóttir, who had been the chairman of the abovementioned Icelandic women's year committee.[72] Women's position in the labor market was one of the main concerns of the new Icelandic Equal Rights law of 1976, stating that "women and men should be provided with equal opportunities for work and education, and that they should be paid the same wages for comparable jobs and jobs of equal value."[73] The legislation prescribed the establishment of an Equal Rights Council which should, if needed, file cases on behalf of workers who were considered to have been subject to discrimination. The first such case was brought to court in 1979 on behalf of an unskilled health worker, Guðrún Emilsdóttir, who complained that she had been paid less than men doing the same job at her workplace, a state-run care home for disabled people. The case was filed against the Icelandic State by Guðrún and the Equal Rights Council. A district court adjudicated in her favor. And while the Supreme Court reversed the verdict due to a technical issue, the court ruling stated that paying Guðrún less than her male counterparts violated the Equal Rights Legislation.[74] It was thus clear that with the new legislation working women

[71] Neunsinger and Warrier, 'Transnational Activism'.

[72] Ástgeirsdóttir K. (2006) '"Þar sem völdin eru, þar eru konurnar ekki": Kvennaráðstefnur og kvennaáratugur Sameinuðu þjóðanna og áhrif þeirra á Íslandi 1975–2005', *Saga*, 44, 2, pp. 23–26.

[73] *Stjórnartíðindi*, 1975 A, 1, p. 88.

[74] Supreme Court judgment in *Hæstaréttardómar*, 117, 1979. On court rulings on equal remuneration in Iceland, see: Konráðsdóttir, S. (2006) 'Jafnaunareglan í íslenskri dómaframkvæmd og dómum Evrópudómstólsins' in Hafstein, P. Kr., Claessen, G and Erlendsdóttir, G. (eds.) *Guðrúnarbók. Afmælisrit til heiðurs Guðrúnu Erlendsdóttur 3. maí 2006* (Reykjavík: Hið íslenska bókmenntafélag), pp. 411–27.

in Iceland had been given an effective tool in their struggle for wage equality.

The Swedish Parliament discussed legislation against discrimination every year since 1970.[75] Government reports about gender equality peaked during the 1970s.[76] In 1972, Prime minister Olof Palme appointed a committee for gender equality (*Jämställdhetsdelegationen*) with the task of investigating gender equality in Sweden. The committee was headed by Social Democrat Tage G. Pettersson, and a feminist researcher carried out the investigation. In 1974, the Swedish government was criticized for the slow progress of the investigation and the government decided to present the results at the upcoming UN women's conference in Mexico City.[77] The report was full of references to international agreements and foreign laws, with the USA as an essential source of inspiration. Still the recommendation published in the report was against the legislation. The report's results were similar to those of the 25 years older investigation of the labor market partners' commission on women (*Arbetsmarknadens kvinnoutredning*). New to it was the methodology to interview individuals to understand the situation at the workplace and inside homes. As in many other countries, the official Swedish report for the UN's International Women's Year published in 1975 was an eye-opener. It showed that wage discrimination still existed, and that the main problem was women's part-time work; it also referred to a report by the union for civil servants, TCO, from 1970 which showed widespread wage discrimination against women.[78] It was clear that the joint forces of the social partners had not ended the discrimination against women in the labor market. In 1977 the Swedish SAF and LO reached an agreement about gender equality in the labor market, and LO's Harry Fjällström

[75] Svenéus, *Konsten att upprätthålla löneskillnader*, p. 159.

[76] Florin and Nilsson, 'Something in the Nature', p. 24.

[77] The report was published in Swedish in 1976: Liljeström, R., Svensson, G. L. and Mellström, G. F. (1976) *Roller i omvandling. En rapport skriven på uppdrag av Delegationen för jämställdhet mellan män och kvinnor* (Stockholm: LiberFörlag/Allmänna förlaget); Florin and Nilsson, 'Something in the Nature', p. 68; and Svenéus, *Konsten att upprätthålla löneskillnader*, p. 161; and Irlinger, *TCO och kvinnorna*, pp. 174, 178–179.

[78] Svenéus, *Konsten att upprätthålla löneskillnader*, pp. 158–163f.; Sandberg, E. (1975) *Målet är jämställdhet: en svensk rapport med anledning av FN:s kvinnoår* (Stockholm: LiberFörlag/Allmänna förlaget).

made it clear that in order to avoid legislation, LO had to show that things could be changed through collective bargaining.[79]

In 1978 the gender equality committee handed over its report to the conservative government. It showed that the 1925 law on equal remuneration for men and women in public employment had yet to be implemented. As a result, the government made clear that it was time to follow the example of other countries, as well as recommendations by international organizations, especially as a new world women's conference was prepared to be held in Copenhagen soon. The conservative government was in favor of the legislation. The new gender equality law came into force on June 1, 1980, the day before Sweden ratified the UN Declaration on the Elimination of Discrimination Against Women (DEDAW) as the first country in the world. The Swedish LO's report on equality and solidarity, published in 1981, became according to Yvonne Hirdman the most crucial document for gender equality in the trade union movement until the 1990s.[80]

Concluding Remarks

Looking at how international political opportunity and mobilization structures worked in interaction with national and local ones, we have intented to demonstrate the importance of situating national equal pay struggles in the broader international context. Despite differences in mobilization structures and political opportunities between Iceland and Sweden they confirm the periodization of global equal pay struggles. Moreover, our results confirm and add to findings in earlier research showing how international organizations and global agreements could be used to substitute missing or limited opportunities for activists on the local and national levels.[81]

[79] Svenéus, *Konsten att upprätthålla löneskillnader*, p. 172; and Hirdman, *Med kluven tunga*, pp. 365f.

[80] Svenéus, *Konsten att upprätthålla löneskillnader*, pp. 151–168; Jämställdhetskommittén. (1978) *Jämställdhet i arbetslivet: Lag om jämställdhet* (Stockholm: LiberFörlag/Allmänna förl.); Hirdman, *Med kluven tunga*.

[81] Zimmermann, S. (2002) 'Frauenbewegungen, Transfer, und Trans-nationalität. Feministisches Denken und Streben im globalen und zentraleuropäischen Kontext des 19. und frühen 20. Jahrhunderts' in Kaelble, H., Kirsch, M. and Schmidt-Gernig, A. (eds.) *Transnationale Öffentlichkeiten und Identitäten im 20. Jahrhundert* (Frankfurt/New York:

The limited mobilization structures for Icelandic labor activists made Icelandic women use international opportunity structures to successfully pressure the Icelandic government and male-dominated institutions. Sweden illustrates a different path. The strong position of labor relations without state intervention, as well as accessible mobilization structures for women inside the labor movement, made it much more difficult for labor feminists to use international opportunities actively. Instead, it is pressure from the international level as well as the moral obligation felt by Swedish labor activists as leaders of the international trade union movement to follow the strategies and agreements of these international organizations, that turned the situation in Sweden in the end.

References

Archives

Swedish Labour Movement Archives and Library (*Arbetarrörelsen arkiv och bibliotek*, ARAB):

Kvinnornas fackförbund, Archive no. 2330.

Serials

Alþingistíðindi
Arbetarhistoria
Arbetsdomstolens domar
Hæstaréttardómar
ILO, Official Bulletin
Riksdagens protkoll (and *Motioner*)
Stjórnartíðindi
Svensk Tidskrift

Literature

Ástgeirsdóttir K. (2006) '"Þar sem völdin eru, þar eru konurnar ekki": Kvennaráðstefnur og kvennaáratugur Sameinuðu þjóðanna og áhrif þeirra á Íslandi 1975–2005', *Saga*, 44, 2, pp. 23–26.

Campus Verlag), p. 275; Neunsinger, 'Translocal Activism'; and Neunsinger and Warrier, 'Transnational Activism'.

Bjørnhaug, I. (2016) 'Likelønn mellom marked, klasse og kjønn. Norsk LOs rolle i ratifiseringen og implementeringen av Den internasjonale arbeidsorganisajons likelønnskonvensjon', *Arbetarhistoria*, 3–4, pp. 36–46.

Boris, E. (2019) *Making the Woman Worker. Precarious Labor and the Fight for Global Standards, 1919–2019* (New York: Oxford University Press).

Cobble, D. S. (2018) 'The Other ILO Founders: 1919 and Its Legacies,' in Boris, E., Hoehtker, D. and Zimmerman, S. (eds.) *Women's ILO. Transnational Networks, Global Labour Standards, and Gender Equity, 1919 to Present* (Leiden/Boston: Brill), pp. 27–49.

Cobble, D. S. (2021) *For the Many. American Feminists and the Global Fight for Democratic Equality* (Princeton: Princeton University Press).

Coenen, M. T. T. (1991) *La grève des femmes de la FN en 1966* (Brussels: De Boeck Supérieur).

Erlendsdóttir, S. Th. (1993) *Veröld sem ég vil* (Reykjavík: KRFÍ).

Erlendsdóttir, S. Th. (1997) '"Til færri fiska metnar". Hlutur Kvenréttindafélags Íslands í kjarabaráttu kvenna 1920–1960' in Kress, H. and Traustadóttir, R. (eds.) *Íslenskar kvennarannsóknir* (Reykjavík: Rannsóknastofa í kvennafræðum), pp. 279–89.

Flood, H. (1939) *Den Socialdemokratiska kvinnorörelsen i Sverige* (Stockholm: Tiden).

Florin, C. (1987) *Kampen om katedern. Feminiserings- och professionaliseringsprocessen inom den svenska folkskolans lärarkår 1860–1906* (Stockholm: Almqvist & Wiksell).

Florin, C. and Nilsson, B. (1999) '"Something in the Nature of a Bloodless Revolution... ": How New Gender Relations Became Gender Equality Policy in Sweden in the Nineteen-Sixties And Seventies' in Torstendahl, R. (ed.) *State Policy and Gender System in the Two German States and Sweden 1945–1989* (Uppsala: Historiska institutionen).

Halldórsdóttir, E. H., Tómasdóttir, K. S., Kristjánsdóttir, R. and Þorvaldsdóttir, Þ. H. (2020) *Konur sem kjósa. Aldarsaga* (Reykjavík: Sögufélag).

Helgadóttir, G. (1951) 'Sömu laun til karla og kvenna fyrir störf af sama verðmæti', *19. Júní*, 1, 1, pp. 19–20.

Hilson, M., Neunsinger, S., Vyff, I. and Kristjánsdóttir, R. (2017) 'Labour, Unions and Politics in the Nordic Countries c. 1700–2000: Introduction' in Hilson, M., Neunsinger, S. and Vyff, I. (eds.) *Labour, Unions and Politics Under the North Star: The Nordic Countries, 1700–2000* (New York: Berghahn Books).

Hirdman, Y. (1998) *Med kluven tunga: LO och genusordningen* (Stockholm: Atlas).

ILO, Record of Proceedings, ILC 60th Session, Geneva (1975) (Geneva: ILO).

ILO Ratifications of C100 – Equal Remuneration Convention, No. 100 (1951) (https://www.ilo.org/dyn/normlex/en/f?p=NORMLEXPUB:11300:0::NO:11300:P11300_INSTRUMENT_ID:312245:NO); retrieved November 13, 2018.

Irlinger, I. (1990) *TCO och kvinnorna: tidsperioden 1944–1974: studie av TCOs och SIFs arbetsmarknadspolitik och behandling av principen lika lön för lika arbete* (Uppsala: Almqvist & Wiksell).

Ísleifsson, S. R. (2013) *Saga Alþýðusambands Íslands*, Vol. I–II (Reykjavík: Forlagið).

Jain, D. (2005) *Women, Development and the UN. A Sixty-Year Quest for Equality and Justice* (Bloomington: Indiana University Press).

Jämställdhetskommittén. (1978) *Jämställdhet i arbetslivet: Lag om jämställdhet* (Stockholm: LiberFörlag/Allmänna förlaget).

Jonsson, P. and Neunsinger S. (2012) *Gendered Money: Financial Organization in Women's Movements, 1880–1933* (New York: Berghahn Books).

Konráðsdóttir, S. (2006) 'Jafnaunareglan í íslenskri dómaframkvæmd og dómum Evrópudómstólsins' in Hafstein, P. Kr., Claessen, G and Erlendsdóttir, G. (eds.) *Guðrúnarbók. Afmælisrit til heiðurs Guðrúnu Erlendsdóttur 3. maí 2006* (Reykjavík: Hið íslenska bókmenntafélag), pp. 411–27.

La grève des femmes de la Fabrique nationale d'armes de guerre de Herstal (1966) (Brussels: FGTB, Centrale des Métallurgistes de Belgique).

Liljeström, R., Svensson, G. L. and Mellström, G. F. (1976) *Roller i omvandling. En rapport skriven på uppdrag av Delegationen för jämställdhet mellan män och kvinnor* (Stockholm: LiberFörlag/Allmänna förlaget).

Lubin, C. and Winslow, A. (1991) *Social Justice for Women: The International Labor Organization and Women* (Durham: Duke University Press).

Lundh, C. (2010) *Spelets regler. Institutioner och lönebildning på den svenska arbetsmarknaden* (Stockholm: SNS).

Määttä, P. (2008) *The ILO Principle of Equal Pay and Its Implementation* (Tampere: Tampere University Press).

Magnúsdóttir, Þ. (2002) *Þörfin knýr. Upphaf verkakvennahreyfingar á Íslandi* (Reykjavík).

McAdam, D., McCarthy, J. D. and Zald, M. N. (eds.) (1996) *Comparative Perspectives on Social Movements, Political Opportunities, Mobilizing Structures, and Cultural Framings* (Cambridge: Cambridge University Press).

Misgeld, K. (1997) *Den fackliga europavägen: LO, det internationella samarbetet och Europas enande 1945–1991* (Stockholm: Atlas).

Neunsinger, S. (2018) 'The Unobtainable Magic of Numbers: Equal Remuneration, the ILO and the International Trade Union Movement 1950s–1980s' in Boris, E., Hoehtker, D. and Zimmerman, S. (eds.) *Women's ILO. Transnational Networks, Global Labour Standards, and Gender Equity, 1919 to Present* (Leiden/Boston: Brill), pp. 121–48.

Neunsinger, S. (2019) 'Translocal Activism and the Implementation of Equal Remuneration for Men and Women. The Case of the South African Textile Industry, 1980–1987', *International Review of Social History*, 64, 1, pp. 37–72.

Neunsinger, S. 'Sigrid Hildur Elvira Ekendahl', *Svenskt kvinnobiografiskt lexikon* (www.skbl.se/sv/artikel/SigridEkendahl); retrieved February 2, 2022.

Neunsinger, S. and Kristjánsdóttir, R. (forthcoming) 'A Global Turning Point for Equal Pay Struggles: International Women's Year, 1975' in Pasolli, L. and Smith, J. (eds.) *Rethinking Feminist History and Theory. Reflections on Gender, Class and Labour* (Toronto: Toronto University Press).

Neunsinger, S. and Waldemarson Y. (2016) 'ILO och kampen för lika lön: en kort introduction till en lång historia', *Arbetarhistoria*, 3–4, pp. 6–10.

Neunsinger, S. and Warrier, M. V. S. (2020) 'Transnational Activism and Equal Remuneration in India During the Twentieth Century' in Bellucci, S. and Weiss, H. (eds.) *The Internationalisation of the Labor Question. Ideological Antagonism, Workers' Movements and the ILO Since 1919* (Cham: Palgrave Macmillan), pp. 329–50.

Nilsson, M., Mazumdar, I. and Neunsinger, S. (eds.) (2021) *Home-Based Work and Home-Based Workers (1800–2021)* (Leiden/Boston: Brill).

Olcott, J. (2017) *International Women's Year: The Greatest Consciousness Raising Event in History* (Oxford: Oxford University Press).

Pietilä, H. (2002) *Engendering the Global Agenda: The Story of Women and the United Nations* (Geneva: UN Non-Governmental Liaison Services).

Pietilä, H. and Vickers, J. (1990) *Making Women Matter: The Role of the United Nations* (London: Zed Books).

Ravesloot, S. (2013) *Exchange of Good Practices on Gender Equality. Equal Pay Day, Estonia, 18–19 June 2013*, discussion paper, Belgium, for the European Commission.

Sandberg, E. (1975) *Målet är jämställdhet: en svensk rapport med anledning av FN:s kvinnoår* (Stockholm: LiberFörlag/Allmänna förlaget).

Sigurðardóttir, A. (1985) *Vinna kvenna í 1100 ár* (Reykjavík: Kvennasögusafn).

Sørensen, A. E. (2018) *Pæne pigers oprør. Ligestillingsprojekter i de kvindedominerede fagforbund 1985–2010* (Aarhus: Aarhus University Press).

Svenéus, L. (2017) *Konsten att upprätthålla löneskillnader mellan kvinnor och män: en rättssociologisk studie av regler i lag och avtal om lika lön* (Lund: Department of Sociology of Law, Lund University).

Tarrow, S. (1998) *Power in Movement. Social Movements and Contentious Politics* (Cambridge: Cambridge University Press).

Tarrow, S. (2010) *The New Transnational Activism* (Cambridge: Cambridge University Press).

Tilly, C. (1978) *From Mobilization to Revolution* (Reading: Addison-Wesley).

Þorsteinsdóttir, R. (1955) 'Jöfn laun karla og kvenna fyrir jafnverðmæt störf', *19. Júní*, 5, 1, pp. 6–9.

Van Hemeldonck, M. (2006) 'De vrouwenstaking van Herstal (1966): in België startschot van het modern feminism, in Europa grondslag van het EU-gelijkheidsrecht', *Brood & Rozen*, 11, 1, pp. 45–51.

Waldemarson, Y. (1998) *Mjukt till formen, hårt till innehållet. LO:s kvinnoråd 1947–1969* (Stockholm: Atlas).

Waldemarson, Y. (2000) *Kvinnor och Klass - en paradoxal skapelseberättelse* (Stockholm: Stockholms universitet).

Wigforss, E. (ed.) (1942) *Kvinnorna på Arbetsmarknaden* (Stockholm: Tiden).

Wikander, U. (2006) *Feminism, familj och medborgarskap. Debatter på internationella kongresser om nattarbetsförbud för kvinnor 1889–1919* (Göteborg: Makadam).

Zimmermann, S. (2021) *Frauenpolitik und Männergewerkschaft Internationale Geschlechterpolitik, IGB-Gewerkschafterinnen und die Arbeiter- und Frauenbewegungen der Zwischenkriegszeit* (Wien: Löcker Verlag).

Correction to: Trade Union Activism in the Nordic Countries since 1900

Jesper Jørgensen and Flemming Mikkelsen

Correction to:
J. Jørgensen and F. Mikkelsen (eds.), *Trade Union Activism in the Nordic Countries since 1900*, Palgrave Studies in the History of Social Movements,
https://doi.org/10.1007/978-3-031-08987-9

The original version of the book was inadvertently published with an incorrect author's name in Chapters 4 and 15, which has now been corrected. The book has been updated with the changes.

The updated original version of these chapters can be found at
https://doi.org/10.1007/978-3-031-08987-9_4
https://doi.org/10.1007/978-3-031-08987-9_15

© The Author(s), under exclusive license to Springer Nature Switzerland AG 2023

J. Jørgensen and F. Mikkelsen (eds.), *Trade Union Activism in the Nordic Countries since 1900*, Palgrave Studies in the History of Social Movements, https://doi.org/10.1007/978-3-031-08987-9_18

Index

© The Editor(s) (if applicable) and The Author(s), under exclusive license to Springer Nature Switzerland AG 2023

J. Jørgensen and F. Mikkelsen (eds.), *Trade Union Activism in the Nordic Countries since 1900*, Palgrave Studies in the History of Social Movements, https://doi.org/10.1007/978-3-031-08987-9

T

The manufacturer's authorised representative in the EU is Springer Nature Customer Service Centre GmbH, Europaplatz 3, 69115 Heidelberg, Germany. If you have any concerns regarding our products, please contact ProductSafety@springernature.com

Printed and bound by CPI Group (UK) Ltd, Croydon, CR0 4YY
30/09/2026
02225490-0017